God Save the USSR

God Save the USSR

Soviet Muslims and the Second World War

JEFF EDEN

OXFORD
UNIVERSITY PRESS

OXFORD
UNIVERSITY PRESS

Oxford University Press is a department of the University of Oxford. It furthers
the University's objective of excellence in research, scholarship, and education
by publishing worldwide. Oxford is a registered trade mark of Oxford University
Press in the UK and certain other countries.

Published in the United States of America by Oxford University Press
198 Madison Avenue, New York, NY 10016, United States of America.

CIP data is on file at the Library of Congress
ISBN 978-0-19-007627-6

DOI: 10.1093/oso/9780190076276.001.0001

1 3 5 7 9 8 6 4 2

Printed by Integrated Books International, United States of America

Contents

Acknowledgments

First and foremost, I want to thank my friend and colleague Allen J. Frank, who has been an inspiration through all phases of researching and writing this book. Allen generously provided me with some of the book's most illuminating sources, and he himself has been a source of motivation and enlightening conversation at every stage. He was also the first to read the completed manuscript and to offer invaluable comments and corrections.

I began writing this book while I was a Mellon Postdoctoral Fellow in Cornell University's Department of Asian Studies. I was kindly welcomed there by Dan Gold, Keith Taylor, Chiara Formichi, Erin Kotmel, Sheila Haddad, and many wonderful students. Two chapter drafts were presented at Cornell's Bret de Bary Interdisciplinary Mellon Working Group, an unusually delightful academic workshop where I enjoyed the great company and suggestions of Benjamin Anderson, Raashid Goyal, Patrick Naeve, David Powers, Danielle Reid, and Aaron Rock-Singer.

Some of the material here was reworked into a "job talk" for the idyllic St. Mary's College of Maryland (SMCM), which I am now very fortunate to call my academic home. I never imagined a department as harmonious and convivial as our Department of History. Greetings and thanks to my SMCM History colleagues Christine Adams, Adriana Brodsky, Garrey Dennie, Chuck Holden, Sarah Malena, Charlie Musgrove, and Gail Savage. Many thanks are also due to Lucy Myers, Adrienne Raines, Kent Randell, Brenda Rodgers, and many other colleagues and friends who have made the college such a welcoming, supportive place.

Some material from Chapter 2 first appeared in an article published in the *Journal of the Economic and Social History of the Orient*. This article was based on a talk I gave at a Harvard conference which I co-organized with Paolo Sartori. Thanks are due to Paolo, to the anonymous reviewers of the *JESHO* article, and to the other attendees of that memorable conference.

Several friends and colleagues have offered valuable advice and support for this project. Thanks in particular to Alfrid Bustanov, Devin DeWeese, and the anonymous reviewers for Oxford University Press. I am also profoundly grateful to Brid Nowlan for her sharp-eyed, diligent work copy-editing the manuscript. I have pestered many other friends and colleagues while working on this project, not with portions of this manuscript specifically, but instead with my caffeinated emails, memes, and dubious comic stylings, and I am endlessly grateful for their indulgence and camaraderie, which can be just as healthy for research morale as any specifically academic encouragement.

In my student days, several great teachers taught me the history of the Soviet Union and/or the languages spoken there. For these great gifts I want to thank Kagan Arik, Anna Bobrov, Bethany Braley, Devin DeWeese, Thaddeus Fortney, Malik Hodjaev, Chad Kia, Oleh Kotsyuba, Terry Martin, Natalia Reed, Ron Sela, Wheeler M. Thackston, and Dalia Yasharpour.

To all of my students, past and present: Being in class with you has been my greatest inspiration and one of the greatest joys of my life.

This book is dedicated to my grandfathers, who were both American veterans of the Second World War: Robert E. Eidelsberg (1921–1998) and Isidore "Irving" Hanin (1918–1991). Pvt. Hanin served in Japan and the Philippines. 1st Lt. Eidelsberg flew B-24 missions into Germany with the 458th Bombardment Group.

Finally, thanks to Ashley, the light of my life.

List of Abbreviations

AkadNkKaz	The National Academy of Sciences of the Republic of Kazakhstan, Almaty
AkadNkTat	The Academy of Sciences of the Republic of Tatarstan, Kazan
CARC	Council for the Affairs of Religious Cults
CAROC	Council for the Affairs of the Russian Orthodox Church
DUMSK	Central Spiritual Directorate of the Muslims of the North Caucasus
DUMZAK	Spiritual Directorate of the Muslims of Transcaucasia
GARF	State Archive of the Russian Federation, Moscow
HPSSS	The Harvard Project on the Soviet Social System, Cambridge, Massachusetts
IIIPP	Boltina, V.D. and L.V. Sheveleva. *Iz istorii islama v Pavlodarskom Priirtysh'e 1919–1999: sbornik dokumentov*. Pavlodar: EKO, 2001.
ISG3	Arapov, D.Iu., and G.G. Kosach, eds. *Islam i sovetskoe gosudarstvo (1944–1990). Sbornik Dokumentov. Vypusk 3.* Moscow: Mardzhani, 2011.
NatArchGE	National Archives of Georgia, Tbilisi
NKGB	People's Commissariat for State Security
NKID	People's Commissariat for Foreign Affairs
NKVD	People's Commissariat for Internal Affairs
OMSA	Orenburg Muslim Spiritual Assembly
PDDUM	Akhmadullin, V.A. *Patrioticheskaia deiatel'nost' dukhovnykh upravlenii musul'man v gody velikoi otechestvennoi voiny*. Moscow: Islamskaia kniga, 2015.
PURKKA	Political Administration of the Workers' and Peasants Red Army
RGASPI	Russian State Archive of Socio-Political History, Moscow
RPTs	Vasil'eva, O.Iu., I.I. Kudriavtsev, L.A. Lykova, eds. *Russkaia pravoslavnaia tserkov v gody Velikoi Otechestvennoi voiny, 1941–1945 gg. Sbornik documentov*. Moscow: Izd. Krutitskogo podvor'ia Obshchestvo liubitelei tserkovnoi istorii, 2009.
RSFSR	Russian Soviet Federal Socialist Republic
SADUM	Spiritual Directorate of the Muslims of Central Asia and Kazakhstan
SNK	Council of People's Commissars

Sovinformburo   Soviet Information Bureau
TsDUM   Central Spiritual Directorate of the Muslims of Russia
TsUNKhU   Central Administration for National Economic Accounting
VRGV   Odintsov, M.I. *Vlast' i religiia v gody voiny. Gosudarstvo i*
                religioznye organizatsii v SSSR v gody Velikoi Otechestvennoi voiny.
                1941–1945. Moscow OOO "Favorit," 2005.
VTsIK   All-Russian Central Executive Committee

A Brief Note on Transliteration

In the interests of keeping diacritics to a minimum, I have omitted them from most proper names as well as from commonplace titles and for words of foreign origin that are widely recognized in English (e.g. *imam*, *mulla*). I have retained diacritics for most transliterated samples of Turkic and Persian. In transliterating Russian, I have followed the Modified Library of Congress system. In transliterating Persian, I have followed the *International Journal of Middle East Studies* (*IJMES*) standard. For Turkic languages, I have generally followed Library of Congress systems when available, but I have made certain small modifications to clarify pronunciation (e.g. I have transliterated some samples of Arabic-script Bashkir to make them more consistent with standardized transliteration from Cyrillic-script Bashkir, in order to make the vocabulary more recognizable to modern Bashkir speakers). For Muslim figures born in the pre-Soviet period who are best known by the "Russified" version of their names, I have opted to use those "Russified" names for the convenience of researchers using search engines. For example, I write Gabdrahman Rasulev rather than ʿAbd al-Raḥman Rasūlī. Similarly, I have opted for Ishan Babakhanov over several alternatives that may yield fewer returns in an English-language keyword search (e.g. Ishan Babakhan, Eshon Boboxon).

Introduction

Debating the Wartime "Religious Revolution"

During the Second World War, the brutal Soviet anti-religious repressions of previous years were ended, and Stalin tasked religious leaders from across the USSR—some newly released from prison camps—with rallying citizens to a "Holy War" against Hitler. Meanwhile, convinced that a new age of religious toleration had arrived, citizens of many faiths participated in what amounted to a revolution in Soviet religious life. Soldiers prayed on the battlefield; entire villages celebrated once-banned holidays; and state-backed religious leaders used their new positions not only to consolidate power over their communities but also to petition for further religious freedoms. This book recounts and interprets this "religious revolution," focusing on Soviet Muslims from Central Asia, the Volga-Urals, and the Caucasus, millions of whom fought for the Red Army or labored on the home front to support the war effort. It is not a book about their fight against the Nazis, but rather about their religion in wartime—the way it was mobilized as a new tool of state propaganda; the way religious repression receded and then changed shape; and the way Soviet Muslim communities responded to the dawn of unprecedented religious freedoms, some of which were shepherded by the state and some of which were achieved thanks to its incompetence or indifference.

Notwithstanding popular myths about the triumph of Soviet atheism, for many citizens religious identity and devotion survived the brutal religious repressions of the 1920s and 1930s—as Stalin clearly realized, and as Soviet officials relentlessly documented, year after year, in panicked or exasperated secret reports. It was precisely the vitality of the religion that Stalin was hoping to exploit when he sought the aid of religious leaders—Christian, Muslim, Buddhist, Jewish, and others—in calling citizens to war.[1] While reviving and promoting religious institutions, the Soviet government established a two-pronged system of propaganda for the country's Muslim "national minorities."[2] On the one hand, the Communist Party of the Soviet Union (CPSU) deluged Muslims with ostensibly secular literature lauding

God Save the USSR. Jeff Eden, Oxford University Press (2021). © Oxford University Press.
DOI: 10.1093/oso/9780190076276.003.0001

the "friendship" of all Soviet peoples and their common cause in defending socialism; on the other, select Muslim elites were delegated the task of issuing a parallel, distinctly Islamic rallying call. In widely circulated speeches and fatwa-like pronouncements, these Muslim elites articulated the war effort in the language of classical Islamic struggles: the Qur'an was quoted liberally; appropriate and familiar samples of *hadith* (the reported words and deeds of the Prophet Muhammad) were deployed; Hitler was declared an enemy of Islam in particular, seeking to destroy not only the world's Muslims but also their customs and sacred places; soldiers were declared "mujahids" (literally, "jihadis"). The war was called a *ghazat* ("holy war") and a jihad. Here is how the state-backed Central Asian Muslim leader Ishan Babakhanov rallied his public to war (in a speech translated here from Arabic-script Uzbek):[3]

> In union with all the Soviet peoples, the Muslims of Turkestan and Kazakhstan have sent their own dear children to join the ranks in this general and sacred jihad (*umūmī va muqaddas jihād*), this holy war (*ghazāt*). And in the manner of fathers (*atalarcha*) they recite to them the noble *fātiḥa* and see them off, hoping with all their heart that they might defeat and destroy the enemy . . . . Every Muslim who sacrifices himself for God in the path of religion is a martyr (*shahīd*). And every single Muslim who slays the accursed and seditious enemy is a *ghāzī* and a *mujāhid*—a warrior for the faith (*dīn uchun urush qiluvchidur*).

Soviet-backed Muslim elites such as Babakhanov were not appointed by the state to "revive" Islam but to channel and control it by tapping into religious currents that were already present in Soviet society. From the state's perspective, "controlling" religion was an important step on the path to overseeing the destruction of religion. That final triumph was still far off, however: the very presumption, echoed repeatedly at the highest levels of government, that a significant market existed for this "religious propaganda" hints that top Soviet officials, including Stalin, believed their decades-long, multifaceted atheist campaigns to have been a failure. This failure was not seen as an isolated problem; rather, it was enmeshed in the state's often-lamented inability to vanquish all the benighted cultural "survivals" (*perezhitki*) of the pre-Soviet past. After the Nazi invasion, as Adeeb Khalid writes, "Stalin banked quite shamelessly on traditional sources of legitimacy for the war effort. The regime resurrected imperial Russian heroes, reinstated traditions of the imperial Russian army, and made peace with religion . . . it suspended the persecution of religious observance. Churches and mosques opened again, and religious organizations had leave to convene again. The regime needed all the help it could get, and religious leaders proved loyal."[4]

In the past several years, the emergence of exciting new sources has made it possible to study the impacts of these wartime developments in unprecedented depth. Compilations of wartime literature, digitized archival documents, published document collections, and local histories have revealed a world of religiously themed poetry and folklore; a rich devotional and ritual life; and the persistence of esteemed sacred lineages, unbroken, through the Soviet period.[5] The emergence of a veritable library of Soviet Muslim literature from archives and private collections is such a recent, sudden phenomenon that the smooth integration of Soviet and Muslim themes in some of this literature retains the power to provoke a double take. Consider, for example, the thematic shift from *ta'ziya* (Muslim ritual mourning, in this case) to the Communist Party in the following Second World War POW poem, translated here from Kumyk and dating to 1942:[6]

> Oh, my life—the black, gray land,
> This land will shroud me.
> My brothers will suffer in their pure hearts,
> My sisters will don their black mourning shrouds,
> My dear mother, weeping, will find the grave,
> And my wife will find herself a husband.
> My sister, Ilmu, will keep on mourning,
> And my friends will stand in *ta'ziya*.
> Long live, long live the Communist Party,
> Which will set this oppression on freedom's path!

This poem was produced "privately" by a Dagestani villager, discovered years later by a Soviet folklorist, and never published in the author's lifetime. There is much more where this comes from, and we will see further samples of poetry like this in Chapter 4.[7]

While "unofficial" Soviet Muslim sources such as letters and unpublished poetry have been coming to light, "official" government sources on Islam have been enjoying a well-deserved reappraisal. On the one hand, many Soviet-era sources on Islam, both bureaucratic and academic, are fraught with inaccurate assumptions, peddling—for example—paranoid fantasies about Sufi mystics conspiring to stage anti-Soviet uprisings.[8] Others traffic in tabloid-like falsehoods about the "primitive barbarity" of Muslim ritual life.[9] It is easy to see, in other words, why the uncritical use of such sources has been lamented by leading historians such as Michael Kemper, who concludes that we should ignore not only such sources as these, but *any* source produced by Soviet non-Muslims concerning Soviet Muslims.[10] On the other hand, while the touted uprising of wandering mystics never came to pass, the more mundane religious activities lamented by bureaucrats are often echoed by other kinds of sources, ranging from interviews to memoirs to petitions written by Muslims. Soviet "atheist sources," moreover, can be read profitably against the grain by readers who are cognizant of their biases. These biases—like most "Soviet-speak" tropes—are rarely subtle and tend to be so formulaic that they are easily recognized. For example, as Devin DeWeese has described, in ritual practices painted by Soviet sources as pagan "shamanism" or "pre-Islamic survivals," the savvy reader can effortlessly identify commonplace and longstanding Islamic traditions found all over the Muslim world.[11]

Finally, the line between "official" and "unofficial" sources can sometimes be blurry (an issue to which we shall return in Chapter 5). Take the sources produced by state-backed Muslim elites in wartime, many of which are showcased in the course of this book. Are these "official" sources? The Muslim elites in question were working for—or at least with the sanction of—a state institution, but their background and orientation is altogether different from that of the average Moscow-based atheist bureaucrat, and lumping the two together obscures more than it explains. Most of the Muslim elites tapped for wartime service by the Soviet government were "elders" from revered Muslim lineages, whose religious leadership and prestige dates back to the Tsarist period, and in many cases even earlier. Babakhanov, quoted earlier, was born in 1858 and served two terms in Soviet prisons; he was released from his second stint shortly before the war began. To say the least, he is a very unusual kind of "Soviet official." The propaganda he provided was not, as we shall see, a "pure" product of Moscow, dictated to him from above; it was a negotiated discourse, a remarkable hybrid of Muslim and Soviet patriotism.

This book draws together a range of voices—"official," "unofficial," and somewhere in between. It also draws on sources in a broad range of languages: Russian, Uzbek, Bashkir, Tatar, Persian, Kazakh, and Kumyk. The effort here, however, is not to survey all of the available evidence on Muslim life in the war era, nor to produce a generalization about what constituted normative "Soviet Islam" at the time, much less over the course of the entire Soviet period.[12] My goal is more modest: to explore the dynamics of Muslim life and state policy in a pivotal four-year period by using evidence drawn from a diverse range of sources, including speeches, eyewitness accounts, memoirs, correspondences, agents' reports, petitions, interviews, and literature.

Two major issues are beyond the immediate scope of the book, although they are deserving of further study. First, I have opted not to cover the important issue of Muslim populations deported from the Caucasus in wartime. Due perhaps to my lack of facility in most Caucasian languages, I have found fewer sources than I hoped to find concerning the religious dimensions of deportation, so I have omitted this broad topic. I hope to return to it again at a later stage, when I have found more sources. Second, while I include much material about Orthodox Christianity, the Soviet Union's most prominent religion, I have opted not to cover the country's many other minority religions, including Judaism, Buddhism, and many other varieties of Christianity (ranging from Catholicism to Renovationism).

While focused specifically on the dynamics of Muslim life, state policy, and propaganda, this book offers a new way of answering the most basic and controversial questions about Soviet religions in this crucial period. Why did the revolution in religious life take place? What role did "popular" religiosity and public religious devotion play? Why did the Soviet state, just a few years after slaughtering religious elites by the tens of thousands during the Great Terror of 1937–38, shift dramatically toward religious tolerance? Why did Stalin revive the Orthodox Christian Patriarchate in wartime, and establish multiple Muslim "muftiates" with official permission to pass fatwas and preside over a vast network of mosques? Addressing these questions at the outset, and in some detail, will help set the stage for many of the themes explored in this book.

Propaganda abroad

One of the most common explanations for the wartime religious revolution is also the most radical: the idea that the shift in Soviet religious policy ultimately had little whatsoever to do with the citizens of the Soviet Union, but was instead a propaganda campaign directed *outward*, toward foreign populations and their leaders.[13] In the first years of the war, anti-Soviet propaganda abroad often focused on religious repression in the USSR— propaganda spread, for example, by the Nazis as part of a broader program of promoting Germany as a defender of religious freedom. As David Motadel and others have shown, the Muslim world in particular was targeted with a robust Nazi propaganda campaign. Sketchy classified plans submitted on September 13, 1941, to V.M. Molotov, minister of foreign affairs, summarize the Soviet Union's predicament, as well as the early game plan:[14]

> To neutralize the anti-Soviet propaganda throughout the Muslim world which has been widespread in recent times, from Berlin and Rome, it would be extremely important for the Soviet Informbiuro, or the NKID, to carry out a series of activities:
>
> 1) Organize and conduct (for example, among the All-Slavic or Jewish [organizations]) a radio-meeting of Eastern representatives/Muslims/peoples of the USSR/Uzbeks, Kazakhs, Turkmens, Tajiks, Tatars, Azerbaijanis, Lezgis, Chechens, Ossetians, with an anti-fascist appeal to the peoples of the East/Muslims/the whole world. The meeting could be held in Moscow, Baku, or Tashkent; and involve the writers Dzhambul, Lakhuti, and others.
> 2) Organize, for example, an address by Metropolitan Sergii/an address to all the Muslim believers of the world from the Muslim religious centers of the USSR. We already have three such appeals.
> 3) Along with these two activities, gather the above materials and hand them over, in accordance with the requests of Stafford Cripps, to the British Ministry of Information to be spread among the Muslims of the Near and Middle East via English propaganda channels.

Already in the first months of the war, in other words, Soviet officials were focused on the need to counter German propaganda with propaganda of their own. The surreal race was on between Hitler and Stalin to win the hearts and minds of the faithful, both at home and abroad. Neither side was above bending the truth to suit its purposes. The radio program alluded to in the classified document just quoted, for example, was a September 6, 1941, Axis broadcast from Rome directed at Soviet Muslims, in which they were warned of a fresh wave of purges on the horizon, including their imminent expulsion from Crimea (this propaganda "prophecy" came true for many) and the conversion of all Russian mosques into cinemas (this was a half-truth, at best).[15] The plan to counter this Axis propaganda with Soviet propaganda was rapidly set in motion. Appeals by Soviet Muslim leaders—among other Soviet religious elites—were circulated not only among the country's own Muslim populations, but also abroad via the British Ministry of Information. Much of this propaganda hailed the Soviet Union as a bastion of religious freedom.

Such Soviet "religious propaganda" would continue to be piped abroad for the remaining years of the war.[16] These dispatches—to which we shall return in Chapter 2—invariably revolved around two points. First, they were calls to support the war against the Nazis, which was described by Soviet religious leaders as a "holy war," as the Nazis were said to threaten religious freedom, religious communities, and the very survival of religion itself (whether it be Islam, Buddhism, or any other faith). Second, they were advertisements for the freedom and prosperity enjoyed by the faithful in the Soviet Union, championing the Soviet state as a catalyst and safeguard of self-determination among religious communities.

Both points are well represented in a 1945 appeal by the Soviet-backed Central Asian Muslim leader and jurist (*mufti*) Ishan Babakhanov to the Muslims of Xinjiang, which was at that time a Soviet-supported state called the East Turkestan Republic—home of the Uyghurs, as well as many Kazakhs and other Central Asian Muslim groups. This text is worth a close look, as it is a fine entry point into the peculiar and remarkable genre of "Soviet Islamic propaganda."[17]

Babakhanov's address begins by acknowledging that the Soviet Union has not enjoyed the best reputation as a happy home for Muslims. "On behalf of all Turkestan's Muslims," Babakhanov begins, "we appeal to the Muslim world with this letter that describes concisely our past and present [circumstances], such as they are, with the goal of dispelling various assumptions and notions about us." The mufti then takes listeners on a whirl-wind tour of Turkestan's sacred Muslim sites, highlighting its holiest shrines, madrasas, mosques, and manuscripts. The "audio tour" leads listeners from large-scale marvels to small-scale ones—from shrine-complexes to books, and from the vastness of the sacred landscape to the modern libraries of the Soviet Union, which, Babakhanov explains, preserve such treasures as a Qur'an written by the Caliph ʿUthman himself. All the while, Babakhanov seamlessly interweaves the story of religion and the story of nations: one especially valuable manuscript, the mufti notes, is written in a medieval Turkic dialect that was the ancestor of Uyghur as well as Uzbek—the idea being that Soviet Central Asia is a historical homeland to the Uyghurs too. "Turkestan," he says, "has been for millennia—and remains—the sacred fatherland of the Uzbeks, Tajiks, Turkmens, Kazakhs, Kyrgyz, Uyghurs, and Karakalpaks."[18]

A lesson in history follows the tour of sacred spaces. "Before the Great Soviet Revolution," Babakhanov explains, "we Muslims of Turkestan were disunited and scattered, lacking our own statehood. Under the banner of the Soviet government we united and established our free republics." In these conditions of independence, Central Asians had thrived—both as modern Soviet citizens and as pious Muslims. Babakhanov blends the two identities into a smooth continuum:[19]

> We now have schools of higher learning for any branch of the sciences, in which thousands of Muslim youths are studying. Shining forth for five hundred years on the threshold of the majestic madrasa of Ulugh Beg in Samarkand is a noble saying of our Prophet: "Striving for knowledge is the duty of every Muslim." Only under the Soviet government is this [saying] embodied in life itself. Now we have our own doctors, teachers, professors, agronomists, engineers, officers, pilots. Turkestan's Muslims have gained the opportunity to apply their skills in all areas of life, and to ensure their prosperity, while remaining firm in the clear faith of Islam.

This progress among Muslims, Babakhanov explains, is not just a by-product of the Bolshevik Revolution but an ongoing process safeguarded by Stalin himself, protected by the Soviet constitution, and now shepherded by the official Soviet muftiates (religious councils, or "spiritual directorates")—which Babakhanov presents as essentially *independent* of the state, a kind of parallel representative government for the faithful:[20]

> Thanks to the constitution of the USSR, the basic law of our state, written by the blessed hand of the great and wise Stalin, we are the masters of our own policies, economy, culture, language, creed, customs, and private lives. Article 124 of the constitution of our state grants every citizen the right to profess whatever religion they please. The clergy and faithful of various denominations have their own Directorates and in matters of the exercise of religious rites the state does not attempt any sort of obstruction.
>
> It is known to Muslims all over the world that the stewardship of Muslim religious activities in Turkestan is entrusted to the Spiritual Directorate of the Muslims of Central Asia and Kazakhstan, elected in the great congress (*kurultai*) of Muslim clergy and believers.

Finally, Babakhanov comes around to the present crisis: the ongoing war against Hitler and his allies, who, he explains, wish "to destroy our home, trample our rights, humiliate and debase our religion, convert Muslims to Protestantism [sic], and leave barren our fragrant gardens, as the great irrigation canals built by the hands of the people flow—along with water, giving life and happiness to our people—with the innocent blood and tears of the elderly, women, and children."[21] The mufti explains that the Crimea, the Caucasus, and other regions have been devastated by the Nazi invasion, and, hailing the accomplishments of Soviet Muslim war heroes, he rallies his audience to support the war effort with a brief selection of Qur'anic verses, including the famous lines, "Fight in the way of Allah those who fight you but do not transgress. Indeed. Allah does not like transgressors. And kill them wherever you overtake them and expel them from wherever they have expelled you . . ."[22] Noting the recent accomplishments of British and American forces, Babakhanov ends his war coverage on an optimistic note:[23]

> The hour of victory against the fascists is near. To accelerate victory against the enemy, we servants of the Muslim religion pray to Allah every day, five times a day, in the mosques. We offer our appeal to all the Muslims of the world. The Hitlerites are the enemies of all freedom-loving peoples, and especially of Muslims. For that reason, we Muslim clergy living in the Soviet Union appeal to the Muslims of all the world to rise up against the wicked fascist enslavers.

Babakhanov concludes by returning to his point of departure: "Do not believe the various heinous slanders circulated about our country by our enemies and yours, may a curse fall upon their heads!"[24]

The existence of many such Soviet Muslim broadcasts directed abroad supports the hypothesis that outward-facing propaganda was a key aspect of wartime religious policy. These broadcasts continued, moreover, after the Nazis were driven from the Soviet Union. In May and June 1945, three top representatives of the USSR's officially sanctioned Transcaucasus muftiate (Spiritual Directorate of the Muslims of Transcaucasia, DUMZAK) visited Iran at the invitation of an Iranian parliamentarian and *shaykh al-islam*. They visited no fewer than ten different Iranian cities, and their activities were carefully monitored all the while by agents of the Soviet Ministry of Foreign Affairs. The agents' reports confirm that the three Soviet Shi'a Muslim elites were ideal envoys, diligently encouraging positive impressions of Muslim life in the Soviet Union, where, in their telling, the faithful enjoyed freedom of conscience and myriad opportunities for advancement. They arrived with gifts for Iranian elites, with pre-approved speeches, and with the remote supervision of I.V. Polianskii, the veteran Soviet anti-religious official then heading the Council for the Affairs of Religious Cults (CARC), the main Soviet organ overseeing religions other than the Orthodox Church.[25] The climax of their visit was a June 13 broadcast by the DUMZAK *shaykh al-islam* Akhund Agha Alizada, directed to all of the envoys' co-religionists in Iran.

This appeal too is worth a close look, as it introduces other key motifs of Soviet Islamic propaganda, including the explicit argument that Soviet Muslim life had been untouched by religious repression; that the new state-backed Muslim muftiates had been (and remained) a "grassroots" initiative; and that Soviet Muslims, represented by their muftiates, enjoyed free exchange and free contact with Muslims around the world.

Though the war had ended, Alizada's address begins with five impassioned paragraphs recounting the recent age of "unprecedented hardship and suffering" during which "flourishing countries have been destroyed, entire peoples have been exterminated *en masse*, the fruits of their labor looted and burned, innocent children murdered along with the elderly, women raped."[26] The Azeri *shaykh al-islam* describes how he and his colleagues had rallied Muslim troops in the Caucasus with appeals that were published both at home and in Iran. "Thank God," he goes on, "that under the brave leadership of His Excellency Marshal Stalin, the treacherous fascists have been dealt crushing blows and unavoidable defeats on all fronts."[27] Among the veterans of this war included two of Alizada's own sons, four of his close relatives, and many Muslim "Heroes of the Soviet Union" (the country's highest honor for courage in battle).

There was another struggle left to fight, however: "After they had fulfilled their duty to humanity and to the Muslim world, we turned to Muslims in 1944 with another appeal, [this time] highlighting their obligations to their faith." Muslims had been bringing these wartime Muslim leaders "religious questions," and it was in order to satisfy their demands, Alizada declares, that he and his colleagues petitioned the Supreme Soviet for permission to create a muftiate. The initiative for all this, in his telling, came firmly from Soviet Muslims and their leaders; the Soviet government's involvement was nothing more than consent. Alizada then introduces his "directorate" with a pure,

exquisite sample of the burgeoning art of Soviet Muslim propaganda—that
seamless yet jarring amalgam of Islamic ethics, Stalinist "Friendship of the
Peoples" motifs, and classic Bolshevik labor-heroism:[28]

> The Directorate of Clerical Affairs is guided in its activities by the teachings
> of the Qur'an and the authentic traditions of Muhammad. In special cases,
> emergency meetings of all members of the directorate are convened. Our
> directorate engages, in its functions, the kind of educational work that
> strengthens friendship and unity among the peoples of the USSR, elevates
> and mobilizes collective farmers for their spring planting, encourages dili-
> gent and productive labor, nurtures feelings of faithfulness to government
> leaders and administration, etc. The responsibilities of our directorate
> include assigning clerical leaders to various tasks, and the safeguarding
> of mausoleums and monuments dedicated to scholars and great figures
> of Islam.

Turning to questions submitted to the envoys by their Iranian hosts,
Alizada introduces the primary personnel of his directorate before trafficking
in some outright lies. "The manner of preaching in the [Soviet] mosques," he
says, "is almost the same as it is anywhere else. Our preachers read chapters
from the Qur'an and discuss the lives of scholars, imams, and prophets. In
each *raion*, the *oblasts* have their own religious scholars and students in religious schools, and at the present time more than 50 Caucasian students are
studying in Iran and at Atabat [in Iraq]. After finishing their studies, they
can lead spiritual activities, with the permission of the government. Our
mosques, religious schools, and meeting-places remain just as they were before."[29] In fact, nearly all of the religious schools in the territory of the Soviet
Union had long since been closed, and hardly any had been reopened by
1945. Thousands of mosques had been closed. As for Soviet Muslims' conspicuous absence from Mecca, Alizada blames "the particularities of the international environment" from keeping them away.[30] The scarcity of Islamic
books printed in Cyrillic is explained away by the fact that the Soviet Union
has plenty of Islamic books in older scripts, and therefore "there is no need
to reprint these books."[31] Nor is there any need to print, import, or translate
the Qur'an, since "There is not a single Muslim home in which one would
not find several copies of the Qur'an."[32] Alizada turns then to the Soviet
government's protection of religious freedom, territory covered in Ishan

Babakhanov's address to Xinjiang's Muslims—but covered here with a more brazen streak of "creativity":[33]

> I want to say a few words about freedom of religion and faith in the Soviet Union. The peoples of the Soviet Union have always enjoyed freedom of conscience and, in particular, in the Soviet Constitution, article 124 underlines the freedom of the conduct [of worship by] religious denominations. In the Soviet Union, religion is separated from the state and the state from religion. We, the faithful scholars, *have always enjoyed complete freedom to practice our religious rites.* In our country the call to prayer is read from the minaret every morning and evening.

Alizada next elaborates on the opportunities for secular education and advancement in the Soviet state, contrasting these circumstances with the Tsarist era, during which the "government did not pay any attention to Muslims, cutting off our path to the mastery of knowledge and science. Our life back then was dark and joyless."[34] Thanks were due to Jafar Baghirov, first secretary of Azerbaijan's Communist Party, but also, of course, "to the great leader of all the nations, Marshal Stalin, who, without distinguishing between nationalities and religions, thinks of the happiness and well-being of all mankind. He casts his attentions upon all the people of the world, and in particular, his friendly attentions are drawn to the Iranian people—the ancient neighbor of our homeland."[35]

Such was the message the Soviet government wished its Muslim leaders to bring abroad: that all was well for Soviet Muslims; that they had united to defeat Hitler; that the Soviet state had facilitated both their self-determination within their "independent" nations and the fraternity of those nations; that Muslims were permitted absolute freedom of religion, a freedom safeguarded by law; that holy places, manuscripts, and traditions were all well preserved; that the Soviet Union's new Muslim muftiates had been formed completely on the initiative of Muslims themselves, for the sole purpose of addressing Muslim concerns and conducting embassies to coreligionists abroad, with no intervention from the government other than a benevolent, paternal nod of assent. There was not any repression of religion in the Soviet Union, nor had there ever been.

Amid the lies here, there are also some intriguing truths. Alizada tells his Iranian audience that some Muslim cemeteries are maintained, that customary prayers and rites for the dead are still performed, and that periods of mourning—far more frequent than usual during the course of the war—are still marked in the traditional Muslim fashion. He mentions that most Muslims working in "secular" occupations came from religious backgrounds: "Almost all scientists of geology [for example] come from families in which, for generations, all members of the family engaged in religious activities. I myself come from such a family."[36] While the claim that religious life had never been negatively impacted by Soviet rule is a grotesque distortion, the *shaykh al-islam's* claim that major aspects of religious experience had persisted in familiar forms rings true. As Alizada claims, and as I will show throughout this book, some strings had never broken, and they resonated in an old, familiar harmony into the war years and beyond.

Not all of the outward-directed Soviet religious propaganda was intended for faithful masses beyond the Soviet Union; some was intended to persuade particular world leaders of the Soviet Union's benevolence toward religion. This became a matter of urgency in the war years, when retaining full support from Britain and the United States sometimes meant assuaging suspicions about Stalinist repression.[37] A substantial proportion of the American public opposed the outlay of material support for the "godless" Soviet Union, and President Franklin Delano Roosevelt (an Episcopalian) was concerned enough to order the US Embassy in Moscow to research the status of the USSR's religious communities.[38] A particularly cruel strategy had been proposed by Harry S. Truman—then a senator in Missouri—in June 1941: "If we see that Germany is winning we ought to help Russia, and if Russia is winning we ought to help Germany, and that way let them kill as many as possible, although I don't want to see Hitler victorious under any circumstances."[39] On the eve of the Tehran Conference of November 1943, Stalin surely felt the urge to dispel any hesitation on the part of his Western allies in working closely with the Soviets or in maintaining the flow of aid. At this conference, Stalin also wished to conclude negotiations to open a second front against Germany, led off by the Allied invasion of northern France—an invasion Stalin had been pushing for since the first months of the war.

Here, the timeline of events proves revealing, and further supports the hypothesis that outward-directed propaganda was a major element of the wartime change in orientation toward religion: the creation of the Soviet Union's newly state-sanctioned religious institutions (including the Orthodox Christian Patriarchate and the Muslim muftiates), which was followed by a wave of speeches and broadcasts such as those described earlier, took place September–October 1943, just weeks before the Tehran Conference.[40] If Stalin's goal was to inspire rumors of thriving religious freedom on the eve of the conference, then deploying several of the country's most eminent religious leaders to sing the USSR's praises was undoubtedly a shrewd move. The implications of this "coincidence" did not go unnoticed by journalists at the time, nor by the Soviet public. One American journalist even predicted the sequence of events: just a few months earlier, when Stalin dissolved the Communist International (Comintern), the primary Soviet organization dedicated to spreading revolution abroad, in order to ease the minds of his allies, the *New York Times* correspondent Harold Callender wrote that "Some of those in closest touch with Russian relations believe that the dissolution of the Communist International may be followed by some gesture in the religious field calculated to allay suspicion of Moscow abroad."[41] Meanwhile, an Irish journalist reported that many Russians regarded the easing of religious restrictions as a way "to please England and America."[42] The effort paid off—or at least it did not backfire: the Tehran Conference was a victory for Stalin; Lend-Lease aid to the Soviet Union increased nearly twofold in 1943; and Roosevelt went so far as to declare, "In so far as I am informed, churches in Russia are open . . ."[43] Cyril Garbett, the Soviet-sympathetic Archbishop of York, followed suit: "There can be no doubt," he announced, "that worship within the churches is fully allowed [in the USSR]."[44]

The foreign tours and broadcasts of Soviet religious leaders were supplemented by a limited propaganda publishing campaign, including the printing of texts intended exclusively for foreign consumption. Perhaps the earliest major publication in this mold was the Orthodox Christian Patriarch Sergii's booklet, *The Truth about Religion in Russia*.[45] As the title hints, the thrust of the book was to set the record straight: religion thrived in Russia, notwithstanding rumors about religious repression. Just as Alizada—among others—would later assert in broadcasts abroad, Patriarch Sergii claims that there had never been any real hindrance to religious freedom in the Soviet Union; indeed, it had been safeguarded by law. Rumors of repression, he claimed, were the concoctions of Russian émigrés who hoped to wring further religious concessions from Stalin by inclining Roosevelt to make religious freedom a key issue in the two states' alliance.[46] *The Truth*, in short, was that everything was just fine. The booklet was printed at the Iskra Revoliutsiei press—until recently, the printer for publications by the League of Militant Atheists.[47] Sergii himself, by the way, had previously been jailed by the Bolsheviks.

Muslim leaders too were enlisted in publishing efforts directed abroad. The broadcast to Muslims in Xinjiang cited earlier, for example, was to be disseminated in a print run of 3,500 copies in Uyghur translation, plus another 1,500 copies in Kazakh (likely for the Kazakh minority population in Xinjiang).[48] A similar appeal to Isma'ili Muslims across Eurasia—in Afghanistan, Iran, China, Syria, and Iraq—would be printed in a run of 2,000 copies, on the initiative of the state security services (then called the NKGB).[49] The speeches of Gabdrahman Rasulev, a top Muslim "loyalist" elite and head of the Central Spiritual Directorate (muftiate), were often tapped for export. In one address, Rasulev lambasted the Palestinian mufti Hajj Amin al-Husseini, an ally of Hitler and disseminator of Nazi propaganda in the Arab World, as a pagan and as a worshiper of "the Nazi god Votan"—a Russified spelling of the German name for Odin.[50] In 1944, plans developed for Rasulev to pen a book about the global Muslim struggle against the Nazis, to be published in India. The plans never came to fruition, but they circulated at the top levels of government, with I.V. Polianskii consulting V.M. Molotov on the particulars.

Muslim and Christian organizations alike continued their foreign publishing ventures well after the war ended. Ishan Babakhanov's Tashkent-based muftiate, SADUM, began publishing its magazine (*Muslims of the Soviet East*) in English. Most of its content blended patriotic Soviet and Islamic themes. Along with reprints of speeches by Stalin, it featured articles such as "The Obligations of the Muslim Clergy before the Motherland in the Current Period" and "On the Patriotic Work of Kazakh Spirituality."[51] Limited runs of Soviet Muslim calendars were also printed for export.[52] These efforts mirrored those of the Orthodox Church, which relaunched its *Journal of the Moscow Patriarchate* in 1943 and issued calendars the next year.[53]

Clearly, the war era and the years that followed were relatively robust periods for Soviet religious propaganda directed toward foreign audiences. This kind of propaganda was seen by Soviet officials not only as a positive step in rallying sympathy for the Soviet Union abroad, but also as a crucial step in countering Nazi anti-Soviet propaganda. It is not surprising, therefore, that many historians have regarded the Soviet religious reforms in the war era to be primarily an *outwardly directed propaganda* enterprise, and that some historians have concluded that the main target of this venture was foreign, not domestic, audiences.

There are good reasons to question these conclusions, however, as we shall see, and another of the most popular hypotheses about the religious policy shift points toward one of these reasons: namely, the fact that a much larger proportion of war-era Soviet religious propaganda was actually disseminated *internally*, to Soviet citizens.

Propaganda at home: Borderlands loyalty and rallying calls to war

This "internal" propaganda, which began in the first months of the war, seems to have been disseminated with particular urgency in Soviet-occupied territories of Eastern Europe and, later, in areas of the Soviet Union under the most immediate threat from advancing German troops. The territories occupied by the USSR in 1939 had already been established, before the war began, as a zone of special permissiveness when it came to religion.[54] In 1941, having been spared from the full intensity of the religious persecutions seen elsewhere in the country, the occupied "borderlands" may have held as many as 70 percent of all functioning Soviet churches.[55] Nevertheless, on the very first day of the German invasion, Nazi radio broadcasts assured Soviet citizens that "one of the first measures of the German administration will be the restoration of religious freedom . . . We will allow you to organize religious parishes. Everyone will be free to pray to God in his own manner."[56] These broadcasts naturally omitted Hitler's personal sentiments concerning Christianity, about which he famously declared: "The heaviest blow that ever struck humanity was the coming of Christianity. Bolshevism is Christianity's illegitimate child. Both are inventions of the Jews."[57]

The German-Soviet propaganda war, *within* the Soviet borderlands, therefore began on the very first day of the war. As we shall see in the chapters to come, as other "fronts" for Soviet religious propaganda opened up in later phases of the war, religious leaders from other regions were enlisted to sound the call to battle. In 1943–45, as the Red Army drove out the Germans and reoccupied Eastern Europe, there was also a strong incentive to broadcast religious tolerance as a way of encouraging loyalty, or at least removing a notable incentive for dissent.[58]

Already in 1942, however, as Red Army battlefield deaths mounted at a staggering rate, an entirely new incentive for domestic propaganda arose: the urgent need to stoke the fighting spirit of Soviet non-Russians. The low morale of many Soviet Muslim "nationalities" was a crisis much discussed among Soviet officials, and discrimination was rampant.[59] Problems emerged quickly, in the early months of the war. In the earliest phases, conscripts were overwhelmingly drawn from among Russians, Belarussians, and Ukrainians, and non-Slavic troops who spoke little or no Russian often found themselves placed into entirely Russian-speaking units, unable to communicate with their own commanding officers and comrades. Soviet officials and military elites generally feared, moreover, that non-Russians were unclear on why they should fight in the first place—a problem presumed to stem as much from lack of patriotism as from lack of knowledge about Hitler's intentions and strength. Indeed, it was observed that Central Asian Muslim soldiers and soldiers from the Caucasus were among the most likely to desert, to self-injure in order to free themselves from service, and to radiate low morale in the early months of the war. They were also among the least likely to volunteer.[60] Soldiers from these regions formed a small minority of the overall Red Army in 1941, but by 1942, as deaths mounted and vast expanses of Belarus and Ukraine suffered under Nazi occupation, more troops and greater momentum from Muslim demographics were desperately needed. In March 1942, E. Schadenko, chief of Red Army staffing and recruitment, had expressed his concern to Stalin that such populations showed an ominous lack of interest in joining the Red Army. Less than a month later, a secret resolution was adopted providing for the emergency recruitment of five hundred thousand additional soldiers, many of whom had formerly had their conscription deferred, and a large proportion of whom would be drawn from Uzbekistan and Kazakhstan.[61]

By the end of 1943, non-Slavic populations would be disproportionately well represented on the battlefield, and also on the casualty registers. All the while, starting in the autumn of 1942, these Soviet minority populations were targeted by propaganda campaigns on a massive scale. As increasing numbers of "national units" were formed from Caucasian, Volga-Urals, and Central Asian populations, for example, wave after wave of national-patriotic literature inundated these regions. Newspapers, bookstores, and theaters showcased tales of war heroes from among the Uzbeks, Kazakhs, Kyrgyz, Turkmens, Tajiks, Bashkirs, Tatars, and other Soviet peoples.

This propaganda tide has been discussed extensively in recent years in groundbreaking work by Brandon Schechter, Boram Shin, Charles Shaw, and Roberto Carmack, among others.[62] These historians generally concur that the intense wartime efforts of the state to align patriotism and ethno-national identity were instrumental in the development of a "hybrid" identity that was both Soviet and "national" (Uzbek, Kyrgyz, Kazakh, etc.). The war, they argue, was simultaneously a crucible for Soviet collective patriotism and for the development of national differentiation, as pantheons of distinctly national heroes were relentlessly hailed by the Soviet propaganda machine and held up as models for a new

generation of heroes to be. The struggle against Hitler was depicted simultaneously as struggle for the Soviet homeland and for the local, ethno-national homeland. The story Schechter, Shin, Shaw, and Carmack tell emphasizes the "secular,"
and much of the propaganda they describe is indeed devoid of explicitly religious
content (especially when compared to the simultaneous, overt religious propaganda showcased throughout this book). "Secular"[63] national propaganda and
Soviet religious propaganda, however, emerged as parallel worlds—the former
disseminated by intelligentsia, sanctioned artists, journalists, agitators, and
propagandists; the latter disseminated mostly by sanctioned religious leaders.

The story of how the Soviet government instrumentalized national identities
in wartime and the story of how it instrumentalized religious identities are two
sides to the very same story. These currents may diverge at the level of the com-
partmentalized Soviet bureaucracy, but they converge in many of the individuals we shall meet in this book, for whom—as Alizada and Ishan Babakhanov
suggest—national identity did not subsume or subvert religious identity, but for
whom, as they both proclaim, "love for Homeland is a part of faith."

Revolution from below

In essence, the hypothesis that the primary catalyst of the wartime "religious
revolution" was the state's desire to rally troops boils down to what Solzhenitsyn
argued in his famous *Letter to the Soviet Leaders* from 1974:[64]

> When the war with Hitler began, Stalin, who had omitted and bungled so
> much in the way of military preparation, did not neglect *that* side, the ideo-
> logical side . . . [F]rom the very first days of the war Stalin refused to rely on
> the putrid, decaying prop of ideology. He wisely discarded it, all but ceased
> to mention it and unfurled instead the old Russian banner—sometimes, in-
> deed, the standard of Orthodoxy—and we conquered!

In this formulation, it is clear that the major wartime changes in religious life
constituted a "revolution from above," not just sanctioned but manufactured
and propagated by the government. When Miner published his *Stalin's Holy
War* in 2003, he could write with good reason that this approach was the most
common—indeed, the "standard"—approach among historians.[65]

An increasingly common approach to the issue takes precisely the opposite perspective, arguing that an upwelling of religious feeling and expression

in wartime moved the hand of the Soviet government, which was motivated by adversity and by pragmatism to open the floodgates of tolerance a crack—only to release a torrent, which then needed to be channeled. In more recent years, especially in Russia, this "bottom-up" approach has supplanted the "top-down" vision in prominence. In fact, it is also Miner's own view, and he elegantly summarizes the approach as follows (with respect to the Orthodox Church):[66]

> Contrary to many accounts, what took place during the war was a mass revival of religion, not of the church. The distinction is important, because the revival of religion erupted spontaneously from below as a response to mass death in wartime and the temporary loosening of Communist atheist bonds. This revival was politically volatile, and so Stalin sanctioned the restoration of the Moscow Patriarchate in hopes of restoring order and stability. Among ethnic Russians, the religious revival took the form of increased grass-roots demands for the reopening of churches, the restoration of church property, and the activation of small religious groups and sects that were often hostile to Soviet power and suspicious of the Moscow Patriarchate, or frankly hostile to it, and thus were beyond state control.

Along similar lines, some historians emphasize what they regard as the utter failure of the Soviet fight against religion in prior decades; for the Muslim case, Shoshanna Keller writes that the "establishment of a new [religious] administration, run by an entirely new generation of Muslim clergy under direct control of the state, was a public admission of what had been apparent for several years—that the fight to eradicate Islam was over."[67] Stalin, in this view, was bargaining from a position of weakness. Victoria Smolkin, by contrast, argues precisely the opposite position, proposing that wartime religious policies came from a position of sheer dominance, strength, and confidence:[68]

> Religion mattered to the Bolsheviks inasmuch as it constituted a threat to Soviet power, and by the end of the 1930s—with the political power of the Orthodox Church as an institution nearly destroyed—they believed that threat to have been effectively neutralized. From this point, the continued existence of religion in the Soviet Union would be on the state's terms. Stalin set those terms in 1943, when his wartime reversal on the religious question and creation of a government bureaucracy to manage religious affairs formalized a new framework for Soviet engagements with religion that remained in place for the rest of the Soviet period.

Inarguably, however, religious devotion among Orthodox frontline soldiers (for example) appears to have been exceedingly common, as described by a many of them in interviews soon after the war and in the decades that followed. The interviews conducted as part of the Harvard Project on the Soviet Social System are especially illuminating here, as they were conducted just a few years after the war (between 1950 and 1953) with Soviet expats and refugees in Austria, Germany, and the United States. Some veterans, such as one forty-three-year-old Ukrainian tractor mechanic, quickly became accustomed to witnessing impromptu religious displays even among committed Communist comrades: "I remember when the bombs were bursting, members of the Komsomol and the Party were saying 'God help me' and would drop down on their knees and pray, right in the street."[69] Another Ukrainian *frontovik*, Ion Lazarovich Degen, interviewed years later, recalled: "Before an attack there were no atheists! All whispered prayers before battle. There is nothing worse than waiting at the starting position for the order to attack. Everything around you stops. A poignant, eerie, maddening silence."[70] Many soldiers describe personally partaking of the religious atmosphere of the war years. "Now I am much more religious than I was before," a young Russian student told her interviewer. "Many people learned to pray during the war."[71] A Mordvin Muslim tractorist recalled: "I didn't believe in God. Only when I came to the front in the war, I started thinking about God."[72] Likewise, a Ukrainian auto mechanic recalled that "During the war I was more religious. I prayed in secret and often would do this by lighting a cigarette and going through the motions of smoking but secretly I would be praying. Communist Party members did that too."[73] A Russian officer in his mid-forties had similar recollections: "[Religion] was outside my attention . . . Until the war. Then came the front. I had very interesting moments which made me think about the existence of God, and even about the existence of religion."[74] We will hear more voices like these in Chapter 4 and elsewhere in this book. Multiplied, at least to some extent, across the Red Army, and across the Soviet Union as a whole, could such voices have influenced Stalin?

Continuity with the past

To these approaches I will add one more: the idea that wartime religious policy was not, in fact, a revolutionary change at all. This approach, which has not yet been argued (to my knowledge) in print but which has emerged repeatedly in my conversations with fellow historians, emphasizes continuity with pre-war policies, casting the Great Terror (1937–38), not the Great Patriotic War, as the outlier in an otherwise linear narrative of Soviet religious policy. It was during the Great Terror that religious leaders (or at least alleged leaders) were arrested and executed in the largest numbers—but the key term here is *leaders*. Elites of all discrete, coherent *groups*—whether it be Uzbek political cadres or Moscow academic economists—were especially vulnerable in these years, while the laborers of the collective farm or factory floor were persecuted at substantially lower rates. This was certainly true among religious "believers" too. There is no reason to believe that alleged religious elites were arrested at a much higher rate than, say, military officers or elite Party members in general, nor any data to support the idea that any given Muslim or Orthodox Christian factory worker was substantially more likely to be arrested than a coworker affiliated with the League of Militant Atheists. An important exception here is those religious minorities whose persecution had been near constant since the Tsarist era, and which increased in the Soviet period, such as Old Believers.[75]

The new alliances between the Soviet government and religious leaders in wartime, moreover, were not *all* new: Metropolitan Sergii was "promoted" to Patriarch in this period, but he had been an outward Soviet loyalist since the 1920s; Gabdrahman Rasulev, as we shall see, had "practiced" for his role at the head of the wartime Central Spiritual Directorate by helming that organization's immediate predecessor for several years until its dissolution in the late 1930s. Nor was the idea of expanding the system of mutually beneficial arrangements between the state and certain hand-selected religious leaders a novel product of the war era: Chapter 1 shows that this too has roots in an earlier period. Moreover, state-led restoration and expansion of the Orthodox Church seems to have begun some two years before the German invasion, in 1939, in occupied Eastern Europe.[76]

Finally, there is the inherent challenge of documenting something as abstract as the ebb and flow of "religious life": beyond statistics of building closures and arrests, our evidence consists largely of the impressionistic reportage of those who lived through the war era. Some of this evidence, as we shall see, likewise points toward ongoing religious activity (such as prayer meetings held in basements and private homes) throughout the darkest years of the 1920s and 1930s. While some holy places reopened in the war era, much communal religious activity continued—during *and* after the war—to take place in the very same secretive venues. In some rural regions, religious locals did not even bother resorting to secrecy. The son of a military physician, interviewed in the early 1950s, recalled that even polygamy and public veiling persisted in rural Tajikistan during the height of the anti-religious repressions:[77]

> The wedding under the Soviets was held in ZAGS [Bureau for the Registration of Acts of Civil Status], and you had to show your face there, and by custom Tadzhik women, as you know, are veiled; yet in ZAGS the women had to remove the veil *and consequently many weddings were not registered there.* In the mountains plural marriage existed; I knew a 78 year old mullah in the Lake Iskandarkul region who in 1936 had one wife age 64, another age 40, and a third, the youngest, was only 23. The Soviet regime fought the paranzha [burqa]; if a woman who had a husband in the Red Army came to the post office to get a letter from him the postal officials would not give it to her if she came wearing a veil. You rarely saw a woman veiled in Stalinabad, but the majority of the women wore veils in the remote kishlaks or village.

Other informants interviewed during the Stalin era avow that anti-religious propaganda had little or no influence in their communities or over their personal feelings. "The strong religious base that I received from my mother," an Orthodox Russian bookkeeper recalls, "in the end withstood all the attacks of Soviet propaganda. I was deeply interested in the question of religion and read a lot about it . . . I believe that the low-class vile anti-religious propaganda did the opposite of what it intended to do. I had friends who turned to religion because of the repulsive character of the propaganda."[78] Similarly, an Avar Muslim tractor-driver asserts in a Stalin-era interview that "Stalin has never changed my religious feelings in the least. It is true of the majority of people in the Soviet Union that they are still religious, in spite of everything the regime has done."[79]

One way to avoid the influence of atheist propaganda was simply to ignore it, as a Chechen laborer recalls: "I did not read Soviet books. Because Soviet books and the newspapers are against God and religion. All of it is a lie. We Caucasian peoples did not want to read that, only scoundrels."[80] A Russian former collective farm worker sums up this dynamic of quiet resistance, which is a common theme in interviews with and memoirs by those who lived through the worst years of repression: "[I was] always religious. The Soviets said that there was no God, but I just kept silent and prayed."[81] Another former farmer, in his fifties at the time of his Stalin-era interview, mocks foreigners for believing Soviet propaganda about the mass "seculari-zation" of the country:[82]

> In 1935–36 all the churches in the Soviet Union were closed down. Only in large cities such as Moscow, Leningrad, Kharkov, Kiev, and Odessa, one church was left open. It was because those cities were visited by different foreigners who asked about churches and religion. "You see, the majority of people don't want religion; therefore, we closed down all large churches, and now we use them for theaters and clubs. That minority which still remained religious has its church over there," they used to say to the igno-rant foreigners. In Odessa there was a small church on the suburban cem-etery which was not closed. Each Sunday there were thousands of people. The entire cemetery was full of people kneeling and praying.

In short, some major aspects of religious life associated with the war-time "revival" doubtless began before and continued long after the era of the Second World War.

Reflecting on five approaches

We have so far seen five distinct explanations for the wartime changes in re-ligious life: 1) it was predominantly an outwardly directed propaganda cam-paign, as the Soviet government used claims of religious freedom to counter Nazi propaganda and in Allied diplomacy (the "propaganda abroad hypo-thesis"); 2) it was predominantly an inwardly directed propaganda cam-paign, as the Soviet government used claims of religious freedom to counter Nazi propaganda in the Eastern Front borderlands (the "borderlands prop-aganda hypothesis"); 3) the Soviet government primarily used religious freedom to rally citizens—such as reluctant "non-Russian nationalities"—to the war effort (the "rallying call hypothesis"); 4) the Soviet government was forced to accommodate and channel a "grassroots" flourishing of religious activity (the "revolution from below" hypothesis); and 5) the war era was not as "revolutionary" as it seems with respect to religious life, as the most signif-icant and commonly identified "changes" actually began before the war (the "continuity hypothesis").

In my view, each hypothesis has significant merits as well as significant drawbacks. First, let us consider the "propaganda abroad hypothesis"—that is, the claim that religious tolerance was predominantly a propaganda tool directed abroad by the Soviet government. As we have seen earlier in this chapter, the need to counter Nazi propaganda broadcast from Rome, Berlin, and Jerusalem was indeed seen as urgent by Soviet officials, as was the need to persuade Roosevelt, Churchill, and their publics that the Soviet Union was not in reality a "godless" empire.[83] Key points in the timeline support the importance of these endeavors: the fact that Soviet religious propaganda was directed abroad so early in the war, for example; the fact that it continued even after the war; and the fact that the first officially sanctioned Muslim "spiritual directorates" made their debut within just a few weeks of the pivotal Tehran Conference in the autumn of 1943.

On the other hand, however, these motivations can explain only a small fraction of the major wartime religious developments described in this book. The vast majority of Soviet religious propaganda was directed inward, toward Soviet citizens, rather than to audiences abroad. The bishops and Patriarch of the newly supported Orthodox Church rarely went abroad, confining almost all of their activities to domestic audiences. More to the point, most of the work of these officially sanctioned religious bodies could not properly be considered propaganda at all, as it involved simply maintaining many of the regularly occurring, traditional functions of religious institutions: conducting weekly services, funerals, marriages, holidays, and so on. In wartime, the Soviet government could surely have attempted to suppress these activities domestically while painting a different picture in propaganda directed abroad. It did not, however.

Second: the "borderlands propaganda hypothesis." A considerable portion of the earliest Soviet religious propaganda, as well as notable state support for religious institutions, took place in territories occupied by the USSR in 1939, and, after June 1941, in borderland areas imminently threatened by Nazi occupation; and a considerable portion of such activities in the later phases of the war took place in areas retaken by the Soviets.[84] As David Motadel and others have demonstrated, Nazi propaganda, especially among Soviet Muslims, was energetic and sometimes remarkably successful; it is sensible to assume that countering it would be a main imperative for Stalin. Beyond the Nazi threat, there were other foreign perspectives to combat within Soviet territory: Yulia Guseva argues, for example, that one of the chief motivations in creating the Muslim muftiates was to oppose pan-Islamic propaganda from South Asia and the Arab world.[85]

On the other hand, however, too much emphasis on these motivations overlooks the fact that the main features of wartime religious policy, including the activities of the muftiates, continued deep into the postwar years—indeed, the muftiates would continue their activities until the end of the Soviet period. As for the war era itself, a substantial proportion of "sanctioned" religious activity, as well as a substantial proportion of religious propaganda, was directed far from the warfront, toward peoples in Central Asia and Siberia, where there was little to fear from Hitler's broadcasts, much less his Panzers.

Third: the "rallying call hypothesis." The Soviet state did indeed need more than sympathy from religious communities—they needed these communities to fight, which is something "non-Russian nationalities," many of them Muslim, had been doing less frequently and less willingly than their Russian counterparts in 1941–42. The tidal wave of "national" propaganda tailored to individual Soviet republics and territories was so immense that several historians have recently speculated that it helped to forge not only a wave of patriotism, but more strongly "hybridized" identities (Soviet-Uzbek, Soviet-Kazakh, Soviet-Bashkir, etc.).

On the other hand, however, the argument that rallying troops was the state's prime motive overlooks the crucial question of why most of these same changes—the sanctioned Patriarchate and muftiates, for example—continued into the postwar era, or even into the final months of the war, when it was clear that the Nazis were in full retreat. The explanatory value of this hypothesis decreases exponentially the further one gets from the Nazi advance.[86]

Fourth: The "revolution from below" hypothesis, which proposes that the Soviet government was either forced or inspired—by popular sentiment, above all—into a position of compromise with enterprising religious leaders, such as Metropolitan (soon-to-be Patriarch) Sergii, whose first wartime address to Soviet populations preceded Stalin's own. A great many sources (including many quoted in the course of this book) highlight the independently inspired nature of religious enthusiasm and activity in wartime; indeed, there is little in what eyewitnesses and participants report about wartime religious life that was clearly *inspired* by government propaganda. On the contrary, the "grassroots" religious revival noted so often in our sources was deeply concerning to the very Soviet officials tasked with monitoring religious activity. A panoply of sources, Muslim and non-Muslim alike, describe wartime religious life in similar terms: what was once hidden emerged from the shadows; what was once forbidden was done with less fear.[87]

On the other hand, this "bottom-up" hypothesis risks ignoring key aspects of the timeline. First, major changes in religious policy began almost immediately, at the very start of the war. Whether this was in response to Nazi propaganda, the need to court foreign allies, or was simply an early, intuitive presentiment that further religious repressions would undermine morale, it is clear that the "grassroots" upwelling of religious feeling noted by Miner would hardly have had time to develop, let alone to influence Stalin, by the time top-down changes were already underway. Second, while the key shift toward tolerance came too early to be linked directly to tangible grassroots developments, the shift toward new, sanctioned religious institutions—such as the Muslim spiritual directorates—came too late. The war had been underway for well over two years by the time Ishan Babakhanov took the stage at the inaugural meeting of his Central Asian muftiate; just shy of three years had passed by the time Akhund Alizada's muftiate for the Transcaucasus was founded. In short, the grassroots hypothesis may help to describe a general *atmosphere* of ongoing toleration throughout the war era, and it may certainly explain (as we shall see) certain specific concessions that seem to have been achieved by religious leaders serving as intermediaries for their communities; but from a chronological vantage point, this hypothesis correlates poorly with the most significant shifts in religious policy.

Fifth: the "continuity hypothesis," which draws meaningful connections between pre-war and wartime developments. On the surface, this hypothesis has much to recommend it. Beyond tallying things like church closures and arrests, it is indeed impossible to assess with scientific precision the impact of previous purges on "religious life," and therefore it is natural to question whether the purges had much impact on religious life *at all*, beyond driving communal religious activities underground. When it comes to Muslim communities, the need for "clergy" and holy places (both targeted by the repressions) can be questioned: unlike Catholics, for example, Muslims are ritually autonomous and need no religious authority to supervise their basic religious observances. This makes Islamic tradition distinctly adaptable in circumstances of persecution. Ideally, a respected and experienced imam would lead prayers or funeral rituals, but if one is absent, a competent replacement could be delegated from the community. It is reasonable, therefore, to object to the confusing use of the word "clergy" in many sources, both English and Russian (*dukhovenstvo*), as a catchall for Muslim religious leaders. Unlike a Catholic cleric, an imam (for example) is not strictly *necessary*; there is no formalized ritual of confession or Holy Communion in Islam. Nor is a mosque necessary: prayers and services can be and were conducted elsewhere, including outside in the open air. (For that matter, there is plentiful evidence that Orthodox Christian religious devotions continued in private homes as well.[88]) How, exactly, can we identify when such traditions have been "repressed"?

One the other hand, to argue that the imprisonment and execution of tens of thousands of religious leaders and the shuttering of centuries-old holy places had minimal impact on religious life is to ignore the testimony of those who lived through these events. The pre-war years of repression are almost invariably remembered by religious individuals who lived through them as catastrophic for religious life *as they themselves envisioned it*.[89] "Religious life" in Islam, for example, as in many other religions, is not only about faith, identity, and private prayers, but likewise about community, lineage, and sacred spaces. During the religious persecutions of the 1920s and 1930s, communities were violently torn apart and infested with informants; many (though certainly not all) esteemed lineages were snuffed out; and sacred buildings that had been at the heart of communal religious life—in some cases, for a matter of centuries—were converted into barns, storage sheds, or museums honoring "Marxist-Leninist scientific atheism." A correlate from our contemporary world resonates here: when members of the devastated Xinjiang Uyghur community of 2020 tell the world that their religion and culture are endangered, they are not referring to private faith in God, nor to ethno-national identity, but more likely to the same deep complex of communal Muslim customs, sacred spaces, lineages, and rituals that the Soviets targeted in the 1920s and 1930s. More to the point, the "continuity hypothesis" contradicts nearly all of the primary sources that emerge from the war era, which—whether produced by atheist officials or religious Soviet citizens—almost invariably point to the *unusual* and novel flourishing of religious activity, broadly defined. It also contradicts later testimony by those who lived through this period.[90]

In Stalin-era interviews, we find Soviet citizens avowing that they maintained their traditions in the age of religious repression—but *still* characterizing the war era as a time of important change for religious life as well as state policy (two things that are, notably, often treated jointly). A Ukrainian railroad engineer recalls: "My grandmother was quite religious, and my mother was, too. As you know, religion was forbidden in the Soviet Union

until this war. Then, at the beginning of this war, you could even pray officially. But before that, it was a scandal if a pioneer or Komsomol [member]
went to church. However, my mother kept ikons in the house and frequently
prayed."[91] A Ukrainian financial inspector elaborates on the cascade-like
quality of the changing state policy:[92]

> The government reopened the churches and ordered the patriarch to agitate
> for the war efforts. The people asked, what sort of thing was this, using the
> churches for militarism . . . During the war the priesthood played a great,
> even a colossal role for the government, for the population; they played
> a huge role. If you registered at the ZAGS for marriage, the government
> would give you one day off, and you would give you [sic] three days off for
> the wedding. The kolkhozes [collective farms] provided transport for the
> wedding personnel free. You see how things changed: The churches are re-
> opened and the people are also given time off and transport for weddings.
> These things go together: one change is made and then a number of others
> follow.

A Chechen Muslim laborer, likewise interviewed in the early 1950s, takes
a darker view, but makes a similar claim about the radical shift in state policy
on holy places: "That scoundrel Stalin now says that he permits churches to be
open when he oppressed them for 25 years and did not believe in God. Now he
says the churches can exist. He is Satan—the devil. He is not a man."[93]

Recently several historians, such as L.A. Koroleva and A.A. Korolev, have
proposed a promising middle ground between some the five approaches just
described, and they have also begun to take stock of the historiography of
Soviet religion in wartime. Koroleva and Korolev describe a three-part development in that historiography: First, historians of the Soviet period tended to
emphasize the spontaneous, patriotic activity of many groups facing the Nazi
threat—a movement that was sanctioned ex post facto by the Soviet state (here,
I have called this the "revolution from below" approach). This is, of course, the
view that emerges in the wartime speeches of Babakhanov, Alizada, and other
Soviet religious leaders. Second, in the first decades of the post-Soviet period,
historians shifted toward exploring ways in which religious groups were given
"special attention" by the state in order to encourage patriotic activities (a "rev-
olution-from-above" approach). Third, the most recent development observed
(and supported) by Koroleva and Korolev is an emerging consensus that the
state "made concessions to believers, but strictly within the political-ideological

framework of the socialist regime."[94] There was give-and-take, in other words, but the state was always in control, and was never *compelled* toward concessions.

This approach offers a promising synthesis, but nevertheless feels unsatisfying, as it leaves little room for some key aspects of religious policy in the war era that will emerge throughout this book: the conceptual vagueness of state policy; its slapdash, inconsistent implementation; and the avenues thereby made possible for independent initiative among religious communities and citizens. The story told in this book, in other words, is hardly the story of a state with firm and constant control over religious life. Indeed, as Chapter 5 shows, the very officials tasked with policing religious life were sometimes baffled over what the state's "control" was supposed to involve.[95]

In short, none of these explanations *alone* is sufficient to explain the fundamental wartime changes in Soviet religious life, and none of these explanations alone can be used as the template for an accurate narrative describing the dynamics of religion in the crucial period between 1941 and 1945. Elements of *all* of these approaches, however, combine to offer a nuanced, dynamic picture of Soviet religious life in the war era. That is the kind of picture I hope to offer in this book, using Islam as a case study. A central assumption of the book is that the religious changes of the war era can be attributed not to a coherent state strategy, but to a *process* informed at different times and to different degrees by all of the variables described in this chapter.

Chapter 1 provides an overview of major developments in Soviet religious life and policy through successive waves of repression in the 1920s and 1930s, concluding with a close look at the "new deal" Stalin struck with religious leaders in wartime. Chapter 2 focuses on the rise of officially sanctioned Muslim elites, revealing how Soviet Muslim leaders were summoned to rally their communities to the war effort. In numerous speeches, these leaders envisioned the struggle against the Nazis in distinctly Islamic terms; they articulated values and interests shared in common with the Soviet state; and they used their novel public platform to define communal Islamic identity using the kind of language that had once been forbidden in the Soviet public sphere. The chapter revolves around several of these remarkable speeches, translated here from Uzbek, Bashkir, Persian, and Russian. Each of them is a call to war delivered by a Soviet Muslim mufti, and each uses language that bridges Soviet wartime propaganda and classical Islamic rhetoric on "Holy War."

The effort to rally Muslims to war was much more than a propaganda campaign, however, and its results were far more wide-ranging than the recruitment of soldiers. As Chapter 3 shows, Soviet Muslim leaders used their newfound freedoms to negotiate with the Soviet state for a range of concessions on behalf of their communities, from the reopening of long-shuttered mosques to permission to celebrate major religious holidays more openly. From the Soviet state's perspective, there were benefits to be gained from this sort of tolerance: newly reopened mosques became major centers of fundraising for the war effort, and Muslim elites disseminated patriotic messages—including praise and thanks to Stalin—in the course of their weekly sermons. Chapter 4 dives deeper into wartime religiosity among Muslims, drawing on sources such as wartime poetry, veterans' memories, eyewitness reports, Soviet officials' classified dispatches, and letters to and from the home front. Here, I identify some aspects of "local" religious change that were particular to the war era, and I show the enduring quality of these changes by tracing them into the postwar years.

As mosques reopened and Muslim devotional practices re-emerged in the public sphere, it became increasingly clear that, even after two decades of militant atheist rule and repression, Muslim identity was widely retained and Muslim traditions were widely observed in the USSR. Some historians have described the emergence of two parallel currents in this period: "official Islam," meaning Soviet-sanctioned religious elites and the activities they oversaw; and "unofficial Islam," meaning unsanctioned or illegal religious activities that nevertheless persisted in the Soviet period. The idea of "parallel" religious worlds, however, presumes that there were clear religious policies in place to distinguish the licit from the illicit, along with "enforcers" who had a firm understanding of those policies. In fact, as Chapter 5 argues, wartime and postwar state policy on Islam was not always clear or well understood—even by the very officials tasked with enforcing it. Using the declassified, recently published correspondences between two such bureaucrats from Kazakhstan, this chapter shows how officials at multiple levels were oblivious about, confused by, and even indifferent to the state's religious policies. As the book's conclusion argues, the growth of these "gray spaces" may have had an even greater impact on the war-era religious revolution than the wave of state-managed religious propaganda or the tireless efforts of state-sanctioned religious elites.

1

The Setting

From the Years of Repression to Stalin's "New Deal"

As early as 1918, prominent Russian Orthodox priests had been subjected to breathtaking cruelties at the hands of Bolshevik supporters, some details of which Alexander N. Yakovlev has recently disinterred from the archives:[1]

> Metropolitan Vladimir of Kiev was mutilated, castrated, and shot, and his corpse was left naked for the public to desecrate. Metropolitan Veniamin of St. Petersburg, in line to succeed the patriarch, was turned into a pillar of ice: he was doused with cold water in the freezing cold. Bishop Germogen of Tobolsk, who had voluntarily accompanied the czar into exile, was strapped alive to the paddlewheel of a steamboat and mangled by the rotating blades. Archbishop Andronnik of Perm, who had been renowned earlier as a missionary and had worked as such in Japan, was buried alive. Archbishop Vasily was crucified and burned.
>
> These documents bear witness to the most savage atrocities against priests, monks, and nuns: they were crucified on the central doors of iconostases, thrown into cauldrons of boiling tar, scalped, strangled with priestly stoles, given Communion with melted lead, drowned in holes in the ice.

Later, in 1921–22, as terrible famines convulsed Russia, the Church's major assets were seized by decree. Lenin reveled at the opportunity: "No other opportunity but the current terrible famine," he wrote, "will give us a mood of the wide masses such as would provide us with their sympathies or at least neutrality . . . Now our victory over the reactionary clergy is guaranteed."[2] Across the country, church bells and precious icons were taken and melted down. Meanwhile, the Bolsheviks had been supporting a rival "Renovationist" Church (the Living Church), hoping to fracture the unity among Orthodox adherents and elevate a loyal "client" clergy to fill the power vacuum.[3] As Narkompros chief A.V. Lunacharskii notified Lenin in a 1921

God Save the USSR. Jeff Eden, Oxford University Press (2021). © Oxford University Press.
DOI: 10.1093/oso/9780190076276.003.0002

telegram: "It could be extremely advantageous to secretly help renovated Orthodoxy [i.e., the Renovationists] with Christian-Socialist leanings and create in the religious arena various transitory states for the peasant masses."[4] In the meantime, Orthodox Patriarch Tikhon was under "house arrest" in a monastery, unable to promote his Church's cause or to respond formally to the Renovationist threat.

In the summer of 1923, after the Patriarch's release (owing to political pressure from abroad), he circulated a statement declaring the Renovationists' aims non-canonical. He fell ill and died the next year, and was immediately hailed by many Orthodox faithful as a martyr. As far as the Bolsheviks were concerned, however, he was no Patriarch at all, but simply a man named Vasilii Bellavin; they had abolished the Patriarchate earlier that same year. Renovationist leaders had been appointed to head the Supreme Ecclesiastical Council, an act intended to elevate them to supreme standing among Russian Christians, but the Renovationist church's popularity among Soviet citizens foundered. Disappointment with the scant influence of Renovationism doubtless played a part in the Soviet government's decision to negotiate a reconciliation with the most prominent Orthodox cleric who had not yet been jailed: Metropolitan Sergii. The son of an archpriest, and a Metropolitan since 1917, the fifty-year-old Sergii was widely admired among bishops, and—thanks to a mission abroad in 1890—fluent in Japanese along with the more traditional priestly languages of Latin, Hebrew, and Greek.[5] On July 29, 1927, Sergii pledged his complete loyalty to the Soviet state. While this conciliation is rumored to have taken place under threat (specifically, the threat to execute all jailed clergy), some Orthodox bishops never forgave Sergii for making peace with the enemy.

At this pivotal point of *rapprochement* with the Orthodox Church, the first major Soviet campaigns against Islam were just beginning.[6] The Special Commission to combat Muslim "clergy"—especially in the Volga-Urals and Crimea—had been established just four months earlier, in February, 1927.[7] The first waves of repression did not fall equally on all Muslim regions, nor were the policies, strategies, and outcomes always coherent to the relevant Soviet local authorities. In a passage that could apply just as well to myriad religious "instructions" offered by anti-religious officials in these years, Shoshanna Keller assesses the vague directives given at a pivotal meeting led by the top atheist official in Central Asia:[8]

His exceptionally opaque bureaucratic language may have caused some problems for his listeners, who were expected to implement his directives, decipher exactly what "ideological re-armament" meant, and move on the clergy at exactly the proper time. The imprecision of language here may have been deliberate . . . since it had the effect of leaving a large gray area in which both local and all-union level party workers could justify a wide range of actions.

Meanwhile, even direct orders could fall on deaf ears: a rural Party cell in Turkmenistan confessed to ignoring most Party memos that reached them because no one in the group could read Russian. The closest translator was 30 *verst*s away, and he didn't come cheap.[9]

The propaganda was more lucid than the policies. The League of Militant Atheists, the top anti-religious propagandists, attempted relentlessly to impress upon the masses that Muslim religious authorities worked arm in arm with oppressor-classes, exploiting the very workers who sought their guidance. The league also urged Muslims to consider that the metaphysical answers religion provided were obsolete thanks to advances in science; and it endlessly reiterated the observation that religion was traditionally—and intractably—oppressive to women. A steady stream of pamphlets and tracts in local languages developed these ideas, oftentimes by drawing direct (unflattering) comparisons between religious norms and Bolshevik alternatives.[10] One tract in Arabic-script Uzbek, for example, compared *shari'a* norms concerning women with parallel Soviet laws in order to demonstrate, point by point, the amenability of the latter to any women who might be willing or compelled to listen.[11] The Bolshevik fixation on Muslim women in this period as—to borrow Gregory J. Massell's famous phrase—a "surrogate proletariat" is now a well-known story among Soviet historians, thanks to a wave of important publications from the early 2000s. A common consensus of these works is that Soviet efforts to force initiatives such as the unveiling of women upon Muslim communities were unsuccessful at best—and, at worst, a disastrous miscalculation and an inspiration for passionate backlash.[12]

A more pernicious, less visible threat to Muslim populations was the work of the secret police. As religious schools, mosques, and other revenue channels for Muslim elites were expropriated by the state in 1927–28,[13] many of the elites (or alleged elites) themselves were also being "liquidated." Meanwhile, those who remained free oftentimes suffered from another harsh tactic of the government: they were driven deliberately to financial ruin.[14] In 1928, Dzhikhangir Abyzgil'din, imam of the First Cathedral Mosque in

Ufa, informed a colleague that the Ufa-based muftiate (which had continued to enjoy official permission to operate) was in a condition that was "not just difficult, but catastrophic." Bankrupted the previous summer, the muftiate's employees now had nothing to eat. Publishing activities were impossible, and the muftiate's ranks were thinned by layoffs.[15]

Many of the victims in this period were Muslim jurists, publishers and teachers who had once considered the Soviet government a potentially enduring ally in the cultural struggle against rival Muslim elites. These self-described reformists, often called "progressive *mullas*" in Soviet sources and "Islamic modernists" by historians, were now regarded as a special danger. Adeeb Khalid aptly sums up the perception of Soviet officials in the mid-late 1920s:[16]

> Shariat [Islamic law] administrations that struggled against incorrect practices, the waqf [pious endowment] administration that claimed to be doing Soviet work, and the new-method schools that pretended to be Soviet schools were all attempts by the bourgeoisie to camouflage itself in the cloak of modern civilization and support for socialism. Traditionalist ulama [Muslim scholars] and the Sufis would go away once the remnants of feudalism were swept away; the real competition came from alternative visions of modernity and progress."

By mid-1928, internal statistics produced by Soviet bureaucrats suggested that up to 8,460 so-called Muslim "clergymen" in Uzbekistan alone had been "eliminated."[17] Like most Soviet statistics, these numbers were likely inflated to advance or protect the livelihoods of the bureaucrats themselves. It is perennially difficult, moreover, to understand what is meant by the term "clergy" as applied to Islam—a religion in which each individual is "ritually autonomous." Nevertheless, it is not a stretch to conclude that thousands of Muslims had by this time been jailed, exiled, or executed for reasons overtly related to their religious activities. As Khalid writes, "No credible statistical data are available for mosques either, but the evidence of destruction was the half-destroyed or disused mosques that dotted the landscape for the rest of the Soviet era."[18] In this same year came the dawn of the First Five-Year Plan, through which, as Smolkin writes, "the Bolsheviks sought to mobilize all resources toward industrialization, collectivization, and cultural revolution. The antireligious campaign was an important part of the broader cultural revolution, since the cultural revolution was about class war, and religion was a class enemy."[19] An Avar Muslim tractor-driver, interviewed during the Stalin era, recalled that "collectivization and the liquidation of religion and the church went together."[20] A local history from Muslim-majority Kazakhstan, where collectivization resulted in one of the twentieth century's worst famines, divides this period into three waves of persecution: a "Great Confiscation" in 1928 that targeted the wealthy; a "Small Confiscation" in 1929 that targeted poor and middle-income nomads; and, beginning in 1930, mass collectivization and famine, which peaked in 1932–33. For these years, the Kazakh author invokes a heartbreaking folk idiom referring to the deaths of entire families of nomadic yurt-dwellers: "There were many smoke-holes whose flaps were left closed."[21]

The next year, in April, 1929, the Soviet Union initiated a law code of 68 Articles concerning religious groups—or, more specifically, establishing rules for their control and surveillance by the state. Certain articles extended massive powers to Moscow as well as to local officials in Muslim-majority regions. The notorious Article 25, for example, provided for the potential sei-zure of *any* building used for religious purposes, effectively nationalizing all such property. Buildings of artistic or historical value would be turned over to the Commissariat of Enlightenment. Muslim communities would techni-cally need to negotiate with local Party executive committees or soviets to re-gain use of their former property. Predictably, many local bureaucrats would be unsympathetic to petitioners—such as a Party secretary in Ghijduvan who forced a local elder to urinate from the minaret of a shuttered mosque at prayer-time.[22]

One of the most significant articles in the Law of 1929 was more dra-matic in practice than on paper: it formalized the mandatory *registration* of religious communities (a process that had begun years earlier,[23] but had remained inconsistent). For the next several decades, the difference between "legal" and "illegal" religious activity would typically be articulated among Soviet officials as the difference between *registered* and *unregistered* activity.[24] Registration paperwork was oftentimes denied, but the submitted paper-work alone served as a means of surveillance: petitioners were expected to submit data on the names and demographics of the Muslims who would form the core of their proposed "community."

In May, 1930, Rizaetdin Fakhretdinov, an officially sanctioned Soviet mufti, lamented that "all religious Muslim organizations are on the eve of their complete destruction."[25] He expressed this fear to the Presidium of the All-Russian Central Executive Committee (VTsIK), to which he was protesting the forced closure of mosques, the heavy taxes imposed on religious organizations, the arrests and fines resulting from nonpayment of those taxes, the seizure of religious books and properties, and the arrest of Muslim "clergy."[26] After hearing this testimony, presidium member P. Smidovich wrote to the chairman of the Central Executive Committee, M.I. Kalinin, with an overview of the state of Muslim "organizations." Unsurprisingly, where Fakhretdinov saw tragedy, Smidovich saw triumph: "The Muslim religious organizations are on the eve of complete disintegration and disappearance off the face of the earth. As of now, 87 percent of Muslim religious centers have closed down, as have more than 10,000 out of 12,000 mosques, and from 90 to 97 percent of the mullahs and muezzins have been left with no means of conducting religious services."[27] Smidovich's concluding claim— that religious services were impossible without mosques—shows typical Soviet official naïveté about Islam, and his statistics should be taken with more than a few grains of salt. Nevertheless, these claims point toward an evident truth that is echoed in innumerable sources and contradicted by none: by the start of the decade, thousands of mosques had been shuttered, and thousands of Muslim leaders had been jailed, exiled or shot.

While some historians estimate that the pace of mosque closures and seizures eased between 1931 and 1935,[28] evidence can be found of ongoing anti-Islamic activity during these years. Between 1930 and 1937, for example, all ten of the once-bustling mosques in Orenburg were shuttered.[29] The practice of "beheading" mosques—that is, destroying their minarets—continued into the 1930s as well. In a recent local history from rural Bashkortostan, A.S. Gaiazov offers a rare, detailed account of such an event, as witnessed by his father:[30]

A characteristic story is the 1930s policy on the "beheading"—so to speak— of mosques. We don't know what was preeminent here: whether it was the desire to fulfill the orders of the "Godless five-year plan," or the desire to turn the people away from centuries-old Islamic tradition, or a sharp turn away from the foundations of morality and goodness . . .

The minaret of one of the mosques (in the center of the village) was removed at the beginning of the 1930s. Among the witnesses to these apocalyptic "measures" was our father, along with other children. It was a day to match the lawlessness underway—sunless, uneasy. Several people (we know who they are but we will not name them, as their children and grandchildren are not to blame) severed the minaret's thinnest beams, and from the ground began pulling on a long rope which had been thrown around the minaret like a noose. The rope broke several times, as if nature itself was resisting evil, but the work was brought to completion. And there on the ground lies a beautiful, brilliant minaret, the crescent moon entirely un-damaged. The children are crying, the elders are voicing their objections, someone is praying . . .

Believe it or not, but not one of those who were first [to undertake] this evil, lawless work lived happily ever after. Some were killed in the war, others in various incidents.

It is frightening to imagine the situation of those who went off to commit such a moral crime. How, [it is] interesting [to imagine], were they able to survive the first night of their deed? How did they come to agree to it—after all, no one paid them, no one gave them anything whatsoever for the act. How did the people agree to this? After all, religion was still strong at that time .

On the international stage, meanwhile, the year 1932 was the first in which not a single Soviet pilgrim was permitted to go on the *hajj* pilgrimage to Mecca. Saudi inquiries into the absence of Soviet pilgrims managed to draw only a series of unlikely (and vaguely comic) excuses. First, Soviet officials claimed that there simply weren't any Soviet Muslims who wanted to go on the pilgrimage. After this, the Soviet diplomat N. Tiuriakulov claimed that the French and British were to blame, as they had been blocking the passage of Soviet pilgrims through the Bosporus and Dardanelles.[31] Even if this was true (which, as far as I can tell, it was not), it was a silly excuse: there was more than one way to get from the Soviet Union to Arabia. Or there would have been, anyway, if the government had permitted it. That same year, mem-bership in the League of Militant Atheists peaked at a stunning 5.2 million members.[32]

The year 1934 saw the notorious murder of the Leningrad "Old Bolshevik" Sergei Kirov, a figure whose popularity and status in the Party led many to believe that he had attracted Stalin's jealousy and wrath. In the months that followed, a wave of "show trials" and repressions began in the Party ranks, but soon extended to such established, cliquish "class enemies" as religious elites. "There was a growing consensus among the Bolsheviks," Smolkin writes, "that religious institutions in general and the Orthodox Church in particular remained politically dangerous, and therefore needed to be defin-itively neutralized."[33]

In 1935, Soviet propaganda outlets began promoting Stalin's idea of "the Friendship of the Peoples"—a concept drawing on the Marxist notion that national or racial antagonism was a product of class antagonism, and that both would decline in proper socialist conditions. That December, at a Kremlin gathering honoring high-performing Tajik and Turkmen collective farmers, Stalin famously declared that the antagonisms that had arisen in the Tsarist era between the Russian colonizers and other now-Soviet peoples had been extirpated by the progress of Bolshevik policy on nationalities. "Today's meeting," Stalin declared, "is a striking proof of the fact that the former distrust between the peoples of the USSR has already come to an end. That distrust has been replaced with a complete mutual trust. The friendship of the peoples of the USSR is growing and strengthening. That, comrades, is the most valuable of all that the Bolshevik nationalities policy has produced."[34] It was not clear what implications—if any—this much-touted "friendship" had for religions, but the following year, in 1936, as the Soviet Union was inundated with images of Stalin sharing a laugh with blank-eyed babies in ethnic garb, a new wave of mosque closures left Bukhara with an estimated 94 percent of its mosques shuttered.[35] That same year, the new Soviet constitution—to which we will soon return—purported to safeguard "freedom of religious worship."

The worst was yet to come. In 1937–38, Stalin's Great Terror disproportionately targeted perceived leaders and elites from communities of every description: military, academic, governmental, industrial, and religious. Minority religious groups, long suspected of being especially susceptible to anti-Soviet agitation, appear to have been hit particularly hard. By one recent estimate, by 1941, thirty-nine out of forty Old Believer bishops had been jailed.[36] Shoshanna Keller writes that, by 1938, "one may conservatively estimate that more than 14,000 Muslim clergy were arrested, killed, exiled from their homes, or driven out of the USSR."[37] The statistics for the Orthodox Church, with its much greater number of Soviet adherents and its more legible system of "clerical" ranks, are still more dramatic. In these years, an estimated 140,000 people associated with the Church were "repressed," of whom as many as 85,300 were executed. In 1939, the total number of Church figures arrested dropped to some 28,300, but the proportion executed increased dramatically: 21,000 of these victims are reported to have been shot.[38]

Local histories are unanimous in describing the years of the Great Terror as an exceptionally difficult period for religious notables. Zaripov and Safarov's recent work on Islam in Soviet Moscow, for example, charts these years through a litany of arrests and executions. The cathedral mosque in Zamoskvorechye district was closed in 1937 after its *imam-khatib*, ʿAbdullah Khasanovich Shamsutdinov, one of the city's most renowned religious scholars, was shot. His wife, a descendant of the Ageev "dynasty" of Moscow imams, died in the Potma gulag. After this, the historic Tatar mosque on Vypolzovy Lane became the main functioning mosque of the city, but its *imam-khatib*, Musa Vakhitov, was soon arrested and shot.[39]

Of the five surviving Muslim leaders who had visited Mecca with Rizaetdin Fakhretdinov as representatives of the Soviet Union at the international All-Muslim Congress of 1926, three were executed in 1937 and a fourth was in exile. Meanwhile, in Central Asia, nearly all members associated with the influential pre-Revolutionary "Jadid" movement of educational and cultural reform had been executed by 1938, including ʿAbdurrauf Fiṭrat (1938), Munawwar Qari ʿAbdurrashid Khan-ughli (1931), ʿAbdullah Qadiri (1938), ʿAbdulhamid Sulayman-ughli ("Cholpan") (1938), and Ishaq Khan Tura Junaydullah-ughli ("ʿIbrat") (1938).

Dzhikhangir Abyzgilʹdin, imam of the First Cathedral Mosque in Ufa, who had complained in 1928 of "catastrophic" conditions for his mosque community, was arrested and shot in June 1938. Like several others associated with the officially sanctioned Soviet muftiate, he was charged with conducting anti-Soviet activities.[40] In 1926, the large swath of Russia under the Ufa muftiate's purview was estimated to have 14,825 operating mosques. By 1941, fewer than one hundred of these buildings had avoided closure, seizure, or destruction.[41] In the language of CARC archival documents, some holy places closed down in this period seemingly on their own, "for lack of a clergyman of the religious denomination" (*za otsutstviem sluzhitelia religioznogo kulʹta*).[42] In Georgia, ninety-six Muslim holy buildings were listed by CARC officials as "inactive" by the 1940s, and their reappointment for other purposes was diligently documented: eighty-six were used as collective farm warehouses; four as schools; one for grain storage; one as a club; and four were empty and unoccupied.[43]

These examples offer just a glimpse of a vast body of evidence covering the most intense periods of religious repression in the Soviet Union. There is another side to this story, however, which is less well known. During these darkest days of repression there was also, undoubtedly, ongoing religious activity. "After all," as A.S. Gaiazov noted, "religion was still strong at that time." Mosques were closed, but prayers continued in private homes, basements, and other safe spaces. As Eren Tasar observes, shuttering mosques and jailing elites was an inherently limited strategy for destroying Muslim devotional life since, in order to carry out religious rituals, "Figures as diverse as Sufi masters, *mullas* performing funerals and other lifecycle or communal rites, circumcision specialists, shamans, sorcerers, traditional healers, and other practitioners who communist bureaucrats associated with religion only required the respect and acknowledgment of the communities they served."[44] A Crimean Tatar refugee, interviewed near the end of the Stalin era, describes this dynamic from an eyewitness perspective:[45]

> Limitations on religious practice led to its prohibition. There were five practices which were effected: a) Namaz—prayer four [*sic*] times a day; since the mosques were closed, and they could not pray in public, they had to do it at home secretly. b) Ramazan—one month a year devoted to fasting, when a person could not eat from sunrise to sunset. c) At weddings, it was forbidden to have a priest officiate. People were to get married at a ZAGS. d) Circumcision—this was forbidden and declared barbaric. e) Religious burial was forbidden. The prohibition of these rites led to the secret practice of these and others. People who had attended the theological seminary before the revolution (the biggest was in Bakchisaray) now acted as Imams. The Imams in the Muslim religion are not appointed from above, but are elected by the local group. Therefore, *anybody could become an Imam*.

Thus, a Kabardian Muslim—likewise interviewed in the late Stalin era—recalls witnessing the reopening of a mosque in Kabardino-Balkaria: "The population reopened its mechet [mosque] by itself. But there was no mullah; instead, those people were used who knew the prayers and procedure. The old folk engaged in religious (Moslem) propaganda among the youth, but I wonder whether it was successful."[46] The ranks of religious specialists could be refreshed, in short, not only by those formally "licensed," but by those willing and able, with the consent of their community.

Repression and anti-religious propaganda, moreover, did not fall equally upon all communities. Shamil Shikhaliev notes that in Dagestan, Soviet anti-religious efforts struck more intensely in areas that had shown particular resistance to collectivization; even communities heavily influenced by Sufi Muslim religious elites could be spared the brunt of such attacks if these elites demonstrated loyalty to the state. More generally, anti-religious propaganda was circulated more intensively among the Lezgin-speaking peoples of southern Dagestan, among Laks, and among the residents of the northern lowlands, while the Avars of the alpine regions, as well as some Dargins and the Kumyks of the piedmont, preserved their traditional Sufi-influenced Islamic practices and endured less government pressure.[47] Among Soviet Christians, meanwhile, ethnographers documented extensive samples of what they called "lived religion" (*zhivaia religiia*) and "folk Orthodoxy" (*narodnoe pravoslavie*) in the countryside throughout the 1920s and 1930s.[48]

Tellingly, officials tasked with monitoring religious life in these years reported persistent "lapses" in diligence, reach, and commitment among their fellow anti-religious authorities. Delegates from the League of Militant Atheists in Sverdlovsk, for example, complained in March 1935 of all manner of ongoing religious "offenses" among Tatar and Bashkir Muslims in the region. A "group" of circumcisers (*sunnatchilar*) was plying its trade in the vicinity. The women in several villages persisted in wearing burkas. The chairman of a collective farm had personally organized the Kurban Bairam holiday for his community.[49] Meanwhile, most of the league's own members in the region were neglecting to pay their membership dues.[50] Sometimes, agitated citizens took it upon themselves to write letters of protest to local newspapers complaining of the poor enforcement of anti-religious norms. For example, a scathing indictment was sent anonymously to the journal *Sotsializm Iuly* in May 1937, under the title "The Regional Council of Atheists Sleeps." The main target of this screed is not the religious "obscurantists" alleged to be up to no good, but rather the ineffectual atheist vanguard.[51]

Some Soviet Muslims, meanwhile, took the brazen step of holding the state to its own constitution. A 1940 petition from Perm called upon Stalin to defend a local mosque:[52]

Dear Iosif Vissarionovich [Stalin]! At this moment, as the new constitution of the Soviet Union is coming to life, some local actors grossly violate this constitution—in particular, Articles 124 and 125. The chairperson of our village council, Comrade Imaikin, took away the key to the mosque, encouraging the arrest of its mullah and parish council chairman, and he avows that in their absence, no one has the right to go to the mosque for prayers. We consider Imaikin's attitude to be making a mockery of us, as well as a mockery of the law. Now it is our month of prayer, during which we must prepare daily to pray in the mosque. But in light of the mosque's closure, we are forced to pray only at home. This fact serves as an instrument of agitation for enemies of the people.

The petitioners received neither key nor mosque; instead, soon after the petition was submitted, the entire mosque community was dismantled and barred from the mosque by the authorities.

Muslim devotional life went on even in the devastated religious landscape of Moscow. After the arrest and execution of *imam-khatib* Abdulla Khasanovich Shamsutdinov of the Zamoskvorechye mosque, *namaz* (daily prayers) and other rituals carried on under the leadership of an imam from Kazan whose family moved into the basement of the prayer hall. At Moscow's Cathedral Mosque, meanwhile, an imam named Khalil Nasretdinov, from the Tatar town of Paranga,[53] took over after the arrest of a previous imam, Musa Vakhitov. According to Zaripov and Safarov, all major memorial rituals, including the washing of the dead, the *janāzah* (funeral) prayer, and the "strict implementation" of the year's memorial observances, were "carried out rigorously," even in the "most difficult years."[54] Undoubtedly, however, as these authors write, the imam Shamsutdinov "took an enormous risk by leading the mosque after the arrest of the previous imam and many parishioners."[55] Shamsutdinov survived these terrible years—but perhaps only because he had a special connection that kept him safe. He was a longtime friend of the Ufa mufti Gabdrahman Rasulev, who would emerge as the most significant Soviet Muslim leader of the Stalin era.

Rasulev had gained his prominent position at the head of the muftiate only in 1936. The circumstances of his promotion were downright tawdry. After the death of his esteemed predecessor, Rizaetdin Fakhretdinov, a brief political struggle erupted between Rasulev and a close companion of the late mufti, Kashshafuddin Tardzhimani. Tardzhimani was the more esteemed scholar of the two and, as Alfrid Bustanov has argued, might have made a more likely successor than the lesser known Rasulev. These are sentiments that Tardzhimani no doubt shared since, without awaiting election, he declared *himself* to be the new mufti, informing M.I. Kalinin of these developments and claiming that his succession had been worked out with Fakhretdinov four days before the latter's death. He did not inform his colleagues in the muftiate, however, and soon the Soviet government was receiving panicked letters about a usurper. According to Rasulev's recounting of events, two muftiate notables informed the government that Tardzhimani had claimed his post by means contrary to *shari'a* law.[56]

The ensuing drama is described—and reached its apex—in a scathing denunciation addressed by Rasulev to Soviet authorities. This document, discovered in a Kazan archive by Alfrid Bustanov, reveals that Rasulev was not only willing to sidle up to Stalin's government (as Chapter 2 will describe), but that he was willing to use classic Stalin-era tactics to destroy his political and social rival. In his denunciation, Rasulev claims that "more than a hundred" telegrams and letters had poured in from muftiate notables across Russia and Kazakhstan demanding Tardzhimani's ousting, and that fifteen "representatives" had come just for the privilege of submitting their condemnations in person. Rasulev then describes his own sudden rise to power, in the middle of this power struggle: he was first appointed to the rank of *qadi* (judge), and soon after this his promotion to "temporary mufti" was forwarded to the Soviet government for registration and confirmation. Meanwhile, "representatives" from Kazakhstan, Tatarstan, and Bashkortostan formally terminated Tardzhimani's membership in the muftiate and had his registration revoked. After this, Rasulev alleges, an audit revealed that Tardzhimani had embezzled money from the muftiate to the tune of 2,000 rubles. Having thus given the Soviet government all the material needed to arrest and execute his rival, and at the very least gutting Tardzhimani's career and reputation, Rasulev clarifies—with a chilling lack of irony—that none of this was meant as a judgment of the man: "My religious honor and conscience do not give me the right to criticism."[57]

Tellingly, as Bustanov observes, Fakhretdinov's testament and Tardzhimani's earlier appeal are absent from Soviet records documenting the case. Rather than weighing the merits of each argument, Soviet officials "decided to use the situation to create conflict among the elites and then to liquidate the entire leadership of the muftiate."[58] This is precisely what they did. Soon enough, however, as Chapter 2 will show, Rasulev would re-emerge and claim his victory. Tardzhimani would not live to see it: soon after being denounced by Rasulev, he was arrested and shot.

This, in short, is how Rasulev took the reins as Stalin's favored Soviet Muslim leader. In 1936, however, Rasulev could not have dreamed of the role he would eventually play. He was at this time the head of an impoverished and marginalized muftiate. He would languish in relative obscurity through the advent of a new constitution, two years of the Great Terror, and the rise of an unprecedented German threat to the West.

Meanwhile, in Moscow, documents from the highest levels of government reveal widespread concerns over ever more widespread "violations" (*narushenie*) of laws concerning religion—evidence of ongoing religious life, visible enough to catch the eye of Soviet officials and agents. Debates over what should be done reached a head after the establishment of the

1936 Constitution, which included a fateful line concerning freedom of religion: "the freedom of the practice of religious denominations and the
freedom of antireligious propaganda are recognized for all citizens."[59] Both
freedoms—that of religion and that of anti-religious propaganda—had
limits, and P.A. Krasikov, deputy chairman of the Supreme Court and former
procurator general of the Soviet Union, was appointed to a commission
tasked with debating and discerning why the ideal balance between them,
which would theoretically result in religion's steady decline, had not yet been
struck.

Krasikov's conclusions were unsparing and unambiguous—and his
criticisms were directed squarely at Soviet bureaucrats. As Krasikov
explained to A.Ia. Vyshinskii, then procurator general, bureaucrats had been
overzealous in their persecution of religion, routinely violating Soviet law.
Religious communities and leaders had suffered the illegal liquidation of
property; the closure of "prayer houses" under false pretexts (for example,
the claim that structural renovations had been demanded and not satisfied);
the denial of registration without cause or proper procedure; and unreasonable fines.[60] The result of all this was the growth of the dangerous religious
underground, beyond the oversight of the Soviet state.

Echoing Krasikov's verdict was A.I. Khatskevich, secretary of the
Central Executive Committee's Soviet of Nationalities, who expressed palpable exasperation: "Materials show the usual phenomena—the closure of
churches by various machinations. The population sees these illegal, fraud-
ulent machinations and becomes terribly outraged. What is the believer to
do? [He is] to go to the leaders of various shadowy sectarian organizations
(*idti k vozhakom raznykh temnykh sektantskikh organizatsii*), to counterrevolutionary organizations, to the underground . . . Religion is being driven
underground."[61] Krasikov's commission even estimated the scale of the "illegal" seizures and closures, albeit from within the limits of the Soviet state's
information-gathering apparatus: of 30,862 legally registered "denominational buildings" in the Soviet Union, fully one third of them (9,954) had been
seized for "administrative" reasons or were otherwise rendered inactive.[62]

How could "illegal" actions have been undertaken on such a massive scale
by the very bureaucrats charged, ostensibly, with enforcing Stalin's religious
laws? The answer boils down to an issue to which this book will repeatedly return—an issue that dogged anti-religious authorities throughout the
Soviet period: the issue of *ambiguity*. Put simply, there was insufficient clarity
in the law, and the expected procedure for making and enforcing religious

policy was often thwarted or avoided. Krasikov lamented the bureaucratic muddle:[63]

> Where there are commissions, their work boils down to discussing the matter of closing prayer houses. *There is no unified law concerning religious associations.* Every union republic makes its own legislation . . . [But] the legislation does not give the right to close prayer houses either to the village council (*sel'sovet*) or to the RIK (*raispolkom*). It is the decision of the regional executive committee (*kraioblispol'kom*), and, upon appeal, of the VTsIK [All-Russian Central Executive Committee] presidium. However, this system is often not respected . . . The majority of churches are closed without carrying out the appropriate mass antireligious work among the population . . . [and] without taking into account the degree of religiosity among the population.

Naturally, some of the blame was bound to fall upon the League of Militant Atheists, the immense—albeit shrinking—"mass organization" fostered by the Party which, with its famous slogan, "The struggle against religion is a struggle for socialism," still had well over three million members and ninety thousand offices in the Soviet Union by the end of the decade. Surely this near-ubiquitous, titularly "militant" organization would object to Krasikov's characterization? Surely the "overzealous" approach to combating religion was, in fact, not only defensible, but a clear step in the right direction? Inevitably, E.M. Iaroslavskii—Old Bolshevik, leader of the league, and editor of *Atheist* (*Bezbozhnik*), its flagship journal—would need to respond emphatically to Krasikov's accusations.

He did indeed respond emphatically, and his response was full-throated agreement with Krasikov's conclusions. At a meeting of the league in December 1936, Iaroslavskii offered a robust *mea culpa*, simultaneously chastening his followers:[64]

> Undoubtedly, we have committed very great excesses (*ochen' bol'shie peregiby*) in terms of administrative interventions. When we became acquainted with the latest data regarding the liquidation of church premises, we arrived at the unanimous opinion that here had been permitted administrative excesses that reveal that systematic antireligious propaganda had not been carried out, but rather they had proceeded along the path of least resistance. Closing churches is easiest of all, it is the shortest path.

People say that there is no reason to occupy ourselves with systematic anti-religious propaganda here, that we can close the remaining churches and with that the issue is settled.

The natural solution, implied by Iaroslavskii, was to stop the "excessive" and ill-considered closing of churches and to focus instead on the anti-religious agitation and propaganda work that had been the league's specialty. With its legions of members in the Party, Komsomol, military, and factories, Iaroslavskii believed that the league could influence hearts and minds without the intervention of church-swiping regional executive committees. That was the league's mandate, after all.

Krasikov's proposed solution was more extreme, however. He proposed not merely ceasing the excessive and arbitrary persecution of religious leaders and communities, but actually *returning* property that had been illegally seized or shuttered. According to the commission's report, this would involve transferring *one third* of the country's temples, mosques, and churches back into the hands of local religious communities. In certain regions these developments, if they came to pass, would be especially significant. In Uzbekistan, for example, where 663 "prayer houses" were still recorded as "active," no fewer than 882 that had been "illegally" seized would be returned. In Azerbaijan, where only 69 "prayer houses" were recorded as "active," 137 would be returned. In Armenia, 45 would be added to the 40 which were "active." Belarus's 239 "active" holy sites would be increased by another 238.[65]

Such was the "soft line" on religion in 1936. Far from a fringe position, it was advanced by some of the top legal authorities of the Soviet Union and echoed by the chief of its primary anti-religious mass organization. It should not be misconstrued as a policy of tolerance, however, nor as a "compromise" with religious communities and their leaders. The goal remained, unequivocally, the elimination of religion from the Soviet Union. The point of contention was not *if* religion should ultimately be eliminated, but rather the best means of eliminating it. As Mikhail Odintsov has observed, Krasikov, Khatskevich, and their sympathizers believed that the most effective strategy was not to drive religious communities underground—which meant driving citizens into the arms of mystic counterrevolutionaries and shadowy fringe elements—but rather to bring them fully into the light, through registration and surveillance, such that they could be monitored, targeted with agitation and propaganda, and made *fully compliant* with laws limiting their activities and finances.[66]

This was not the only perspective among top Party officials, however. There was also a "hard line." G.M. Malenkov, for example, Stalin's trusted confidant and former personal secretary, bluntly urged Stalin to "do away with . . . the governing bodies of the churchgoers, with the church hierarchy."[67] He was not alone. In the end, Stalin himself took the hard line. Krasikov's commission was terminated in April 1938. (Krasikov himself escaped Stalin's 1937–38 Great Terror with his life, only to die of natural causes in the summer of 1939.) Religious affairs were now subsumed entirely under the purview of the NKVD. As the era of the Great Terror reached its horrific climax in 1938, a hint of the organization's disposition toward religion can be gleaned—as Odintsov observes—from the title of one of its top-secret departments: the department (*otdel*) "for the fight against church and sectarian counterrevolutionaries."[68]

Through it all, the League of Militant Atheists' Iaroslavskii held to the "soft line." As late as 1939, he continued to reiterate that wherever major religious "organizations" did not have a foothold, the religious "underground"—a much more dangerous force, and one more difficult to patrol and surveil—proliferated. Iaroslavskii reiterated his vision at a meeting of Moscow atheists in April 1939: "The enemies of socialism act through religious organizations," he explained. "And in those *raions* where there are no religious organizations, where there are neither churches nor mosques nor synagogues, there is not infrequently a 'wandering priest' (*brodiachii pop*) or 'itinerant priest' (*pop-peredvizhka*), moving from place to place; or the inhabitants of former monasteries settle there, and they are at work discrediting the leaders of the religious sects, the former church elders and other former[ly powerful] people."[69]

Such was Iaroslavskii's notion of the relative influence of rival religious currents, but the bigger-picture issue for Soviet atheist authorities concerned the very existence of religion in the Soviet Union. Historians making a case for the strength of religion in this period often cite the 1937 All-Union Census, which was the state's most ambitious effort to gauge the self-described religious orientation of its citizens. The census did not start out with this goal, however. In the original version of the census questionnaire prepared by the Central Administration for National Economic Accounting (TsUNKhU), there were no questions whatsoever concerning religion. On the theme of identity, the original census draft asked citizens only for their nationality and mother tongue. This section was revised to ask respondents' nationality, mother tongue, and *religion* by Stalin himself.[70]

It is no surprise, given Stalin's seminary education, that he would have taken a personal interest in issues concerning religion. By all accounts, Stalin anticipated that the census would reveal a sea change toward atheism, the results of nearly two decades in pursuit of the New Soviet Person—or at least, perhaps, evidence that Soviet people ("New" or otherwise) would recognize the need to show deference to the official religious orientation of an atheist state, at least in such an official venue as a census.

Of the 80 percent of census respondents who provided an answer to the question, fully 56.7 percent of citizens over sixteen years old reported a specific religious affiliation; 43.79 percent of these reported their religion as Orthodox Christian. The second most prominent religion reported was Islam, with 8.39 percent of respondents describing themselves as Muslim.[71] What can we assume about the 20 percent who left this question blank? Certainly some respondents intended this to mean "no religious affiliation." It is equally likely, however, that some of these citizens did indeed align with a religion but—for obvious reasons—shied away from reporting it. Citizens self-reporting as atheists, finally, constituted no more than 43.3 percent of respondents.[72] In the world's first militant atheist state, after two decades of Bolshevik rule, atheism remained a minority perspective.

Given Soviet state employees' well-deserved reputation for chronically manipulating data, falsifying data, credulously discussing unreliable data, and generally making a mess (deliberately or otherwise) of data-driven investigations, it would be wrong to make too much of this census or to take its findings strictly at face value. Self-reported data on religious affiliation gathered by a militantly atheistic government does not, to say the least, satisfy even the most modest standards of scientific rigor.

It would also be wrong to make too little of this data, however. Undoubtedly, tens of millions of Soviet citizens really did take part in the census. And while it is generally the case that when a totalitarian government commissions data gathering, it gets the results it wants, the All-Union Census of 1937 was not such a case. The results, obviously greatly displeasing to Stalin, were immediately classified and buried in the archives, condemned as a "gross violation of the elementary foundations of statistical science." Within three months, the head of the census bureau (O.A. Kvitkin) and the researcher who prepared instructions for the question on religion (L.S. Brandgendler) were arrested, along with at least ten statisticians and data processors. Not only the census-takers, but even the Orthodox Church itself was blamed for "distortion" of the census results.[73] According to archival files on the census uncovered in the post-Soviet period, Stalin had hoped the census would show clear evidence of the Soviet state's massive shift into atheism.[74] It showed precisely the opposite. For the next census, in 1939, the question of religion was excluded.

A census is a bird's-eye view, however, and an ambiguous one at that. When it comes to evidence of religiosity on the eve of the Second World War, we are fortunate to have more lucid and intimate sources. We find in the archives, for example, hundreds of letters sent and received by Red Army soldiers or prisoners-of-war in the course of the Soviet-Finnish "Winter War" of 1939–40, typically brimming with explicitly religious sentiments and formulas. In the 542 such letters examined by V.M. Zenzinova, one finds prayers, pleas for God's help, and parental blessings.[75] As we shall see in the chapters to come, evidence of religious devotion among soldiers would continue throughout the Second World War.

On June 22, 1941, Hitler's forces invaded Soviet territory in what amounted to the largest ground invasion in human history. Over the next four years, the Red Army would face up to 70 percent of Germany's total fighting forces on the battlefield. The fighting, along with the disease and starvation that came in its wake, would leave some twenty-five million dead.

Hitler also came bearing gifts, however. On the very day of the German invasion, German radio broadcast in the borderlands that "one of the first measures of the German administration will be the restoration of religious freedom . . . We will allow you to organize religious parishes. Everyone will be free to pray to God in his own manner."[76] Even as Nazi forces in the borderlands were immolating civilians in locked barns and burying them alive in mass graves, they hoped to enlist the sympathies of some Soviet citizens as a force of liberation, granting freedoms that Stalin had denied them. The strategy had notable but limited successes, as tens of thousands of Christian and Muslim populations voiced support for, or even joined, the Axis military. During the first summer of the invasion, four Baltic bishops hailed Hitler with a letter of welcome.[77] A Ukrainian railroad worker, interviewed shortly after the war, recalled the contrast between Soviet rule and Nazi occupation:[78]

> My parents were very religious people. Three kilometers from our village stood the Orthodox church. My parents always went to the church; they took me along and taught me to pray and live according to God's laws. But Stalin does not like God's laws. In 1929 our church was destroyed totally by the Communists and the place where the church stood was ploughed by the

anti-Christs. I never stopped believing in God and praying. Although later I had no opportunity to go to the church, I prayed at home and I taught my children to believe in God and to pray. Especially my daughter followed me and prayed at home. When during the German occupation in 1942 and 1943 the church was open again, I was very glad.

Stalin had clearly been aware that the issue of religion was particularly delicate in the borderlands. Soviet anti-religious repression had targeted these territories less vigorously, such that, by 1941, they contained an estimated 70 percent of all remaining Soviet churches.[79] This region even experienced a limited but noticeable Soviet-backed "restoration" of previously closed churches between 1939 and the beginning of the German invasion—a tactic that Stephen Merritt Miner proposes as a template for the much more ambitious religious restorations to come.[80]

On the day of the Nazi invasion, some leaders of the Russian Orthodox Church sprang into action. Indeed, Metropolitan Sergii beat Stalin to the punch: as Stalin retreated to his dacha in a daze, emerging to lead the country only after a few days of silence, Sergii sermonized on the defense of the Fatherland, instructing all Orthodox faithful that it was their duty to resist the Germans. This mass is reported to have drawn a crowd of some 12,000 packed inside the cathedral, with thousands more gathered outside.[81] Similarly, on June 26, four days after the invasion, a prayer gathering for the victory of the Red Army drew huge crowds at Moscow's Yelokhovo Cathedral. Here, Sergii warned that the enemy targeted not only the Soviet Union, but Christianity itself. The Nazis brought idolatry, slavery, the destruction of Orthodox holy places and, ultimately, the very religion of Orthodoxy.[82] Over the course of the war, Sergii would deliver such public addresses on twenty-four occasions.[83] Other top church leaders followed suit, including Metropolitan Alexii of Leningrad and Novgorod; Metropolitan Nikolai of Kiev; and Filipp, Archbishop of Astrakhan.[84]

The initiative taken by church leaders in the first days of the war has been cited by some historians as evidence that patriotic efforts by Church elites were undertaken independently and with no explicit support from the Soviet state until the fateful autumn of 1943 (to which we will soon return), in which Stalin made his "New Deal" establishing a formal alliance with Church leaders and granting a concession to elect a new Patriarch. The broader narrative suggested by this approach is that it was *only* the dedicated patriotism of church leaders and their faithful that opened Stalin's eyes to the value of religious "toleration." In fact, we have reason to hesitate before accepting this chronology. Within weeks of the invasion, an essay was published informing Soviet citizens of an alleged consensus among religious leaders: that Hitler posed a threat to religion itself and that combating him would be the duty of every believer. Titled "Why Religious Figures Oppose Hitler," the essay summarized and expanded upon the sentiments Sergii and other church leaders had been expressing in their sermons.[85] The author had an unusual name: Katsii Adamiani. Who was this hitherto-unknown Adamiani, who took it upon himself to speak for the leaders of *all* religions in the Soviet Union and managed to have his proclamations widely and immediately circulated?

Adamiani was the pen-name of Iaroslavskii, chief of the League of Militant Atheists, the Soviet Union's leading anti-religious ideologue. We can trace the fateful merger of atheist administrators and patriotic religious propaganda, in other words, to the very start of the war.

The early patriotic appeals by Orthodox Church leaders made their way into Soviet mass media soon afterward. The first of these was published in *Pravda* on August 16, 1941, and thereafter such appeals became fairly commonplace in major newspapers.[86] Meanwhile, newsreels shown to soldiers at the front sometimes showed clergy bearing icons; clergy meeting with troops; clergy encouraging the Red Army in sermons; and clergy leading religious processions.[87] One wartime propaganda film, titled *District Committee Secretary*, shows a heroic priest aiding Soviet partisans; near the end of the film, the chiming of church bells calls citizens forth to defend the Fatherland.[88]

Meanwhile, as we shall see, the anti-religious activities of the Soviet state were sharply curtailed. Iaroslavskii's League of Militant Atheists ceased publication of its venerable *Bezbozhnik* (*Atheist*) magazine and reallocated all resources toward anti-German agitation and patriotic propaganda. The wave of church, temple, and mosque closures which, in the Soviet Union as a whole, had been at high ebb over the past three years, suddenly ceased. The Germans took notice, and internal Nazi documents reveal a tone of alarm: the German promise to uphold religious freedom would be less potent, after all, if religious freedom had already been restored. "In recent months," one German internal report warned in May 1942, "the Soviet government has increasingly restricted activities hostile to the church. Recently, the freedom of the church has even been announced [by the government]. All surviving temples are [now] open, and they are visited by many people. Regular holy services are held in which prayers for Russia's liberation can be heard."[89] Indeed, along with the palpable lightening of restrictions on religious activity, a wave of church reopenings had begun in the territories most immediately threatened by the advancing German troops.[90]

Borderland populations were now subjected to dueling propaganda campaigns: Hitler claimed to liberate holy places from Stalin; Stalin claimed to safeguard them from Hitler. The propaganda war was not limited to regions in the line of fire, however. On September 6, 1941, radio programs broadcast from Berlin and Rome targeted Soviet Muslims, warning them about the Soviet state's plans to inflict further repression on its Muslim populations. As noted in the Introduction to this book, one of their claims was disingenuous: all Russian mosques, the radio program alleged, were going to be converted into cinemas; but another claim was chillingly prescient—Crimean Muslims were to be forcibly deported. This latter nightmare came to pass.

Within a week, a response was mobilized at the highest levels of the Soviet state. V.M. Molotov, Stalin's foreign minister, personally planned the response in consultation with Soviet Information Bureau (Sovinformburo) chief A.S. Shcherbakov, and G. Saksin, the Sovinformburo's head of international affairs. Saksin showed his comrades drafts of an appeal to the world's Muslims by Gabdrahman Rasulev, at that time the chairman of the Soviet Union's minimally active Central Spiritual Directorate of the Muslims of Russia. Rasulev's appeal, the officials resolved, would serve two purposes. First, it would be broadcast on the radio for the benefit of Soviet Muslims. Second, it would be dispatched to Britain's Ministry of Information, with instructions to circulate it among the Muslims of the Middle East.[91] In the months to come, Christian appeals would likewise be broadcast and shipped abroad: Sergii circulated his calls to war among soldiers in Romania, Yugoslavia, Czechoslovakia, and Greece.[92]

We will return to the theme of Soviet religious "patriotic appeals" in the Chapter 2. Suffice to say, in the meantime, that the landmark moment in Soviet religious policy arrived only in the third year of the war. In August and September 1943, Stalin personally oversaw the development of official Soviet religious "directorates," each led by venerable religious leaders working in close consultation with state security services. While it is clear that concern over borderland propaganda and the urge to rally diverse populations to the war effort inspired Soviet religious propaganda campaigns in 1941 and 1942, it is not as clear what immediate pressure or inspiration gave rise to this sea change in Soviet policy in 1943. It is possible (as Chapter 2 describes) that the intensification of the war played a part: the latter half of 1943 marked the deadliest phase of the war for the Soviets, even as the tide turned against the Germans. It is also possible, on the other hand, that the Nazi retreat inspired Stalin to ponder the *long term* relationship between state and religion. The "open" approach toward religion that characterized the war years could not continue forever.

Nor, according to Stalin, could the Soviet Union return to the religious policy that had existed prior to the Great Terror—that is, the formation of a department for religious affairs overseen by the Supreme Soviet. Such a "loose" system was impossible in wartime conditions. The new system would need to be simultaneously more expansive in its outreach to religious communities *and* more rigorously patrolled (in order to reduce the incidence of independent religious activity going unreported).[93] Stalin communicated as much to G.G. Karpov, a rising state security official, who was summoned to meet with the dictator on the night of September 4, 1943.[94] It was to be the most momentous meeting in the history of religion in the Soviet Union.

Karpov was no celebrity in the Soviet government, but he was a veteran in the security services with extensive experience monitoring religious activity. As far back as the 1920s, he had monitored such activity in northwestern Russia for the Cheka, and subsequently for its successor organizations, the GPU and NKVD. He was awarded the Order of the Red Star in 1938 and, in 1940, promoted to the NKVD's Main Directorate of State Security in Moscow. Further promotions followed in the war years, first to the rank of major, in 1941, and then to the rank of colonel.[95]

While much pertaining to Soviet policy in the Stalin era remains shrouded in mystery, we are immensely fortunate when it comes to Stalin's fateful meeting with Karpov: an extremely detailed account of the meeting has been left to us by Karpov himself. Also present at the meeting were Malenkov, whose hardline position on religion had likely helped to encourage Stalin's ruthlessness in the era of the Great Terror; and Lavrentii Beria, the minister of internal affairs and chief of the NKVD.

"On 4.09.43," Karpov recalls, "I was summoned to Comrade Stalin['s office], where I was tasked with addressing the following questions:"[96]

a) What is Metropolitan Sergii like (age, physical characteristics, his authority in the church, his relationship with the government);
b) A brief characterization of Metropolitans Aleksii and Nikolai;
c) When and how Tikhon was elected patriarch;

d) What kind of relationship the Russian Orthodox Church has with [churches] abroad;

e) Who is the patriarch of [the] Constantinople [patriarchate], Jerusalem, and others;

f) What do I know about the leadership of the orthodox church in Bulgaria, Yugoslavia, and Romania;

g) What are the present material conditions of the Metropolitans Sergey, Aleksii, and Nikolai;

h) The number of parishes under the Orthodox Church in the USSR and the number of episcopates.

This "quiz" seems to have served the double purpose of debriefing Stalin on current church-related issues and evaluating the depth of Karpov's knowledge. If Karpov had any idea at the time that he was, in fact, being interviewed for a job, there is no evidence of it in his account. After these preliminary questions had been dispensed with, Stalin cut right to the chase: "A special organ must be created which would undertake relations with the church leadership. What suggestions do you have?"

Karpov writes that he was unprepared for the question, but nevertheless he had a ready answer: he proposed a "department for the affairs of denominations" (*otdel po delam kul'tov*) under the Supreme Soviet and, following this, a permanent commission—perhaps, we may assume, something like the commission that had been abolished five years earlier.[97] Stalin dismissed the suggestion and countered with one of his own, summarized as follows by Karpov. The third point is the most striking:[98]

1) We need to organize under the Union Government, that is, under Sovnarkom, a Council—let's call it the Council for the affairs of the Russian Orthodox Church,

2) The council will be entrusted with conducting relations between the Soviet government and the Patriarch,

3) The council does not make independent decisions; it reports to and receives instructions from the Government.

At this point Stalin conferred with Malenkov and Beria about the possibility of meeting with the three leading figures of the Orthodox Church: Sergii, Nikolai, and Aleksii. (Aleksii would later succeed Sergii as head of the church after the latter's death in May 1944.) All three considered it a positive option.

It is not clear if Karpov realized at the time that Stalin meant it should happen *that very night*. "After this," Karpov writes, "right there in Comrade Stalin's office, I received the order to call Metropolitan Sergii and in the name of the Government give him the following [message]: 'The chairman of the Supreme Soviet [Stalin] will speak with you. The chairman wishes to receive you, and also Metropolitans Aleksii and Nikolai, to listen to your needs and allow for any questions you may have.'" If the Metropolitans could make it, the meeting would happen that same night, in an hour and a half.[99]

Two hours later, all three Metropolitans were gathered before Stalin. Beria and Malenkov had evidently departed, but Molotov, Stalin's foreign minister, who had collaborated on religious propaganda efforts since the first months of the war, joined Karpov, Stalin, and the three holy men for a meeting that lasted, by Karpov's watch, an hour and fifty-five minutes. Stalin began the meeting by applauding the patriotic works of the Church in wartime, recognizing their efforts to gather donations as well as "the position occupied by the church with respect to the state." He then asked if the Metropolitans had any questions to raise that were pressing but hitherto "not permitted."[100]

Sergii took the lead, bluntly raising the issue of gathering bishops to elect a church Patriarch. He himself had served for almost eighteen years as Patriarch *locum tenens*—that is, a "substitute" or "placeholder" Patriarch— but technically the church was without a proper head. Aleksii and Nikolai seconded the request, which Stalin had surely predicted. Stalin not only agreed to the gathering (*sobor'*) of bishops and the election of a patriarch, but even offered logistical support in securing a venue, transportation, and funding. Stalin also enquired about the would-be Patriarch's title. The previous Patriarch, Tikhon, had styled himself "Patriarch of Moscow and All Russia." Sergii offered a more expansive option, hinting perhaps at outreach to the borderlands: "Partiarch of Moscow and All Russians." Stalin agreed that this title would be "proper." As to the convening of the *sobor'*, however, Stalin objected to Sergii's reply that it could be convened within a month. Stalin smiled: "Is it possible to do it at a Bolshevik tempo?" With Karpov's reassurances, the date was set for September 8, just four days away.[101]

Sergii and Aleksii then raised the possibility of organizing theology classes to begin training new cadres of clergy. To this too, Stalin consented, and then went still further, offering permission to open "religious academies" as well as "seminaries in all dioceses that need them." The Metropolitans demurred, explaining that the church did not yet have the manpower for such an ambitious project. "Well, as you wish," Stalin replied. "This is your matter, and if you want theological courses—start with those, but the Government will have no objection to the opening of seminaries and academies."[102] Stalin was equally obliging when it came to their next request: the publication of a monthly journal featuring "such things as a chronicle of the church, essays, and speeches of a theological and patriotic character." To this, Stalin replied simply: "The journal can and should be released."

At this point, with the meeting clearly going well for the Metropolitans, Sergii waded into more sensitive territory: the reopening of churches that had been shuttered during the decades of religious repression. Supporting their comrade, Aleksii and Nikolai noted the uneven distribution of churches in the Soviet Union. Here Stalin's response was, in retrospect, a blatant lie: on the reopening of churches, Stalin promised that the state would offer *no obstacles*.[103]

Thus satisfied, Aleksii edged into still more sensitive territory, raising the issue of liberating the several bishops who were in exile, in prison, or in the Gulag. Here, Stalin was less obliging: "Furnish a list of them," he replied, "and I will take it into consideration." Stalin's reply to the Metropolitans' next proposal (voiced by Sergii), concerning freedom of movement and a liberalized "passport regime" for priests, was similarly vague and noncommittal.[104]

Stalin soon steered the conversation to the Metropolitans' personal circumstances: "Comrade Karpov reported to me," Stalin told them, "that you are living very badly (*vy ochen' plokho zhivete*): cramped apartments, buying groceries at the market, you have no transportation. For that reason the Government would like to know what your present needs are, and what you would like to receive from the Government."[105] Buying groceries at the market was no problem, Sergii replied, but transportation assistance would be welcome. A bigger request followed, one that may well have felt to the Metropolitan like a veritable Hail Mary (so to speak): that Stalin return to the church's hands the spectacular sixteenth-century Novodevichii Monastery, in Moscow. This palatial complex encompassed a cathedral, multiple churches, monastic and convent facilities, apartments, and a cemetery holding the graves of Chekhov, Gogol, and many other notables. Since the 1920s, its state-appropriated buildings had served as art and history museums, including a Museum of Women's Emancipation. And it was entirely unsuitable, Stalin explained, as a church residence. Instead, he offered them a furnished three-story mansion, ready at a moment's notice. As luxurious as the mansion sounds, we can safely assume that it was infested with bugs—of the surveillance kind, that is. After all, the mansion had until 1941 housed the German ambassador Friedrich-Werner Graf von der Shulenburg. No wonder that it was now vacant. Stalin offered the Metropolitans a private viewing of the residence the very next day.[106]

Karpov does not record the Metropolitans' response to Stalin's offer, but he hardly needed to: this meeting was not, despite all appearances, a negotiation. Stalin was dictating terms. Some of the terms were clearly convenient to the Metropolitans, and perhaps unexpected: they would no longer be doing their own grocery shopping at the market. The markets nowadays Stalin explained, are uncomfortable, expensive, and poorly supplied by collective farmers. The state would instead provide them with goods "at the state price" (*po gosudarstvennym tsenam*), along with two passenger cars at their disposal.[107]

What was it all for? Stalin already had the loyalty of the Metropolitans, their diligent work in rallying their public to the war effort, and their steady routing of donations into government hands. The newly permitted election of a Patriarch was certainly of great symbolic significance for the church, but it could not have been immediately clear how, specifically, it would have fundamentally altered church activities or granted the church greater independence. Aside from this profound—but inherently limited—symbolic concession, did Stalin really call three of the most powerful religious leaders in Eurasia into his office in the middle of the night just to offer discount groceries and bugged apartments?

It was nearly two o'clock in the morning before Stalin revealed the central purpose of the meeting. After confirming that the Metropolitans had nothing more to ask, Stalin made his big announcement: "Well, if you have no further questions for the Government, then perhaps you will have [questions] later on. The Government suggests the formation of a special state apparat, which will be called the Council for the Affairs of the Russian Orthodox Church, and it suggests appointing Comrade Karpov as the chairman of the Council. What do you think of that?"

All three Metropolitans, Karpov recalls, "declared that they looked very favorably upon the appointment of Comrade Karpov to this post." Then they departed—and it would be half a century before any head of the Soviet Communist Party would host another official meeting with the heads of the Orthodox Church.[108]

The creation of a new intermediary organization between church and state had been agreed upon, a career security official had been appointed to lead it, and now Stalin had the consent of the church's leading lights. This was the crux of the "New Deal." It is likely that the Metropolitans were not familiar with Karpov's history and skillset. Nevertheless, Stalin gave Karpov a warning in their presence: "[J]ust remember: first of all, you are not a chief prosecutor (*ober-prokuror*); second, in [the Council's] activities you should greatly emphasize the church's independence (*samostoiatel'nost'*)."[109]

Stalin then tasked Molotov with drafting a communiqué for newspapers and radio, "during the preparation of which the appropriate comments, amendments, and additions were made on the part of Comrade Stalin and on the parts of Metropolitans Sergii and Aleksii." The resulting announcement— published in *Izvestiia* the very next day—was undoubtedly the most significant public proclamation ever issued by the Soviet government on the matter of religion, but for all that, it conveys all the drama and fanfare of a revision to the state procurement price of buckwheat:[110]

> This year, on the 4th of September, the Chairman of the Council of People's Commissars of the USSR, Comrade I.V. Stalin, held a meeting during which he had a conversation with the patriarch *locum tenens* Metropolitan Sergii; the Leningrad Metropolitan, Aleksii; and the Exarch of Ukraine, Kiev, and Galicia, Metropolitan Nikolai.
>
> During this discussion, Metropolitan Sergii brought to the attention of the Chairman of Sovnarkom that the leadership circles of the Orthodox church intend to assemble a *sobor'* of bishops to elect a Patriarch of Moscow and All Russians, and to found under this patriarch a Holy Synod.
>
> The head of the Government, Comrade I.V. Stalin, is sympathetic to this proposal and declares that, on the part of the government, there would not be any manner of obstruction. Present at the meeting was the Deputy Chairman of Sovnarkom, Comrade V.M. Molotov.

The emphasis on Sergii's role in the negotiations is, of course, slightly disingenuous. He came to Stalin not to inform him of a decision already taken by the leaders of the church but because he was summoned and prompted to make an inquiry. In any case, the communiqué's presentation of the church-state relationship is clear in its implications: the church was *free* to make this momentous decision for itself, and the role of Stalin (here representing the government as a whole) was simply to have final oversight of decisions taken independently by the church. No doubt the staid language of the circular was likewise deliberate and well considered: it reflects *toleration* of religion without demonstrating any particular *support*, let alone enthusiasm.

As Stalin and the Metropolitans exchanged final pleasantries, their historic meeting concluded without so much as a photo op. Molotov asked Stalin: "Maybe a photographer should be called in?" Stalin replied: "No, it's already too late, two in the morning, we'll do it another time."[111] That time would never come. Nevertheless, as Karpov recalled, "This meeting was a historic event for the church, and made big impressions on the metropolitans Sergii, Aleksii, and Nikolai, as was obvious to all who knew and saw Sergii in those days and afterwards."[112]

The resolution creating the Council for the Affairs of the Russian Orthodox Church (CAROC) was adopted by the Sovnarkom within ten days, on September 14, 1943. The council's powers, according to its founding document, support Odintsov's observation that, from now on, "not a single important issue in the life of the church could be resolved" without prior discussion and approval from CAROC.[113] Along with the power of "preliminary consideration" of any issues raised by the church, the council would also, in theory, receive comprehensive data on church activities, oversee registration of local churches, and monitor the implementation of state laws on religion.[114] CAROC's most fundamental function, however, would be as an intermediary: unable to draft or enforce any legislation itself, the council was to defer to higher authorities in the government—a requirement that likewise implied consistent sharing of information between CAROC and more directly impactful state organs (such as the NKVD). Strictly speaking, in other words, the council was a bureaucratic apparatus for monitoring church activities, but it was not a *supervisory* organization. Its primary purpose, notwithstanding Stalin's description of the council to the Metropolitans, was not to help or support the church, but to help the security services monitor the church.

Other than the right to convene a *sobor'* and elect a Patriarch, moreover, it is not clear that the establishment of CAROC provided the Church with any new rights or freedoms. Rather, it provided the state with a new layer of oversight for a church that had already been taking robust advantage of wartime freedoms for nearly two years. It also provided the state with a new mechanism for coercing the Church's transparency, deference, and participation. It is hard to accept without a caveat, therefore, the arguments of those historians who describe the autumn of 1943 as the first landmark in the development of "religious tolerance" on the part of the Soviet government.

Naturally, the ambiguities of Stalin's wartime religious policy caught many Communists off guard. E.F. Krinko provides three illustrative vignettes:[115]

The "machine-builder" communists Dziabchenko and Mashchenko won-
dered: "how are we supposed to conduct ourselves? Before, we learned
that religion is the opium of the people, but now the government itself
is going toward the clergy (*idet navstrechu sviashchennosluzhiteliam*)."
Party-members Koniashkin, Zaitsev, and Kolpakov, workers in Moscow's
"Komintern" factory, in conversation amongst themselves, came to the
conclusion that "now, the communists can go to church unhindered, pray
to God, baptise their children, and get married." But a third [perspective]
saw this as a further deception on the part of the government. In the words
of Shapiro, an engineer at the Institute of Nitrogen Industry: "One cannot
read Comrade Karpov's speech without irony. According to his words, it
turns out that the government is sympathetic to religion and the clergy, but
in reality this is a deception (*obman*)."

The abrupt pivot could never overcome, moreover, the darkest suspicions
and disdain of some Soviet faithful—nor would the "sanctioned" church ever
earn their trust. One Russian bookkeeper, interviewed in the late Stalin era,
cautioned that "The church which exists in Russia today is a sinister branch
(*levaia storona*) of the NKVD and works for the government. Most of the
priests are active members of the NKVD."[116] Likewise, a refugee Russian psy-
chiatrist told her interviewer, "I would not recognize a single priest or patriarch who is working now in the Soviet Union . . . Because now in their
prayers they pray for Stalin and all the horrors that took place in the last years
are forgotten."[117]

The sense among many Soviet citizens that they were receiving mixed
messages would continue for the remaining war years (and beyond), not
least because the main government organs tasked, after 1943, with overseeing them—CAROC for the Orthodox Church and, for other religions,
CARC—remained chronically understaffed and underfunded (an issue to
which we will return in Chapter 5). Throughout the remaining months of
1943, and all through 1944, only twenty-five to twenty-seven people worked
in CAROC's central "apparat," though forty were deemed necessary for its
basic functioning. The target of forty employees was not achieved until 1945,
and the problem with finding "qualified" people for the task of monitoring
religion would be a consistent burden well into the postwar years.[118]

One of the most basic functions of CAROC, meanwhile, was hin-
dered by Molotov himself, despite the fact that he was ostensibly one of its
founders. Consulted by Karpov about the issue of opening new churches—a

development eagerly expected by many Orthodox, who had begun petitioning the government by the hundreds—Molotov replied: "*Do not give
any kind of permission to open churches.*"[119] The central government, rather
than local executive committees answerable to the councils, was to retain
sole power over permitting church openings. In November 1943, the council
attempted by more formal means to incline Sovnarkom to facilitate more
church openings. In a draft resolution titled "On the System for Opening
Churches," it was proposed that diocese bishops could serve as intermediaries
for petitions concerning church openings. Bishops would have first oversight
of petitions, deciding which ones to support and which to deny. Supportable
petitions would then be passed along to the council and Karpov and Sergii
(now Patriarch) would have the final say.[120] Despite Karpov's best efforts,
only a small fraction of the thousands of petitions received would be satisfied. In 1944, no fewer than 6,402 petitions for the opening of churches were
submitted; 207 churches were opened that year. The following year, in 1945,
the openings more than doubled to total 509, but by the end of that year another 6,025 petitions had been received. In 1946, both petitions and openings
dipped, with 369 church openings and 5,101 petitions received.[121]

There are two divergent ways of translating this data into plain language.
On the one hand, one might observe that over *one thousand* churches were
opened under the close watch of the atheist Soviet government in a period of
just three years. This is far from trivial; indeed, it could be seen as a veritable
revolution in Soviet religious life.

On the other hand, a mere 6 percent of petitions came to fruition over
these three years. Local efforts to open new churches using official channels
were rejected 94 percent of the time.[122] A Soviet citizen had vastly better
odds of surviving uninjured through the Stalingrad or Leningrad sieges than
of securing permission to open a church. How was the average Soviet citizen
supposed to interpret this ambiguous kind of "tolerance"?

We know, at least, how Karpov himself interpreted it. In a revealing letter
to Molotov, he highlighted the success of the new Orthodox Church–state
alliance while warning about the growth of a teeming and ominous religious
"underground" in those places where Church authority was still weak and
churches were not available:[123]

In oblasts with an insignificant number of active churches and in raions
where there are in large part, activists of such unregistered church groups
and clergy, in their consistency, are in an adversarial relationship with legal

patriarchate Orthodox churches, condemning the latter for their legal relationship to the Soviet government and the patriotic position of their activities.

The majority of believer-fanatics, being under the influence of these groups, for the lack of legal active churches in the raions where they are active, are in their disposition distinctly different from the groups of believers under the influence of the patriotically-disposed clergy of the legal churches. This circumstance gives rise to all kinds of "recidivism" in terms of a significant revival of religious sentiment, in the form of the so-called "renewal" of icons, the distribution of "holy letters," conducting public prayers in the fields and at wells, various kinds of soothsaying, and agitation concerning the persecution in the USSR of religion and the church.

As for the main part of the clergy of the legal Orthodox Church, both in the city and in the village, there is no clear evidence of this kind of perversion of religious activities.

Fighting such phenomena presents a major difficulty, because the administrative restriction and non-satisfaction of petitions for the opening of churches often leads to believers going off to satisfy their religious demands (*zaprosy*) in the underground (*v podpol'e*), setting up "forest," "cave," and "catacomb" churches.

Here, we come full circle: back to the "soft line" on religion from the mid- to late 1930s, the approach that had been subverted by Stalin on the eve of the Great Terror. Now, however, without the threat of mass arrests and church closures that had loomed throughout the late 1920s to 1930s, there was nothing to prevent the rapid spread of "underground" religious activity. For Karpov, to go only halfway in developing "loyal" churches under CAROC's watch would only exacerbate the danger.

Church openings would never reach the level implicitly suggested by Karpov. Within months, however, as Chapter 2 will show, the "new deal" between Stalin and Soviet religious elites would be extended to every major religion in the country. This "deal" would form the basis of Soviet religious policy for the next half century, until the fall of the Soviet Union, and serve as a model for state policy toward religion well into the post-Soviet period, throughout the former Soviet Union, and down to the present day. In Chapter 2, we will turn to the Muslim institutions created in this milieu and to the Muslim leaders who leapt into a newly carved space between the Muslim faithful and the Soviet government.

2

Praying with Stalin

Soviet Islamic Propaganda of the Second World War

Stalin invited the Sufi master to Moscow, a Bashkir folktale relates, and asked him who would win the Second World War. "I'll pray on it," the master said. When he had finished his prayers, he returned his verdict: "We shall win." But to make this happen, the master explained, Stalin needed to do two things: "Pray, and give the order not to retreat!" According to the tale, the Sufi master then helped Stalin to do ritual ablutions in the Muslim fashion and afterward had him pronounce the profession of faith: "There is no God but God, and Muhammad is His messenger." Having thus converted to Islam, Stalin prayed to God that the Red Army should win the war. A few years later the Sufi master's prediction came true, and Stalin turned to him in gratitude. He asked, "What can I do to reward you?" The Sufi master explained that whatever wealth Stalin could provide would be wasted on him, as he had no need of it. Instead, he made a demand on behalf of his community: "Religion must be strengthened. Permit the Muslims to go on the pilgrimage to Mecca!"[1]

This strange tale contains a kernel of truth. The Sufi master in question is real, and we have met him already: his name is Gabdrahman Rasulev. Stalin summoned him to Moscow to help win the war—that part is true, too. We can assume that Stalin stopped short of converting to Islam, but he did indeed need the master's help, and he got it. Rasulev aided Stalin not only by praying on behalf of the Red Army but by rallying his community to the war effort. In exchange, Rasulev and other religious elites were not only given leverage to negotiate with the Soviet regime—they were also given leverage and power within the Soviet Muslim community.

In this chapter, we will see how Rasulev, his Central Asian counterpart Ishan Babakhanov, and other Soviet Muslim leaders were called upon to rally their communities in wartime; how they articulated the fight against Hitler in Islamic terms; how they attempted to advance a platform of shared values

God Save the USSR. Jeff Eden, Oxford University Press (2021). © Oxford University Press.
DOI: 10.1093/oso/9780190076276.003.0003

and shared interests with the Soviet state; and how they used the novel occasion of addressing their followers to define communal religious identity in terms that, just a few years earlier, could well have earned these same elites a trip to the Gulag and a bullet in the head.

At the heart of this chapter are several remarkable speeches, translated here from Uzbek, Bashkir, Persian, and Russian—each one a call to the war against Hitler issued by Soviet Muslim muftis in language that bridges Soviet wartime propaganda and classical Islamic rhetoric on "Holy War."[2]

Rasulev's rise

Gabdrahman Rasulev was a Bashkir who came from an esteemed family of religious elites in the Volga-Urals. He was the son of Shaykh Zaynullah Rasuli, a Sufi master of the Khalidi Naqshbandi order who was one of the major figures associated with what is often called "Jadidism," a movement to revise madrasa education and expand literacy.[3] A few of Zaynullah's famous disciples would die in the Gulag, a fate Zaynullah too might have suffered had he not died in 1917, years before the anti-Islamic purges began. Among Zaynullah's seven sons, Gabdrahman ('Abd al-Rahman) appears to have been his chosen *khalifa* (successor) in the Khalidi Naqshbandi order. Despite his prominence as a Muslim community leader,[4] it is no longer any mystery how Rasulev avoided the prisons that had swallowed so many of his contemporaries: as described in the Chapter 1, Rasulev became a Bolshevik collaborator, snitching on fellow Muslim elites—at least one of whom ended up dead as a direct result of Rasulev's denunciations. In 1937, following those same grim events, he was appointed to serve as supreme mufti of TsDUM.

We do not know precisely when Rasulev was first summoned to meet with Stalin, or if it was the mufti who made first contact, but their initial wartime contact likely happened soon after the German invasion. Metropolitan Sergii met with Stalin almost immediately after the start of Operation Barbarossa in late June 1941; he pledged to help rally Christian followers to the war effort. Rasulev was apparently close behind him, since, on July 18, 1941, as Smolensk fell to Nazi troops, he published the first of his wartime appeals to Soviet Muslims.[5] The next month, Rasulev received a visitor who came to deliver a surprising message (events recounted in a remarkable—but tiringly flattering—post-Soviet family history authored by the mufti's own daughter):[6]

In August, 1941, a chief representative (*rukovoditel'*) of the Bashkir government came to our house and conversed for a long time with my father. The guest reported that the Soviet government decided to allow freedom for the religion of Islam, not to repress the activities of the religious community, and to open previously-closed mosques. A new phase began in the activities of the Central Spiritual Directorate of the Muslims of the USSR. It changed from being an institution unnecessary for the Soviet government to being very useful.

Meanwhile, behind closed doors, the bureaucrats on the frontlines of the war on religion began advocating a gentler approach—albeit not in so many words—to enforcing atheism. As early as June 27, 1941, just five days after the Nazi invasion had begun, a directive circulated within the central council of the League of Militant Atheists urged the restructuring of the league's efforts in wartime to focus on anti-fascist propaganda and aid to the frontlines. This aid included the gathering of scrap metal for war industries; collecting clothing for the Red Army; collecting charity for hospitals; and generally raising defense funds. In other words, the Militant Atheists' activities were to be divested of explicitly atheist content for the time being.[7]

This did not mean, however, that the league was to stop functioning as a "mass organization." In a letter to a local Party official from March 26, 1942, the league's director E.M. Iaroslavskii clarified that its change of orientation did not reflect the dissolution of the league, or even a permanent policy shift, but simply a wartime strategy.[8] The task of eradicating religion remained a long-term goal; no fundamental change in Militant Atheist ideology would be required.

On September 2, 1941, scarcely three months after the Nazi invasion, Rasulev released a fervent appeal:[9]

Dear Muslim brothers!
It is known to all that the war was begun by a cunning, merciless, relentless enemy; that they attacked our dear homeland (*rodina*) without warning—humanity cannot even recollect a similar outrage. The homeland suffers now, as our friends and our brothers die on the frontlines, their wives and children bereft. The aggressors are guilty of all this. With their attack on our homeland, sisters and children are doomed to misfortune. This religious assembly (*dukhovnoe sobranie*) therefore asks you to defend the homeland in the name of religion (*vo imia religii*); and also that you ask your fellow

Muslims to defend the homeland. In the mosques and prayer-houses, it is necessary to ask God to aid the Red Army in the defeat of the enemy.

Dear Muslims! It is known that this is [truly] a war—a war for the homeland. Therefore, on the frontlines and on the home front, Muslims are beholden by their religion (*s tochki zreniia religii obiazany*) to fight until the enemy is annihilated. The Qur'an says: Kill in the name of God, never retreating before the enemy, for God does not love those who retreat. Do to them as they have done to you, driving you from your native cities and villages. Vengeance is worse than death. The enemy exacts vengeance upon us, and God will forgive the destruction [of the enemy].[10] Do not tire. If there are a hundred of you, then you will prevail over two hundred [of them]. If there are a thousand of you, then you will prevail over two thousand [of them] by the grace of God. God helps those who persevere in their struggle. You are at war with those who made war upon you without any declaration of war. God does not love those who make war upon the peaceful. Those who make war upon you: destroy them where you find them, drive them out from where they drove you out. The unrest [they cause] is worse than war itself—the outrages of the enemy upon women and children. The Prophet Muhammad said: "Love for country is a part of faith."

According to Rasulev's daughter, this appeal was read aloud not only in mosques but also in factories and at trade union meetings. The mufti received bags full of letters expressing gratitude—not for the mufti's efforts on behalf of the war effort, but rather for the appeal's apparent subtext: "that the religion of Islam," as Rasulev's daughter explains it, "would no longer be repressed."[11]

In fact, audiences more likely greeted the very first samples of "official" Soviet Islamic propaganda with a mixture of bewilderment and suspicion. Striking indeed is Rasulev's summons to the mosques and prayer-houses, most of which had been shuttered or demolished over the previous two decades; his quotations from the Qur'an, the public brandishing of which could attract police scrutiny; and his call for Muslims to fight *for* their homeland but *inspired* by their religion and its traditional prescriptions on the nature of war—ideas long officially derided as at best benighted and at worst reactionary. In any case, this appeal is equally remarkable for what it does *not* say: while much of the content concerning the Nazis' cowardly sneak-attack, betrayal, and atrocities against civilians could just as easily be found in the "secular" propaganda that was simultaneously being circulated—mostly in the Russian language—throughout the Soviet Union, many key motifs of that propaganda are missing here. There is no contrast (either implied or explicit) between socialism and fascism; no mention of toilers, colonialism and anti-colonialism, heroes ("national" or otherwise), or friendship-of-the-peoples. The distinctly Soviet vision of history reiterated incessantly in wartime propaganda, by which the Bolsheviks liberated and then safeguarded sundry Eurasian peoples from colonial aggression, is here replaced by a "deeper" and less specific kind of history: the Nazis are the unnamed "enemies" mentioned in the Qur'an, nothing other than a great evil to be vanquished by the pious. Later in the war, propaganda directed at Soviet Muslims would begin to absorb more of the typical traits of Soviet wartime propaganda directed at "general" audiences—especially its political content. In these early days, however, only the refrain-like repetition of the word "homeland" (*rodina*), here clearly indicating the Soviet Union, hints at the existence of a community other than the Muslim community.

In any case, in the early months of the war, the combination of such limited-but-ambitious propaganda efforts by Rasulev and the merely "passive" official support for Islam (via momentary relief from anti-religious purges) seems to have had a negligible effect on the fighting morale of Soviet Muslim soldiers. An internal report by the Main Political Administration of the Red Army revealed that some 80 percent of soldiers deserting their posts between February and April 1942 were from "non-Russian" (i.e., non-Slavic) backgrounds.[12] "Yusup" (a common Muslim name, in its Russified spelling) and "Yoldosh" (Turkic for "comrade") became sneering terms of derision for non-Slavic soldiers,[13] while some commanders joked that non-Slavs could say only two words: "*Korsak bolit*" ("My stomach hurts").[14] The majority of non-Russian soldiers served in mixed battalions and under Slavic commanders, and their homesickness and sense of alienation must have been profound. One Uzbek soldier reportedly wept upon hearing his native language.[15] A Kazakh soldier who had become a hero in the defense of Moscow lamented: "I think it's a crime that Kazakh fighters at the front do not receive the most elementary scanty ration from the arsenal of their native language, native literature, and native music."[16] Meanwhile, Slavic commanders suffered the frustrations of attempting to communicate with Caucasian and Central Asian Muslim soldiers who, in many cases, did not speak Russian. "Let them be crushed by tanks and shot by the enemy," one commander reportedly said. "That way we'll get sent to the rear for restaffing. We need to save the Cossacks and Russians, they are useful."[17]

To some in Moscow, the problem was simple: propaganda efforts among non-Slavs had been far too limited. These efforts were failing, and they were failing because, in the early phases of the war, most of the propaganda was still in the Russian language and spoke to distinctly "Russian" concerns. Even those propaganda efforts which mentioned the diverse peoples of the Soviet Union tended to take a Russian chauvinist tone, emphasizing the "elder brother" status of Slavs: "Ivan" leads; "Yusup" follows. Still more maddening, while the Soviet government had proven inadequate in providing propaganda to non-Slavic soldiers, the Nazis were making direct contact with Soviet Muslim citizens with appeals to join the their "liberation" campaign.

Such observations were made by no lesser authority than L.P. Beria, the notorious chief of the NKVD. In early March 1942, as he presided over Gulags filled with Muslim prisoners of religious conscience, Beria observed that the Nazis were making headway in the propaganda war for the minds of Muslims.[18] Stronger countermeasures were urgently needed. Rasulev's outreach to Soviet Muslims was precisely the kind of thing Beria was looking for.

Meanwhile, throughout the autumn and winter of 1942, the Political Administration of the Red Army (PURKKA)—the chief source of wartime propaganda—likewise aimed to establish a plan of action. While military officers were sometimes lambasted for their insensitivity toward their non-Slavic subordinates, the low ebb of these soldiers' morale mostly prompted finger-pointing and self-criticism within Party ranks; "weakness of party-political and educational work" was identified as the culprit in the "insubordination, self-inflicted wounds, desertion, and treason on the part of a certain portion of Red Army men of non-Russian nationality."[19]

We may detect some arrogance in the conviction of these propagandists that increasing Muslim morale was simply a matter of running a better ad campaign. But there can be no doubt that the officials were onto something: *why*, after all, should Muslims fight at Stalin's behest? One can imagine the kinds of questions that may have arisen around Central Asian dinner tables in the first year of the war: Does Hitler hate Soviet citizens or only the Soviet regime? Would he treat us cruelly? Is he crueler than Stalin? Does Hitler hate Islam? Does he hate it as much as Stalin does? These would have been good questions, and they remain good questions, especially since, as Motadel shows, Hitler appears to have held Islam in particularly high regard among world religions,[20] and, in any case, he never clarified his long-term plans for (or racial theories on) the Muslim peoples of Central Asia.

Whatever Hitler's plans, Soviet propagandists hoped to impress upon Muslims clearly and forcefully that the Red Army was their army too; that the Soviet Union was their homeland too; and that they too could—and should—be heroes in the struggle. An order by Shcherbakov from September 17, 1942, sketched out an eight-point platform around which the new wave of propaganda directed at "non-Russians" would revolve:[21]

a) The Red Army—army of brotherhood between the peoples of our country. b) What Soviet power gave to the peoples of the USSR. c) what the Hitlerites will bring upon the peoples of the Soviet Union. d) Defend the independence of all the national republics on the fronts of the Great Patriotic War. e) The iron discipline and steadfastness of soviet warriors— the guarantee of victory. f) Heroes of the Soviet Union Mil'dzikov, Kurban-Derby, and others. g) The role of the Great Russian People in the struggle for freedom and independence of the peoples of the USSR and for the building of socialism in the brotherly Soviet republics. h) The role of the Great Russian People in the Fatherland War of the peoples of the Soviet Union against Hitlerite Germany.

On most of these fronts, Rasulev was way ahead of him. He had hammered home these points—as well as some other, more original messages—in an appeal from May 1942, published in *Trud*, a prominent official newspaper based in Moscow. This address, ostensibly penned for the benefit of the other members of the Central Spiritual Directorate, was immediately translated into Tatar, Bashkir, Kazakh, Uzbek, Arabic, Turkish, Persian, and Hindi, and circulated widely at home and abroad:[22]

Dear Muslim Brothers!
The proclamations of God and His prophet, the great Muhammad, exhort you Muslims to fight unsparingly on the battlefield for the liberation of the great Homeland (*rodina*), of all humanity, and of the Muslim world from the yoke of the fascist villains. To the men and women on the home front: do not succumb to cowardice and panic; give all your strength to doing what is necessary for the successful conduct of the War for the Fatherland and the security and the lives of its people.

In this holy War for the Fatherland (*v etoi sviatoi Otechestvennoi voiny*) against fascist Germany and her henchmen, show before all the world your loyalty to the Homeland, proving your righteousness. Pray in the mosques and prayer-houses for the victory of the Red Army.

We scholars of Islam (*uchenye islama*) and spiritual leaders living in the Soviet Union call all Muslims to the unanimous defense of the beloved homeland as well as the Muslim world from the German fascists and their henchmen. Pray to great and gracious God to hasten the deliverance of all humanity and the Muslim world from the tyranny of the misanthrope-fascists (*chelovekonenavistnikov-fashistov*).

There is not one true believer (*pravovernyi*) whose son, brother, or father does not fight today against the Germans, or who lags behind in taking up arms for our common homeland. Likewise, there is probably no one on the home front who has not aided in victory through their labor in the factories and plants. For we Muslims well recall the words of the Prophet Muhammad (peace be upon him!): "Love for the homeland is a part of faith."

Just as in Rasulev's appeal from the previous year, published just days after the war began, this rallying call implies that it was not just the Soviet government calling Muslims to war, but God Himself along with His prophet. Once again, the "War for the Fatherland" is depicted as the unanimous concern of all Soviet Muslims. Once again, Muslims are directed to the few available mosques to pray for the Red Army. And once again, Rasulev concludes with a famous formula equating the Arabic *watan*—which has alternately been understood to mean country, nation, or homeland—with the Russian *rodina* (homeland, i.e., in this case, the entire Soviet Union).

But there is something new and remarkable here: unlike in Rasulev's appeal from the summer of 1941, his message in *Trud* presents the war as an *international* Muslim struggle. He is not subtle on this point. While the Muslims of the Soviet Union were the focus of the earlier rallying call, here Rasulev reiterates no fewer than three times that it is not just the immediate "homeland" that needs saving, but the entire "Muslim world" (*musul'manskii mir*). Given that Soviet secular propaganda was steadfastly focused on the "Friendship of the [Soviet] Peoples," as it would remain for years to come, Rasulev's appeal to Muslims' sense of membership in a *global* community seems a shocking departure. Just four or five years earlier, publicly proclaiming this kind of "bourgeois internationalism," and couched in religion no less, could probably have earned Rasulev a trip to the Gulag, or worse. Now, such language was circulating with tacit Party approval in one of the state's major newspapers.

Soviet propaganda masters were, as Schechter and others point out, skilled in the art of modulating a single message to suit the needs of specific communities, tailoring their message by naming nation-specific heroes of legend, history, and the Red Army. However, the professional propagandists of PURKKA were not the only elites to have mastered the art of modulating a message to suit the crowd. In the same month—May 1942—Rasulev addressed the Muslims of Ufa with what he called a "pious appeal to Muslims" (*nāsīkhāt bän musulmānlargha murāja'at*), delivered at a major congress (*qurultay/kurultai*) of Muslim elites.[23] Here, Rasulev doubles down on the "internationalist" message of the *Trud* appeal while elaborating dramatically on Muslims' shared history. Speaking in the Bashkir language to his immediate community of Volga-Urals Muslims, Rasulev presents the war effort as, above all else, a global Muslim struggle against imperialism. The "Friendship of the [Soviet] Peoples," and even the Soviet "homeland," are secondary concerns.

In this Ufa appeal, Rasulev paints the Nazis and their allies as the direct descendants of the "imperialist governments, enemies of Islam" (*islām dushpandari imperyalist ükumattar*) in Germany, Italy, and France, which had swept a refined Muslim culture from southern Spain (al-Andalus) in the medieval era; and of the "imperialist" Crusaders who attacked the Middle East, identified likewise as the governments (*ükumattar*) of Germany, Italy, and France. Rasulev writes that these "German fascists and their European puppets" (*german fashistlar va ularning qurshaqlari*) went on to conquer the entire world in later periods, wiping out religions, cultures, customs, and traditions, and seeking to make only "pure German law" and the "Protestant" religion supreme.[24] In the process, they laid waste to *maktab*s (primary schools) and mosques.

More recently, Rasulev writes, the Germans and Italians had devastated the Muslim culture of Tripoli (Ṭarabulus) in Libya, "land of Islam," where they tyrannized the populace, including elders, women, and children.[25] After noting also the ruin brought upon Muslims in Abyssinia and Albania, the mufti warns that the Germans and their "puppets" have turned to the land of the Tatars, destroying maktabs and terrorizing the people. In Crimea, he writes, the German fascists destroyed many mosques, replacing the Islamic crescent atop the mosques with their fascist symbol: a "black cross" (*qara karas*).[26] They forbade Muslims from *namaz* (prayer), ridiculed Islamic customs and practices, ruined the chastity of young women, shuttered maktabs, and destroyed countless works and buildings in an effort to wipe

out "Tatar-Turk" customs (*tatar-turk adattarin*). Muslim children, claims
Rasulev, have been forbidden from wearing Tatar "national" clothing and
have been prevented from receiving names drawn from Islamic literature—
the children are taken before the "German priests" (*nemis pöpdar*) and given
German names instead. The streets of Crimea, the mufti says, are filled with
starving, impoverished Muslims.[27]

Following a selection of Qur'anic verses,[28] Rasulev appeals to all the
Muslims of the world (not only of the Soviet Union) to join in the "sacred
struggle" (*muqaddas küräsh*) against the Germans and their allies. He calls
for continued prayers on behalf of the Red Army in the mosques and places
of religious observance (*ibādat jāylar*) and warns that the enemy threatens to
cast the country into ruin, putting an end to Muslims' learning and culture,
their religion, their countries, their languages, and their customs. Rasulev
concludes by calling on all Muslims to join the struggle and hasten to engage
the enemy in battle, begging God's mercy and assistance.[29]

While Rasulev paints a grave picture of German offenses in Crimea, the
Reich had, in fact, been engaged in quite the opposite program, implementing
what Motadel justifiably calls a "radical pro-Muslim policy" in the region.[30]
Mosques were reopened; madrasas were returned to Muslim ownership and
control; previously banned Islamic ceremonies were permitted and even
encouraged. A German-led bureaucracy to oversee Muslim affairs was established in the Crimea and planned in the Caucasus. One Caucasus correspondent surveyed the scene: "Next to the flag of the Reich waves the green
banner with crescent and star, under which once Muhammad prevailed over
the Jews."[31]

In any event, the international and anti-colonial orientation of Rasulev's
commentary here emerges in clear relief: the pre-Soviet world is separated
into European "imperialists" and their victims, most notably the world's
Muslims.[32] Anti-colonial resistance was, by this time, a familiar language
of protest in Eurasia, and certainly in the Soviet Union. It was also a language the Germans employed, both in North Africa and on the Eastern
Front, when attempting to rally Muslims to wage jihad alongside the
Reich.[33]

Surprising and novel in the context of Soviet propaganda, however, is
Rasulev's almost complete lack of reference to the Soviet Union itself, save for
its Red Army. Gone are the relentless mentions of the "homeland" (*rodina*);
claims of shared purpose between Muslims and other Soviet citizens; and
any clear articulation of the fact that the Nazi threat concerned non-Muslims

too. In short, Rasulev calls on Muslims to fight *with* the Red Army but *for* the entire Muslim world.

In this way, Rasulev carves out a distinctive space for himself and his community of Volga-Urals Muslims. The broader Soviet public—the readers of *Trud*—got one kind of message from Rasulev, packaged as a "general" appeal to Muslims; but Rasulev's constituents, the Muslims assembled immediately in front of him, got something else entirely. His words to this community assert the validity of an international Muslim identity—one that clearly, at least in Rasulev's reckoning, takes precedence over any Soviet identity or solidarity with non-Muslim Soviet peoples. In Rasulev's drastically condensed summary of Operation Barbarossa, for example, it is not just any Soviet citizens whom the Nazis attacked, but Muslims and only Muslims. In short, a new public space had been created in which a Muslim leader could safely articulate his community's collective distinctiveness to an extent unthinkable at any other time since the pre-Soviet period. For Muslims in the audience who, since the 1920s, would only have dared to express such sentiments behind closed doors, Rasulev's address must have been surprising indeed.

It must also have been fundamentally confusing. Was this now the official *Party line*? Somehow, it had to be—after all, Rasulev was able to mount the pulpit only by the grace of the Party. His organization, TsDUM, received and addressed Muslims' concerns, but it was unabashedly an organ of the state, no more likely to go "rogue" than any other creature of the thoroughly terrorized Stalinist bureaucracy.

Nevertheless, the fact remained: Rasulev's message was profoundly different from the one being circulated by "secular" authorities. The secular authorities urged Muslims to fight for their country; Rasulev urged them to fight for their religion. The secular authorities urged them to fight for their Soviet brothers; Rasulev urged them to fight for the entire Muslim world. The messages contradicted one another on two fronts. First, the secular message was resolutely "Unionist"; Rasulev's was just as plainly "internationalist." Second, the secular message seemed strenuously to divest Muslim cultural touchstones (legendary infidel-slaying heroes, monuments of distinctly Islamic architecture) of any religious significance; Rasulev's message sought to restore the sacred landscape and its history. Could it be that one authority figure was suddenly and bravely speaking—in the Bashkir language, at least—without the approval of his higher-ups?

The more likely explanation is that the Soviet central government condoned and collaborated in Rasulev's radical discursive departure. There is evidence for this on three fronts. First, Party archives preserve drafts of Rasulev's speeches, showing clearly that Soviet officials monitored and signed off on his major addresses; it was the Party, after all, which oversaw their translation, reprinting, and export. Second, Rasulev's spiritual directorate not only managed to avoid censure (and Rasulev arrest); indeed, rather than shutting down this muftiate, Party officials sought to duplicate it in other regions of the Soviet Union. Third, while Party officials were collaborating in the drafting of religious propaganda, the state's security apparatus did not turn a blind eye to Rasulev's activities; on the contrary, agents of Stalin's NKGB (and later the NKVD) were widely attested to be a common presence at his patriotic gatherings.

Ishan Babakhanov's war

In May 1943, Vsevolod Merkulov, chief of the much-feared NKGB (People's Commissariat for State Security), wrote to Stalin with a bold proposal. His primary concern at the time was "To suppress attempts by foreign intelligence and anti-Soviet elements within the USSR to use the Muslim clergy against the Soviet government." One way to combat this, Merkulov believed, was by "providing the patriotic elements of the Muslim clergy of Central Asia and Kazakhstan with the ability to organize patriotic works among Muslim believers." Therefore, he requested that Stalin "entrust the NKGB of the USSR with carrying out appropriate practical activities for the organization of a Spiritual Directorate of the Muslims of Central Asia and Kazakhstan."[34] There was, in any case, a precedent here: back in 1923, Rasulev's Central Spiritual Directorate had itself been created with the direct oversight of Soviet state security (the NKVD, in that case).[35]

Over the next two months, Moscow acted quickly to satisfy Merkulov's request. On June 10, the Politburo published a decree requesting that officials "permit the establishment of the Spiritual Directorate of the Muslims of Central Asia and Kazakhstan."[36] Just two days later, a group of Muslim leaders in Central Asia received a message from M.I. Kalinin, chairman of the Presidium of the Supreme Soviet of the USSR, laying out what was to be expected of them. "For the duration of the Great War for the Fatherland," he wrote, "all honorable representatives of the Muslim clergy have taken a strongly patriotic position, urging faithful Muslims to rise up in defense of the homeland (*rodina*) and render service to the warfront. The Muslim

Spiritual Directorate [of Central Asia and Kazakhstan] will dedicate all efforts toward the goal of more quickly vanquishing the enemy." Thus far, Kalinin explained, "the lack of a single spiritual center for Muslims in Central Asia has not allowed the Muslim clergy to provide more organizational support to our government in its efforts on the frontlines and the home-front."[37] Make no mistake, Kalinin seemed to say: the Muslim elites' newfound power and platform would have everything to do with the war effort and nothing to do with any ideological turn by Moscow toward religious toleration. The "clergy" had their muftiate, but they also had their marching orders.

The chief of Uzbekistan's Supreme Soviet, Yoldash Akhunbabayev, summoned Ishan Babakhanov—recently released from the Gulag—and urged him to write to Kalinin, evidently to request the establishment of the proposed spiritual directorate.[38] A petition submitted to Stalin by Babakhanov and three other Central Asian Muslim leaders around this time has been preserved in the archives.[39] Finally, on July 31, the Presidium of the Supreme Soviet of the USSR resolved to "satisfy" the request to create a spiritual directorate based in Tashkent and to hold a "convocation, in Tashkent, of a congress of representatives of Muslim clergy and believers from the Uzbek, Tajik, Turkmen, Kazak, and Kyrgyz SSRs."[40] Like Rasulev, Ishan Babakhanov was summoned to Moscow to meet with Stalin himself. The mufti's daughter, Sofiya, later recalled the circumstances of the historic visit:[41]

> I. V. Stalin granted an audience in Moscow only to my father. After coming back home, he told us that the conversation took place in Stalin's office with the assistance of a translator. With respect and sincerity, he inquired about the mood of the Muslims, their life, and suggested organizing a *qurultoy* for the Muslims, a Spiritual Board, that would call upon Muslims to help the front and resolutely struggle with the invaders. They offered tea and grapes to father. He noticed that the leader's office was very modest.

The occasion must have inspired mixed emotions for Ishan Babakhanov. He was, after all, receiving a promotion from a dictator whose reign had been hell for him: he had been imprisoned in 1937 and again in 1940. Babakhanov was at least seventy-three at the time of his first arrest, and nearly eighty when he was appointed to take charge of the muftiate. Descended from a long line of esteemed Sufi shaykhs, he attended Tashkent's Barakkhan madrasa as well as the Saray Tash madrasa in Bukhara, and went on *hajj* in 1912. Stalin could easily have found a young, loyal Muslim Party member to take charge of the muftiate, but he must have wanted precisely the opposite. While no documents have come to light to explain how Babakhanov was chosen, we might guess that his elder status and his previous estrangement from the Soviet system were seen as positives: who better to rally Muslims to the war effort than an "authentic," venerable figure whom even anti-Soviet Muslims might be inclined to respect?

Babakhanov later recalled that one of his prison interrogators had shouted at him in anger: "You will fizzle out in this prison!" To this, he replied: "Everything in this world happens according to the will of Allah. I entrust myself to the Almighty and the fate He has prepared for me."[42] Could either of them have imagined that, just a few years later, Babakhanov would be sharing tea and grapes with Stalin?[43]

SADUM's founding congress, held on October 20, 1943, came at a pivotal time. By then, the tide of war on the Eastern Front had turned decisively against the Axis forces. Eight months earlier, the Battle of Stalingrad had ended with the formal surrender of German commanders. This, Winston Churchill wrote, was "the end of the beginning" for the Nazis. The territory around Belgorod and Kharkov that the Germans captured in the coming weeks would serve as their last significant conquest in Soviet territory. Then, throughout July and August, the Germans suffered massive losses of life and territory in the Battle of Kursk; they lost Belgorod and Kharkov. This, Churchill wrote, was "the beginning of the end."[44]

The number of Soviet soldiers killed and wounded in the first two quarters of 1943 has been estimated at 2,834,947.[45] The greatest territorial gains were still to come, but so was the greatest loss of life; the "beginning of the end" for the Nazis also marked, for the Red Army soldier, the beginning of the war's deadliest phase. The tally of dead and wounded from the year's third quarter exceeded those from the first two combined: an estimated 2,864,661 Soviet soldiers were killed or wounded between July and September, the deadliest three months of the entire war for the Red Army. Another 2,157,895 were killed or wounded between October and the year's end. That autumn, the Red Army needed resources and recruits as badly as it had ever needed them.

This was the context in which Ishan Babakhanov addressed Central Asian Muslims in October 1943. In calling them to the war effort, he probably intended to appeal to the broadest possible demographic. It is partly for this reason that the contents of his opening remarks are so striking. Unlike Rasulev, who appealed to the Muslims of the Volga-Urals region on distinctly pan-Islamic, "internationalist" grounds, Babakhanov's appeal is resolutely local in character. He emphasizes the sacredness and primacy of an aspect of Central Asian Islam that had long been targeted for destruction by Soviet officials: the veneration of local shrines and saints. These centuries-old traditions had, for nearly two decades, been denigrated in Soviet anti-religious literature and official decrees as dangerous and primitive features; as retrograde "pre-Islamic survivals" of paganism; and as corrupting evils to be torn up by the roots. Ironically, Babakhanov himself was no great fan of these mystical traditions; he had long been associated with reformist Muslim currents *against* such practices as shrine-veneration.[46] Perhaps this is one of the traits that endeared him to the Soviet government. In any case, as Babakhanov addresses his public, then, he appears to herald a new era for Islam in the region. After a short statement recounting how the "enemy wolves of Hitler" had invaded Soviet territory, had "drenched all of Europe in blood," and had pushed into the North Caucasus and attacked Krasnodar, Babakhanov tells his audience that the Nazis (whom he calls *gitlerchilar*, Hitlerites) intend to press on into Central Asia, threatening not only its people but its precious Sufi shrines:

> They wish to bring Samarkand to ruin, the historic [city] of fame and renown where Qusam b. ʿAbbas[47] and Khwaja Ahrar[48] (God's mercy be upon them!), *ʿulamāʾ* of Islam, lived and are buried, [the former] in the shrine of Shah-i Zinda. They intend to burn our city of Bukhara, home to the shrines (*mazārlar*) of such blessed persons as the hadith-transmitter Muhammad b. Ismaʿil Bukhari[49]; Bahaʾ al-Din Naqshband,[50] esteemed among the saints; Sayyid Amir Kulal[51]; *shaykh al-ʿālam* Bakharzi,[52] and Agha-yi Buzurg.[53] And they intend to destroy and bring to ruin sacred Ferghana, home to the shrine of ʿAli (God's blessings be upon him)—follower of our Prophet Muhammad (peace be upon him), beloved of God—at famed Shahimardan.[54] They intend to bring to ruin the city of Turkestan, home to the radiant shrines of such shaykhs as Khwaja Ahmad Yasavi,[55] Abu ʿUbayda b. al-Haraj Khwaja Tarabi,[56] and Khwaja Ghazi.[57] And they likewise seek to capture, turn to ashes, and scatter to the wind the city of Tashkent, home to the shrines of such eminent saints and great men as Imam Abu Bakr Muhammad Qaffal Shashi,[58] Shaykh Khavand-i Tahur,[59] and Shaykh Zayn al-Din,[60] as well as the burial place of the radiant, sacred body of ʿUkasha,[61] one of the close companions of our Prophet.[62]

Here, at the inaugural congress of the region's highest "official" Islamic institution, we find the region's religious life tied inextricably to its local shrines. Central Asian Islam, in Babakhanov's formulation, is embodied in its shrines, a constellation of which shape the region's sacred landscape.

Following this, Babakhanov warns that the Germans "intend to turn our maktabs into dungeons, to turn our places of higher learning into brothels, and to make a mockery of our mosques, our sacred places of pilgrimage (*muqaddas ziyāratgāhlarimiz*), and the shrines of our saints." Here, shrines are combined with mosques and maktabs as a basic unit of religious life in the region.

Babakhanov then cautions that the Germans will annihilate the "national cultures" (*millī madanyatlar*) of the people of Turkestan and Kazakhstan and will cast into the flames "eminently valuable works by the '*ulama*' and other "treasuries of knowledge" safeguarded in the libraries of Bukhara, Urgench, Samarkand, Tashkent, Ashgabat, Khujand, Awliya Ata, and Frunze (Bishkek). It is at this point, after elaborating on the German threat to Central Asian religious life, that the possible sufferings of the region's populace enter the picture: the Germans, Babakhanov says, will "violate the chastity of our virtuous women and innocent girls. They will ridicule and bring to grief the happy dreams of our children, the peaceful lives of our elders, and the hearths of our domestic contentment."

The mufti now turns to the subject of Soviet nationalities, finally echoing some of the propaganda pitches familiar from "secular" publications:[63]

> For a thousand years, Turkestan has consisted of the sacred homelands (*muqaddas vaṭanlar*) of the Uzbek, Tajik, Turkmen, Kazakh, Kyrgyz , and Karakalpak peoples, and so it will [continue]. The people of Turkestan, in accordance with the counsel and charge of the elders (*ata va bābālar*) of their respective homelands, as well as in the interests of liberty and progress (*ḥurriyat va taraqiyāt*), in the interests of religion and law, in the interests of conscience and reputation, have joined together in union with the other peoples of the Soviet Union and are conducting a great war against the fascist murderers.

The Soviet state, in Babakhanov's familiar formulation, preserves the self-determination of preexisting Muslim groups. (As evidence of this self-determination, it is the "elders" who resolved to join the war effort, rather than Soviet-appointed local and national officials who were, in reality, often young.) The mufti then cites and explains a Qur'anic passage permitting Muslims to make defensive war on those who have attacked them,[64] returning afterward to the subject of nationalities: "From the first day that the Soviet state came into being as a homeland for all the peoples of the Soviet Union," he writes, "its people were freed from tyranny and lawlessness, from poverty and penury, from backwardness and from darkness. And regardless of their differences of nation (*millat*), religion and custom, the law has been passed for them to conduct themselves independently, and a broad path has been opened for them to achieve national progress (*millī taraqiyāt*), happiness, and prosperity."[65]

To this, Babakhanov adds the familiar formula: "Love for your country is a part of faith." The implication here seems to be that the Soviet state has created the conditions under which Muslims can best live out the example of the Prophet—in this case, by fighting bravely in the Soviet Union's defense. Babakhanov immediately contrasts this with Hitler's ideology: "Hitler has set forth a theory of the purity and domination of the German race (*nemets irqi*). He considers all the [other] people of the world to be a lowly race, and he considers any Eastern peoples to be monkeys (*maymūnlar*). Using this theory, the Germans intend to conquer other peoples and annihilate their countries."

Babakhanov then stresses the peaceful orientation of the Soviet people prior to Hitler's attack, and he offers an optimistic appraisal of the current war effort, reassuring his constituents that "Hitler and his sympathizers (*fikrdāshlar*) have brought about their own demise." What follows this is one of the speech's most striking passages (also quoted in the Introduction):[66]

> In union with all the Soviet peoples, the Muslims of Turkistan and Kazakhstan have sent their own dear children to join the ranks in this general and sacred jihad (*umūmī va muqaddas jihād*), this holy war (*ghazāt*). And in the manner of fathers (*atalarcha*) they recite to them the noble *fātiḥa* and see them off, hoping with all their heart that they might defeat and destroy the enemy . . . . Every Muslim who sacrifices himself for God in the path of religion is a martyr (*shahīd*). And every single Muslim who slays the accursed and seditious enemy is a *ghāzī* and a *mujāhid*—a warrior for the faith (*dīn uchun urush qiluvchidur*).

Here is Babakhanov's boldest rallying call—and his starkest declaration of Muslims' fundamental separateness from other Soviet citizens. What does it mean to wage jihad "in union" with non-Muslims? Surely, the non-Muslims of the Soviet Union cannot be among those sacrificing themselves "in the path of religion"; nor can their dead be "martyrs" in the same sense as the Muslim dead. Whatever the non-Muslim Soviet citizens may be fighting for, it is clear that, in Babakhanov's formulation, Central Asian Muslims' communal survival and their communal identity are inextricably linked to Islam—and to the Soviet Union.

Following another Qur'anic verse condoning defensive warfare,[67] Babakhanov continues with the theme of holy warriors in the ranks of the Red Army. First, he cites a hadith of the Prophet: "Every honorable person who loves his country must make war against and destroy the enemy. May our *ghāzīs* [holy warriors] be courageous and never turn and flee from the enemy." Then he provides the names of nine "true sons and daughters of Turkestan" who have fought with the Red Army and "gained the noble rank of heroes of the Soviet Union." Finally, all of the foregoing having set the stage, Babakhanov arrives at what is ostensibly the central purpose of his speech, calling directly on Muslims to join the war effort:[68]

> Join hands in union with the brother-nations of our country (*mamlakat*), and, in perfect friendship and with the zeal and intensity of lions, struggle against Hitler's accursed [army]; annihilate the vile fascists without mercy; wipe them from the face of the earth; protect every last inch of the Soviet land with every last drop of your blood; fight with perfect loyalty and intensely, that it will not fall into the hands of the enemy; make your battle lines firm like iron; be steadfast in your military discipline; follow the orders of your commanders, never shrinking from [your duty], and execute your orders with all haste and perfect loyalty.

After a hadith cautioning against desertion from battle,[69] Babakhanov turns his attention to those at home, far from the front, urging them to "give more, so that there will be raw provisions and cooked meals for our Red Army soldiers; labor truly and devotedly at the collective farm (*kolkhoz*) and the state farm (*sovkhoz*), at the factory and the company."[70] A Qur'anic quotation urging the reinforcement of battle lines[71] is then followed by a hadith praising those who support their local *ghāzī*s: "He who equips a *ghāzī* in the way of God is as if he has taken part in the fighting himself; and he who looks after the dependents of a *ghāzī* in his absence is as if he has taken part in the fighting himself." In other words, even those at home are able to join the jihad, as long as they perform a vital function in support of the front.

At this point, Babakhanov begins his concluding words, addressing directly, for the first time, the Muslim leaders of the region of whom he has now taken charge: "Esteemed imams and leaders of Muslims! Hasten the hour of victory by your devotion and loyal labors, by [engendering] the courage and zeal of the Muslims and believers at the front." What he then asks of the Muslim community at large is more elaborate, if also more concrete:[72]

> O Muslim men and women! Every day, perform *namāz* five times without error (*nuqṣānsiz*), ask victory from God for our soldiers, and pray. Ask for victory and aid for your sons. So that our country, which has given you peace and safety, will be stable and prosperous, give earnest assistance by way of your earthly possessions as well as through your devoted and untiring labor and service.

Babakhanov ends his speech on a triumphal note, promising that victory is near, reassuring his constituents that their sacrifice would not be in vain:

> Praise and thanks to Eternal and Almighty God, that we have begun to see the fruits of our prayers and labors. We are hearing news of victory. The [inevitable] defeat of the damned enemy and the accursed murderers is today, in the world's view, as bright and plain to see as the sun. Each day our Red Army soldiers in their tens and hundreds are liberating villages and cities, and they do not rest. The enemy intends to flee to the West, but we will close off every last inch of our land to them, we will be ready to risk our lives, and we will stand against them. Our famed [Soviet] allies (*shuhratli ittifāqchilarimiz*) will strike Germany's manufacturing centers from the air and flatten them to the ground, and we will drive their soldiers back to the Italian border. But victory will not come of its own volition. In order to hasten victory, we must redouble our aid to the Front, and our soldiers must show still more of their greatness and courage. O Almighty and Glorious God, save and liberate us from the wretched crimes of the man-eating, accursed, savage enemy.[73] Amen, O Master of Worlds.[74]

If the Soviet state had wanted a Muslim authority capable of grounding the call to war in locally resonant terms, they had chosen wisely. Did Central Asian audiences really believe that Hitler posed an immediate threat to Samarkand's shrines? It seems unlikely. In any case, the message that the Nazis were out to destroy the entire Soviet Union would not have been the novel aspect of the speech for Babakhanov's audience. Rather, it is the message between the lines that resounds here: Babakhanov was honoring the very shrines that the Soviet government had previously spent two decades converting into barns, storage sheds, and museums of "Marxist-Leninist scientific atheism." For some, the choice of a twice-imprisoned mufti to render the message that the Nazis—and not the Soviets—posed an existential threat to Islam may have seemed ironic, tone-deaf, even absurd. But in fact it was a stroke of genius. Babakhanov, a living link to pre-Soviet Sufi traditions, was here to announce that times had changed. Sacred ground was sacred again—with Stalin's assent.

An appeal to Isma'ilis

Moscow must have been pleased with the results of Babakhanov and Rasulev's work. In less than a year, two additional spiritual directorates were founded on the model of the two existing organizations. A mufti named Khizri Gebekov was elected to lead the newly founded Central Spiritual Directorate of the Muslims of the North Caucasus (DUMSK), while the Shi'i *shaykh al-islam* Akhund Agha Mamed Jafar-oghli 'Alizada (Alizada Akhund) took the helm of DUMZAK. The leaders of DUMZAK promptly reassured Stalin, in a letter, that they had "blessed their brother Mohammedans in their military deeds and called them to stand in defense of the sacred soil of their ancestors, together with all the other peoples of the Soviet land."[75]

Like Ishan Babakhanov, Gebekov and Alizada had faced persecution in the earlier Soviet anti-religious campaigns before finding themselves "rehabilitated." At the founding congress of DUMZAK, a now-familiar message was delivered, albeit one lacking Rasulev's bold pan-Islamism and Babakhanov's tributes to Sufi tradition:[76]

[F]rom the first day that the Patriotic War made clear to faithful Muslims that the defense of the homeland was their sacred duty . . . We have called for—and [we still] call for—all faithful men and women serving in the army and working on the home front, to fight against the enemy, not sparing your own life, until it is completely exterminated; to work on the home front, sparing no effort, so as to multiply the strength of our army and our homeland . . . Onward, strengthening your prayers to hasten the hour when the criminal Hitlerian state and its brigandly war will be trampled into dust,

and [to hasten] the bestowing of victory upon our Soviet state and its glorious allies.

Clearly the Soviet state, by creating four distinct spiritual directorates in
four different regions, hoped to reach the broadest possible demographic
of Soviet Muslims.[77] But what about those Muslim groups that fell outside
the mainstream? One conspicuous example is the Nizari Isma'ili Shi'a of
Tajikistan, probably numbering several thousand, concentrated mostly in
the mountainous region sometimes called "right-bank Badakhshan" (now
within the Gorno-Badakhshan Autonomous Province)—one of the poorest
expanses of the Soviet Union. These Isma'ilis—who nowadays constitute
an estimated 3 percent of Tajikistan's total population—regard the heredi-
tary Aga Khan as the spiritual leader of their community. At the time of the
Second World War, Sultan Muhammad Shah (1877–1957) was the third Aga
Khan. Knighted by the British queen and famed in the West for his racehorse
stables, Aga Khan III had precious little communication with the Soviet
government despite holding supreme spiritual authority over thousands of
its citizens. Moreover, just a few years previously, Soviet officials had been
preoccupied by paranoid, preposterous fantasies about a supposed plot by
the Aga Khan to foment an uprising among his Badakhshan followers.[78] As
early as the mid-1920s, Soviet agents were expressing their concern that the
Isma'ilis were "influenced and patronized by governments that are hostile
to us."[79] This was not entirely off-base: as an agent reported in June 1927, the
Aga Khan had made speeches in which he accused the Bolsheviks, among
other things, of intending "to destroy the most sacred principles of religion
and nature" and attended at least one conference crowned by a joint resolution among global elites to fight Communism.[80]

There were broader paranoias, too: Iulia Guseva has argued that one of the
primary motivations in creating the four spiritual directorates was to counter
the "pan-Islamic" propaganda supposedly entering the Soviet Union from
South Asia as well as the Arab world—although there is no evidence that any
appreciable amount of such propaganda was really making its way into the
USSR.[81] If indeed the threat of Muslim "internationalism" was as acute as
Guseva says, then the Isma'ilis—occupying a barely accessible borderland
and unambiguously devoted to a foreign leader with strong ties to capitalist
governments—must have seemed uniquely vulnerable to it. Any religious
appeal to this community on behalf of the Soviet government would have to
walk the line between stressing allegiance to the Soviet state and allegiance to

a non-Soviet leader. While being a pious Muslim, in the propaganda formula of the day, was supposed to mean supporting Stalin's Red Army, being a pious Isma'ili Muslim would always mean supporting a man whose assemblage of stables and palaces spoke volumes about his feelings for Bolshevism.

An attempt was made to reach these Isma'ilis, however. In a remarkable document discovered by Kawahara Yayoi and Umed Mamadsherzodoshev during their recent expeditions in the Pamirs, we find a Persian-language wartime appeal that synthesizes earlier appeals while unflinchingly asserting the community's devotion to the Aga Khan.[82] Even before the customary evocation of God ("In the name of God, the compassionate, the merciful"), this document hails the Imam: "O Mullah! O Your Excellency Mawlana Sultan Muhammad Shah!" Its authors[83] then appear to speak to a broad demographic of Muslims, addressing their statement "to all the believers of Kuhistan, Badakhshan, Turkestan, Bukhara, the God-given country of Afghanistan, Iran, China, Syria, Iraq, and other countries." The subsequent lines, however, reveal that only a very particular Muslim audience is intended: namely, "all Isma'ili believers, all over the world."

"To all of our co-faithful," the document goes on, "we assert that we are the proponents of the pure religion of the Isma'iliya and in the shadow of His Excellency the Mawlana [Aga Khan] we should be alone and without equal. And we know loving him as our obligation, and each one of us has taken up his own occupation [in] aiding the Mawlana in the Pamirs, Kuhistan, and Badakhshan." The Isma'ili community, in other words, is being addressed as an international community, distinct from other Muslims. The message then begins in earnest, with a familiar summary of Nazi atrocities:[84]

> Hitler, the executioner of peoples, along with his sympathizers, has plundered all of Europe. He has filled it with blood and tears. He has inflicted death upon thousands of poor people.
>
> Wheresoever the detested footsteps of fascism should pass, the bodies of slain people are stacked high; the moans of the children and elderly who have been afflicted with misery and lost their lives go unheard, as do the cries and groans of women and girls who have been brought to dishonor and tormented. The [fascists] starve people to death and then flee the scene.

It is not just the violence of the Nazis that is to be detested, however, but also their ideology, which, the appeal explains (just as Babakhanov's speech had done), threatens fundamental Soviet principles:[85]

Hitler proclaims the "ideology" of the purity and domination of the German race, [which holds] that all the [other] people of the world are one race, and considers Muslims of the east to be monkeys (*maymūn*). In actualizing this "ideology," the Germans want to enslave other peoples and eliminate their [self]-governance. Hitler and his allies have revealed themselves as enemies of learning and culture, and as enemies of the freedom of conscience (*azādī-yi vijdān*).

The lines which follow likewise appear to be drawn directly from Babakhanov's speech, or perhaps from a common template:[86]

The Nazi state . . . destroyed its pact (*mu'āhada*) with the Soviet Union and [attacked] without declaring war, with the intention of enslaving our men and women, of leaving our children orphaned and alone, of destroying our homes, of establishing vice and debauchery (*barpā kardan-i fisq o fujūr*) in our homes, of trampling our laws, of disdaining and insulting our religion, of reducing our gardens to wastelands and our country to dust, and of breaking their oath in carrying out an assault upon our country.

Rather than following Babakhanov's lead in describing Central Asia's sacred landscape, however, the Isma'ili leaders borrow a page (quite literally) from Rasulev, providing an account of Nazi depredations in the Caucasus and Crimea which are strikingly similar to those found in Rasulev's appeal from a year earlier:[87]

In the North Caucasus, a region where in bygone days believers and warriors-for-the-faith (*ghazīyān*) used to win fame, the Nazis have perpetrated astonishing crimes. They have pillaged the people; the homes of the mountain-dwellers have been burned and blown up; thousands of men and women have been taken and enslaved. In Krasnodar and its environs, in the city of Kharkov, and in other places, in accordance with the orders of German commanders, thousands of people, including the sick, the elderly, women, and children, have been asphyxiated with gas and poisoned. The Germans intend for blood and orphans' tears to flow instead of water in the great canals and watercourses our people built with their own hands. These dogs are ravenous for the blood of these innocent people; what God do they know, and what book do they consider holy, that it does not forbid this tyranny and cruelty and bloodthirstiness?

Now, in the typical manner of wartime propaganda (secular or otherwise), the perspective suddenly shifts from victimhood to heroism, highlighting the common Soviet struggle: "The people of the Soviet Union—the Tajiks, Uzbeks, Turkmens, Tatars, Russians, Ukrainians and others—have stood up in defense of our dear country, in league against their common enemy." In a striking inversion of "secular" propaganda strategies, however, the Muslim populations are not united with other Soviet citizens in a "secular" struggle; instead, it is the non-Muslim populations who have joined a Holy War which here appears to be led by Muslims:[88]

> The peoples of Europe who are now oppressed or will be oppressed by fas-cism, whether they be Muslim or otherwise, cannot withstand the tyranny and cruelty. They come out for the sacred jihad (jihād-i muqaddas) against bloodthirsty fascism, extending the hand of aid to one-another, with one soul and one body. Muslim brothers, [imbued] with that greatest sentiment of mankind—the sentiment of patriotism (vaṭan-dūstī)—have banded to-gether to wage a true revolt against fascism. They have extended the hand of aid to the oppressed peoples of Europe.
>
> Muslim brothers are acting in [accordance with] the foundation of their sacred heritage, understanding as they do that finding freedom and salva-tion is possible only through true and earnest struggle.
>
> We, the Mulla-revering [i.e. Aga Khan-revering] believers in the Pamirs and Kuhistan and Badakhshan and the Soviet Union, appeal to all of the Muslims of the world, and we pray for a true struggle against German fas-cism, that treacherous enemy of humanity. We ask that peace be achieved through the defense of our sacred country.

After a few lines affirming Ismaʿilis' commitment to eliminating the Nazis ("They must be blasted from the face of the earth!"), now in league with "all the Muslims of the world" and "with the aid of the noble religion,"[89] the appeal fi-nally addresses the elephant in the room: the Aga Khan's close and longstanding relationship with the capitalist West, and in particular with England. It does so unflinchingly, and then turns abruptly to hailing the friendship and alliance of all the Soviet peoples:[90]

> Be aware that His Excellency the Mawlana [the Aga Khan] has entered the hospitable country of the English people and is residing there; he bestows his kindness upon it. That is, he is living in a country that is fighting fascism in league with America and Russia. This is highly significant.

In the holy book it says: "By rights, Almighty God does not love the aggressors."

We—the Mulla-revering people of the religion of Islam who are residing in the socialist republics of the Soviet Union—purposefully take up the sacred duty of believers, and we appeal to you with this brotherly call to action.

Rise up and struggle against Hitler the bloodthirsty one, and against his plundering armies. Give aid to the fraternal peoples of the Soviet Union who heroically stand and fight on every front to free their own country and all humanity from the ignorant fascists.

The Aga Khan's warm, lifelong relationship with English royalty and elites is depicted here as a temporary residency for the benefit of the war effort. The leader himself, this appeal hints, has generously granted his favor on England as it joins the Allied struggle. The significance of this is not spelled out explicitly, but it is nevertheless clear enough: the Aga Khan had joined the war effort on behalf of the Allies. (In fact, the Aga Khan's relationship to the Allied war effort was rather complicated and remains a point of debate and controversy.)

Superficially, this Isma'ili call to war shares much in common with the earlier appeals by Rasulev and Babakhanov; indeed, certain passages appear spliced in, nearly unaltered, from those appeals. But the aspects which make this appeal unique are hardly subtle. Rasulev's vision of the Muslim struggle was relentlessly international in its orientation; the Muslims of his own Volga-Urals region are never mentioned specifically, whether by ethnicity or by region. In Babakhanov's appeal, meanwhile, the global Muslim community is an afterthought; the local sacred landscape, sacred history, and Sufi traditions of Central Asia take center stage—not as the purview of a distinct or particular Central Asian ethnic group however, but rather as the shared inheritance of all Muslims in the region. By contrast, these Isma'ili leaders hammer home the distinctiveness of their community, muting pan-Islamism and defining a core audience in the Soviet regions where Isma'ilis lived. It would seem, in other words, that this decree underscored every trait that would have made the Isma'ili particularly suspect in the eyes of the Soviet state: their presumably divided loyalties; their "internationalist" orientation; their likely ties to the capitalist West; the precedence of their communal religious identity over "secular" ethnic categories such as Tajik or Uzbek.

Meanwhile, the Isma'ili community remained the subject of intense suspicion on the part of the state. In July 1942, Malenkov and other top Soviet officials were alerted to allegations that "during the war, in the Pamirs and in several other border regions, the Isma'ili sect has considerably strengthened its counterrevolutionary activities. The Isma'ili sect is closely connected with coreligionists in Afghanistan. The sect systematically conducts meetings, which are often attended by Komsomol members and even Communists."[91] Two years later, in a secret Party memo to Malenkov lambasting a speech by Tajikistan's Party Secretary, the latter is said to have "passed over in complete silence the acute fact of counterrevolutionary activities among the Isma'ili sect, which has an especially extensive network (*set'*) in the Pamirs and carries out Afghan intelligence work."[92]

In sum, Soviet Muslim rallying calls to the war against Hitler served, for the leaders of multiple Muslim communities, as an opportunity to define the nature and concerns of those communities—even when these concerns were fundamentally at odds with the ostensible position of the state. Common Soviet propaganda themes were parroted and the basic task of summoning Muslims to war was accomplished, but Muslim leaders accomplished much more with the templates they were given. They reasserted the primacy of Muslim identity (whether Sufi, Isma'ili, or otherwise) and attempted to reconnect Soviet Muslims rhetorically to the broader Muslim world—a world from which they were still, of course, completely cordoned off. They advanced positions—pan-Islamist, internationalist, shrine-focused—which not only skirted the boundaries of previous government proscriptions, but flouted them in flamboyant fashion. Given an inch, in other words, Muslim leaders like Babakhanov and Rasulev took a mile.

Decades later, another folktale would circulate among the Bashkirs concerning the initial meeting between Stalin and Rasulev. According to this tale, Stalin sought Rasulev's advice on how to conduct the war, asking him why the Soviets could not seem to get the upper hand over the Nazis.

"It is because we do not pray to God," Rasulev replied.

"Well then, pray!" Stalin said.[93]

3

Negotiating Stalin's Tolerance

Muslim Institutions in Wartime

"I say 'salaam' to you, with much satisfaction, on behalf of the Muslims of the USSR!" So begins a public "telegram" from Gabdrahman Rasulev to Stalin, published in the state newspaper *Izvestiia* on March 3, 1943. The cause of Rasulev's satisfaction was the stunning success of his fundraising efforts among Volga-Urals Muslims. "Inspired by the success of our glorious Red Army," he wrote, "I personally bring 50,000 rubles for the construction of a tank column, as well as a special message inviting Muslim believers to donate towards the construction of [additional] columns of tanks." The mufti signed off: "Praying to God, and sincerely wishing good health to you as well as the prompt defeat of the enemy."[1]

To envision the magnitude of the mufti's donation, consider the fact that the average annual wage of a Soviet worker in 1944 ranged from 435 to 822 rubles.[2] Now consider the fact that the mufti's "personal" contribution was a mere fraction of the total revenue that his spiritual directorate had collected for the Red Army's new tank column. The total revenue collected for this column has been estimated at no less than *ten million* rubles, a sum that may have been roughly equivalent at that time to the entire yearly earnings of 12,165 workers. Stalin thanked Rasulev personally, via a reply telegram in the pages of the same newspaper.[3]

Not to be outdone, Ishan Babakhanov's muftiate (SADUM) allegedly matched the donation.[4] Meanwhile, Muslim elites in the Caucasus and Central Asia submitted "personal" donations that put Rasulev's 50,000-ruble gift to shame. The Azerbaijani Amir Kara-Ogly Suleimanov donated 250,000 rubles; the Kazakh Kulash Baymagambetov handed over a staggering 325,000 rubles.[5] Animals were fair game too: in October 1943, Muslims from Kazakhstan were on the register for 700 hens, 80 rams, and 10 head of "large livestock."[6] Turkmenistan reportedly contributed, in all, 110 million rubles and over seven *tons* of "national silver jewelry."[7]

God Save the USSR. Jeff Eden, Oxford University Press (2021). © Oxford University Press.
DOI: 10.1093/oso/9780190076276.003.0004

While some "donations" were likely covers for bribery or extortion, and while the overall tallies were almost certainly exaggerated (perhaps even comically so), the sheer number of documented donations channeled through Muslim institutions suggests that Stalin's effort to rally Muslim support had quite literally paid off. The donations started flowing in from Soviet Muslims practically from the moment Stalin began his new alliance with Muslim leaders, and they continued to flow for the remainder of the war. Newly opened or reopened mosques and other once-repressed Islamic institutions served as conduits for these funds. No doubt some of these donations were coerced and figures were probably inflated—perhaps even grotesquely inflated. There is no doubt, however, that some religious Soviet citizens believed that their generosity would be rewarded.[8]

As this chapter will show, wartime patriotism among religious populations was developed not just through rousing speeches and concessions; it was developed by knitting patriotic activities (such as donations) and devotional activities together so tightly that it was not clear where one ended and the other began. By channeling traditional Muslim charity (*zakat*) payments into the war effort, for example, *zakat* became both pious and patriotic; by weaving patriotism into the fabric of Friday sermons, visiting a newly reopened mosque allowed Muslims to embody and enact that line quoted so often by the leading muftis: "Love for country is a part of faith." In short, the war era was an age in which Islamic devotion itself could become—for some—an expression of Soviet patriotism.

Donations had begun pouring in immediately after Rasulev delivered his initial appeal to Soviet Muslims in the summer of 1941. According to his daughter, "Cash contributions to aid the Muslim front were handed over to banks on the spot, and receipts received [by the donors] were sent to the Central Spiritual Directorate. Later, special people came from the Bashkir government and calculated the sum total of these receipts. So much money was collected in the name of the Muslims of the Soviet Union that it greatly surprised the Soviet government."[9]

While it is clear enough that elites could gain Stalin's favor (and perhaps also his protection) by turning over vast fortunes, it is not immediately clear how "ordinary," non-elite Muslim citizens benefited from these lavish demonstrations of loyalty and support for the Soviet state. Given all the "secular" avenues available for supporting the Red Army, what did a Muslim collective-farm laborer, tailor, or mason gain by donating money to the local mosque? As we shall see, those Muslims who valued their mosques and local religious leaders had quite a lot to gain. The early success of fundraising efforts produced a chain reaction: as Muslim elites such as Babakhanov, recently freed from the Gulag, generated more funding through donations, local Soviet Muslims and their newly empowered leaders began to negotiate for the opening of more mosques; as new mosques were opened (albeit in limited numbers), more Islamic religious specialists were promoted or freed from prison to staff them—and so on. The Soviet state gained donations as well as a new propaganda foothold; Muslim elites and their public gained modest but unprecedented leverage in bargaining for the permission of things previously forbidden.

The social and psychological impact of these developments is more difficult to estimate than the number of mosques reopened and the number of tank columns funded, but it too must be considered. Before the war, having a traditional religious education or experience as an imam, muezzin, or qadi could doom a citizen to the Gulag, or to a fate still worse. In wartime, however, arrests of religious elites essentially ceased.[10] These elites—many of them educated in the Tsarist period—were permitted to re-emerge on the scene as professional religious specialists, effectively reconstituting an Islamic public sphere that, just a few years ago, had been circumscribed nearly to the point of oblivion.

Take the Muslim community in Orenburg, for example. Long a major trade and transport center between Moscow and Central Asia, this diverse southern-Urals city hosted no fewer than ten mosques in Tsarist times. Activity at these mosques was drastically reduced in the 1920s, and between 1930 and 1937, as mentioned in Chapter 1, all ten of them were shuttered.[11] The story of how Islamic public life returned to Orenburg in the war years is preserved in local histories of mosque communities that have been published in Orenburg in the post-Soviet era. These histories offer biographies of Muslim leaders appointed to work at the mosques that reopened in wartime and shed some light on their lives. They also solve an intriguing mystery: while scores of religious elites were jailed or killed in the early Soviet period, many—likely even the majority—survived and even remained free; these sources offer a rare glimpse of their interwar activities, revealing what they had been doing and how they had been supporting themselves during the two decades in which the job of muezzin or imam had become impossible. Much attention has been devoted to the many religious elites imprisoned or executed under Stalin, but a great many others simply retreated from formal religious work, laboring instead as masons, beekeepers, clerks, and in many other jobs.[12]

Before religious personnel could be appointed to the mosques, however, the mosques themselves needed to be reopened. Rasulev's daughter recalls her father playing an active part in this process, both as an intermediary and as a gatekeeper for the state:[13]

> My father corresponded with people who had previously served as imams, but who had been forced to give up that work since the time when the mosques were closed. Many imams, knowing that formerly closed mosques would be revived, wrote of their desire to serve as imams once more. Some came at once to the Central Spiritual Directorate. My father issued them documents with a seal and his signature. On the basis of this document, the imams applied to the local organs of power and initiated efforts to restore previously closed mosques.

The offices of the Central Spiritual Directorate were busy with visitors in those days. The doors never closed, and the many visitors—old and young—included wounded soldiers returning from the front. Journalists and foreign observers came to visit as well, and Rasulev's daughter recalls at least one guest from abroad expressing surprise that the chief mufti of such a large country was working out of such cramped quarters: the chancery occupied a single small room; there was no "office" space to speak of; there was no doorman of any kind by the large, open front door. Rasulev seems to have taken the modest space as a point of pride, suggesting to the visitor that to live the Muslim way is to live simply.[14] The more likely explanation for the dainty space, however, was a simple lack of funds—a problem common (as we shall see in Chapter 5) throughout the state's newly established infrastructure for religions.

As for the opening of mosques, however, that was a gradual and sensitive process, and not the kind of business to which state security agencies such as the NKGB or NKVD were accustomed. To oversee such work, an entirely new government organ had been created. On May 19, 1944, the Council of People's Commissars (SNK) had established—as we have seen—the CARC, headed by I.V. Polianskii. According to the decree that brought the new council into existence, its purpose was "implementing the link between the government of the USSR and the leaders of religious associations of the Georgian Armenian, Old Believer, [Roman] Catholic, Greek Catholic, and Lutheran churches, and of the Muslim, Jewish, Buddhist, and Sectarian faiths on questions of these faiths that require resolution by the

USSR government."[15] The council's founding statute elaborated on its extensive powers, which included the right to draft laws concerning these religions and, if passed by the government, to supervise their implementation; to provide the government with information on religious activities and issues; and to keep "statistical reports" concerning religious communities across the Soviet Union.[16]

The activities of religious communities were to be enfranchised by the Soviet state to an unprecedented extent—but they were also to be surveilled to an unprecedented extent. At the heart of this surveillance was the long-established system of registration. In order to operate legally in the Soviet Union, Muslim institutions and their personnel would have to register with CARC. In theory, all unregistered "clergy" remained forbidden from plying their trade, and all unregistered mosques were operating illegally. In practice, unregistered personnel often worked side by side with registered, "official" religious leaders without facing arrest or censure.[17] Nevertheless, monitoring registration and keeping track of registered citizens' activities appears to have constituted a substantial share of CARC's work; indeed, in Yaacov Ro'i's *Islam in the Soviet Union*, which offers an expansive history of CARC's Muslim affairs on the basis on its own internal correspondences, the subject of registration seems to appear on nearly every page—often more than once.[18] CARC would also serve as a mediator between Muslim leaders and the Soviet state. While it was responsible for monitoring activities, it was also responsible for receiving requests and passing those requests up the chain of command.

The requests of local Muslim communities sometimes came to fruition in remarkable fashion. On August 6, 1944, Baymukhamet Tuguzbaev, secretary of the Central Spiritual Directorate, addressed a crowd in the central cemetery of Orenburg (then Chkalov) during the ceremony of 'Eid al-Fitr, marking the end of Ramadan. He updated the audience on the muftiate's activities and called on them to raise funds for the Red Army ("for the defense of our country and the rapid defeat of our common enemy"). Having dispensed with this ordinary business, he proceeded into more delicate territory: he expressed a desire to see more mosques opened in the city.[19] He had no government permission to open new mosques, nor did he offer any hints about how this was to be accomplished. But local Muslims evidently took the speech as a call to action. As they donated 5,700 rubles for the Red Army and bought up 20,460 rubles' worth of war bonds, they also gathered signatures for a petition. In all, some 8,000 Muslims appealed to city council deputies to open a new mosque in the city.[20] The petition was accepted by local authorities for submission to CARC within seven months, and just one month after this (March 1945), CARC gave its approval.[21] By Soviet standards, the petition had moved through the bureaucracy like greased lightning. The old, shuttered mosques of the city were examined, and one was deemed most appropriate. Ziyatdin Mukhamedzhanovich Rakhmankulov (b. 1881) was appointed its chief imam in April.

Like nearly all religious personnel newly promoted in wartime, Rakhmankulov's career path had been a meandering one. It had auspicious beginnings: Rakhmankulov was a scion of one of the region's most esteemed Muslim families. His father, brother, and uncle were imams in his hometown of Troitsk; two cousins were also imams. He received his madrasa education in Troitsk and served its Third Mosque in various capacities—as "second mullah," *imam-khatib*, and *mudarris*—starting in 1906. A celebrated orator and respected scholar, Rakhmankulov is said to have been fluent in Arabic, Persian, Turkish, Russian, and Tatar, with some proficiency in English and German too. Many Muslims who had rarely visited the mosque except on holidays made a point to show up for his sermons. After his mosque was shuttered by the Soviet government, Rakhmankulov moved to Tashkent, where he found work in the local bureaucracy as a government interpreter. He did not last in the job, however: from 1934 to 1937, he was jobless, forced to depend on his son to support him. After this, he resumed working for the government as a low-ranking clerk.[22] His sudden promotion from clerk to head the Orenburg Mosque was surely a pleasant surprise.[23] He would suffer terribly in the war years, however: three of his sons were killed at the front.[24]

Two common features shared by Rakhmankulev and Rasulev—as well as many other leaders whose religious work was "revived" during or after the war—were their Tsarist-era religious education and their impeccable family bona fides in pre-Soviet religious hierarchy. With religious education gutted over the previous two decades, there was a shortage of imams trained in the Soviet period who could truly "replace" such experts—or, at least, who could be seen as sufficient replacements by older generations of Soviet Muslim citizens. In any case, the appointment of "traditional" elites had the incidental-but-profound effect of reasserting the prestige of certain elite families with deep historical roots in the region.[25] With Rasulevs, Babakhanovs, and Rakhmankulevs once again taking their place at the center of religious hierarchies, ties to the Tsarist period that had deliberately been severed were connected once more. Perhaps this was because Soviet officials wished to draw on these figures' prestige and legitimacy, but certainly it was also because they had few convincing alternatives.

Rasulev, for one, was offered "VIP treatment." His daughter recalls:[26]

> The Bashkir government down to the start of the war indifferently watched the difficulties of the Central Spiritual Directorate's work. It was oppressed with taxes and humiliated, evicted from its two-story buildings. Now [the government] was suddenly very attentive to my father. They appointed a special doctor to look after the health of our parents. This was Doctor Zarifzhan Zagidulin. The doctor came once a week, examined my father, and brought the necessary medicines.

The rigorous medical attention was not without sense, evidently: the war had taken a severe toll on Rasulev and his wife. Their daughter observes that they lived in a state of constant anxiety and frequently fell ill during the war. Their son, Gabdrauf, had been sent to Sevastopol soon after being drafted, and as the city was besieged by the enemy, they had no news of his fate. An entire year and a half passed without word of him. It turned out that he had been wounded.[27] Their son-in-law likewise disappeared on the frontlines for many months without a word.[28]

Meanwhile, Rasulev buried the sons of others and prayed with the wounded. In a mosque near the muftiate's headquarters, Rasulev led prayer services five times per day, and in mild weather—when so many came to pray that services needed to be held in the outdoor courtyard—many of those assembled came from the military hospital down the street. They would show up to pray in their hospital gowns and slippers.[29]

Between services, Rasulev, along with one of his comrades, would often walk around the cemetery where soldiers from the hospital were buried. Taking down names, they would attempt to track down the families of those Muslims who had died on the frontlines. They would send letters to whichever families could be found, informing their loved ones that the *janazah* funerary prayer had been spoken over the dead. Sometimes the documentation identifying the dead was so sparse that it revealed only the recruitment office through which they had been drafted. In such cases they had no choice but to send their letters to those offices. On many occasions, they received notes of confirmation that workers in the recruitment offices had tracked down the families of the deceased and delivered the mufti's letter.[30]

In other words, the ailing, aggrieved Rasulev, Stalin's longtime loyalist and snitch, was no mere propaganda mouthpiece. He was likewise, to all appearances, a diligent and empathetic leader.

Whatever the day-to-day religious activities of men like Rasulev, one of the state's most urgent tasks was to have him bring in soldiers and revenue for the war effort. In this, there can be no doubt that the wartime wave of "manufactured" religious tolerance was a success. Muslim citizens not only donated hard currency and bought treasury bonds at the prompting of their local mosque officials, as we have seen; they also donated clothing, supplies, and provisions in support of the Red Army and the struggling families of soldiers.[31] One area of need was the support of war widows, whose numbers increased from day to day in all regions of the Soviet Union. The Spiritual Directorate of the North Caucasus (DUMSK) under mufti Khizri Gebekov established a special fund for widows in November 1944 and quickly raised 50,000 rubles in donations. These efforts garnered the mufti a telegram of thanks from Stalin.[32]

Such telegrams were always cause for celebration. The villagers of Akush, Dagestan, having raised some funds for frontline soldiers and the restoration of Sevastopol, held a gathering to welcome Stalin's telegram of gratitude. The occasion was used to appoint a new muezzin to the village mosque, and this man—Magomed Omarov—hailed Stalin for permitting the mosque to be opened; called upon his neighbors to work diligently on the collective farms and donate generously to the war effort; and led by example, contributing 3,000 rubles to the Sevastopol fund. On that single day, 50,000 rubles were collected from the people of Akush.[33]

Indeed, praise of Stalin and similar "patriotic" activities regularly accompanied mosque gatherings. The very next month saw the reopening of Dagestan's historic Derbent Mosque—said to be the oldest mosque in all of Russia. It was, in fact, opened before official permission had been granted. In any event, the imam, Mirakhmed Seidov, proved keenly aware of his new duties: in his first sermon, he called on Muslims to pray to God to endow Comrade Stalin, "Marshal of the Soviet Union," with many years of life; to grant the Red Army a prompt victory; and to curse the Nazis. These themes would apparently become a fixture of Seidov's preaching: four days later, he enlivened the day's holy proceedings with a prayer "for the long life of that wise leader of the peoples and great commander, Comrade Stalin."[34]

While many of the donations collected at the newly reopened mosques were channeled to central government funds or redistributed among needy local families, Muslim leaders sometimes intervened in local cases of need, taking the initiative to redirect funds themselves. Not far from Ufa, the home base of Rasulev's Central Spiritual Directorate, Central Asian soldiers labored in horrific conditions to construct new factories for the defense industry. Most did not speak Russian, and they dressed in traditional Central Asian clothes that were ill-suited to the brutally cold Ural mountain climate. There were no hospitals for those who fell ill, and many died. Rasulev learned of their circumstances and, after paying a visit to the work camp, appealed for help to local Bashkir citizens as well as to his colleague Ishan Babakhanov. Donations of clothing, shoes, food, and even honey poured in. An imam from Ufa came to lead Friday prayers for the laborers—a rare respite from midday work, permitted by the camp officers at Rasulev's request.[35]

Red Army soldiers on the frontlines, their families at home, and the "labor units" tasked with reconstructing Soviet industry beyond German striking distance were not the only demographics in need of aid. With millions of collective farmworkers deployed to the frontlines, there was also a dire need for manpower in agriculture. Here too the mosques played a part. In September 1944, for example, Sakhratullah Mirzaev, qadi at a mosque in the alpine village of Botlikh, Dagestan, mobilized his entire community—including schoolchildren—to help take in the year's fruit harvest. Even after the harvest, the qadi's morale-raising efforts were credited with a decline in thefts from collective farms as well as an increase in school attendance among local children.[36] This was quite literally the stuff that Stalin-era propaganda films were made of—with the crucial differences that 1) these events were not staged for the camera, and 2) it was a venerable Islamic shariʿa judge, rather than a fresh-faced Party functionary, leading the way. On one memorable occasion, at the Botlikh mosque, a ninety-year-old man named Magomed-Yakubov Magomed-Ali rose to offer a prayer for the victory of the Red Army and the health of the Soviet government.[37]

The events in Botlikh point to the fact that changes were happening not only in larger towns with substantial religious communities, but also at the village level. Some of these small communities made truly outsized contributions to the war. In January 1945, for example, the village of Verkhnie Chebenki, in the district of Chkalov (now Orenburg), allegedly collected 22,780 rubles' worth of treasury bonds, along with 1,680 rubles in cash. (The sale of treasury bonds in this Muslim community actually increased after the end of the war, with 30,000 rubles' worth being purchased over the course of 1946.[38])

Admittedly, such tallies of rubles and treasury bonds do not make for swashbuckling reading. Nevertheless, recognizing what Muslims on the home front contributed to the collective war effort is necessary for understanding the other side of the story: namely, what Muslim religious institutions got from the new toleration policies. The reciprocal nature of these two phenomena was acknowledged explicitly by Muslim leaders when addressing public: "My dear fellow townsmen and brothers of the true faith," DUMSK mufti Khizri Gebekov announced to the citizens of Nizhni Kazanishcha, *"In return for the care and attention of our government to the needs of the religion of Islam*, we must strengthen our aid to the Red Army in order to hasten the moment of victory over the enemy, which is so joyful for all humanity. We must improve and better organize our toiling in the collective farm fields, increase labor productivity, and deliver the products of agriculture to the Red Army and to the country [as a whole]."[39]

The effectiveness of this new reciprocal relationship between Muslim communities and the state was hailed not only in Stalin's concise telegrams, but also by local Party officials and regional chiefs of the security service, including (perhaps grudgingly) resolute atheists.[40] M. Kalininskii, the People's Commissar of State Security in Dagestan, sent a special message to the secretary of the republic's Regional Party Committee in January 1945 to explain that the creation of the region's Spiritual Directorate had already brought about positive changes—not only in fundraising efforts, but in the overall social life of Dagestan. He praised the clergy for leading local Muslims in patriotic ventures, for aiding collective farms in the fields, and for directing prayers toward the Red Army.[41] While his positive feedback certainly does not represent unanimous opinion among local officials, one can say, at least, that it helps address the question of why, in many parts of the Soviet Union, Muslim communities were so bold as to open mosques and prayer-houses without bothering to register them.[42]

How else, besides reopening mosques, could the state reward the excellent work of patriotic Muslim leaders? The leaders themselves had some ideas, naturally. Ishan Babakhanov suggested to the CARC chief I.V. Polianskii that certain particularly distinguished Muslim leaders be recognized with a state award (*gosudarstvennyi nagrad*) for their contribution to the war effort. (Here it is tempting to imagine the mufti gesturing none too subtly in the direction of his own beard.) The request was initially declined, but in February 1945 Soviet Muslim leaders received a far more valuable gift from the state: a special commission under the SNK liberated "laborers of the Muslim denomination" (*sluzhiteli musulmanskogo kulta*)—as well as "clergy" from other major religions—from being conscripted into the Red Army. And this with heavy fighting still to be done: the Battle of Berlin was then two months away. Later, after the war, they got their medals too.[43]

At times, the motivations and impacts of religious toleration (on the one hand) and Muslim institutional fundraising (on the other) overlapped in remarkable ways. One traditional strategy by which mosques generate charitable donations is through the custom of *zakat*—a type of alms-giving considered by Muslims to be a fundamental religious obligation. Traditionally, the annual payment of *zakat* would be tallied as one-fortieth of the total value of an individual's possessions. Collecting and redistributing these alms would typically have been the purview of local religious authorities. Unsurprisingly, this practice was suppressed in the Soviet state's antireligious campaigns of the 1920s–1930s. In wartime, however, with mosques goaded to raise donations, the utility of *zakat* was obvious. Rasulev's Central Spiritual Directorate acted quickly on this front, passing two fatwas to emphasize the importance of paying *zakat* for every Muslim. The subtext, of course, was that the practice of collecting *zakat* had been legalized by the Soviet state.[44] According to these fatwas, however, the burden of charity was to be taken up particularly by wealthier families, no doubt to avoid straining the resources of the already struggling masses. Any family with over 16,000 rubles' worth of possessions—excluding the value of its winter and summer clothing, bedding, revenue-producing cattle, and a ten-day emergency supply of food—would pay one ruble annually for every forty rubles' worth of money and property in its possession.[45] Babakhan's SADUM quickly followed suit, issuing a parallel fatwa.[46]

Religious festivities such as ʿEid al-Adha (the Feast of the Sacrifice, generally called Kurban Bayram in Central Asia and the Volga-Urals) also served as points of harmonious convergence between government revenue-raising interests and the efforts of local Muslim elites to carve out and secure new spaces for public religious life. Some of the charity provided by local Muslims was redistributed by the government for the purpose of buying livestock for the sacrifice. After the sacrifice, the meat of this livestock was provided to families in need.[47] Through such endeavors, the mosque became, as A.A. Nurullaev argues, the primary source of charity for poor Muslim families whose primary wage earner(s) were away on the frontlines.[48]

As the usefulness of Islamic institutions in the war effort was proven over and over again, the space carved by Islamic elites for sanctioned religious endeavors steadily grew. As mentioned in the Introduction, this included outreach and publishing activities in areas that would once have been strictly illegal. A February 1944 document concerning "special activities" by Babakhanov's SADUM organization allowed for:[49]

1. The issue of a monthly Muslim journal in two printed sheets in a circulation of 5000 copies, of which 1500 will be in Uzbek, 1500 in Kazakh, 1400 in Tajik, and 700 in Turkmen and Kirghiz.
2. The release of a Muslim calendar for 1944 (5000 copies) in the five abovementioned languages.

Islamic publishing, absent from the region for nearly two decades, had been revived—albeit in very circumscribed fashion.[50] Within a year, Rasulev would publish his *Islam Dine'* ("The Religion of Islam")—a landmark, inasmuch as it is the first substantial, original Islamic text to be published legally in the Soviet Union.[51]

Even more striking than the rise of (limited) Islamic publishing was a third permission issuing from the same 1944 decree:[52]

3. The opening of a spiritual school (madrasa) in Tashkent for 60 people and in Bukhara for 40 people for the training of Muslim clergy, including no less than 50% NKGB agents (*kuda vkliuchit' ne menee 50% agentury NKGB*) with the goal of furthering their use in the interests of the Soviet Republics.

The scale of this new school was certainly small, and the profusion of "agents" among its students must have made for a comical—if also intimidating—"open secret" on campus. Nevertheless, even a modest, cynical revival of traditional Islamic education under the auspices of the militant atheist Soviet state is a watershed moment, both surreal and evocative.

Of the so-called Five Pillars of Sunni Islam—pronouncing the profession of faith (*shahadah*), *zakat*, fasting during Ramadan, performing one's daily prayers, and undertaking the pilgrimage to Mecca (*hajj*)—four were now legalized in the Soviet Union. The one pillar that remained completely off limits was the pilgrimage to Mecca. A refugee from Tajikistan, interviewed in the late Stalin era, reported that the pilgrimage was still managed by a few, but only in secret and under conditions of great danger: "[the illicit pilgrims] bring back sacred water from the spring at Mecca together with some soil from Arabia. If they get caught by the NKVD border guards on returning they get article 58, paragraph 6, and they can be shot or sent to labor camp. The NKVD empties the bottle of water for which they traveled thousands of kilometers."[53]

Being barred from the *hajj* is no small thing; many Muslims who have completed the pilgrimage consider it one of the pinnacle moments of their lives, and some amend their names afterward with the honorific *Hajji*. Pilgrimage to Mecca from the Soviet Union had dried up by the early 1920s. At that time, British agents based in the Arabian Peninsula kept a close watch on the comings and goings of the Soviet envoy Karim Khakimov, who came by from time to time in an attempt to win Sharif Hussein, the bumbling, British-backed ruler of the Hijaz, for the Soviet cause. Things were not going well. The classified British "Jeddah Report" from July 31, 1924, which notes the arrival of Khakimov and his retinue, adds that "Their information about Jeddah must have been bad, for they had no house to go to, no furniture of any kind (there is none to be got in Jeddah), and only European clothes such as can be worn on perhaps five days in the year in Jeddah."[54] These overdressed visitors were among the only Soviets to see Mecca in quite some time:[55]

> Being a Muslim, M. Hakimov has one advantage of his foreign colleagues: he can go to Mecca. He went there, in a car provided by the King, soon after his arrival . . . There have been no (Russian) Bokhariot [sic] or other Russian pilgrims, so far as we know, since the war, and M. Hakimov does not seem to expect many, since he says that few if any Russian subjects have at present as much money as would buy a ticket for Jeddah, and if they had they would spend it on something else.

The British agents were only half right, however. After Ibn Saʿud's militants drove Sharif Hussein from the Hijaz, Khakimov himself paid a visit in the guise of a pilgrim—a rather unconvincing pretext that evidently aroused due suspicion:[56]

> M. Khakimov, the Soviet agent in Jeddah, is paying a visit to Mecca, nominally in the private capacity of a Moslem desirous of performing the minor pilgrimage. As he scoffs openly at the Muslim religion, one may suppose that his visit is not prompted by piety alone. He is taking with him a young Persian, the son of a merchant, who is at present in charge of Persian interests. This boy is completely in M. Khakimov's pocket, and repeats

all the Bolshevik cant about Persia having been saved by the noble Soviet Government from the imperialistic claws of Great Britain. They had some little difficulty in getting permission from the Hejaz government, but Ibn Saud replied to their application in a few hours, giving them permission to go to Mecca.

The strain of so much devoutness evidently took its toll on the ambassador. The "Jeddah Report" observes that "The Soviet and Persian representatives returned after spending five or six days in Mecca. With M. Khakimov the reaction after this prolonged period of piety was very severe; he drank steadily for twenty-four hours and was more or less unconscious for forty-eight."[57]

But where were all the other Soviet pilgrims? Khakimov's claim about Soviet Muslims preferring to spend the little money they had elsewhere is no more convincing than the explanation of his successor N. Tiuriakulov, who served as Consul General in the Hijaz from 1928 to 1932 (and later as Soviet ambassador to Saudi Arabia from 1932 to 1936): according to Tiuriakulov, the British and French were to blame for stanching the flow of pilgrims, since they had been blockading the passage of ships through the Bosporus and Dardanelles.[58] Putting this explanation aside (which overlooks, among other things, the existence of airplane travel, not to mention the fact that the British and French were not actually blockading the Bosporus and Dardanelles), it is clear that Soviet Muslims' pilgrimage to Mecca—like pretty much all other travel deemed "non-essential"—had been stamped out by the Soviet regime.

In August 1944, however, an emboldened Ishan Babakhanov sent a message to CARC chief Polianskii requesting permission for Muslims to resume the *hajj*. Polianskii seems to have been drawn to the idea, though not for the same reasons as Babakhanov. He kicked it up the chain of command to V.M. Molotov, then minister of foreign affairs, proposing that sending some pilgrims could increase Soviet prestige in the Middle East while also increasing the authority of the spiritual directorate.[59] More dubiously, he went so far as to suggest that sending as few as six pilgrims could demonstrate to the Muslim Middle East that the Soviet Union did indeed provide space for freedom of conscience.[60] It is possible that Polianskii was seeking a clever new spin on Khakimov's earlier excuse to account for the low pilgrimage tallies from twenty years prior—in both cases, the alleged implications of the low turnout were that Soviet Muslims were simply uninterested.

In any case, six pilgrims set out for Mecca on November 7, 1944—four from Uzbekistan, one from Tajikistan, and one from Kazakhstan. They enjoyed an elaborate road trip together, traveling by car through Mashhad, Tehran, Baghdad, Mecca, Medina, and Jeddah, and taking a plane to visit Cairo (an excursion aided by British diplomats).[61] While it is doubtful that this voyage impressed upon their Middle Eastern hosts that freedom of conscience reigned in the USSR, it is likely that those eminent religious scholars hand selected for the voyage left a good impression among their foreign counterparts.

The next year, 1945, saw seventeen Soviet Muslims embarking on the *hajj*. Among them was Gabdrahman Rasulev, whose daughter recalls:[62]

> A special airplane was provided by the Soviet government to bring the pilgrims to Arabia and back. The plane needed to stop in Ankara to refuel, but the Turkish government refused to receive a plane with pilgrims from the Soviet Union. So the plane landed in Tehran to refuel. The Soviet pilgrims were welcomed amiably and respectfully by representatives of Iran's Muslim clergy. Shah Pahlavi arranged a grand reception in honor of the pilgrims. After visiting Mecca and Medina, they made a trip to other cities in Saudi Arabia.
>
> In Iran and Saudi Arabia, the Soviet pilgrims were met and received as envoys from the Soviet Union—the great country which had played a large part in the defeat of fascist Germany. In Tehran, in a large square, they held a special memorial service dedicated to the memory of those Muslims from the Soviet Union killed in the struggle against fascism.

The planning stages were not without awkwardness, however. According to the records of the trip's doctor, M.S. Karimov, Rasulev was jealous that Babakhanov—thanks, evidently, to his superior Arabic and Persian skills—had been appointed to head the delegation. So jealous was Rasulev, in fact, that he leaned on Karimov to have Babakhanov declared "medically unfit" for the role, and the official list of visitors received by the king of Saudi Arabia shows Babakhanov at a lesser rank. Notwithstanding Rasulev's foolproof scheme, Babakhanov reportedly attracted especially positive attention in the Kingdom thanks to his superb Arabic.[63]

In 1946, thirty pilgrims were selected, though their journey was cancelled on the pretext of severe weather. In a meeting held by CARC the next summer, it was noted—with approval, evidently—that the *hajj* carried out in previous years had "helped to expose anti-Soviet slander in the countries of the East."[64] Permitting the limited *hajj* was no doubt both a concession to the broader trend of expanding religious tolerance as well as a rather shameless publicity stunt, but foreign observers had probably perceived only the latter.

Nevertheless, the trips to Mecca continued to be planned. Forty pilgrims were chosen for 1947; one of them was Ziyatdin Rakhmankulov, the hard-working imam of Chkalov. Unfortunately for the pilgrims, this *hajj* too was cancelled—this time on the pretext of cholera quarantines in the Middle East.[65]

If the urgent goal of raising funds, troops, and morale for the war ef-fort had been the only incentive in the Soviet state's expansion of religious privileges, one would expect those new privileges to evaporate quickly after the end of the war. It was well within Stalin's power to insist on a new wave of mosque closures and arrests. Babakhanov had been jailed twice before—he could certainly be jailed a third time. As the hammer and sickle waved above the ruined Reichstag in Berlin, a rapid reversal in religious policy must have seemed, to many, quite likely—perhaps even inevitable.

As Soviet citizens turned to the grueling effort of rebuilding, however, the new purge of religious elites did not materialize. 1945 turned to 1946, and the mosques stayed open. In fact, some additional mosques opened. In Chkalov district alone, Rakhmankulov oversaw the opening of mosques in the villages of Staro-Kul'sharylovo (October 1945), Sultakay (December 1945), Sol'-Iletsk (October 1946), Kargala (December 1946), Starogumerovo (December 1946), and Novomusino (January 1947).[66] Central Asia like-wise saw new mosques open: a January 1945 resolution permitting—at Babakhanov's request—the use of seven previously shuttered shrines was never repealed, and in October of that year, after the war's end, the opening of madrasas in Tashkent and Bukhara was permitted.[67]

Although there was no longer any need to issue a war-cry from the pulpits, Muslim leaders continued to carry out their patriotic duty: donations continued to be collected for the national defense fund, and sermons still praised both God and Stalin.[68] The mosques' finances, too, were bound up in the state: in 1946, the Chkalov Muslim community took out a government loan of some 30,000 rubles; and a sometimes substantial portion of *zakat* donations was funneled toward securing further state loans.[69] Meanwhile, local religious authorities dutifully urged Muslims never to let prayer and gatherings interfere in their labor requirements and not to carry out reli-gious ceremonies without first securing written permission from a registra-tion office.[70] Some new and visible accommodations were granted: in 1946, the Executive Committee of the Orenburg City Council agreed to allocate separate buildings for the sale of beef, lamb, horsemeat, and pork—a concession to Muslims' preference that pork be cordoned off from licit meats.[71]

Nevertheless, by the end of 1946, there was evidence of changing tides. In the first quarter of that year, the Soviet government received 125 formal requests for the opening of mosques and prayer-houses. Of these, nearly half (fifty-seven requests) were reviewed and eighteen (14 percent of all requests) were granted. In the second quarter of the year, total requests jumped to 150, of which nearly two-thirds (ninety-four requests) were reviewed. The number of requests granted rose substantially, to 40 percent (sixty-one granted overall). The fourth quarter of the year saw these numbers plummet dramatically across the board: only fifteen requests were received; six were reviewed; none were granted.[72] For the most part, the window for opening mosques and prayer-houses was closing.

Throughout 1947–48, evidence of this shift—as preserved in internal documents—circulated through CARC offices. One such document insists that the registering of new Muslim communities should categorically cease.[73] A Muslim community in Tiumen *oblast'* which—somehow—managed successfully to register a mosque in 1947 became a flashpoint of concern within CARC: while the number of Muslims effected by the registration was estimated at seven thousand, CARC officials feared a two-fold increase in the number of "active" Muslims in the immediate area of the mosque (whatever that might mean) and worried that news of its opening and expansion would feed still more applications.[74]

Still, the mosques that had been opened in wartime stayed open. The religious elites freed from prison stayed free. The new strictures represented a belt-tightening, but not a renewed purge. The freedoms granted by the state in wartime were strikingly durable, as were the concessions gained by Muslim leaders and their communities. As we shall see in Chapter 5, some of these enduring freedoms can be explained by the ongoing "soft line" strategy on the part of the Soviet state; others are better explained by official confusion—and even, in some cases, indifference—about the nature of Soviet religious policy during and after the war. First, however, in the next chapter, we will venture beyond the mosques, elites, and petitions to get a more intimate glimpse of Soviet Muslim religious life in wartime.

4

Red Army Prayers and Homefront Lyrics

Glimpses of Soviet Muslim Life in Wartime

Kharis Salikh uly Salikhov, a Tatar from a small village and an NKVD man, saw combat in Hungary and Vienna, and he went to the front with a certain prayer near to his heart. It was a chapter of the Qur'an, sewn into his coat by his grandmother. Salikhov later recalled: "My grandmother told me, 'I sewed the Yasin *surah* into your *bishmät* [padded coat-lining]; don't lose it!' Indeed, I did not lose it. I've kept it to this day."[1] More than once, Salikhov came within inches of death or capture, and he emphatically credits prayer with keeping him safe. For him, this is the key lesson of his wartime experience, and his war stories emphasize his efforts to share this lesson with his comrades while under fire. He does not draw attention to the remarkable irony that calls out to the foreign observer—an NKVD man teaching religion on the battlefield— but it would be wrong to say that the irony was lost on him. For Salikhov, in the war years, faith and state service simply were not in conflict: "During the war," Salikhov recalls, "religion was not forbidden (*sugysh vakytynda dinne tyiu bulmady*). In the years '43–'45, no one in any branch (and I was in the NKVD branch at the time) was touched [for religious reasons]."[2]

Salikhov's recollections of the war, told to a journalist years later, provide vivid accounts of religious devotion among Soviet soldiers—accounts so vivid, indeed, that one might dismiss them offhand as fictions. Given that NKVD men were often despised by Red Army soldiers, this veteran's "sacred history" of his wartime experience could even be an effort to come to terms with his own guilt by (as we shall see) recasting himself as a beloved battlefield "holy man." On the other hand, Salikhov's reminiscences are made much more compelling by the scores of distinctly similar reminiscences offered by other Red Army veterans. Indeed, the climate of frequent and commonplace battlefield devotions described by Salikhov is hardly unique to his accounts; it seems, rather, broadly representative of the kind of wartime experience recalled by a great many

God Save the USSR. Jeff Eden, Oxford University Press (2021). © Oxford University Press.
DOI: 10.1093/oso/9780190076276.003.0005

veterans (even if, to be sure, very few of those devotions were led by NKVD agents!).

This chapter offers a rare glimpse of Muslim devotional life in the war era and the immediate postwar years, drawing on sources such as the memories of veterans like Salikhov, Islamic war poetry, eyewitness reportage, Soviet agents' dispatches, and letters to and from Muslim Red Army soldiers. Here, I argue that it is not only possible to reconstruct some aspects of religious change that were particular to the war era but also to trace these changes into the postwar years. In other words, this chapter proposes that the war era is a turning point not only in Soviet religious policy but in Soviet Muslim life more generally. These changes include the flourishing of Soviet Muslim poetry (much of it devoted to wartime experiences) and the increasing level of women's participation and leadership in ritual life. Salikhov, the self-described NKVD "imam," offers a nice entry point into a world of sources that often seamlessly blend Muslim faith and Soviet patriotism in wartime.

According to Salikhov, his wartime devotion was shared and mirrored by his Muslim and Christian comrades alike, sometimes with his encouragement. He describes a pivotal moment for his regiment while it was under bombardment in Hungary:[3]

> The Nazis bombed us continuously. A young comrade named Sagdulla said, "The passage for the dying—go on, recite it!" (*üterälär bit, äydä, uky äle!*). I recited it. I recited the "alham" *surah*.[4] Sagdulla said again: "Recite!" I recited it again . . . He said, "Recite, recite!" The crisis passed, and I recited until the end. Thanks to Allah, no one died from our detachment, and just one soldier, named Nurgaian Karimov, was wounded in the leg. And the dead were innumerable [overall]. After that incident, the Tatar boys sensed it: when you recite, you apparently remain unharmed. Even the ones who, until that time, did not believe at all [started to believe]. After that, many of them started to stay close by my side. Before each battle Sagdulla, Nurgali, or some others would say, "Recite!"

Soon enough, Salikhov recalls, he had become a kind of imam in his unit, regularly leading his fellow Muslim troops in prayer. There were around thirty Tatars in his battalion, which found itself under heavy fire once more during the Vienna Offensive (April 2–15, 1945), in which the Red Army advanced on Vienna from the south and besieged the Panzer corps guarding the city. On the eve of battle, Salikhov recounts, the Tatar troops asked him to lead them in prayer (*namaz*): "Every soldier has a *plashch'-palatka* (rain poncho), and we stand on these in place of prayer-rugs. I'm the imam. What I did, the boys did. They asked, 'If I do namaz, might I survive?' I said, 'You might survive. If you attain sincere devotion—ask this of Allah.' The boys, stepping up to their prayer rugs, cried '*ya Allah, ya Allah*.'"[5]

Their NKVD imam did not dare carry on this prayer service in the open, however—they all stayed out of sight, behind the bushes, where they were soon discovered by a non-Muslim commanding officer named Sorokin, who demanded an explanation. Salikhov recreated their awkward conversation: "What are you doing there?" "Where?" "Were you whispering something in the bushes?" "We were performing namaz." "What is namaz?" "Namaz—it's a prayer (*morazhegat'*)." "To whom?" Thus on the spot, Salikhov "thought to say it was to Iusif Vissarionovich Stalin." This explanation, we can imagine, would not have been very convincing to the officer. Nevertheless, Salikhov could barely bring himself to confess. He recounts, "I was afraid to say that it was an entreaty to Allah. Standing there like that, not knowing what to do, I pointed my finger at the sky and said, 'There, to the one sitting up there.'" The officer replied, "To God, or what?" "That's right, to God."[6] To Salikhov's relief, the officer seemed more curious than angry, and a friendly theological dispute ensued[7]:

> After this, thanks be to Allah, he said to me:
> "What do you ask him?"
> "We ask that we—Comrade Sorokin, Red Army Soldier Salikhov— should not die during the operation."
> "What else do you ask?"
> After I said the names of all the Tatar boys, I said, "we also ask that Pashka should not die, though his God is different." He said with surprise, "Different how?" I explained that the Russians have their own God, and we Tatars have ours. And he said to me, "You'd better remember well: you do not have your own Allah! Your Allah and our God (*bog*) are one and the same, I'm telling you." And isn't it so!? Right here is a senior sergeant, a Communist!

Like all distant war memories (indeed, like all memories, distant or otherwise), Salikhov's vivid recollections may—and should—arouse a healthy dose of suspicion. Nevertheless, every individual element of these narratives is mirrored by other Muslim soldiers' recollections, from other regions of the front.[8] Salikhov's assertion that he prayed throughout the war, for example, is a common theme in the recollections of Muslim soldiers. Gabdulgariai Galliamov, from the town of Kizel in Perm' (then called Molotov) *oblast'*, was wounded in battle, but explains that things would have been much worse if not for his prayers: "During the war, it was specifically the uncomplicated words '*bismillah al-rahman al-rahim*'[9] which saved me more than once. The bombing starts, you fall to the bottom of a trench, and, without stopping, you repeat them. Shells are bursting all around, but the Almighty saves [you] from death."[10]

Gaziz Gabidullovich Murzagalimov, a gunner and self-described atheist from the village of Nakaevo in Cheliabinsk *oblast'*, found himself praying for his life while wading across the cold Dnieper in October 1943, as Nazi shells churned the water around him. "The enemy opened fire with all kinds of weapons," he recalls. "The water all around seemed to boil. Boats were tossed about like woodchips. The maingun (*orudiia*) goes down into the dark waters of the Dnieper. Dead, mutilated bodies slowly drift by on the current. I, of course, as a Komsomol member, did not believe in Allah, but here I remembered some words of prayer that my grandmother taught me: '*la illaha il'Allah, Muhammad rasul Allah, a'udhu billahi, rahmani . . . Allahu akbar!*' "[11] Murzagalimov survived and was later decorated as a "Hero of the Soviet Union" for his heroism in the Battle of the Dnieper.

Salikhov describes praying his way through a similar ordeal: during the Vienna campaign, he and his comrades were blown from a boat into the freezing Danube. Under German bombardment, trapped in the icy water, and unable to make out whether the approaching boats were Allied, Hungarian, or German, Salikhov recited the Yasin *surah* over and over, prompted again by his comrades, until they were finally saved by a Yugoslav boat.[12]

Mukhamet Saifullovich Saifullin, from the village of Seliaevo, near Cheliabinsk, who was recruited at eighteen, recounts—like Murzagalimov—some tension between his Komsomol ideology and his faith in wartime. A paratrooper, he made twenty-eight jumps during the war and more than once found himself praying for his life: "At the front, although I was a Komsomol member, at a moment of mortal danger I would recite to myself a brief prayer: '*alhamdulillah*.'[13] Soldiers of different nationalities were fighting beside me, and I, of course, could not recite the prayer aloud."[14] He later became a member of the Communist Party.

Sayfullin, like Salikhov, recalls his parents sending him off to war with prayers—specifically, his father recited prayers for him as he set off for war.[15] His fellow native of Cheliabinsk *oblast'* Gilmitdin Khisamovich Nizamov recalls a similar parting: his mother prayed for him all night, "asking Allah to save her eighteen-year-old son."[16]

Fasyikh Gafiev, a parachutist and veteran of the defense of Moscow, the Siege of Stalingrad, and the liberation of Rostov, among other conflicts, recalls praying for his life as he lay in a ditch in Zaporozhye. As his damaged plane was plummeting from the sky, he managed to parachute out—but then his parachute was struck, perhaps by bullets. He landed hard in a crater, shattering both femurs and three ribs, and lay there for four hours as German troops moved past, sometimes coming within a few steps of him. He thought of God and waited to die, before he was finally saved by an old man from a captured company, who found him and offered some basic first aid.[17]

Gafiev notes that prayer was a constant for him, not only in moments of imminent death, but throughout the war. In an interview with the journalist Ainaz Mukhametzianova, he recalls:[18]

I loved jumping out of the bomb-bay [doors]. And always, when I would jump out of an airplane, I would pray. It used to be like this—we're sitting in the plane, and my comrades-in-arms are saying, "there's Gafiev, starting up with his muttering" . . . There was a time when German planes were flying over Bataysk and starting bombing . . . I jumped onto the sunken platform and another man jumped on top of me, and then another. We had to sit down—when they bomb, the earth starts to shake all over. I started repeating out loud, "*la illaha ila allah*."[19] The major who was overtop of me also started repeating, "Lord have mercy, Lord have mercy!" and crossing himself. The third turned out to be a lieutenant colonel, and after the bombing ended, he said to him, "Well, you came out with it, major!" He answered him by pointing to me: "He over there also called out [to God], in his own way."

The sight of Christian counterparts in moments of prayer would have come as no surprise—it was evidently commonplace. As Salikhov recalls: "The Russian boys had prayers with them written out from the Bible (*Bibliyadän yazyp alyngan dogalary*). Some of them carried icons in their pockets. They would take them in their hands and pray, "God save us." I said, "How are we given such freedom in matters of religion?" (*Nichek bezgä din mäsäläsendä irek birälär ikän!?*) I was surprised. Not one person forbade it— they even defended it."[20] Many Christian veterans recall carrying prayers, amulets, icons, and crosses to the front. "They burned their Party cards if they were going to die," one veteran recalled, "but they did not throw away the crosses."[21] Cavalryman Vladimir Annenkov recalls wearing an overshirt into which "my mother, taking a needle and thread, sewed a prayer for me so that I could survive all the difficulties of the war."[22] Infantryman Stepan Stiazhkin—who carried a cross given to him by his mother—recalls a comrade who made a business of selling crosses he crafted out of duralumin alloy (*diural'*) taken from downed planes, both German and Soviet.[23] The ninetieth psalm ("Living Aid"), in particular, was often pinned by parents and spouses to the collars of soldiers heading off to war, or else sewn into their overcoats. This "amulet" was believed to offer protection to its wearers.[24] A veteran and former NKVD agent, interviewed a few years after the war, recalled: "During the war every soldier had a prayer written and sent to him by his mother. Every soldier thinks: maybe there is something to that after all. It was after the propaganda against the church had stopped."[25]

Wearing religious artifacts as part of the Red Army uniform ensemble could sometimes—so the legend goes—provide more than just spiritual salvation. Sadyk Galiullin, another young draftee from Cheliabinsk *oblast'*, kept a prayer-amulet in the bundle of personal documents he wore in a breast pocket; under fire in Koenigsberg, the "sanctified" bundle caught a bullet and saved Galiullin's life. Decades later, his family still had the damaged amulet, kept as a memento.[26]

At the home front and on the frontlines, witnesses report dramatic religious displays from people who had never previously engaged in such things. A.K. Agarkov recalls: "My parents never [stood before] icons, did not go to church, let's say, and I was never baptized. But when the bombs whistled (*kogda svisteli bomby*) in wartime, my mom flung herself [into church]: 'Mother of God, carry us and have mercy on us!' And all of us, not even understanding such things, also cried out: 'Blessed Virgin, help us and carry us! Lord, have mercy on us!' "[27] The tank driver Ion Lazarevich Degen recalls pouring vodka with his comrades before their final battle in January 1945, at which point his gunner, "a great joker, a funny fellow and drinker, suddenly covered his mug with his palm and said sternly, 'I am a Muslim. I should not drink before my death.' No one told him anything in response. We realized that he was serious."[28] Many soldiers recall praying silently, sometimes with embarrassment.[29] The scout Fedor Beliaev recalls: "When you hear today that everyone was an atheist, it's rubbish. The thing is, though, that since religion was unfashionable, everyone tried to keep his pleadings to God to himself, so that no one would see it. Of course, no one prayed openly!"[30]

Soldiers of higher rank—including celebrated generals—also showed no-table displays of devotion, as historian M.V. Shkarovskii describes:[31]

> In liberated Vienna, in 1945, at the orders of Marshal F.I. Tolbukhin (whose brother was an archpriest who served through the Leningrad siege), the stained-glass windows of the Russian Orthodox Cathedral were restored, and a bell was cast as a gift to the temple, with the inscription, "To the Russian Orthodox Church, from the Victorious Red Army." Marshal L.A. Govorov, commander of the Leningrad front, repeatedly made a public display of his religious feelings; and after the Battle of Stalingrad, Marshal V.N. Chuikov began attending Orthodox Church [services]. It was widely believed among the faithful that Marshal Zhukov carried with him in his car, throughout the entire war, the image of Our Lady of Kazan.

The scout Grigorii Krasnonos recalls the scene in the quiet moments before battle, when soldiers of different faiths would pray, in groups, not far from one another: "I did not believe in God, but I did not blaspheme, and I treated the believers with sympathy. Always before a combat outing we were given time to check the weapons, recover, get ourselves together. Some of the guys used this time to pray; they knelt and crossed themselves. The Muslims gathered together in groups and likewise recited their prayers."[32]

Soldiers' memories and firsthand recollections are a precious but imperfect barometer of events long past, even when many accounts are in harmony. One wishes, of course, for contemporary sources: soldiers' letters from the warfront with religious content, for example, or religious literature produced during the war. Fortunately, such sources are abundant, and they help to confirm veterans' perception of the war as a religiously resonant experience for many Soviet soldiers. One of the most common themes in soldiers' letters—both Christian and Muslim—is the request for prayers on a soldier's behalf. One soldier, wounded in Stalingrad in September 1942, implored his mother from his hospital bed: "Please, go to church for me, pray for me, and put a few candles in front of the icon. Pray to God for a quick end to the war, for the long-suffering Russian people, and for a new world.[33]

The presence of openly religious language in letters to and from the warfront is striking, since all Soviet citizens knew that such letters could fall under the censor's eye. Indeed, the NKVD maintained a vast trove of "redacted" wartime letters. One finds in former Soviet archives, for example, massive compendia of letters of complaint or entreaty (*zhaloba*) exchanged between soldiers and their families, as well as "case files" showing how NKVD agents targeted some letter writers for further investigation. Sometimes an effort was made to provide supplies to families complaining of deprivation. These fortunate ones were relatively few, it seems, and they risked a delicate balance: less fortunate complainants could find themselves under investigation for expressing "anti-Soviet" sentiments. I read hundreds of such "complaints" in the Communist Party archives in Tbilisi in the summer of 2019, expecting to find ample evidence of "subversive" religious sentiment being flagged for persecution by NKVD censors.

I found nothing of the sort. Censors were clearly preoccupied with letters complaining of starvation, shortages of clothing or heating fuel, and allegation of misdirected aid; they also "flagged" letters from soldiers who indicated dissatisfaction with commanding officers. The flagged letters were invariably devoid of religious content, and I concluded that the reason was a general awareness among soldiers and their families that incorporating even the most basic religious language in their letters would be dangerous.

I was wrong, and I should have taken more seriously the claims of veterans like Salikhov that religious expressions were scarcely subject to persecution during the war. The place to look for religious content in soldiers' letters, it turns out, is not in the NKVD files, but in the homes of veterans' families. Religion was *not* generally among the topics flagged for investigation or censorship by NKVD agents in wartime.[34] Two examples will suffice to give a sense of letters that were received, with "blessings," by their intended recipients. The first is especially notable for its casual, unselfconscious mingling of pleasantries both Soviet and Islamic.

Gussam Mingazetdinovich Mingazov, an eighteen year-old rifleman from Tatarstan, began his letter home in the manner typical of Soviet soldiers' letters—that is to say, with a charming but stilted patriotism likely copied from the "ideal" frontline letters that were widely reproduced in Soviet newspapers for propaganda purposes. "This letter," Mingazov writes, "filled with deeply-felt respect and love, is written by your son, a soldier in the Red Army who fights the despised enemy, defending our Motherland." The young soldier goes on to evoke the formulaic greetings of a different tradition: "Dear father and mother, ask the elders to perform *duʿa* (prayers), that I might return from the war alive and unharmed. By the grace of Almighty Allah, after my return home I will thank them properly for this."[35]

Iarulla Galiullin, another young recruit from Tatarstan, had especially good reason to request the prayers on his behalf: recruited in 1942, he had been wounded on three separate occasions, returning to the front after each subsequent recuperation. In February 1945, he wrote home to reassure his family: "As for me, don't worry. I'm alive and well, thank Allah, and I don't need anything. My wounds are almost healed . . . Having received this letter, ask someone, if possible, from among the elders, to read the Qur'an and dedicate prayers (du'a) to me, your son, for the mercy of Almighty Allah is limitless."[36]

Along with memories and letters, the religious experience of the Second World War is expressed in a vast trove of wartime poetry. In recent years, this religiously themed wartime poetry has emerged in great quantities from archives and private collections, especially in Kazakhstan and Tatarstan. Much is written in the traditional verse genres of Central Asia, the Volga-Urals, and the Caucasus—the *bayt*, for example, a catchall term for lyric and epic "songs" (both sung and recited); and the *munajat* (a pious poetic entreaty or lament). Khakimov observes that there was an efflorescence of this kind of verse writing among, for example, villagers in Sverdlovsk *oblast'* during the war. In one village, residents composed wartime *bayt*s with a common repeating refrain: "Hey Lord, give us patience; Hey Lord, give us patience . . . !"[37] The most prolific authors of this traditional literature, however, were Muslim soldiers. Many of these poems are preserved in manuscript form or in letters from the war era, and many others were recited to family members after the war and written down later. A great number have been collected by anthropologists and folklorists, and in the last several years these extraordinary literary works have begun to emerge in published compendia.[38]

An intensive study of this literature is currently underway: at the time of writing, Allen J. Frank has just completed a monograph on the Kazakh Islamic poetry of the Second World War, for which he has translated dozens of poems into English. Among them, for example, are these moving lines from Shämshï, a poet from the city of Turkestan, on the pain of leaving for war:[39]

> I handed over, first to God, my children
> And to the young and old who were there.
> All of them were young like chicks
> I raised them and put them in my palm!
> I thought, "If [God] accepts the tears in their eyes
> I will return, like the breaking dawn.

The poetry of the war experience often addresses the listener in the first person, most often with the narrative voice of a memoir. Indeed, a great many of these poems were actually *letters* to family members. Others recount firsthand experiences for a more general audience. The following Tatar *bayt*, with a traditional "bismillah" ("In the name of God") as well as an evocation of the Muslim "feast of the sacrifice" at its outset, describes the experiences of a mulla who, after a career of itinerant teaching, was "billeted" in a Tatar village on his way to the warfront:[40]

> *Bismillahi va billahi!*
> ʿEid Qurban has arrived.
> Let's tell it—listen!—
> The song of Zofar Mulla.
>
> They go with horses,
> We go with fear.
> Hearing the sound of the rifle,
> The heart burns with flames.
>
> After I arrived at the village of Denis,[41]
> They issued our billets.[42]
> I could not drink two cups of tea
> Before they made us go to shoot.
>
> After I entered the village of Denis,
> They issued my billet.
> Oh Lord, give me your help
> To return to my native home.
>
> [When] I was a young man, I was clever.
> I saw many villages, cities!
> Although things were hard for me,
> I taught the children.
>
> The desks in the madrasa
> Were bought by the government treasury.
> And don't cry, Asgade,
> It was Mokaddir's fate.

> My house is all of pine,
> The place I lie is a bed.
> O Sälimä, oh Nailä,
> We are scared!

This "song of the wandering mulla" evokes a venerable genre of Sufi folk poetry dating to pre-Soviet eras. Most striking here is the implications of the speaker's consolation to his loved one ("Don't cry, Asgade"): The idea he appears to convey to them is that, while the speaker was fated to go off, terrified, to war, the local madrasa would still be supported—by the Soviet government!

Another poetic theme often rendered in the first person is the experience of captivity in German Prisoner of War (POW) camps. Wartime "prison poetry" often recounts, in mournful and concise terms, the entirety of the prisoner's wartime experience, from enlistment to their present predicament. The following poem by the Dagestani Red Army soldier Sultan Daudov, quoted briefly in the Introduction, is translated here from Kumyk and was composed in 1942. It is a remarkable sample of the "prison poetry" genre:[43]

> I was [indeed] a Sultan, living in Dorgeli,
> Ay, I was like the wing of the falcon.
> In this [war], I fell into the fascists' net,
> I was scorched in smoldering, flameless fire.
> Who doesn't see both hardship and relief?
> Every heart is sick for the Motherland.
> If I'm told today about my past life,
> My brain will melt, blood will run from my eyes!
> In the Taiga, where in dark nights nothing is seen,
> The sons-of-bitches run riot.
> Ay, my body suffers every moment.
> My friends and countrymen don't know my state.
> Three months of summer—the sun bakes;
> Nine months of winter—bodyparts fall off.
> I shot at my enemy with a rifle.
> Many burdens bring pain to my heart.
> The winds struck, the fog rose,
> The cold struck—what's alive starts to die.

In some unknown country, in Finland,
I set off shouting, "my Motherland!"
I, without wings to fly through the air,
I, without blood to pump through my chest.
A tiger blocked my way,
Which today I'm not armed to slay.
My Motherland is across the blue sea,
And my mother awaits her son's return.
Foreign land, open your belly, hide my body!
I'm vanishing, as if the world never was.
The moon doesn't scatter its light for my sake;
The flowers don't bloom for my sake.
Oh, my life—the black, gray land,
This land will shroud me.
My brothers will suffer in their pure hearts,
My sisters will don their black mourning shrouds,
My dear mother, weeping, will find the grave,
And my wife will find herself a husband.
My sister, Ilmu, will keep on mourning,
And my friends will stand in *ta῾ziyah*.[44]
Long live, long live the Communist Party,
Which will set this oppression on freedom's path!
Farewell, live happily, my friends,
Forget about the way I was.
Don't the winds and birds carry
My final testament to you today?

While soldiers on the warfront or in captivity penned poems pining away for their families, their families were composing verses that mirrored their elegiac despair—such as the following Avar poem (translated here from Russian), from a mother to a well-beloved child:[45]

Clever, with a beautiful name,
Accomplishing many glorious deeds,
Obliterating fascists, with tired hands,
The support of his family, a true brave man,
Dreaming of driving off the enemy from the land of his fathers.
He was a splinter in the eye of Hitler's troops,

> With a heart of steel, feeling no fear.
> Did a mother [really] bear you?
> He never turned his back on the enemy;
> [He was] beautiful in speech and manner.
> He who shot at you knew no peace!
> Oh, Allah, may black Hitler be burned
> In the flame burning in this mother's chest!

While the poems composed by soldiers span several themes, ranging from enlistment to parting to battle to imprisonment to hospitalization, the Muslim war poems composed on the home front almost invariably evoke the agony of parting and loss. In the following Avar poem by Kh.S. Navruzbekova (recorded by the folklorist F.M. Ibragimova in the village of Rutul in 1974) a woman worries not only about her beloved's fate, but also about how she can support herself now that her Magomed has gone to war:[46]

> My serious-eyed Magomed,
> Will you read the Qur'an over my grave?
> My Magomed, light of my eyes,
> Will you pray behind my bier?
> In the chancellery, where they revered you,
> There is not a man left who might take pity on me.
> With your vulpine and cunning eyes,
> Be on guard from the enemy,
> Quick-footed like the lynx,
> Be ready to fend off the enemy.

In contrast with these deeply personal verses, some home front Muslim poetry is distinctly impersonal, general, and formulaic, such as the following two quatrains—the first Avar, the second Rutul, but translated here from Russian—collected by folklorists in the postwar period:[47]

> Ease up, Allah, the suffering of my heart,
> Bring back alive those who've gone [to the front].
> Heal, Allah, our inner wounds,
> [By] returning our sons from the war.

. . .

> Let no snow fall on this mountain,
> And if it does fall, let it never melt.
> Let no Muslim anywhere in the world
> Forget the dear Motherland!

At the opposite end of the poetic spectrum from these plainspoken verses is the following Avar poem passed down to the folklorist F.Z. Abakarova in 1980 by M. Alieva, then seventy years old, in the mountain village of Tidib. With its alpine setting and lush, exotic imagery of rubies and apricots, it is distinctly evocative of a Dagestani folk lyric:[48]

> My God, what a state my breast is in,
> Like a garden in the valley at the time of ripening apricots!
> Didn't the mountains and rivers start to weep, Allah,
> When your son departed, leaving me in tears?
> Didn't the mountains start to weep, Almighty Allah,
> When you shook my hand in parting?
> Isn't the door-handle I lost made of silver?
> Constantly you appear before me!
> The home from which you're absent—isn't it made of ruby?
> And isn't it in dreams that I wander around it?

Finally, in contrast with these florid verses, there is home front poetry of stark, heartbreaking immediacy, such as the following Rutul lament evoking a brother's death at the front:[49]

> Oh, is that how it should be?
> Should there be a bird without wings?
> I lost my beloved brother—
> Does this please Allah?
>
> The heart of the bard (*ashug*) was burned up, Allah,
> His chest was smashed, Allah.
> [My] only brother came forth,
> And they killed him in the war, Allah!

These samples—nearly all drawn from Dagestan—serve as a mere hint of the lyrical and stylistic diversity of Soviet Muslim wartime poetry. As vast troves of such poetry have emerged from the archives, Allen J. Frank has identified sub-genres and themes of peculiar specificity.[50] For example, multiple poems by multiple, unrelated Red Army authors are *munajat*s (laments, or pious entreaties) on the theme of the authors' severed arms, in which they ask God for the occasion to be reunited with their lost limbs on Judgment Day.

Notwithstanding their exotic blend of Soviet and Muslim themes, the *traditional* character of Soviet Muslim poetry is striking. Similar poetry in identical genres, as Frank shows in his forthcoming book, was written throughout the First World War, the Russo-Japanese War, and the conflicts of prior centuries. In short, these Second World War poems represent the unbroken passage of classical Islamic literary genres into the Stalin era—with all their typical religious language and symbolism intact and explicit. As in the warfront letter of the eighteen-year-old Mingazov, just quoted, these poems often show a smooth liaison between traditional religious formulae and the of-the-moment experience of serving in the Red Army. Take, for example, these verses (translated here from Tatar) by Nizametdin Minapov from Shentalinsky *raion*, Tatarsan, completed in April 1944, while the author was a prisoner in Lviv (then called L'vov):[51]

I have begun this *bayt*
With *bismillah*[52]
And have begun briefly to write
About the things I have experienced.

In the year
1941,
On the second of November,
I set out on the road.

When I say "the road," it means
Getting up and setting off for war.
I left my wife and seven children
In hardship.

At the recruitment office
They put me in a labor battalion.
In my heart I always knew
That I wouldn't be spared from battle.

When we got to Bol'shanka,
We started working hard.
We went four versts per day,
Digging tank emplacements.

On the sixth of June we left for battle
And reached the warfront.
At that heavy moment,
I lost my mind to sadness.

. . .

Gas filled the air,
Shells rained down.
When they landed, the earth
Looked like a potato field after harvest.

This poem is "sanctified" at the outset by its traditional opening, a formula so typical of the *bayt* genre that it even inspired an atheistic (ironic?) variant in wartime *bayt*s produced by Bashkirs opting to write in Russian—as in this *bayt*, titled "We Left the *Aul* and Headed to Berlin":[53]

We begin our *bayt*
Without any *bismillah*
(*Nachinaem svoi bayt my*
Bezo vsiakoi 'bismilly')

The survival of *bayt* and *munajat* genres in the Volga-Urals and Central Asia is mirrored by the survival of the *nazm* (broadly, "rhymed verse") genre in the Caucasus, from which hundreds of thousands of Muslims were forcibly deported by Stalin during and after the war. Some of the most moving Caucasian literature of deportation and exile finds expression in this genre, such as the following verses, passed down by Liuba Ausheva Mukhtarovna from Ala-Yurt, Ingushetia:[54]

The Caucasus' roads are forlorn today
Of the Ingush heroes who've gone to do ablutions in blood.
The longing eyes of mothers, filled with sadness,

See their sons battling the enemy,
[While] here in gray Siberia their fathers are cut down,
Their little daughters writhe in their death-throes,
The exhausted hearts of the maidens are torn to pieces.
O Allah, give us strength! O Allah, give us strength!

Another poem of deportation—likewise preserved by villagers and later documented by folklorists—more clearly identifies "the enemy" as Stalin and his agents:[55]

This is a story of great grief,
Of the great grief of the entire nation,
Of those who died in a foreign land, dreaming of their homeland.
Their cruel enemy exiled them to Siberia.
Cry for them, our homeland,
Pray to God for them, our Motherland ! . . .
They starved to death, as they had no food,
They froze to death, as they had no warmth,
They died of disease, as they had no cures.
Cry for them, our Motherland,
Pray to God for them, our Motherland!

Is it fair to conclude that these poetic genres, with their traditionally explicit Islamic content intact, survived from earlier periods, or were they "revived" in wartime? There is a promising middle ground that accommodates both conclusions. On the one hand, many of these poems represent an *oral* tradition that would have been exceedingly difficult to patrol even in the age of the Great Terror. Many of the Second World War–themed poems later documented by folklorists had been memorized, not written; indeed, some poems were even passed on to folklorists from veterans' children, who had memorized them. Oral literature can hide away more easily than *samizdat*. We can be sure that classical Islamic poetic genres survived the decades of religious repression in part through oral preservation. On the other hand, however, when compared with the vast trove of Second World War–themed religious poetry that has recently emerged from archives and memories, there is thus far a relative scarcity of extant religious poetry concerning the interwar decades (collectivization, for example). If this imbalance reflects a reality in literary production rather than merely a quirk of preservation, then it may very well be true that the war inspired an outpouring of creativity among its participants and victims—a revival, in other words, independent of changes in Soviet policy. After all, two great themes dominate Eurasian Muslim poetic traditions: the poetry of war, and the poetry of love (including "divine" love). It is no surprise, then, that we should have a particularly rich Islamic poetic literature from the Second World War, the First World War, and the Russo-Japanese War.

Other plausible explanations are worth noting. Perhaps Soviet "official" encouragement of patriotic poetry in wartime inspired Soviet Muslims to trumpet their work (even when religiously themed) more confidently than in previous decades. Or perhaps the anti-religious repressions, that age of jailed imams and informants, really did inspire reticence among Soviet Muslim poets, who then started to loosen up again as they saw imams freed and harsh consequences lessened.

All of these possibilities point toward a fundamental question about religion in the war period: is it best to regard the war era as a *turning-point* for religious expression, or did it merely facilitate the *re-emergence* of a fundamentally unchanged devotional life from the shadows? One can find sources pointing in both directions. Recall, for example, Fatima Galim'ianova's oral history of a Bashkir Muslim family in the Soviet period, which includes the recollection that "Despite the difficult living conditions, the Muslim community continued to operate. All services, ceremonies, weddings, naming, were held at home. During the ʿeids [holidays], they gathered together with someone, performed a prayer, recited *surah*s from the Koran."[56] If, as this suggests, the war period simply made more visible what was once less public, then it could be concluded that, notwithstanding the standard depiction, this period does not have much significance in the religious history of the Soviet Union. The story of Islam in the country becomes, in this view, simplified into a linear formula about the fundamentally irrepressible nature of faith and its survival, unimpeded, even in adverse conditions.

The vast majority of sources, however, whether produced by Muslims or by the Soviet bureaucrats monitoring them, clearly identify the war era as a watershed moment.[57] The essential context for this significance was not merely the establishment of official religious organizations working for the Soviet government, but the *perception* among many Muslims that previously forbidden religious activity and expression was no longer illicit. This change of mentality was not only embodied by the proliferating "registered" religious figures, but literally shouted from the *minbar*: take Mulla Avzal

Khusnutdinov, for example, of the Bashkir SSR, who informed a gathering of one hundred, assembled at a formerly closed mosque, that "In high government circles there is permission for the right to conduct prayers (*est' razreshenie na pravo soversheniia molitvy*), and likewise permission to return, for believers' use, closed mosques. In the near future, under the leadership of Comrade Stalin, the enemy will be defeated and the war will end. We will conduct prayers once again for many years to come."[58]

A change of atmosphere and mentality was felt both in the countryside and in the city. According to Zaripov and Safarov—whose recent book on the Soviet Muslim leader Akhmetzian Mustafin is a fine contribution to the almost entirely unstudied topic of *urban* Soviet Muslim life—Moscow Cathedral Mosque, the main mosque of the city, had emptied out by the late 1930s, as arrests and fears of appearing at collective prayers gutted attendance. In wartime, however, according to these authors' informants from the mosque, "Muslim life" was slowly and carefully "legalized" in the city, and the mosque once again filled with regular visitors. (Most of these visitors, Zaripov and Safarov note, were elderly, perhaps because of demographic differences in the popularity of religious ritual, but perhaps also because so many younger men were away at the warfront.)[59] Crucially, the authors note that, while major changes in official state policy came only in 1943, the decrease of "total control" was already felt within the first months of the war.[60]

In the remote countryside, local memory of the war era follows the same pattern. Vladimir Bobrovnikov, who has conducted years of fieldwork in and around the Dagestani village of Khushtada, reports that—according to locals—the village's mosque was never formally shut down, even "during the peak of Stalin's repressions." Nevertheless, the war era saw significant changes. First, a new pilgrimage site was constructed at the village outskirts: a shrine dedicated to three Naqshbandi Sufi masters. As in Moscow, changes were felt even before changes in *official* policy took effect. "By the mid-1940s," Bobrovnikov's informants report, "life returned to a more normal course. Well before the mosque's official opening, the believers had begun to pray in its precincts. People were gathering there for evening prayers and for recitations of *tarawih* in the Ramadan month. The celebration of the Qurban and Uraza-Bayram festivals resumed, as well as male and female Naqshbandi *dhikrs*, and collective prayers for rain at the pilgrimage of the three Sufi masters."[61]

This proliferation of religious gatherings did not go unnoticed by the authorities, whose internal documents from the late war period range in tone from concerned to panicked. As Miner notes, "Beginning in 1943, and even more so during 1944, the Soviets faced what was, for them, an alarming growth in the numbers of spontaneous religious manifestations; Soviet sources uniformly testify to this phenomenon throughout the USSR, both in areas occupied by the Germans and in the Soviet rear."[62] A top-secret report by I.V. Polianskii sums up the situation across all religious communities circa 1945:[63]

> *On the growth of the religious activity of believers.* The growth of the reli-
> gious activity of believers is observed *everywhere and in all religious cults.*
> Moreover, in some republics, oblasts, and krais, this growth is slower, and
> in some more rapid; in one place sectarians are active (e.g. Evangelists,
> Baptists, Seventh Day Adventists, Pentecostals, etc.), whereas in others, it's
> Muslims, Old Believers, Jews, Catholics, etc. The activeness of believers is
> expressed in their submission of applications to the Council for the reg-
> istration of religious communities; in the increase of religious rituals
> (baptisms, weddings), in the involvement of children and adolescents in
> religious activities of one cult or another, etc.

There is broad consensus about a "resurgence" of devotional life in some of its major visible forms—but did the *character* of Muslim religious expression change in any significant way during the war? A range of sources—again, both Muslim and Soviet-bureaucratic—answer in the affirmative, and they highlight several areas of change.

The role of Sufism, for example, changed in fundamental ways. According to a since disproven trope among Soviet bureaucrats, Sufi "brotherhoods" constituted a large-scale subversive movement with ambitions of insur-
rection against the state. Militant "ishans" (Sufi masters) were allegedly committed to training subversives, and secretive "brotherhoods" were tan-
tamount to sleeper cells. In retrospect, as several researchers have observed, there is no evidence for this phenomenon.[64] There is evidence, however, that certain Sufi practices changed shape and scope. *Dhikr*, for example, the ritual chanting closely associated with Eurasian Sufi practice, had in at least one Dagestani village "come out of the limits of the brotherhood and become a public Muslim ritual."[65] Perhaps this was due in part to a phenomenon noted in the same village: the most prestigious local religious lineage—the Shamkhal-gay clan, from which the village's three Naqshbandi Sufi saints were all descended—had been so devastated by the repressions of the 1930s

that not a single lineal descendant had survived into the war years;[66] the most legitimate leaders of private "brotherhoods," in other words, were not around to claim leadership roles, and with no legitimate heirs to their initiatory lineage, those inclined to do *dhikr* perhaps felt free to carry on the tradition outside the confines of the formerly exclusive group. Like so many other elements of Sufism in Russia, the Caucasus, and Central Asia, *dhikr* therefore became "common property" rather than the exclusive purview of any specific brotherhood requiring formal initiation. Devin DeWeese has described this phenomenon emerging already in the pre-Soviet period,[67] and no doubt these preexisting patterns laid groundwork for such ongoing changes and helped to normalize them; but what is novel here is the new context and its distinctive pressures—the pressures of deliberate and sustained persecution. This devastation of noble Sufi lineages was not universal in the Soviet Union, however, and in places where prestigious lines of descent were unsevered, local *dhikr* practices may have remained a more exclusive affair. There is also a simpler possible explanation for the spread of *dhikr* practices in some areas: as some Soviet bureaucrats feared (and reported in panicked tones), perhaps the closure of thousands of mosques really did bolster the popularity of rituals traditionally associated with the old Sufi "brotherhood" tradition, which had always thrived beyond the mosques.

Another shift was the rising profile and frequency of *mawlids*—a term that traditionally refers to celebrations commemorating the birthday of the Prophet Muhammad, but in some regions includes ceremonies celebrating the birthdays of Sufi saints. In the Soviet period, it seems that these "saint celebrations" were arranged to coincide with typically Soviet community gatherings, such as collectively seeing off soldiers headed to the warfront. According to Shamil Shikhaliev's informants in the Caucasus, the elders overseeing these *mawlid* ceremonies would oftentimes seize the opportunity to offer instruction for the community on basic Islamic norms. Shikhaliev observes that these events represent "a certain fusion of Islamic and new Soviet traditions."[68]

The most significant wartime change, however, according to many accounts, was an unusual shift toward women's participation and visibility in the mosques. In Moscow's Cathedral Mosque, for the first time ever, a significant portion of regular attendees were women—they prayed separately, on the top floor.[69] Zaripov and Safarov describe how, after prayer, women would gather in the courtyard outside to compare notes and share news about loved ones on the frontlines and about the progress of the war.[70]

Elsewhere, the proportion of women attending mass prayer gatherings was even more striking: in one Ufa holiday prayer meeting, which drew a crowd of some three thousand, the attendees were predominantly either women or demobilized male soldiers.[71]

Some sources attest to the phenomenon of women leading or attending women-only prayer groups in private homes during wartime. In these meetings, women prayed together and also gained instruction on, for example, how to read Arabic script.[72] Some of these groups were led by women, and others by men—such as one group of five to ten women who gathered regularly with an imam from a Kamyshly mosque to hear recitations from the Qur'an. This imam was interviewed by Soviet authorities and remained unapologetic, explaining simply that these women "also want to hear the word of God."[73] Sometimes women led such gatherings. Anthropologists have collected reports, for example, of a Tatar woman regularly conducting the prayer-session known as *namaz-istikhar*;[74] other Tatar women performed naming ceremonies (Tat. *isem kushu*) and the traditional washing of dead women. While it had not previously been expressly forbidden for women to perform and lead these specific rites, there is scant evidence of women doing so before the war years.[75]

War-era reports on religious life describe women hosting large-scale religious gatherings as well as smaller, more secretive ones. In the former category, for example, a Bashkir *kolkhoz* notable named Mazitovaia was reported as having hosted eighty comrades at her home in December 1943, for Kurban Bairam ('Eid al-Adha) ceremonies led by a mulla named Talip Kasimov, who urged those assembled to support the Red Army.[76] In the latter category, the Cheliabinsk-based historian R.Sh. Khakimov describes wartime women-led prayer sessions in his region that were held at eight or nine in the evening, after the collective farm administration and unsympathetic Party leaders had gone home. With no meat to share among them due to widespread shortages, those assembled shared humble milk soup (*halma*).[77] (Elsewhere, such secrecy would hardly have been necessary: in Dagestan, in January 1942, a regional Party agit-prop director complained bitterly to his superiors about the Communists in his purview: "many of the 23 Komsomol members pray, and the Communist and agitator Akhma Akhmaev also prays."[78])

Perhaps the most striking examples of the atmosphere and mentality of increasing religious "openness" are found in the petitions written by Muslims to local or regional Party officials, of which we have already seen several samples. One of the most extraordinary petitions was received by Party officials in the Ferghana region of the Uzbek SSR "on behalf of" (*ot imeni*) fifty women and girls. The petition reads, in part:[79]

> Our Government issued a decree on giving [aid] to women with many children and material assistance to children of frontline soldiers. We are not opposed to this decree, but we want to say the following. Many of our husbands have been missing for four or five years, some of them have already been killed, most of our daughters have already grown, and they have no suitors. In our region there are very few men left, and it is forbidden and shameful to us to give birth out of wedlock (*bez muzhei rozhat'*). Formerly, according to our religion (*po nashei religii*), it was possible for men to marry two or three girls, but now, by law, this is impossible. We could still have two or three children [each], so it is necessary that the government give orders that the men marry two or three women (*neobkhodimo, chtoby Pravitel'stvo dalo rasporiazhenie muzhchinam zhenit'sia na 2-3 zhenshchinakh*).

Stranger than fiction: a petition from Uzbek Muslim women requesting that the Soviet government *order* men to engage in religiously sanctioned polygamy.

We can safely assume that this petition went unsatisfied, but sometimes, in cases of particular urgency, local Communist authorities took the issue of satisfying religious norms into their own hands. An internal government report from January 1944 expresses alarm over a veritable frenzy of circumcisions in Kuibyshev region:[80]

> In January, a Bashkir girl refused to marry a collective farm worker of the Kuibyshev region's "Kzyl-Iulduz" [*sic*] collective farm, the Komsomol member Gali Akirov due to the fact that he had not been circumcised. In order to carry out this rite, the collective farm chairman Shagaev, a member of the Communist Party, dispatched a collective farm worker to Chkalov oblast', Teshgov *raion*, for a "circumcision specialist" (*za 'spetsialistom' po obrezaniiu*). A 78-year-old old Bashkir, Kushan Shekov, was brought from Teplov *raion*, who circumcised not only the Komsomol member Akirov, but also another 255 boys, including two sons of the collective farm chairman Shagaev.

While some government observers alleged that participation in religious communal rituals was prevalent mostly among collective farm workers,[81]

other sources observe precisely the opposite, hinting—as in the panicked report on "circumcision mania" just quoted—that, in some regions, a proportion of Party officials were known for taking part. I. Terentiev, the chairman
of the Ulianovsk Regional Party Committee, reported to superiors in 1947
that performing "religious rites" had become common in the postwar years
among Party members and their families; on a single collective farm in
Kliuchi, "out of eleven [registered] communists, seven have embarked on the
path of religious worship (*vstali na put' otpravleniia religioznykh obriadov*)."[82]

When it comes to collective religious activity in wartime among women
specifically, perhaps the most remarkable single example is the work undertaken by the Muslim women of the village of Koianovo, in Perm' *oblast'*, to
save their local mosque. Informed that the mosque—dating to 1898—would
need to be requisitioned to provide wood for a new school, a group of these
women harvested a large amount of timber from the forest and used it to
build a school with their own hands. The mosque, which in an earlier period
would probably have been taken nonetheless, was saved.[83]

Back in Moscow, meanwhile, women were also seen more frequently at
what Zaripov and Safarov describe (as noted earlier) as the most important
site at which their presence had previously been limited: the Danilovsky
Muslim cemetery, where women began—as they had never done before—
to participate in funeral rites for their relatives. (This trend continued into
the postwar period, and when a new Muslim cemetery was opened in 1956,
to the southeast of the city, women continued to form a significant proportion of its visitors.[84]) In this same Danilovsky cemetery, the famous Tatar
Bolshevik Shaimardan Nurimanovich Ibragimov (1899–1957), Moscow
City Council member and longtime resident of Moscow's notorious "House
of Government," buried his parents, with full Muslim ceremonial rites.[85] In
the estimation of Zaripov and Safarov, "it would be no exaggeration to say
that funeral ceremonies occupied the most important place" in the activities of Moscow imams, as a large number of Muslims who did not attend
the mosque still regularly took part in traditional burial and grave-visitation
rites.[86]

"Population transfer"—whether of individuals or of larger populations—
was another major driver of religious change in the war era and in the years
immediately afterward. It is interesting to consider, for example, the massive growth of the Muslim population in the Urals throughout the 1930s
and 1940s. The first catalyst of this shift was the rapid industrialization of
the Urals throughout the 1930s; the second was the wartime repression and

deportations of Tatars in the Crimea and Caucasus, leading many to settle (sometimes voluntarily, but more often forcibly) in the Urals. Sverdlovsk alone saw its Tatar population grow by a factor of ten between 1926 and 1939. The industrialization of the region's cities—Cheliabinsk's population grew by 500 percent, Nizhnyi Tagil's population by 400 percent, and Perm's by 300 percent in the same period—was driven to a significant degree by Tatar and Bashkir resettlements.[87] A number of workers at a major Urals machine factory (*mashzavod*) operating in wartime recall the close relationship that developed between Muslim Uzbek laborers and resettled Tatars and Bashkirs; oftentimes, they would perform *namaz* together.[88] In Dagestan, meanwhile, where isolated mountain communities were forcibly resettled in the plains, partly in hopes of exposing the mountaineers to the alleged "secularizing" influence of lowland populations, Michael Kemper and Shamil Shikhaliev have documented how the result for both communities was not secularization, but rather religious cross-pollination between the older methods of religious instruction popular in the mountains and the more recently developed "new method" (or *usul-i jadīd*) curricula popular in the plains:[89]

> [P]aradoxically, through this measure the religious elites of the mountain areas got into closer contact with the local population in the target places, where they influenced and enhanced the transmission of Islamic knowledge. Theologians and Islamic scholars from the resettled population thus began to work in lowland *kolkhozes*, sometimes several of them in one settlement . . . Thus Islamic manuscripts that had been copied in the Avar mountains were now also studied by Kumyks of the plains. At the same time theologians and students relocated from the Avar mountains got familiar with the new method textbooks . . . that had been in use in the lowlands since the early twentieth century. As a result, the resettlement areas produced a new amalgamated system of elements from two types of Islamic education that had hitherto been more or less separated.

Restrictions on collective worship also had some unintended consequences. A Tatar village imam who held leadership posts on collective farms in the immediate postwar years recalled: "Of course, in Soviet times it was very difficult to follow religious regulations, especially if you were in some leadership role, however small. In those days people gathered in private homes together to perform *namaz*, almost in secret."[90] Needless to say, confinement to private homes did not critically hinder the prayer meetings, but we can go much further than this: in rural Dagestan, Bobrovnikov has noted new mosque construction in the post-Soviet period that takes its inspiration not from classical Caucasian mosque designs, nor from the mosques of the Middle East, but rather from the village-style *residential homes* that, for decades, served as houses of prayer. As the activities of shuttered mosques moved into domestic homes, domestic architecture became a viable inspiration for "sacred" architecture.

The mosque environment too, both in wartime and in the first postwar decade, was undergoing radical changes. In Moscow, in 1954, a group of women sent a letter of complaint to the Commissioner of the Council for the Affairs of Religious Cults—a petition that would have been unfathomable in the pre-war years. It is a distinctly Soviet Muslim production, molded by and suffused with a Soviet Muslim identity, and crafted in the context of those fundamental changes to women's religious participation—described in this chapter—that emerged in the war years. These women wanted to hear their imam, and they appealed to Soviet religious tolerance, feminism, patriotism, and the spirit of the Bolshevik Revolution to make it happen:[91]

> To Comrade Besshaposhnikov, Commissioner of the Council for Religious Cults under Mossovet:
>
> For many years, we Muslim women of Moscow have been praying on the top floor of the mosque. In early 1954, we were transferred by an organ of the Muslim religious community to the basement of the mosque, where the voice of the imam and his sermon are completely inaudible.
>
> We know that after the Great October Socialist Revolution, the Soviet government created for us, women, equal rights with men in all areas of our lives. We, the defenders of our Motherland, with the goal of satisfying our prayer needs, and knowing of your benevolent disposition towards Muslims, ask that a microphone be placed in our mosque, with at least one speaker.
>
> Otherwise, we ask that you direct the leaders of the mosque to transfer us to the top floor of the mosque, where we prayed before.

Extraordinary petitions like this one became increasingly common throughout the final years of the war and into the early postwar period. In the course of the war, as we saw in earlier chapters, the Soviet state created a new bureaucracy to deal with such petitions; to oversee the registration of religious specialists, communities, and buildings; and to monitor religious life as a liaison for the state. As we shall see in Chapter 5, this bureaucracy was in shambles—a fact that served as a prodigious advantage for religious Soviet citizens.

5

Bureaucrats Bewildered

Monitoring Muslims in Postwar Kazakhstan

In 1949, after years of dedicated service monitoring religious activity for the Soviet bureaucracy, Kh.S. Bagaev, commissioner of the CARC of the Tatar Autonomous Soviet Socialist Republic (ASSR) was fired from his post and condemned for "misconduct" in a damning internal memo. Bagaev, the memo reported, "in a number of cases did not carry out the policy of our Party with respect to religion, and remained indifferent to the actions of unregistered *mullas*." He permitted "a significant number" of unregistered mosques to operate with impunity. In several cases, he became an "accomplice" of local religious leaders: he helped one mosque to get a new telephone, the memo stated, and allowed for the purchase of a vehicle by Muslims in Kazan to transport the dead to their burying-grounds. The denunciation concluded: "These facts speak to the point that Bagaev has worn out his welcome as a commissioner for the [Council for the] Affairs of Religious Cults, and has in several cases encouraged *mullas* and leaders of other religious communities to disseminate their influence among the workers. For this reason, in the future, he will be unable to implement the policy of our Bolshevik Party with respect to religion, and he must be removed from his post."[1]

Considering Bagaev's resume, these are shocking allegations. After all, he was both a veteran bureaucrat and a committed atheist. An economist by training, Bagaev had previously served as the chairman of the League of Militant Atheists in the Tatar ASSR, a post to which he had been promoted at the apex of Stalin's Great Terror in 1938. He held that post until 1944, when he was appointed republican CARC commissioner. Could this man really have been an "accomplice" of renegade Islamic elites?

The "offenses" blamed on Bagaev's negligence—the proliferation of unregistered religious communities, for example—were hardly limited to Tatarstan, and, as this chapter will show, they were symptomatic of a general confusion among officials and local populations alike concerning religious

God Save the USSR. Jeff Eden, Oxford University Press (2021). © Oxford University Press.
DOI: 10.1093/oso/9780190076276.003.0006

policy during and after the war. Such ambiguities, misunderstandings, and frustrations about the enforcement of religious policy are strikingly demonstrated in a series of remarkable documents that will be the focus of this chapter: the declassified, recently published correspondences between N. Guliaeva and N. Sabitov, two CARC bureaucrats from Kazakhstan. These officials, like Bagaev, were on the frontlines of enforcing Soviet religious policy, and yet they too—like Bagaev—were unable to keep track of the policy, let alone enforce it.

How, in the end, could there be an "official" Islam when the policies on Islam were neither enforced nor understood by the officials themselves? Indeed, the case studies presented here undermine the distinction that has long been drawn between "official" and "unofficial" Soviet Islam. This distinction has recently been challenged on the basis of new evidence proving that the spiritual directorates and "registered" elites consistently interacted with unregistered elites and communities that, at least in theory, were engaged in illegal religious activities. In other words, historians have insightfully blurred the distinction between "official" and "unofficial" spheres. One takeaway from these recent revelations is the implication that the divide between "official" and "unofficial" activity existed mostly in the minds of those Soviet officials tasked with monitoring religious life (and in the minds of historians adopting these categories uncritically). It is tempting, then, to presume that such conceptual distinctions seemed clear-cut for these officials. After all, they created the distinctions and reinforced them with incessant discussion of "registered" versus "unregistered" activity.

As this chapter will show, however, even CARC bureaucrats could easily lose track of the religious policies they were tasked with enforcing. Meanwhile, officials at the level of the district and regional executive committees could be oblivious or even indifferent to those policies. Beyond the bureaucratic confusion and malaise, there was also significant confusion, as we shall see, over the very nature of Islam in Central Asia (to say nothing of the broader Soviet Union). What was the point of "registering" mosques, for example, if Kazakh Muslims, with their legacy of nomadism, did not need mosques? What was the point of monitoring *mullas* and other Islamic leaders when each Muslim is, according to tradition, ritually autonomous?

From the perspective of atheist Soviet bureaucrats, the unprecedented permissiveness of religious policy in wartime came with a compelling strategic justification: appearing to "foster" religious institutions would allow the state to supervise and surveil them. From this perspective, the broadening of personal freedoms also broadened and empowered the surveillance state. At the heart of this strategy was the system of *registration* mentioned in Chapter 3. Newly opened mosques would need to be registered with the government. The personnel and attendees of the mosques, collectively referred to as the religious "community" (*obshchina*) needed to be registered too. During and after the registration process, bureaucrats employed by CARC were expected to seek information about the activities of these communities and their leaders. While the CARC was in constant contact with representatives of the spiritual directorates, it relied heavily upon its own agents for intelligence gathering and local surveillance operations among Muslims. On paper, it was a brilliant system: "patriotic," state-supported imams would serve simultaneously as "religious clergy" (*sluzhiteli kul'ta*) and as informants for the regime, while local religious communities were surveilled by non-Muslim Soviet agents.

On the ground, however, chaos reigned. For one thing, unregistered communities consistently outnumbered their registered counterparts. In the Tatar ASSR, by the mid-1940s, officials counted twenty-five unregistered communities, compared with just sixteen registered ones; eighteen of these unregistered communities had their own imam, and their alleged "membership" varied from twenty to 130 Muslims. Neighboring Ul'ianovsk district had thirty-five unregistered communities, while only ten had been registered. K.F. Rabotalov, the CARC commissioner for Kuibyshev (Samara) district, which had as many as eighteen unregistered communities as of 1945,[2] observed that the unregistered groups "in some respects . . . are in a more advantageous position compared to the registered communities, because they act essentially without any control."[3]

The arrival of these Muslim communities, whether registered or unregistered, on the state's proverbial radar screen came in the midst of what many CARC officials saw as an ongoing "revival and revitalization" of communal religious activities among Muslim populations—a revival that had started in wartime.[4] And while numerous officials alleged that the average "religious" (*veruiushchii*) Soviet Muslim tended to be elderly,[5] a younger demographic of demobilized soldiers gained visibility at the mosques in the postwar years. According to one estimate, these military veterans came to constitute as much as 15–20 percent of the mosque-going population. Respectful of their elders and idolized by their juniors, the veterans were a focus of concern for CARC officials, who offered frequent updates on the "spread" of religious influence.[6]

Meanwhile, major Muslim holidays could be counted upon to bring large and diverse crowds to the mosques as well as widespread festivities beyond them. According to some officials' reports, occasions like Uraza Bairam ('Eid al-Fitr) were celebrated by the entirety of the Soviet Muslim population, including local Party bosses. In Kuibyshev district, for example, the Oblast Council commissioner reported to Moscow that "All the Muslims of the Tatar population are faithfully observing [Uraza Bairam], from the elderly to children of school and preschool age."[7] While Communist Party officials usually avoided taking part in religious ceremonies, such holidays could be an exception. The 1949 Kurban Bairam ('Eid al-Adha) celebration for Kuibyshev oblast's V.M. Molotov Collective Farm was held at the home of the *kolkhoz* boss and attended by multiple Party "assets," including the local Party secretary himself, as well as the head of the local grain-processing station and the chairman of the *kolkhoz* auditing committee. Unfortunately, as a CARC representative reported, "a fight broke out amid all the boozing."[8]

Notwithstanding the proliferation of "unregistered" activity, some religious leaders found it expedient to register with the government in order to gain access to previously shuttered mosques. On September 17, 1944, local officials in Pavlodar received a modest request from a man named Rakhmetolla Kulmagambetov, who claimed to speak for all the "believing" Muslims of the town:[9]

In the name of the Pavlodar Muslim community, we ask permission that 'Eid-Ramadan should be celebrated; it falls on 18 [September] 1944. On that day we will:

1) Pray to God and ask Allah to send victory to our heroic Red Army over the German-Fascist invaders.

2) Collect donations for the defense fund.

This is what we shall do on that day. The Muslim community asks that you not reject this request.

The requested permissions were granted, and CARC officials monitored the celebrations and kept track of the promised donations, which totaled 6,225 rubles. As it turned out, local officials failed—perhaps deliberately—to submit these donations to the Gosbank, prompting a chiding from the CARC regional office.[10] In any case, the sum gathered during Ramadan was just a fraction of the total sum that had been donated to the Red Army by Pavlodar's Muslim community. These donations would be at the heart of

Kulmagambetov's next request, which he and two colleagues submitted to Pavlodar's *oblispolkom* (executive committee) on December 19, 1944:[11]

We, the Muslim believers of the city of Pavlodar, who number 3,000 people, together with all the people of our Homeland (*Rodina*), rejoice in the valiant successes of the Red Army on the frontlines of the Great Patriotic War. We support these successes with our donations to the defense fund, and we ask God that, alongside our comrades' armies, He should accomplish the work of smashing German-fascist Germany [*sic*] as promptly as possible. We (that is, the Muslims of Pavlodar) have already collected and delivered 115,000 rubles to Gosbank, for which we received a congratulatory telegram from Comrade Stalin, reinforcing our commitment to strengthening the Red Army with any aid possible in the effort to deliver a crushing blow against the enemy.

Fundraising among believers continues. But to this day, we do not have a mosque in the city, such that we are not given a chance to conduct services according to our religion. For that reason, we ask you to give us the ability to perform *namaz* for our victory in the struggle with fascist Germany; to open a mosque; and to register our Muslim community. The most appropriate "housing stock" (*zhilfond*) in the city for the location of the mosque—1st of May Street, No. 76—is the old Kazakh Mosque with an area of 300 square meters; it would fully accommodate us.

At the same time, we ask that Rakhmetolla Kulmagambetov be registered as imam at the opening of the Pavlodar mosque. We sincerely request that our application not be denied.

[All this was resolved at] a meeting of the believers of Pavlodar, at which 45 believers were present.

Just one week later—a lightning-fast reaction by the standards of the Soviet provincial bureaucracy—the request was recognized and accepted in a memo from the local executive committee, which noted in passing that the former mosque building at 1st of May Street was, at that time, a sewing workshop, having been seized for conversion in 1937. The city's other shuttered mosque was occupied by the orchestra.[12]

Unfortunately for Kulmagambetov and the Pavlodar Muslims, however, this was just the first step in the bureaucratic process. First, some faulty paperwork needed to be redone and resubmitted before it could be brought before the CARC (a first attempt did "not meet the requirements for the opening of prayer houses of religious denominations . . . Lacking, for example, is the information stipulated in paragraph 5 of the resolution"[13]). Next, a background check was evidently carried out for all forty-five of the local Muslims mentioned in Kulmagambetov's initial appeal.[14] Meanwhile, the building hosting the sewing workshop was evidently deemed unsuitable, so that Kulmagambetov had to petition for the space occupied by the orchestra.[15] Months passed.

With the status of the Pavlodar mosque in limbo, the state took steps to restrict Pavlodar's Muslim leaders from traveling and "spreading influence" in neighboring districts. In recent years, they had gotten used to traveling freely. This had to be stopped.

Enter N. Guliaeva, a local CARC representative based in Pavlodar whose declassified correspondences with her superiors show a striking, thoughtful frankness. In a letter to the main CARC office in the Kazakh SSR from April 1945, Guliaeva shrewdly observed that the restrictions on travel were not without sacrifices on the government's part:[16]

Patriotic work by Muslim believers was [previously] expressed particularly through fundraising for the country's defense fund. In truth, fundraising primarily took place in 1944; in the first quarter of 1945, very little of it took place. This can be explained by the fact that the leaders of the community of faithful citizens in the city [previously] carried out fundraising not only within the boundaries of the city, but also journeyed out to [other] *raions*, with travel permissions issued by the executive committee. Recently, [the practice of] issuing this kind of permission to representatives of communities of believers has been discontinued, with the explanation that they should carry out their activities only among the believers of the city of Pavlodar.

Guliaeva had taken up her post with CARC the previous autumn, but she was an experienced bureaucrat, having served before that as deputy chairman of social-cultural affairs for the *oblispolkom*. She was, moreover, no great enthusiast when it came to Muslim religious activities, and notwithstanding the potential loss of state revenue that she herself pointed out, she hastened to clarify that measures to circumscribe Muslim leaders' movements were, in her view, entirely justified. "It must be mentioned," she wrote, "that representatives of groups of Muslim believers of the city have an inclination to spread their religious activities in the territories of all oblasts."

In particular, she warned that they had been attempting to enlist Muslims in various *raions* in the effort to petition the government for the opening of provincial mosques.[17]

Registering and opening a local mosque in Pavlodar could facilitate not only the surveillance of the mosque community, but perhaps also the "anchoring" of a formerly itinerant imam. On May 30, 1945, just a few weeks after the surrender of Germany and the end of the Second World War, permission was finally granted for the opening of the mosque, which would occupy the space recently held by the sewing workshop.[18] Two weeks later, the community was provided with "all remaining denominational property on the inventory list," which included the modest furnishings of the mosque property itself.[19] The list in question describes a humble building with simple features, each detail of which was scrupulously documented and itemized as "denominational property":[20]

1) A carved-wood house (*dom*) atop a brick foundation
2) A roof partly covered in iron, and the rest—that is, the larger portion—with boards
3) Interior walls finished with whitewashed clay, [topped by] plank ceilings
4) Timber flooring, old, unpainted
5) Two windows, glazed, missing three winter frames
6) Two stoves, Dutch-style, with plating and cast-iron furnace and dampers
7) Four doors of timber, simple, with iron instruments [i.e. locks and handles]
8) Two wooden partitions, simple, unpainted
9) Two partition walls, new, as recorded in the present document

Upon receiving their new space, Kulmagambetov and his colleagues signed a contract that specified their new responsibilities. They would, of course, care for the property and pay for its upkeep (including renovations, heating, insurance, security, debt repayment, taxes, local dues, and so on). But they also agreed to some open-ended concessions to state surveillance. The contract confirms that the community would allow, "without hindrance," visitation and scrutiny of the property by representatives of the Pavlodar City Council of Workers' Deputies as well as CARC officials. More ambiguously, the contract called upon its signatories to "undertake to use the house and the religious objects in it exclusively for the satisfaction of religious needs and not to allow for clergy of the denomination to undertake religious rites which have not been registered" with CARC representatives.[21] In other words, all religious endeavors undertaken by the mosque community needed to be approved and documented by CARC officials. The mosque opened on June 20, 1945.[22]

These concessions on surveillance would, at first glance, appear to be a victory for Soviet intelligence agencies, and for all officials who hoped to yoke the novel policies of religious toleration to an expansion of direct control over religious communities. Indeed, Yaacov Ro'i's deeply researched *Islam in the Soviet Union*, based on vast collections of internal correspondences on Muslim groups written by Soviet bureaucrats, clearly lends support to the notion that religious toleration was, above all, a strategy for growing the "surveillance state," with the goal of policing Muslims' behavior and gaining supervisory powers over religious life. The evidence presented by Ro'i also sheds light on a dualism envisioned (albeit implicitly) by Soviet officials, and later articulated by historians: "Official Islam" vs. "Unofficial Islam." The official side is represented by the sanctioned spiritual directorates and "registered" religious leaders and the unofficial by unregistered figures operating illegally, allegedly at the fringes of society, and often with anti-Soviet motives. The internal Party documents and correspondences detailed by Ro'i reveal, for example, a preoccupation with the allegedly anti-Soviet activities of "ishans" (*īshān* being a common regional term for a Sufi master), many of whom were suspected of spreading anti-state propaganda. Sufi orders and "wandering clerics" were thought to compete with the official establishment for the sympathies of Soviet Muslims. (Certain "ishanist" groups—such as the so-called Hairy Ishans of Kirghizia—were evidently especially worrisome.) Beyond the assumed threat from established Sufi organizations, an expansive complex of religious observances, often deemed "pre-Islamic survivals," was associated with these unofficial channels and thought to be a danger to the state, as well as to the progress and "modernization" of Muslims.

These divisions have long been predicated on two intertwined ideas that can be found both among Soviet bureaucrats and among historians of religion in the Soviet Union: first, that the Muslim authorities sanctioned by the Soviet Union—often called "Red *mullas*"—had, as their primary goal, the undermining of traditional, "popular" forms of Islam; and, second, that these authorities were widely rejected by Soviet Muslims. They have thus been considered, as Walter Kolarz writes, "generals without soldiers."[23]

While unregistered religious activity appears to have been wide-spread among Soviet Muslims—a fact that is made abundantly clear in the correspondences by some of the same CARC bureaucrats who attempted to depict such activity as "marginal"—anti-Soviet mobilization does not appear to have been a common feature of such activities. As the case of Pavlodar will show, when it came to asserting state control over religious communities, the Soviet government was faced with a much more pervasive problem, as articulated by its own CARC bureaucrats: local communities simply did not understand the new religious policies which had been developed in wartime—and neither did many Soviet officials.

On June 28, 1945, scarcely a week after the opening of the Pavlodar mosque, N. Guliaeva, in a strikingly frank, classified dispatch, alerted her superiors to the proliferation of "unregistered" activity in the region. According to her, it was caused not by anti-Soviet agitation among religious leaders, but rather by widespread confusion at every level, from local Muslim citizens to schoolteachers to government organs:[24]

> We have information that, in a number of *raions*, there are districts where Muslim believers are conducting services without registering their communities, and the local organs of government are entirely unaware of this.
>
> The indifferent regard toward the activities of Muslim believers on the part of *raion* organizations is explained by the fact that many leaders *do not understand how this question has been resolved by our government*, [and] how to understand the allowance given by the government of "the right to pray freely" (*pravo svobodno molit'sia*). There are leaders who understand it thus: "if the freedom to act on their religious feelings has been permitted to believers by the government," they say, "then let them pray when and where they please."
>
> Here, for example, is such a case (granted, this does not issue from the side of the *raion* or city leadership). In one of the schools of Pavlodar, a female history teacher taught the pupils that church and state are not separate, i.e. that there are representatives of the executive committee who permit questions of religion [to be raised] at the committee's meetings.

The very same day, Guliaeva sent a memo to officials in a nearby district alerting them that an unregistered group of Muslims had been conducting communal religious ceremonies. Guliaeva requested that the officials clarify for these Muslims that religious services could only take place once the community had a prayer-house or mosque that had been registered with the government. "Until the government's permission for the opening of a prayer house has been granted," Guliaeva wrote, "group services must be terminated."[25]

Meanwhile, Guliaeva's superiors—in particular, N. Sabitov of the CARC's main Kazakh SSR office—were pushing her to investigate reports of unregistered activity and to collect detailed intelligence on the communities involved. When it came to "illegal" religious communities, Sabitov wrote to Guliaeva, "it is necessary to identify all of them and to make a determination on their continued existence."[26] Once identified, the CARC could either call for the termination of their gatherings or permit them to petition for registration. These petitions took the form of an application for the opening of a mosque or other prayer-house and needed to include a detailed list of all "believers" in the community at hand. Before being presented to the CARC, the petition needed the approval of the local executive committee.

Few such applications were received, however, and Guliaeva's reportage on local religious activities carried a tone of deepening concern as the months passed. In the autumn of 1945, she alerted Sabitov that although illegal Islamic activities in Pavlodar had not recently been detected, "it must be said that the influence of this community on the entire Muslim population has manifested itself in a negative way." For example, during a recent Muslim holiday,[27] Muslim workers ceased their labors entirely "and cast the day as a holiday for themselves." Three entire factories shut down for the day. "Most agitating of all," Guliaeva wrote, "the directors of these companies made concessions in this respect, instead of explaining things to the working masses."[28]

Meanwhile, the patriotic works for which religious communities had been widely praised during wartime were in conspicuous decline. In the third quarter of 1945, the Muslims of Pavlodar had contributed just 2,000 rubles toward the defense fund. In Guliaeva's view, the opening of the Pavlodar mosque had a negative impact on patriotic donations. As she explained to Sabitov, those Muslims who had actively been gathering donations before the opening of the mosque had done so with a "view to merit such authorization," and, after it had opened, "there was no particular zeal [remaining], since, in their minds, the goal had been accomplished."[29]

In the rural districts surrounding Pavlodar, meanwhile, illegal religious activities continued, as did—Guliaeva claimed—the utter disregard among local officials. She explained the situation to Sabitov with palpable exasperation:[30]

> The indifference of the *raion* organizations to the activities of believers continues. Notwithstanding our repeated commands and warnings to *raion* leaders, the latter continue to be indifferent. We have detected, in several *raions*, organized Muslim prayer services under the leadership of some *mulla*, with *raion* leaders not attaching any importance to this whatsoever . . . We have sent a warning to these districts once again.

Some local Muslim leaders seemed, to Guliaeva, equally indifferent—or perhaps just confused—about the official policy on religious activity. Though travel permissions for Muslim leaders had been restricted in an avowed effort to interfere with their "influence" over neighboring populations, Guliaeva reported to Sabitov that a Muslim leader in Semipalatinsk "gave instructions— conflicting with our instructions—that the leader of the Muslim community in Pavlodar [Kulmagambetov] should spread his activities throughout the territories of all oblasts."[31]

Sabitov evidently chalked up some of these problems to a lack of rigor in the process of intelligence gathering, or, at the very least, a lack of clarity concerning the kinds of intelligence CARC agents were supposed to be collecting. To clarify things, on November 16, 1945, he circulated a request detailing eleven specific points that needed to be illuminated in future intelligence reports. This list offers a remarkable window on the kinds of surveillance the CARC hoped to undertake among Muslims:[32]

1) The characteristics of the principal denominations.
2) The number of prayer houses: a) opened with the Council's approval; b) registered as actually existing.
3) Revealing data about the social composition of the believers.
4) The proportion of believers and the degree of their influence over the masses.
5) The social-political character of the clergy: a) social makeup; b) religious knowledge; c) degree of influence over the masses; d) behavior in wartime and at the present time.
6) The political coloring and orientation of religious organizations: a) forms of religious activities; b) recruitment efforts and propaganda activities;

c) methods of gaining exposure among the masses; d) attitude toward agricultural campaigns [i.e. collectivization].

7) Specific features of individual denominations.

8) The religious underworld (*podpol'e*).

9) The principal shortcomings and difficulties in your work.

10) The method of your work.

11) Your conclusions and recommendations concerning all of these questions.

Guliaeva was given one month to submit the requested report. She delivered it on time—on December 15, 1945—but it was filled with bad news. "It is difficult to give an answer to the questions in your outline," Guliaeva wrote, "especially concerning the number of believers and their social composition, as there has been no kind of record of this and it is not possible to conduct [such a survey] across all oblasts." She could say only that the Pavlodar Muslim community consisted of between two thousand and two thousand five hundred people. "It is practically impossible to say anything about the believers' social composition," she wrote.[33] The social background of the "clergy" was easier to summarize, though Guliaeva—like many other CARC agents—found their religious credentials underwhelming. According to Guliaeva, Muslim leaders in Pavlodar were predominantly from cattle-rearing backgrounds (ordinary Kazakhs, in other words), had studied in madrasas, and had worked for some time as secular teachers (*mugalim*) among Kazakhs. They then nominated themselves as *mullas* and managed to win the support of some proportion of the population. In any case, in Guliaeva's view, these self-appointed *mullas* could do little more than recite a few appropriate verses over the deceased, or during prayers, and otherwise, "for the most part, they know nothing about the religion."[34]

Guliaeva concluded her report by reiterating the fact that patriotic donations had declined substantially, owing at least partly to the newly imposed travel restrictions on religious leaders, and that the "influence of clergy" was reflected negatively in the widespread trend of abandoning factory work on Muslim holidays. For this, once again, Guliaeva blamed not only the "clergy," but also the factory managers. "This speaks to the fact," Guliaeva wrote, "that a number of managers *do not know the policies of the Soviet state concerning the religious question*."[35] Meanwhile, the "series of warnings" Guliaeva had sent to local officials concerning the proliferation of illegal religious gatherings and services had apparently been ignored. These gatherings continued, entirely unhindered.[36] How could the local Muslims take such risks? Didn't they know they were breaking the law?

Apparently not. In her report from the next month—January 1946—Guliaeva clarified that these gatherings continued "because, on the one hand, [local Muslims] do not yet know the procedure for registering a community, and, on the other, because the local *ispolkom* pays no attention to this [kind of activity]." She reiterated that she had "repeatedly sent instructions to the *raispolkom* concerning the prohibition against carrying out group prayer services," but that these instructions continued to be ignored.[37] Meanwhile, she was getting precious little support from local *raispolkom* officials: no one on that executive committee was working on the issue of "religious denominations," so Guliaeva's only point of contact in the local government was *raispolkom*'s chairman—"who, as you know," she wrote to Sabitov, "is more preoccupied with other issues. Thus, naturally, to get some information or to demand that some instructions be carried out is very difficult."[38]

Things were no better at the level of the regional government (*oblispolkom*). Guliaeva complained to Sabitov that, as of January 1946, she did not even have a place to work in the *oblispolkom* offices, and therefore had no formal place to receive visitors. How could she be expected to host local religious leaders and informants if she did not even have a chair to offer them? She beseeched her CARC superiors to intervene on her behalf in order to improve her working conditions.[39]

Instead of support, Guliaeva received a coldly worded rebuke from the main CARC offices in Moscow. In a stinging letter addressed to both Guliaeva and Sabitov, CARC deputy chairman Iurii Sadovskii acknowledged the receipt of "much factual information" from the two of them but added that "all of this is unsatisfactory due to its lack of political information and statistical data." When it came to their reports of unregistered activity, Sadovskii wrote that they "did not provide any kind of concrete data which might also interest the Council." He demanded that future reports indicate, among other things, "why the Muslims do not turn to you with petitions to open mosques, and prefer instead to conduct religious rites in the open air are or in private homes, without registering religious organizations in the manner established for them." Moreover, they should always be on the lookout for "the religious underground" that, Sadovskii wrote, consisted of "those religious groups that engage in anti-Soviet activities."[40] Guliaeva had no trouble responding to Sadovskii's dispatch:[41]

Why do the Muslims not come to the representative with petitions to open mosques, but prefer instead to pray in private homes? First, because no one has prevented them from conducting prayer services in private homes. The local government does not pay attention to this, and, additionally, the Muslims do not know all the rules about opening mosques. And among them there is no more-or-less literate person who might fill out the petition and supply all the documents.

Guliaeva illustrated this state of affairs by recounting a recent "success story" which, despite its satisfactory conclusion, nevertheless revealed something of her predicament. She had been informed that a group of Muslims at a local mine had been conducting services both in a private home and in a canteen basement that had been serving as an unregistered mosque. A "local representative of the organs of state security" informed this community that they needed to register if they wanted to continue conducting prayer services. At this point, Guliaeva reports, their imam, "if he could be called that," turned to her to seek information on how to register the community. As it turned out, he was illiterate. She helped register the community, but, above all, she was struck by the fact that, before being contacted by state security, they had all been perfectly "content with conducting services in a private home under the leadership of an illiterate imam."[42] They had been, in other words, entirely unaware of the government's policy on religious gatherings.

Meanwhile, Guliaeva's working conditions continued to deteriorate. In April 1946, she pleaded with Sabitov:[43]

I must once again mention the difficult working conditions. This is not mere sniveling on my part . . . What will you say if I tell you that I am ejected from my workplace almost every day? I have tried and failed to explain the value of my work—that the representatives of the community come to me as before a representative of the government, that I must not receive them out in the hallway—but none of it helps. Evidently, since religion has "stepped aside," it has no authority, and neither does the worker who conducts this business [of supervising religious communities].

Regarding my appeal for help in improving my working conditions, neither the Council [for the Affairs of Religious Cults of the USSR], nor the [regional] representative of the Council for Kazakhstan has come to my aid.

Along with these basic and tangible daily challenges, Guliaeva faced others that were harder to articulate. If the Muslims of Pavlodar and its surrounding districts had failed to comprehend the need for registered mosques, it was not only because the laws on mosque registration had been inadequately clarified for them. As Sabitov explained to her in an uncharacteristically "ethnographic" letter from November 1945, the region's Kazakhs may simply have been unused to the idea that mosques—registered or otherwise—were strictly necessary for communal religious activities. Before the revolution, Sabitov explained, Kazakh mosques were found in towns and cities—and only in towns and cities. Among the nomads of rural spaces—the majority of Kazakhs, in other words—"mosques were few, since, given the conditions of the nomadic way of life, there was no need for them." In these circumstances "a stable tradition developed among the formerly-nomadic Kazakhs of managing without stationary mosques to serve as sites of prayer-gatherings." When it came to registering new Muslim communities, then, Sabitov anticipated petitions from "mosqueless *mullas*" seeking permission to carry out religious services in the open air or in private homes.[44]

Registering a "mosqueless" Muslim community would mean departing from the established policy on registering religious communities. Previously, a Muslim community was identified with a particular mosque, just as a labor union was identified with a particular factory. This not only situated the community and its activities in a circumscribed space; it also facilitated the kind of surveillance regime that justified the permissive orientation toward religion. In order to surveil a community, one had to locate it. Registering a community *to* a mosque made this process easy. Indeed, registering communities and mosques in tandem had been perhaps the *only* crystal-clear procedure in the new age of religious "toleration." This was the message Guliaeva had repeatedly sent to local officials (and which, according to her, they had repeatedly ignored): group religious activities needed to take place in the setting of a registered mosque. Indeed, such were the marching orders that had come directly from Stalin himself. Namely, CARC officials were ordered to:[45]

1) unswervingly guide the activities of religious associations in the direction of a wholesale narrowing of their scope;
2) restrict the activities of religious associations within the limits of prayer-houses and only [for the purposes of] worship;
3) carry out relentless surveillance on the activities of religious centers;
4) relentlessly suppress the activities of all kinds of [unregistered] religious formations.

But if many Kazakhs had no need of mosques or other prayer-houses, how—and *what*—would they go about registering in order to legalize their communal prayers, ceremonies, and other activities?

On this point, Sabitov's letter grows distinctly enigmatic. "Thence arises before the representatives," he wrote, "the necessity of reviewing the matter in order to arrive at an appropriate conclusion." Beyond this, all Sabitov could do was punt the ball:[46]

Toward these ends, the representative is entrusted with carrying out special interviews with members of the Spiritual Directorate of the Muslims of Central Asia and Kazakhstan; with members of the revolutionary committee of said Spiritual Directorate; and with local elders (Muslim "aksakals") on the following theme: [should] the auls, kishlaks, villages, and similar population centers in the oblast, which previously had no mosques, [continue] not to have them in the present day? After conducting interviews with the abovementioned competent individuals concerning these matters, the representative must furnish the following information:

1) The names of *raions*, which previously had no mosques, along with approximate data on the number of believers in them.
2) Where (whether in a tent, yurt, or in the open air) and with which *mullas* collective prayers are carried out . . . [and] who leads these prayers (whether *mullas* or, for lack of them, elders or other laity literate in religious matters).
3) The approximate number of *mullas* in the auls, kishlaks, and villages where there are still no mosques, and their degree of training.

Forward this information no later than 25 December.

Suffice to say Guliaeva was unable to provide the information requested of her. With no help whatsoever from local governments, how was Guliaeva to discover prayers that took place in private homes, basements, tents, or open fields? All she could gather were scattered rumors. The "peculiarity" of Kazakh Muslim culture—as Guliaeva described it—also helped to explain the lack of petitions in her provincial, majority-Kazakh region for the opening of mosques. In a report to Sabitov from January 1946, she confirmed in more straightforward terms the circumstances he had already described for her:[47]

A peculiarity of Kazakh Muslim believers must be noted. Kazakh believers can conduct prayer services regardless of whether there is a mosque present or not. As per longstanding tradition among nomadic peoples, they can carry out prayer services in the open air. Thus they adhere to these traditions and nowadays make no particular effort to achieve the opening of mosques. Besides, their clergy may be anyone who has at least some familiarity with religion or who can recite a few verses of the Koran during prayer services.

All this makes it very easy for them to organize prayer services.

And all of this made it practically impossible to register mosques in the vast rural expanses of the Kazakh SSR.

The problems described by Guliaeva were not limited to her office—or, more properly, her hallway—in provincial Kazakhstan. CARC officials throughout the Soviet Union complained of rampant unregistered activity. Examples of their anxiety are legion; indeed, a great deal of the evidence presented in Ro'i's six-hundred-page *Islam in the Soviet Union* concerns bureaucratic hand-wringing over such activities. According to Koroleva and Korolev, leading historians of Soviet-era Islam in the Volga-Urals, the archival record proves that most religious activities, whether life-cycle ceremonies or daily prayers, took place in private or out-of-the-way spaces, beyond the oversight of officials—a conclusion echoed by other researchers as well.[48] "Illegal" religious gatherings took place in private homes, open fields, and cemeteries. Most of these gatherings appear to have been led by elderly men, but some were led by women.[49] Women were also alleged to have led female-only prayer- and study-groups, where they studied religious texts and learned to read the Arabic script.[50] In a confidential report submitted to I.V. Polianskii on religious activities in Kuibyshev oblast in 1945, a local CARC agent observed that even some registered *mullas* stepped outside Soviet law when it came to women:[51]

> In order to increase the reach of their influence over the population, the clergy will engage in spiritual discourse not only in the mosques, but also in [private] homes, and, most significantly, with women. Thus, it is known that the *mulla* of the Kamyshlinskii mosque sometimes collects 5–10 women, mostly elderly ones, in a private home, who, as he explains it, "also want to hear the word of God." On these occasions he reads them the Qur'an.

A still greater concern was the phenomenon of registered authorities using their "official" platform to preach against fundamental Soviet social projects—especially collectivization. As the Kuibyshev agent explained, most registered "*mullas*" were patriotic types, but among them lurked subversives:[52]

> As can be seen from the data provided, a significant proportion of the *mullas* had no specialized [religious] training and came to this line of work after the October Revolution—and, mainly, during the Great Patriotic War. Hence their moral-political orientation. The majority of the *mullas* are extremely loyal to the Soviet government and to the activities it carries out, and take an active part in the work of the *kolkhoz*[53] ... But among the *mullas* and such, there are those who have not yet reconciled themselves to the collective farm system in our village[s]. For example, the *mulla* of the Bakaev Mosque of Kamyshlinsky district, Galimov Ady, born in 1882, himself an independent peasant farmer (*krest'ianii-edinolichnik*), leads efforts against collective farm construction. Sometimes, in the midst of vigorous collective farm labor, he deliberately initiates religious services in order to disrupt the work on the collective farm. (Presently, the NKVD is occupied [with investigating] this *mulla*.) Moreover, he goes about his work slyly. Outwardly, he appears completely loyal with respect to the Soviet government, but in private conversation with believers he consistently engages in his anti-*kolkhoz* interpretations.

Another pernicious problem with registered *mullas*—and doubtless one that was challenging to monitor—was the issue of their alleged influence over Muslims beyond their immediate constituency at the mosque. In Penza, officials were disturbed by obvious signs of the high status of local imams in the eyes of the population. Villagers had been building houses for their imams without seeking permission from the local government. During major holidays, these citizens would only go to work when the imams gave them the go-ahead. In the autumn, at the imam's request, citizens provided the mosque with ample firewood—while the local school had none.[54] Some imams had plans for schools of a different kind: "At the present time," the Kuibyshev agent wrote, "all of the servants of the Muslim denomination are occupied with the question of how to involve young people in prayer meetings and the study of the Qur'an. Several times, various representatives of the clergy have raised the issue of the possibility of teaching children to read the Qur'an, at school or at home, as well as the issue of organizing special Muslim religious schools."[55]

In Pavlodar, Guliaeva alerted her superiors that local Muslims had been all too self-sacrificing in donating funds to the mosque: "people who, paying no mind to their poor material circumstances, give away their last kopeks." Meanwhile, she had not only observed Party members frequenting the mosque, but, among them, even Stakhanovites and other elites. Their rationale, in her formulation, was: "I not only fulfill the work of the state—I overfulfill it. So what harm could come from the fact that I go to pray?" Guliaeva warned her superiors: "if the Muslim religion has influence on those at the vanguard, then it will have a much greater influence upon the rest of the population."[56]

In Tiumen oblast, whose first and only Soviet-sanctioned Muslim community was registered to a mosque in 1947, officials cautioned that the mosque's opening could increase the number of "believers" in the region by two or even two-and-a-half times, and that more petitions for mosque openings were sure to follow. Indeed, several petitions were submitted in 1948–49, all of which were denied on the pretense that space or funds were lacking.[57]

Pavlodar's imam Kulmagambetov, meanwhile, despite enjoying the good graces of the state for his patriotic disposition and registered status, continued to grate on regional CARC officials due to his habit of spreading his "influence" in neighboring regions.[58] As early as November 1945 he had already earned the censure of Sabitov, who urged Guliaeva to inform him that he ought to restrict his travels to Pavlodar and its immediate surroundings, since his activities "should be carried out only in the territory of the religious community to which he is registered."[59] By June of the next year, Kulmagambetov was likewise on the outs with his own community and could hardly rely on the support of CARC officials to guarantee his position. Reflecting on this imam's downfall, Guliaeva blamed inter-tribal Kazakh feuds as well as "the struggle among their own denominational clergy to seize the profitable post of imam." She explained to Sabitov:[60]

> These problems find clear expression in the appointing of a new imam to the Pavlodar mosque. When the newly-appointed imam, Bektasov, arrived, the former imam, Kulmagambetov, did not want to give up his seat by any means. The matter almost came to a big scandal and, roughly speaking, to a scuffle. Imam Kulmagambetov did not recognize any rules; the way he saw it, the people had chosen him and only the people could depose him. With this goal in mind, he walked from door to door and collected the signatures of supporters.

The nuances of tribal politics, like so much else concerning the "inner life" of religious communities, would remain opaque for Guliaeva. She could offer few insights about such issues, and, even after many months of service as a CARC official, the information she provided for her CARC superiors about religious life in Pavlodar and its surrounding areas was—as her superiors complained—distinctly meager. In theory, local CARC representatives were expected to create a network of informants, as well as alliances with local officials in the district executive committees. As the CARC commissioner for the Penza region explained, information was to be gathered through "the representatives and secretaries of district executive committees; through conversations with visitors ([that is, with] believers, clerics, and people who came [to discuss] various issues concerning the denominations), and through interviews with representatives of Soviet organs and individual believers at the time of field visits."[61] In practice, as Guliaeva's experience shows, such connections could be difficult to forge. Local officials had no interest in Guliaeva, no respect for her work, no understanding of the religious policies she hoped to enforce. They had—quite literally—no room for her. She appears to have had better luck getting information from local citizens, but mostly she was exasperated that they so reliably failed to comprehend the need to register.

Elsewhere, local CARC officials suffered a still more basic impediment to intelligence gathering: in the Tatar-majority Kuibyshev region, where practically all aspects of Muslim religious life (aside from Arabic prayers) were conducted in the Tatar language, the CARC representative spoke no Tatar.[62]

Meanwhile, the state's ever-vague policy on religion—a moving target since the start of the war—kept shifting beneath the CARC officials' feet. Over the last two decades, a number of historians have concluded that the era of official religious "toleration" ended in 1948–49, the period in which Kh.S. Bagaev, whom we met at the beginning of this chapter, was fired for his "misconduct" as an "accomplice" of renegade religious elites.[63] Indeed, in 1948, an internal document that was circulated among CARC officials proposed that registration of new religious communities should utterly cease;[64] and in August of the next year, an order personally signed by Stalin repealed permission to open a madrasa in Tashkent.[65] (Yaacov Ro'i and Bakhtiyar Babazhanov propose an earlier shift toward stricter religious policies, noting that hints of a firmer approach began to appear within a year or two of the war's end.[66])

A January 1946 decision from Moscow, attributed to Stalin and circulated among CARC officials, appears to validate the idea that "tolerant" wartime policies continued into the postwar period, as it allows—albeit only with the CARC's permission—for the opening of new mosques and prayer-houses. Amazingly, this document even allowed registered Muslim leaders to engage in limited private enterprise (i.e. "capitalist" activity) toward the upkeep of their communities, including the manufacture and sale of religious "utensils" (*utvari*) and other religious objects as well as the construction, lease, and sale of private property (*sobstvennost'*) other than their "prayer-houses."[67] Less than a year had passed, however, before strong hints of a more restrictive policy began issuing from Moscow.[68]

The lack of agreement among historians concerning the chronology of religious policies mirrors the consistent vagueness of the policies themselves.[69] According to Stalin's 1946 directive, CARC officials were permitted to sanction the opening of registered mosques—but did that mean they *should* sanction them? And if so, how often? Registered groups were allowed to purchase and sell certain items with the permission of CARC officials, but does that mean CARC officials were *supposed* to give their permission? Or were these ostensibly "tolerant" policies merely a strategy for *monitoring* the requests, as part of the larger strategy of surveilling activities among religious groups? CARC officials and leaders of the spiritual directorates were evidently left to negotiate these issues among themselves.

When Bagaev was reprimanded and removed from his post in 1949, a central piece of evidence used to paint him as the "accomplice" of religious deviants was the fact that he had helped Muslim leaders in Kazan purchase a vehicle. In doing so, he had allegedly strayed far from the Party's religious policies. In fact, however, the purchase of a vehicle by registered religious leaders—with the consent of a CARC official (like Bagaev)—had been expressly permitted *by Stalin himself* in Article 7 of his order from January 1946.[70] To my knowledge, this article was never afterward repealed.

Nevertheless, during Bagaev's tenure in the CARC offices, the ground had shifted beneath his feet. It is doubtful that he had missed any major policy memos, but he had obviously missed some whispers. If the top CARC official in the Tatar ASSR could "misunderstand" the state's policy on religion, what could lesser officials be expected to understand of that policy—let alone ordinary Muslim citizens?

Conclusion

This book tells two convergent stories about Soviet Muslims in the Second World War. One is about the devotional life of Muslim citizens, including soldiers, their families on the home front, and local religious leaders. Theirs is a story of widespread religious resurgence in the war era. That resurgence is evidenced through wartime literature, veterans' memories, letters to and from the warfront, eyewitness accounts, petitions, and the reports of Soviet agents who were oftentimes exasperated over the unprecedented preponderance of religious life in its visible forms. This was a modest but meaningful social revolution that, to some extent, came to be sanctioned by the state—first implicitly, through toleration, and then explicitly through state support, however limited. The other story is about those state dynamics: the evolution of state priorities and strategies regarding religion; the interface between the state and Muslim elites; the propaganda they pioneered together and effectively co-authored; and the ways in which state-sanctioned institutions became a conduit for popular participation, manifested through such examples as petitions for registration, attendance at registered and newly reopened mosques, *zakat* payments and Ramadan charity, and donations to the war effort through religious channels.

These two stories converge at the level of any given Soviet Muslim citizen, as both the subject of their own devotional life as well as the intended "object" acted upon by propaganda. It must be asked, however: Did wartime religious propaganda have any impact on Soviet Muslims? Why, after all, did Soviet Muslims fight in the war?

Speaking for himself, at least, the Kyrgyz machine-gunner Asral Kalychev had a simple answer: "For the homeland, for Stalin. Stalin—he's the man thanks to whom the country stood strong. He was a strong man." His interviewer, doubtless surprised by the bearded elder's answer, followed up with a question about religion: "Did you believe in Allah at the front?" "We do not forget Allah. And at the front too, Allah."[1]

Kalychev's response about Stalin is remarkable because it is at once both representative and unrepresentative: some soldiers' poetry and memories speak often of homeland, family, and comrades, and very rarely of Stalin,[2]

God Save the USSR. Jeff Eden, Oxford University Press (2021). © Oxford University Press.
DOI: 10.1093/oso/9780190076276.003.0007

while others speak of him more often. This very diversity, however, is one clear point of difference between the Stalin-heavy state propaganda and the words and writings of eyewitnesses. There are other differences too. Soviet wartime propaganda was almost invariably triumphant, focused on the ultimate victory over Hitler, the joy of liberated regions, and the glory of success in battle. Red Army heroes are not permitted any tears. By contrast, Muslim poetry from the war, like the contents of many interviews with veterans, is dense with bereavement, parting, violence, and despair. At the same time, the war in question is invariably shown as Hitler's doing, not Stalin's. Stalin is only *sometimes* praised, but neither is he blamed. To ask what the soldiers were fighting *for* is, in this sense, the less relevant question, since it was perfectly clear what they were fighting *against*. It was a defensive war, justified by self-preservation. A relatively small proportion of Soviet Muslims volunteered to fight at first, and—like the Red Army as a whole—their morale and conviction in the first year of the war appeared extremely low. As Hitler made headway and news spread of the atrocities committed by Axis soldiers against citizens of all religions, the existential character of the war became clearer to soldiers and citizens across the Soviet Union. In many of our Muslim sources, it was not a war *for* Stalin, but a war *against* Hitler. This struggle was not unanimously depicted as a defense of Stalin or the Soviet government. It was almost always depicted as a defense of things far more sacred: home, family, and community. Shared religious devotion was a pillar of many Soviet communities, families, and homes, albeit certainly not of all.

If the goal of Soviet state propaganda was to rally soldiers behind Stalin and Communism, then we may reasonably suspect that the wartime propaganda was in many cases a failure, as private and family documents, as well as memoirs and memories, reflect an inconsistent interest among soldiers in these pillars. More resonant with many of are the words of poet and frontline veteran Iurii Belash:[3]

> To be honest about it—
> In the trenches the last thing we thought about
> Was Stalin.
> God was on our minds more.
> Stalin played no part at all
> In our soldier's war
> And even to talk about him—
>   There was simply no call for it.

If, however, the goal of Soviet wartime propaganda was to articulate a compelling vision of the "homeland"—the "we"—that was worth defending, then perhaps it achieved some limited success. There is no doubt that propaganda tropes and motifs show up even in the private writings of frontline soldiers, writings intended only for family and loved ones. Among Muslim soldiers, these propaganda motifs are sometimes twinned with Muslim themes—a mirror, or at least a faint echo, of the Soviet Muslim propaganda that emerged with state backing in the final years of the war.

Nevertheless, the Soviet religious propaganda campaign was limited in scope, late to arrive, and riddled with blatant disingenuousness. Citizens who certainly knew better were told that the Soviet Union had always been a happy home for Muslims, sheltering their religion and ensuring their self-determination. The propaganda speeches of leaders like Babakhanov and Rasulev were broadcast in major venues, but—as Karel Berkhoff observes—not very often.[4] These leaders' muftiates came into existence less than two years before the end of the war; the broad scope of their influence in the decades to come has been described at length by Eren Tasar, but it seems unlikely that their influence and visibility among Muslim populations could have been very extensive while the muftiates themselves were still in their infancy.

For all this, can we really say that the muftiates, let alone the propaganda they circulated, were a significant force during the Second World War? For some historians, indeed, the muftiates were never anything more than a marginal, barely visible force, even in the decades that followed.[5] By contrast, I argue that the muftiates are a crucial touchstone for understanding Soviet Muslim life in the Stalin era and beyond. Indeed, I can think of at least fifteen ways in which the subject of the muftiates, in their broader foundational context of wartime religious revolution, illuminates Soviet religious history.

First, the muftiates served, for Soviet Muslim citizens, as the most dramatic example of how religious repression was reduced and religious policy reversed during the war, just as Sergii's re-emergence as a sanctioned Patriarch served as a symbolic turning point among Orthodox Christians—as it is still remembered today, nearly eighty years later.

Second, the propaganda developed by the state in cooperation with respected, "authentic" pre-Soviet elites (such as Babakhanov) offers a remarkable window into what those elites believed would resonate with the largest proportion of Soviet Muslims. No one alive today understands the values of pre-Soviet Central Asian Muslim culture as intimately as did

Ishan Babakhanov, the heir to one of the region's most esteemed Muslim lineages and already nearly sixty years old at the time of the October Revolution. Within Soviet society, Babakhanov was the farthest thing from a Moscow-born, Soviet-educated atheist. We can learn much, therefore, from Babakhanov's *perception* of what would inspire his community. This is especially true since Babakhanov promoted, for propaganda purposes, aspects of Muslim life that he himself had previously condemned, such as shrine visitation and Sufi mystical traditions. He was telling his audience what he thought *they* wanted to hear, and his assumptions were backed by personal experience and lifelong immersion, not by the formulas and prescriptions of Marxist-Leninist scientific atheism.

Third, while Berkhoff argues that the most unique thing about Soviet wartime propaganda is the state's absolute control over its expressions,[6] the Soviet religious propaganda of the muftiates reveals a type of propaganda that was not exclusively a Moscow product. This "genre" is an example of state propaganda as a negotiated discourse, with Moscow able to give directives on context but, when it came to content, forced to follow the lead of religious elites. As Chapter 2 argues, these negotiated spaces allowed religious leaders to articulate perspectives and values that would have been taboo—even dangerous—just a few years earlier.

Fourth, the creation of the muftiates prompted a flood of petitions from Soviet Muslims, who requested everything from the reopening of mosques to the return of religious ceremonial objects. This hints, at the very least, at a widespread awareness of these new institutions, as well as a willingness on the part of some citizens to test them as channels for expanding religious activity in novel, ostensibly "legal" contexts. As modest as this sounds, it amounts to nothing less than a new vision of the Soviet state's relationship to the rights and privileges of each individual.

Fifth, we can observe that the muftiates and their leaders were no mere propaganda mouthpieces or bureaucratic liaisons; their formal religious responsibilities were vast. Even in the first two years of the muftiates' existence, in the war years, their leaders fulfilled the traditional functions of Muslim religious elites. These leaders, and others affiliated with the muftiates (whether through registration or through more informal connections), presided over funerals, circumcisions, and weddings. They delivered regular sermons and tended to the day-to-day functions of newly reopened mosques. Altogether, they contributed substantively to day-to-day religious life in wartime. This also had some bearing on the war effort: demobilized Red Army soldiers were conspicuous among mosque attendees, and many casualties of the war were buried according to Muslim customs.

Sixth, as Chapter 3 shows, the muftiates also contributed to the war effort in more concrete ways. Muslim leaders raised immense amounts of capital through donations promoted at, and routed through, the mosques. Many of these "patriotic" donations were explicitly tied to traditional Muslim charity, as they were oftentimes offered in the form of *zakat*. Naturally, Soviet sources cite donation tallies that appear inflated, and varieties of coercion and corruption surely played a part. We may reasonably ask how many of these "donations" were *de facto* bribes—efforts, for example, by individuals to secure the support of the state, or to pay shady "operating costs." Nevertheless, the evidence that Muslim institutions (like their Christian counterparts) were donating immense sums to the war effort is undeniable; this was a point conceded even by militantly atheist officials. Soviet Muslim leaders worked to channel not only hearts and minds to the fight against Hitler, but also tanks, guns, and bombs.

Seventh, by serving as a nexus between Muslims and the atheist state, the muftiates bolstered perceptions of the Stalinist Soviet Union as a kind of "participatory" state—a perception Stalin cultivated by many means.[7] The mere fact of the muftiates' existence, to say nothing of their diverse activities, signaled to citizens that a new, limited space for agency had been opened. A clear signal cut through the policy haze: participating in public religious life would no longer be an act of inherent dissent. On the contrary, religious life could be consonant with state law, with state values, with the fight against Hitler—and even with Soviet patriotism.

Eighth, this new space created more than just a new mentality toward the faith-state relationship; it created tangible opportunities for social mobility in the religious sphere. At its most dramatic, this meant that some recent "prisoners of conscience"—such as Babakhanov—were pulled practically straight from the Gulag to staff religious posts. On a broader level, this meant that scores of former religious functionaries who had transitioned into "secular" jobs could return to open religious service. Local histories offer plentiful biographies of individuals who had worked as government clerks or farmers throughout the 1920s and 1930s only to find themselves employed as imams or muftiate *qadis* in the 1940s and 1950s.

Ninth, while Cold War–era historians typically divided Soviet Islam into two discreet religious spheres, the "official" (state-sanctioned) and the "unofficial" (unregistered), more recent studies—starting with a landmark essay by

Devin DeWeese[8]—have articulated the muftiates as a point of convergence for diverse religious currents. Sanctioned and registered Muslim leaders had extensive, complicated, and oftentimes productive relations with their unregistered counterparts. As Zaripov and Safarov write, "Unofficial imams were usually well-known to the imams of registered mosques; in cities where there were mosques, they were the most active parishioners (such is how it was in Moscow, in particular)."[9] Meanwhile, the mere fact of registration did not hinder the registered imams from engaging in activities of dubious legality, as Bobrovnikov observes: "[T]he imams submitted to DUMSK's authority were at the same time illegally teaching the youth in their *hujras*, whilst accredited clerics like Muhammad-Sayyid could be adepts of unauthorized Sufi *shaykhs*."[10] The point here is not that the muftiates were regarded as legitimate by *all* Soviet Muslims; indeed, as one might expect, their proximity to state power inspired suspicion and contempt among many. Inarguably, however, the muftiates' significance was more than just symbolic, and their functions involved more than just government gatekeeping.

Tenth, the muftiates consolidated and reinforced the authority of sacred Muslim lineages throughout Russia, the Caucasus, and Central Asia. Rasulev and Babakhanov are themselves examples of this, and Babakhanov's case is especially dramatic, as the once-jailed mufti passed down his post at the helm of SADUM to his son Ziyauddin Babakhanov, who then passed it down to his son Shamsuddin-Khan Babakhanov. On a more local level, the remarkable, recently translated autobiography of the Kazakh *mulla* Saduaqas Ghïlmani provides a veritable who's who of such religious "dynasties" throughout the Kazakh steppe, impressing one with the sense that few Kazakh communities were lacking for local "holy families" in the mid-Soviet period and that these figures drew their prestige as much from lineage as from learning.[11]

Eleventh, the muftiates reinforced not only literal Muslim lineages, but also intellectual and conceptual lineages that can be traced deep into previous eras. During the war, the fatwas issued by the muftiates mostly concerned the war effort, but in the decade to come, they would turn their attention to articulating a distinctive (and, in some cases, restrictive) vision of Islam rooted in distinctly pre-Soviet debates. Perhaps the defining feature of this vision is its opposition to shrine-pilgrimage, a centuries-old hallmark of Eurasian Islam and a characteristic feature of Sufism. These anti-shrine efforts found expression, for example, in a series of SADUM fatwas over the course of the mid-Soviet period, during which the muftiate was led by Ishan Babakhanov's son and successor, Ziyauddin. Historians have offered multiple hypotheses about the intellectual genealogy of these efforts and about the doctrinal orientation of SADUM more generally (the other muftiates are ripe for, but still awaiting, similar study). Tasar draws a link between the Babakhanov dynasty's religious ideology and the Naqshbandi-Mujaddidi tradition, associated with the South Asian Naqshbandi *shaykh* Ahmad Sirhindi and his successors.[12] Khalid finds their heritage among the Jadids of the early twentieth century.[13] Sartori traces a line from SADUM to non-Jadid "rigorists" of Russian colonial Central Asia.[14] The key point, for these purposes, is what all three historians have in common: they show plausible linkages between the muftiates and pre-Soviet Islamic intellectual traditions—links to traditions, moreover, whose nuances their atheist patrons in Moscow and in the CARC could hardly have comprehended. "Indeed," Sartori concludes, "while it is plain that CARC did request fatwas from SADUM, it is equally clear that the latter enjoyed an agency of its own and often manipulated the Council's requests to pursue its own cultural agenda."[15]

Twelfth, by carving out such a distinctive theological space, by monopolizing access to state resources, and by maintaining ties with state security, the muftiates were able to enfranchise certain Muslim leaders and marginalize others. Notably, they were able to accomplish this within a distinctly Islamic (rather than atheist and state-focused) ideological framework.

Thirteenth, while the muftiates were thus shifting conceptual borders for Muslims inside the Soviet Union, they were also crossing borders that few others could cross: as ambassadors to other parts of the Muslim world, muftiate leaders were able to articulate their peculiar hybrid of Soviet and religious propaganda to Muslims in Saudi Arabia, Iran, China, and beyond. It is easy to scoff at these trips, which saw Muslim leaders tailed by "minders" and touting blatant lies about Soviet religious freedom. It is difficult, too, to know what foreign audiences made of their visits. Nevertheless, we know that the sight of Soviet Orthodox Christian envoys abroad made a big impact on American and British audiences, and we can sensibly imagine that the news of, say, Babakhanov and Rasulev in Mecca was more than trivial for some of their Soviet followers and, perhaps, for Saudi audiences too.

Fourteenth, as several other historians have observed, the muftiates' creation renewed a relationship of "controlled mediation" between Eurasian Muslims and the state that can be traced all the way back to the founding of the Orenburg Muslim Spiritual Assembly in the 1780s.[16] Several parallels between this Tsarist administrative structure and the Soviet muftiates are significant: the Spiritual Assembly, like the Soviet muftiates, served as a bureaucracy for extending state oversight to Muslims and their religious institutions; it served to entrench a mutually beneficial relationship between Muslim elites and the state, offering these elites, as Tasar writes, "an avenue toward acquiring a stake in the systems' welfare";[17] and it served to promote a kind of Soviet Muslim "orthodoxy" by elevating the religious ideas of the muftiates above rival religious currents. For all the similarities, however, we should hesitate to regard the revised and newly-constituted muftiates of the 1940s as a mere reprise of the Tsarist-era religious institution. After all, the Soviet state created the war-era muftiates—unlike the Spiritual Assembly of old—with the explicit endgame of destroying religion still firmly in mind. Moreover, the new infrastructure created for the Orthodox Church was a more immediate and obvious model for the new muftiates. This much is clear even from the look-alike titles of the government branches monitoring each: the Council for the Affairs of Religious Cults (CARC, for Muslims, Buddhists, and others) and the Council for the Affairs of the Russian Orthodox Church (CAROC). We have no evidence that Stalin made any special study of the Orenburg Muslim Spiritual Assembly before meeting with Rasulev; we do know, however, as Chapter 1 describes, that he had already worked out his "New Deal" with church leaders months prior, and that he apparently offered Rasulev much the same "deal." In short, the connection between the muftiates and the Orenburg Muslim Spiritual Assembly is likely more vivid for historians than it was for Stalin, Molotov, Karpov, or anyone else directly involved in crafting the new policy. Nevertheless, the historical connections are remarkable for the study of Eurasian religious history over the longue durée—and they would surely have been meaningful for Rasulev himself (for example).

Fifteenth, just as we can draw links between the Soviet muftiates and the pre-Soviet past, we can also draw them with the post-Soviet present. Soon after the collapse of the Soviet Union, multiple post-Soviet states created religious "boards" that essentially replicated the state-muftiate relationships of the Soviet era. In Uzbekistan, for example, president Islam Karimov (d. 2016) employed a well-known Islamic scholar named Muhammad Sodiq Muhammad Yusuf (d. 2015) for many years as the republic's de facto "chief mufti." The appointment was not a stretch: Muhammad Sodiq had been elected chief mufti by SADUM in 1989 (in the same year, he also became an elected deputy to the USSR's Supreme Soviet).[18] The shaykh was a "pure" product of the Soviet Muslim establishment: born in the Fergana Valley, he received his Islamic education at Tashkent's Imam al-Bukhari Islamic

Institute and at Bukhara's historic Mir-i Arab *madrasa*; afterward, he worked as editor of SADUM's official journal, *Muslims of the Soviet East*; and, like most Soviet Muslim elites, he was heir to a prestigious pre-Soviet lineage of Muslim jurists and scholars (in this case, from the famously devout region of Andijan). Prolific, well-connected, and impeccable in his distinctly *Soviet*-Muslim bona fides, Muhammad Sodiq was well placed to become one of the most influential Islamic figures of the post-Soviet period. While the "official" religious institutions of post-Soviet states no longer labor under militant atheists longing for their ultimate destruction, it is clear that Stalin's wartime "New Deal" continues to echo into post-Soviet religious politics.

These points focus on conditions, institutions, and roles that were *created* during the wartime religious revolution. However, what the state removed during the war was just as important as what it created. It removed the constant threat of arrests and executions, the punitive taxation of religious leaders, and the seizures and shutdowns of communally held religious property. At no other time since the 1920s had so many Soviet citizens been so free to practice their religion openly. The state did not so much "raise the banner" of religion, as Solzhenitsyn would have it, as remove its chains.

The religious resurgence, and the state's tolerance, were clearly vexing to many Soviet atheists, including the chronically underfunded, baffled bureaucrats of CARC. Controls on religious expression, once slapdash but often brutal, were now ineffectual, even inscrutable. This too was crucial: Stalin gave believers an inch, and they gladly took a mile. No one stopped them. The wartime revolution in religious life came not from the energy of the state's religious propaganda but from millions of faithful citizens eager and ready to take advantage of the state's tolerance as well as the state's absence.

Here, I have sketched many arguments for the significance of the Soviet muftiates (some elaborated over the course of this book, some elaborated in recent work by Tasar, Sartori, DeWeese, and others), and throughout the book I have shown how and why the muftiates emerged during the war era, demonstrating their broader significance as part of a wartime religious revolution. My goal has not been to produce a single, normative vision of Soviet Islam, much less to project that vision forward into the four remaining decades of the Soviet period. Nevertheless, this book joins other recent studies in challenging nearly every piece of "common knowledge" that has prevailed about Islam in the Soviet Union for the past several decades. Paolo

Sartori and Bakhtiyar Babadjanov summarize these longstanding points of consensus in a recent article:[19]

> When asked to explain what historical forces of change affected Muslimness in Soviet Central Asia, historians and anthropologists alike unfailingly agree on the fact that [1] a sizeable number of scholars (*'ulamā'*) either fell victim to the Red Terror or lost social prominence, thereby impeding the transmission of specialized religious knowledge; [2] that *sharī'a* ceased to be viewed as a source of proper conduct and a yardstick to measure justice; [3] that such important institutions as charitable endowments were abolished; [4] that religiosity became confined to the sequestrated space of the family; [5] that moral self-discipline, renunciant behavior and ascetic lifestyle as traditionally embodied by figures such as dervishes and *qalandars* capitulated before the allure of modernization; and [6] that education lost most of its local religious principles and began to convey mainly national and secular values.

On the first point, it is true that a great many Muslim scholars fell victim to the religious repressions described in Chapter 1; however, this book shows that many survived the purges and continued their devotional work. After the wartime religious revolution, many of these figures received the sanction of the state, and many others who were not formally sanctioned nevertheless took advantage of the new religious climate.

On the second point, while the Soviet state eliminated the pre-Soviet Islamic courts, Islamic "law," more broadly conceived, continued throughout the Soviet period in the form of the fatwa-issuing muftiates—as well as at more local levels, in communities that were home to influential Muslim elites.

On the third point, while mosques and other religious structures were no longer supported by formal pious endowments of the classical Muslim sort (called *waqf*), Chapter 5 shows how religious property came to be endowed, ironically, by the Soviet state itself, which sometimes administered this property cooperatively with Muslim leaders and CARC officials.

The fourth point—that Soviet religiosity was confined to the family—is the point most thoroughly contested by the evidence in this book, almost all of which concerns religious life in contexts outside the immediate household. Here, we see religion mobilized as an instrument of the state; we find it seized upon by Muslim leaders to incite mass action; we find it shared among soldiers on the battlefield; and we find it preserved in both urban and rural spaces as a community-wide phenomenon engaging communal identity and ritual life. We find Muslim identity articulated at the level of the family, but also at the level of the village, the town, the Red Army, the Soviet Union as a whole, and—in the speeches discussed in Chapter 2—even at the level of the broader Muslim world, past and present.

The fifth and sixth points, concerning the survival of Sufi asceticism and of Islamic education, are dealt with more indirectly in this book but, to be sure, there is evidence here that challenges both points. First, while the traditional "dervish" behaviors associated with pre-Soviet mystics declined in prominence during the Soviet period, the broader heritage of Sufism clearly survived—including many esteemed Sufi lineages and the widespread practice of shrine-pilgrimage.[20] As DeWeese writes:[21]

> even quite public manifestations of religiosity with roots in "Sufism" continued throughout the 19th and 20th centuries, not merely as part of an unchanging "tradition" that is sometimes posed as an alternative to "modernity," but as part of an ongoing negotiation about religious propriety that had deep roots in Muslim society in Central Asia, and had been "activated" at various times by political and social shifts, but continued to unfold, dynamically and (we might say) "innovatively," within new social, political, and religious frameworks entailed first by Tsarist rule, and then by the Soviet state."

Sufi tradition and Islamic education encompass all of these dynamics—and in this broad sense they most certainly survived the Soviet period. (As for *madrasas*, a couple of those survived too.)

A final, closely related point is worth adding to the list: the claim that the Soviet state succeeded in its attempt at isolating religion and reducing it to a mere component of ethnicity or national identity—divesting it, in other words, of any function as a source of ethical or moral values, spirituality, or meaningful knowledge about this world or the hereafter.[22] While the evidence in this book clearly points in other directions (as I will describe later), this vision of Soviet "secularization" is not baseless. On the contrary, is an insightful reading of what the Soviet state hoped to accomplish, and it accurately renders the self-described perceptions and experiences of many Soviet citizens. It is, moreover, an accurate reading of the secular propaganda directed at Soviet Muslims in wartime, which, for example, strenuously denuded legendary Muslim heroes of their traditional religious "baggage," just as the Orthodox saint Alexander Nevskii was desacralized for Russian audiences. Thus, a Muslim from Balkaria, interviewed shortly after the war, recalls:[23]

> We had tales (*rasskazy*) regarding old heroes; many of them had a religious basis. The Soviet regime did not use all folklore because much of it had religious aspects. The Soviet regime did not collect and publish our folklore because they could not use it. For instance, in one of our tales we have Asireb-Ali who raises his sword and causes the ocean to divide in order to get his troops across and his pursuers become porpoises. This kind of folklore the Soviets obviously could not use.

Moreover, there can be no doubt that many citizens who grew up in religious homes came to embrace Soviet atheism and its norms. Some Red Army veterans deny outright that religion played any substantive part in their own wartime experience. The scout Grigorii Konstantinovich Kudriavtsev tells us that "There was no relationship with religion in the war. We didn't know anything [about it], either. Nothing was mentioned anywhere. After the Revolution, the churches were ruined, destroyed; the priests were taken away somewhere ... It was later, at the end, that religion seemingly started to help in the war, something [happened] and Stalin started to relate to religion better."[24] The recollections of the Bashkir signalman Farit Minrahmanovich Kagarmanov, meanwhile, reflect a religiously diverse family life that is not easily reducible to the binary religious vs. secular:[25]

> We were utterly young, we didn't think about God. Moreover, our family was not at all devout (sovsem ne nabozhnaia byla). Mama still knew something, but papa was far from it. All they taught me was how to say "*yappar*" after eating, and I didn't know anything more. True, when I went into the army, upon parting, mama gave me a piece of paper on which something was written in Arabic letters. Throughout the entire war, I carried it in the pocket of my uniform (*gimnasterka*), but I didn't even know what was written there. A prayer, probably.

The religious landscape was varied, in other words, and the story of secularism in the Soviet Union is likewise a story worth telling. It is not the *only* story worth telling, however, and this book tells a much different story. As

Chapter 1 shows, not even Soviet atheist officials—Stalin foremost among them—believed that the state's anti-religious campaigns had been a success. There is a cunning, cynical pragmatism in the state's instrumentalizing of religion during the war—but there is also more than a hint of desperation. In a sense, the persistence of religious devotion into the war years is intuitive, especially among, say, the Muslims of Central Asia, for whom the anti-religious campaigns did not even begin in earnest until the late 1920s. A child born on the night of the October Revolution, in 1917, would have been just twenty-three years old when the war began. The first "Soviet generation," in other words, was still very young at the start of the war (and it is worth noting that some Soviet Muslim regions had been incorporated into the Bolshevik state only later, several years after 1917). Therefore, the "traditional" life that the state evoked in its wartime propaganda was not a hazy, unknowable past; rather, it constituted a past that most Soviet citizens had grown up with and knew intimately—a past that, as Stalin realized, was not even "past," but present, visible, and in some ways cherished.

It did not take a professional Soviet propagandist, much less a premier, to recognize these dynamics. Shortly after the war, a thirty-two-year-old Russian émigré engineer, the descendent of pre-Revolutionary gentry, reflected on these developments to an interviewer at the Hotel Midway in New York. His wry, compelling insights are worth quoting at length:[26]

Before the war, they used to speak about Soviet patriotism. After the war was under way, they soon learned that there was no such thing as Soviet patriotism and they returned to Russian patriotism. It was discovered that no one was willing to fight for Stalin. They delved into history to find traditional anti-German feeling. They brought up the First World War and the German invasion. They went back to Alexander Nevski and told how gloriously he had defended Russia against the German invader. Of course, Alexander Nevski is a saint of the Orthodox Church, but they neglected that aspect of him, and concentrated on his military exploits. They went back to using shoulder epaulets and kind of let people feel that this was a return to something dear, something familiar . . . Churches were opened all over. Metropolitan Sergeii was received in the Kremlin by Stalin. They rediscovered the story of the Novgorod merchant, Minin, and the noble, Pozharski, who, during the Time of Troubles, when Moscow was occupied by the Poles, organized a campaign which freed Moscow and drove out the Polish invader. They revived such historical figures as Suvorov, Alexander

Nevski, and Bogdan Khmelnitski and created new military decorations in their name. Somewhere or other they dug up an old man who had won a lot of decorations in the Tsarist army, including four St. George crosses. They had a picture of him in "Ogonyok." All this had an effect; people saw in it a return to the old, which played on their emotions. Of course, not as many will believe it if they try it again.

Indeed, while the religious revolution was perhaps its most enduring and consequential feature, the state's wartime bricolage of "tradition" was about much more than religion, and it amounted not only to a recognition that devotional life had survived, but to a broader appreciation, however grudging, that the fabled New Soviet Person still contained multitudes.

The result of this collision between expectation and reality was a historic negotiation. This book has focused on the religious dimensions of that negotiation, showing how Soviet Muslims carved out a space for their devotional life in the context of a fundamentally hostile state ideology. They achieved this not through dissent or covert "anti-Soviet activity," but by learning how to blend the state's dependable values and its more novel concessions into a distinctly *religious* patriotism that they could present—or take for granted—as entirely compatible with Soviet ideals.

Soviet Religious Propaganda and Wartime Documents

A Selection

The following documents are samples of one of the twentieth century's most unusual literary genres: Soviet religious propaganda. Dating to the Second World War or the years immediately afterward, these documents showcase the language by which Soviet Muslim, Jewish, and Buddhist leaders attempted to rally their communities to the war effort, to communicate with coreligionists abroad, and to curry favor with Stalin.

Document 1

A patriotic appeal to the Muslims of Transcaucasia (May, 1944)

In the name of God, the Merciful, the Compassionate
"Thank God, Lord of the world, the merciful, the compassionate."
Muslim ʿUlama and Clergy, Fellow Believers, Brothers and Sisters—Muslims!

We representatives of the Muslim clergy and believers of Azerbaijan, Georgia, and Armenia—having convened a sacred *kurultai* held from 2 to 5 Jumada al-Thani, 1363 (May 25–28, 1944), in the city of Baku—appeal to you on this day, when the fates of Muslims and all humanity are decided.

Our *kurultai* discussed, among other questions of paramount significance for the Muslims of Transcaucasia, the question of the atrocities of the damned Hitlerites (*Gitlerovtsy*) and their wicked henchmen in the sacred fatherland of the people of the Soviet Union.

For three years the world has burned in the fire of a war unprecedented in history, which has spawned horrors and deprivations as great as any humankind has ever experienced.

Obsessed by thirst for human blood, the butcher Hitler and his despicable henchmen have carried out malicious crimes and atrocities in almost all the countries of the world for the purpose of seizing these countries and turning their freedom-loving peoples into slaves.

The bloodthirsty hordes of Hitler have flooded the fertile lands of many countries with blood and tears; they have exterminated millions of people; they have turned hundreds of flourishing cities into ruins.

Treacherously breaking the contract it had made with the Soviet state, Hitler's Germany, with criminal treachery, attacked our great homeland.

Muslim brothers!

The brutal fascist hordes, driven and instigated by Hitler the executioner, have defiled our cherished land, have committed and continue to commit heinous crimes and atrocities on Soviet land.

Having annihilated everything in their path by fire and sword, Hitler's hordes came like a sandstorm (*samum*) through fertile cornfields and flourishing gardens—the gardens and cities of our homeland.

Millions of honest and free laborers of the Soviet Union, and among them our coreligionist brothers, have been subjected to merciless abuse and torture only because they did not wish to be slaves.

The gray beards of our fathers, the dear faces of our mothers, wives, sisters, and daughters, the breasts of the young, are drenched in their own innocent blood. Many holy buildings have been destroyed by fascist bombs and shells.

All the world has witnessed the bloody atrocities of the fascist butchers upon the war captives of the Red Army and the peaceful inhabitants of Soviet regions now under occupation. Millions of peaceful Soviet people have been driven into fascist labor [camps], and languish under the yoke of Hitler's butchers.

In the year 1361 (1942), Hitler's hordes reached the foothills of the Caucasus. The fascist beasts hoped to empty our flourishing, sunny Transcaucasian republics—Soviet Azerbaijan, Georgia, and Armenia. Hitler wanted to enslave the people of Transcaucasia, to annihilate and defile the mosques and prayer-houses in the blessed home of our ancestors, and, with the criminal hands of the German soldiers, dishonor our wives, sisters, and brides.

The fascists wished to stain the waters of the Kura and Araks with the blood of our babies and mothers.

But they were unable to carry out their black intentions. God's mercy dawned on the Muslims of Transcaucasia. The valor of our soldiers saved us from the enemy invasion.

The treacherous attack on the Soviet Union, the atrocities of the fascists on the sacred ground of our Homeland, have caused great anger among all the Soviet people. At the call of their Leader, the great Stalin, the Soviet people have called out as one, transforming the country into an impregnable fortress in the enemy's path.

The Muslim clergy of the Soviet Union, witnessing the atrocities of the Germans, unheard of in history, and carrying out the instructions of the sacred Qur'an, called upon Muslims to defend the Homeland—the Soviet Union, where all people are equal; where there is no place for enmity and discord between nations; where all, without exception, are given complete freedom of conscience (*pol'naia svoboda sovesti*). We called on our soldiers to annihilate the enemies of our Homeland, just as it is written in the holy Qur'an: "Fight them. God will punish them by your hands and will disgrace them and give you victory over them and satisfy the breasts of a believing people" (Qur'an 9:14).

Recognizing the defense of the Homeland as our sacred duty, the ulama and clergy of the Muslims of Transcaucasia, by the example of the Muslim clergy of other republics of the Soviet Union, issued a patriotic address to Muslims and called them to a merciless struggle with the bloodthirsty enemy of Islam and of all humankind—Hitlerite Germany.

We blessed our children and Muslim brothers for their combat exploits in battles with the fascist blood-drinkers and villains, and we gave them this mandate: be fearless heroes, crush the enemy, wipe the fascist beasts from the face of the earth.

We admonished them with the well-known hadith of the great messenger of God, Muhammad: "Love for the Homeland is a part of faith." Truly, whosoever is not a lover of their Homeland cannot be a believer.

Our call found a lively response in the hearts of our Muslim brothers. The fraternal people of Azerbaijan, Georgia, and Armenia, in unity and concord with all the people of the Soviet Union, have carried out a merciless war with the enemy. Our heroic sons and brothers, in fearsome battles, are fighting courageously for the freedom and honor of their homeland.

Who in the Soviet Union does not know about the feats of the 416 Taganrog, the 77 Simferopol, and other divisions of Azerbaijanis? And who has not heard of the amazing victories of these divisions as they smashed and drove out the fascist invaders from Taganrog, Melitopol', Simferopol, and other cities? We are proud before the homeland and the Soviet government to have such courageous sons—honored with the title Hero of the Soviet Union—as Hazi Aslanov, Salatdin Kizimov, Melik Mageramov, Museib Aliev, Fariz Safarov, Mekhti Guliev, Idris Suleimanov, Israil Chincharadze, Khidir Mustafaev, and others.

Our great prophet Muhammad, sending his soldiers into battle with the enemy, said to them:

"Discipline, devotion, obedience to orders, love for the art of war, a desire to raise the glory of your homelands [*rodiny*] and state—[this] will bring us victory."

Muslims at the home front are making all efforts to work selflessly in the [state] enterprises, factories, and fields, as is their duty before the homeland, and in every possible way rendering necessary aid to the Red Army and the country.

The blessed task of the Soviet people, the task of our Muslim brothers, has borne fruit. The courageous Red Army has rescued from the hateful enemy hundreds of cities and thousands of villages, and in a day not far away, she will completely cleanse the sacred Soviet land of the fascist invaders—led by their brilliant Commander, the Great Leader of all the peoples of the Soviet Union, the hope of all the world, the defender of the freedom of conscience (*zashchitnik svobodi sovesti*), Iusif Vissarionovich Stalin, steeped in the glory of the Red Army whose reach extends westward to the borders of our Fatherland, who continues to chase the enemy into the territory of Romania and brings liberation to the enslaved peoples of Europe.

We representatives of the clergy and believers of Azerbaijan, Georgia, and Armenia, gathered at the congress, appeal to you, dear brothers and sons, valiant warriors of the Red Army, to carry out the fight bravely, hand in hand and shoulder to shoulder with all the people of the Soviet Union, and to annihilate mercilessly the German invaders, to drive them from the sacred homeland, just as the Noble Word (Qurʾan) says:

"Fight in the path of God with those who fight with you; kill them wherever you overtake them, drive them out from wherever they drove you out."[1]

Dear brothers and sisters, sons and daughters on the home front!

We call upon you to work at your post still more selflessly and still better, and by your labors strengthen aid to the Red Army through equipment, munitions, and provisions. In this way you will fulfill the covenant of the sacred Qurʾan:

"Against them make ready your strength to the utmost of your power, including steeds of war, to strike terror into (the hearts of) the enemies, of Allah and your enemies."[2]

Esteemed ʿulama and Muslim clergy!

We shall fulfill our sacred duty to the homeland. We bring forth feverish prayers for the rapid annihilation of the enemy.

We urge faithful Muslims to bravery and heroism on the front of the War for the Fatherland; to selfless and honest labor on the home-front to aid the conclusive destruction of the enemy-of-all-humanity.

Pray and ask Almighty God to endow our great homeland with happiness and well-being.

Raise feverish prayers for the health and long life of the Great Leader of the people, Iusif Vissarionivich Stalin.

Battles to come between Hitler's solders, the Red Army, and the soldiers of our great allies, England and America, will justify our hopes for the liberation of humanity from the damned enemy and the restoration of peace and justice throughout the world.

May an eternal curse fall upon the evil Hitler and his accomplices.

With the help of great Allah, the enemy will be defeated and annihilated. AMEN.

On behalf of the *kurultai* of the Muslim clergy and believers of Transcaucasia:

Shaykh al-Islam: Ali Zade Akhund Aga, chairman (*predsedatel'*) of DUMZ

Mufti: Efendi Zade Ibrahim Efendi, Deputy Chairman of DUMZ

Members of the DUMZ from Azerbaijan:

Kazi Pishnamaz Zade Akhund Faradkulla

Kazi Akhundov Abdul Ragim

Kazi Magomedov Ramazan Efendi

Members of DUMZ from Georgia:

Kazi Beridze Rasim Suleiman Ogli

Kazi Bakirov Molla Nadershakh Usta Darvish Ogli

Members of DUMZ from Armenia

Kazi Bairamov Mirza Alekder

Kazi Magerramov Shaykh Alesker Abbas Ogli[3]

Document 2

Address from the leaders of the Spiritual Administration of the Muslims of Transcaucasia (DUMZAK) to the Muslims of Iran (June 13th, 1945)

We, the representatives of the Council for the Affairs of the Clergy of Transcaucasia, on behalf of the Muslims of Transcaucasia, and in particular on behalf of the Muslims of Soviet Azerbaijan, welcome our faithful brother-citizens of the Iranian state of the Shah-of-Shahs, and convey our sincere, heartfelt gratitude for their hospitality. As it says in the Qur'an: "All believers are brothers." Since olden times there have been the most amiable and neighborly relations between us and the Muslims of Iran, and this, of course, is entirely understandable. Now, as *shaykh al-islam* Malaeri, respected deputy (*deputat*) of the parliament, has graciously and hospitably received us at his home, we think that this friendship will be strengthened all the more. We hope that this friendship will continue always.

Today I want to tell my faithful brothers a few words about the lives and circumstances of the Muslims of Transcaucasia. You know, of course, that for more than four years the people of Europe, like the people of Russia and Transcaucasia, have been embroiled by the German fascists in a great calamity. Humanity has experienced, at the hand of bloody Hitler, unprecedented hardship and suffering. In this time flourishing countries have been destroyed, entire peoples have been exterminated *en masse*, the fruits of their labor looted and burned, innocent children murdered along with the elderly, women raped. Mad Hitler has thought to conquer the world, enslaving and subduing its peoples. Hitler's insolence has reached such a degree that after seizing several European countries, he attacked the sacred Muslim countries of Algeria, Tunisia, and Egypt, and finally, contrary to international law, he deceitfully violated his non-aggression pact with the Soviet Union and suddenly attacked it. He managed to seize several oblasts in Russia, and in those territories he proceeded to commit such evils and atrocities that words cannot describe them. Wherever the fascists set foot, cities and towns were reduced to ashes; the flourishing gardens and fields were left barren; peaceful populations were exterminated; and children, women, and the elderly were subjected to unprecedented abuses.

The Soviet state bravely defended our homeland, but all the same the fascists strove to conquer the Caucasus. When the insolence of the fascists reached such a degree, we Muslim scholars, along with the faithful among all the peoples of the Soviet Union, and on the basis of the teachings of the Qur'an, which reads "love for homeland is a part of faith,"[4] could not stand aside and regard such atrocities with indifference. As *shaykh al-islam* of the Caucasus, I, together with Shaykh Abdurakhim, the *qazi* of Baku, and the outstanding scholar Akhund Mirza Faradzhola Pishnemazada, after discussing the issue with other representatives of the clergy, decided to help our homeland and the allies of the Soviet government with all our strength and to the best of our abilities, contributing to the deliverance and salvation of the people of the world from the nightmare of fascist hegemony. Therefore, in 1942, we turned to faithful Muslims all over the world with an appeal to stand in defense of their homelands. Our appeal was published and circulated in the Soviet Union as well as in Iran. Thank God that under the brave leadership of His Excellency Marshal Stalin, the treacherous fascists have been dealt crushing blows and unavoidable defeats on all fronts. Muslim soldiers in particular have distinguished themselves in this struggle, steadfastly defending their sacred homeland with their own bodies.

After they had fulfilled their duty to humanity and to the Muslim world, we turned to Muslims in 1944 with another appeal, [this time] highlighting their obligations to their faith. It should be mentioned that the Muslim soldiers, like all the soldiers of the peoples of the USSR, have realized remarkable achievements in the mastery of the military arts. Many of them have attained the rank of general. Among them should be mentioned Hazi Aslamov, that glorious son of Azerbaijan, who fought bravely against the enemy of his homeland and died a hero's death on the battlefield. His death was a heavy loss for our people. For his service to his country and for his great military talent, fourteen government awards were bestowed upon this valiant general. His contributions were truly great.

On the fronts of the Great Patriotic War, the 416th Taganrog and 77th Simferopol divisions—whose fame has spread around the world—were particularly distinguished. But there are very many divisions similarly experienced and heroic, divisions that have rescued the peoples of the Soviet Union and Western Europe from captivity under the German fascists.

I want also to mention that four of the sons of Akhund Mirza Faradzhola Pishnemazada, two of my own sons, and four of my close relatives participated in these battles. We are duly proud of the bravery of heroes such as Salahaddin Kazimov, Melik Mageramov, Museib Aliev, Fariz Safarov, Mehdi Kuliev, Idris Suleimanov, Zuber Mustafaev, Aziz Abdurakhmanov, Nadzhafkoli Rafiev, Marvan Musaev, Adil Kuliev—among other Muslim heroes.

After the publication of this appeal [in 1944], faithful Muslims began turning to us with religious questions, and in order to satisfy the needs of the Muslim clergy we established a special directorate (*upravlenie*). In 1944 we turned to the Supreme Soviet, petitioning for permission to arrange the Directorate of Clerical Affairs. The Supreme Soviet promptly granted our petition, and by the end of last year we convened a conference of Muslim clergy in Baku. At that conference, honorary guests [included] Ziyauddin Babakhan from Tashkent; Mufti Rasuli from Ufa, Mufti Kadari from the Caucasus, Khizri Efendi from the North Caucasus, and Nasreddinov from Moscow.

The Directorate of Clerical Affairs is guided in its activities by the teachings of the Qur'an and the authentic traditions of Muhammad. In special cases, emergency meetings of all members of the directorate are convened. Our directorate engages in its functions the kind of educational work that strengthens friendship and unity among the peoples of the USSR; elevates and mobilizes collective farmers for their spring planting; encourages diligent and productive labor; nurtures feelings of faithfulness to government leaders and administration, etc.

The responsibilities of our directorate include assigning clerical leaders to various tasks and the safeguarding (*okhrana*) of mausoleums and monuments dedicated to scholars and great figures of Islam.

Now I can turn to answering the questions which have been presented to me by the chairman of the Society of Islamic Propaganda and the representative of Iran's Main Directorate of Propaganda Affairs and Publications.

The composition of the Directorate of Clerical Affairs for the Caucasus includes the following nine members: The chairman of the department is me, *shaykh al-islam* Alizada; the deputy chairmen are mufti Ibrahim Efendizada; Akhund Mulla Abdurrahim Akhundzada; Akhund Mirza Faradzhula Pishnemazada; Ramazan Efendi Mirza Aga Bala; Shaykh Ali Askar Maharramov; Mirza Ali Akbar Nemaz Ogly; Rahes Efendi; and Mulla Yunus. The first four members are based in Baku and directly supervise the affairs of the directorate. About 35 million Muslims live in the republics of the Soviet Union. All the above-mentioned scholars, along with many others, signed our wartime appeal to the Muslims of the world.

The manner of preaching in the [Soviet] mosques is almost the same as it is anywhere else. Our preachers read chapters from the Qur'an and discuss the lives of scholars, imams, and prophets. In each *raion*, the *oblast*s have their own religious scholars and students in religious schools, and at the present time more than 50 Caucasian students are studying in Iran and in Atabat (Iraq). After finishing their studies, they can lead spiritual activities, with the permission of the government. Our mosques, religious schools, and meeting-places remain just as they were before.

In the near future, the Directorate of Clerical Affairs will open a special religious school in which modern sciences and foreign languages will be taught alongside religious disciplines. A special building will be constructed for this school.

[Soviet] Muslims have their own special cemeteries, both new and old.

In light of the particularities of the international [political] environment, in recent years our Muslims have not embarked on the pilgrimage to Mecca.

In our country we have very many books and literatures in the Arabic language, printed in the old script, and there is no need to reprint these books in the newer script [i.e. Cyrillic]. However, all textbooks for middle and high schools are printed in the new script. In some educational institutions, the old script is taught along with the new script.

The same applies to the Qur'an. In the Soviet Union there are so many Qur'ans that there is no need to print them. There is not a single Muslim home in which one would not find several copies of the Qur'an. Almost all scientists of geology [*sic*] come from families in which, for generations, all members of the family engaged in religious activities. I myself come from such a family.

I want to say a few words about freedom of religion and faith in the Soviet Union. The peoples of the Soviet Union have always enjoyed freedom of conscience and, in particular, in the Soviet Constitution, Article 124 underlines the freedom of the conduct [of worship by] religious cults. In the Soviet Union, religion is separated from the state and the state from religion. We, the faithful scholars, have always enjoyed complete freedom to practice our religious rites. In our country the call to prayer is read from the minaret every morning and evening. In the mosques and at religious gatherings, sermons are delivered. Marriage and divorce proceedings are carried out by the scholars in accordance with the laws of the country. Prayers for the dead, charity, and other religious rites are carried out as in former times.

During mourning periods, sermons are composed and stories read about the martyrdom of the Imams. During the month of Muharram, the faithful perform mourning rites.

Believers are given all possible assistance by the government. In fact, if you compare Soviet times with the former, despotic regime, the difference is huge. The former [Tsarist] government did not pay any attention to Muslims, cutting off our path to the mastery of knowledge and science. Our life back then was dark and joyless. Muslim children and adolescents were deprived of the right to study, and we were not given access to state institutions and enterprises. Now the Soviet Union, without distinguishing between nationalities and religions, lovingly instructs all, without exception, in new sciences and teachings. Our young boys and girls study in first-rate educational institutions. The Muslims of our country show such a strong inclination to study that there is no need for coercion. [Even] in villages and hamlets it is rare to meet an illiterate person. In the republics there are thousands of primary schools, educational institutions, institutes, and technical schools. We have our own local cadres of highly skilled specialists, who are experts in various industries. We have such celebrated academics as Mir Kasymov, Topchibashev, Huseinov, Mir Ali Qashqai, Professor Karaev, Professor Fuad Efendiev, Professor Abdulaev, Professor Mammad Emin Efendiev, Professor Mammad Aliev, Professor Shamkhal Mammadov, and others.

In all institutions and higher organs of government, Muslim sons and daughters have proven themselves capable of fulfilling any task or duty in [various] enterprises, and it can be said that they have surpassed some other peoples in this respect.

The Azerbaijani people owe all these brilliant achievements to their dear leader, Jafar Baghirov, who, like a father, gives all his strength to the cause of educating the Azerbaijani people, not for a moment resting on successes already achieved. May God grant him a long life for the benefit of our homeland.

Of course, to a considerable extent, we owe all these accomplishments to the great leader of all the nations, Marshal Stalin, who, without distinguishing between nationalities and religions, thinks of the happiness and well-being of all mankind.

He casts his attentions upon all the people of the world, and in particular, his friendly attentions are drawn to the Iranian people—the ancient neighbor of our homeland. May God grant that the friendship between these two countries shall be durable and unending.

To conclude, I wish to express my sincere gratitude to His Majesty the Shah, to the spiritual leaders of Iran, and to all my Iranian friends for the courtesy and hospitality extended to me and my companions.[5]

Document 3

A patriotic appeal from a group of authorities from among the Buddhist clergy and believers (undated)

Om! May peace and happiness reign on earth!

From those who follow in the footsteps of the teachings of the great, omnipotent Burkhan Buddha, from his true students, having taken vows of chastity (*tselomudriia*),

To you, believer and student of the all-forgiving Burkhan Buddha; to you, beneath the blessed light of our sacred religion—to you we dedicate these words of revelation, these words of entreaty.

Yea, we give ourselves up to the mercy of the Almighty Burkhan! Yea, have mercy on us, Lord Buddha!

In 1941, in the middle of the month of June, on the 22nd day, the unfaithful (*nepravovernii*) German fascists—followers of the heretical teachings of the devil race of Chomnos[6] and their leader, Hitler, the hateful monster of the lineage of Abilgachin[7]—attacked our fatherland with treachery and inhumane cruelty; [they attacked] our family of peoples [joined] in friendship , followers of many different teachings and religions. Prompted by the most abominable and sinful notions, they destroyed our happy, peaceful life and commenced a bloody, criminal war with the goal of enslaving us and our children and grandchildren.

All of the people populating our vast land, the followers of all faiths and religions, rose to [make] sacred and uncompromising war against the fascist monsters [to safeguard] their future happiness, and for the honor and freedom of their country.

The *Bators*—soldiers of our mighty Red Army—have dealt crushing blows against the heretic fascists, day by day driving them back to their animal lair (*v ikh zverinoe logovo*). In 1943, in the span of just five months, the Red Army has liberated and returned to the people 160 cities, including Donbass and Kiev, the capital of Ukraine, and 38,000 settlements; and also 82 cities [*sic*] and 320 railway stations. With growing force they continue to drive the heretic troops back to the west, restoring our blessed land for the good of the people.

The German bloodsuckers (*krovopiitsy*), during the previous 100 years, have more than once attacked our blessed people, [each time] failing to seize our extensive grainholdings, to take possession of the rich soil of our land, and to capture and enslave our freedom-loving, peaceful people.

Instead, by the will of the Almighty and by the strength of the radiant hero-ancestors (*bogatyrei-predkov*), more than once they were betrayed by death and dishonor.

Thus, in 1242 they found themselves entombed in Chudskoe Lake beneath the sword of the luminous Russian *bogatyr* Alexander Nevskii. In 1760 the Russian army under the leadership of the famous *bator* Suvorov smashed the Germans and took Berlin.

In 1914 they attacked our homeland three times, and the Buryat-Mongol people—followers of the Buddhist religion from time immemorial—took part in our victory over them. Their sons, blessed by the sacred fathers of our religion, spilled their own blood on the fields of battle, displaying their high military valor and bravery.

Everyone knows how our religious leaders, the Pandita Khambo [Lamas] IROLTUEV and ITIGILOV [*sic*], along with other leading lamas and other *dachans*, on behalf of the faithful populations, laid sundry, precious sacrifices upon the altar of the father-land, and how they also organized charitable institutions to help wounded and disabled soldiers.

All the people residing in our great, blessed Soviet Union, the followers of many different faiths and religions, including our Buryat-Mongols (followers of the sacred Buddhist religion and since time immemorial), together with the great Russian people, have stood [together] more than once in the face of great threats on the part of foreign interventionists (*so storony inostrannykh interventov*), and, hand in hand and heart to heart, with unprecedented selflessness, they have endured hard days of adversity and suffering.

So too now, when the German heretic fascists and their ringleader, the monster of the Chomnos, Hitler, have bloodthirsty intentions for us, we Buryat-Mongols, together with other peoples, take part in the sacred war for the liberation of our land.

The unfaithful heretic Hitler boastfully speaks of himself as a venerator of Christ [*sic!*], but everywhere he has set foot, there has been unbelievable evil: the barbaric destruction of Christian churches and cathedrals, the malicious despoilment of all that is good concerning the spirit and traditions of the people, the heartless slaughter of the elderly, women, and children, the disgusting picture of violence, looting, and arson in peaceful towns and villages, the destruction of the cultural values and monuments of the elders—all of this shows with inescapable clarity the beastly and devilish face of these brigands.

Thus we, the followers of the Buddhist religion, and its true students, having taken the vows of chastity—to you, the believers and students of the salvific power of the three jewels of Burkhan, to all of you, the suffering and the thirsty, the men and the women, we turn with an appeal.

Give all your strength, all your knowledge and thoughts, to the great, sacred, godly effort of the defense of the homeland. In the name of Burkhan we bless you in new struggles and military feats. Work in the *kolkhoz*, *sovkhoz*, and [state] enterprises bravely and in good faith for the sake of the homeland. Multiply your strength and everything needed for a rapid victory over the enemy.

Swear before Burkhan that our selfless faith, our courageous labor, and our purehearted thoughts will always be directed toward the most sacred task: the task of defending the fatherland. We will remember that our slightest laxity, carelessness, and idleness is a retreat from the sacred task of helping the homeland—it is apostasy (*bogootstupnichestvo*), a scourge of the blackest evil.

Those who selflessly believe in the blessed Buddhist faith and honor the precious *arshan*s, the scholars of the Buddha—they will never retreat from their true, sacred mission: to sacrifice all of their lives on the altar of the fatherland (*na altar' otechestva*).

Follow the path of the scholars of almighty Burkhan, be true to your luminous oath—that is the sole mission for the faithful in this life.

"If they have the will to pursue the truth, then people's lives will be happy and they will be able to defend their country, their valor, and their freedom"—thus taught the Buddha.

Faithful Buddhists!

We shall labor selflessly, and god will send a prompt victory over the tribe of Chomnos and their evil leader, Hitler. Our effort will lead soon enough to their being cast into a bottomless hell for all of their evil deeds.

Day and night we shall pray to the three jewels for salvation and to all the Burkhans for peace and a future happy life in a land without the Chomnos. We shall pray that our valiant Red Army will cut the enemies of humanity into pieces with their radiant, fiery sword.

The war's turning point has come. Still more will we bring all our might to securing victory, and the enemy shall be defeated.

Your labor shall bear fruit for as long as you shall live!

Glossary [reproduced from the original document]:
Chomnos: The Devil
Abilgachin: The death-bringer
Bator: hero
Bandido-khambo [*Pandita Hambo*]: A rank among Buryat Buddhist lamas
Datsan: Buddhist monastery
Burkhan: god
Arshan: Holy water[8]

Document 4

A Rosh Hashanah greeting to Stalin, from "the Chairman (*predsedatel'*) of Moscow's Religious Jews" (1943)

To I.V. Stalin (Moscow, Kremlin):
  Dear Iusif Vissarionovich!
  On the 29th of this month, we religious Jews (*religioznye evrei*) mark the new year—5704 by our reckoning—and on that day, referred to as the day of spiritual cleansing and renewal and filled with important and sacred content for every faithful Jew, we turn to you, our wise leader and great commander, with an entreaty, and with cordial wishes for your happiness, fortune, health, and well-being in the coming year. May God keep you and be with you hereinafter in all your thoughts and deeds, which are directed exclusively for the benefit of our homelands (*rodiny*) and our Soviet people (*narod*).

  By established tradition, on the day of the New Year every faithful Jew looks into his soul, considers his actions, and answers before God and before his conscience for the deeds he committed over the past year, and he prepares his path for the year to come. On this day he communicates with his heavenly father, and in his prayers he asks for peace to descend upon all the world, for justice to triumph, and for the victory of goodness and reason. We Soviet religious Jews, on this day of cleansing, dedicate all our thoughts and feelings to our beloved country; we pray to the Almighty for the prosperity of our great state—the homelands of fraternal peoples, the fatherland of truth and justice—and for the granting of health and long life to its supreme leader, whose wise leadership has granted us the boundless possibility to lead the full and beneficial lives of worthy and proud Soviet citizens.

  Now we are celebrating the third New Year under conditions of war. For three years now we Jews, shoulder to shoulder with all the fraternal peoples of our country, have borne the hardships of this cruel, bloody war. Alongside all the others, we, with great eagerness, make huge sacrifices in the name of our Homelands (*Rodiny*) and along with the others we, with great exultation and pride, celebrate the success of our courageous Red Army, in which there are more than a few sons from among our own people, going from victory to victory under your brilliant leadership and bringing us closer to the day of final celebration. And on this third New Year's day of the war we—taking stock of our deeds and giving an account before our own conscience of our actions and thoughts— can bravely say what is in our hearts: in the past year we fought with great love and de- votion to our homeland, for our heroic Red Army, and for you, our beloved leader; our blood boiled over with hate for the fascist enemy; and we gave all our might and ability to the task of war and victory. In this present New Year, we once again offer our prayers to the heavenly father; we promise still more and still more resolutely to strain our might to reach the final victory—the complete banishment of the despised enemy from the boundaries of our homeland. We assure you, dear leader and teacher, that our New Year's prayers are dedicated to one goal and one wish: that the coming year of 5704 is—for you, and for our heroic Red Army, at whose head you stand, and also for all of us—a year of brilliant victory; a year of shining happiness, gladness, and well-being; a year of won- drous progress; a year in which you are destined to see the realization of all of your ideals and reap the benefits of your great, tireless concerns and labors for the benefit of our homeland and all of our Soviet people.

On behalf of the religious Jews,
The Chairman (*predsedatel'*) of Moscow's Religious Jews
Samuil Solomonovich Chobrutskii[9]

Document 5

Gabdrahman Rasulev, a patriotic appeal to
Soviet Muslims (May, 1942)

Dear Muslim Brothers!

The foregoing statements of God and His prophet, the great Muhammad, exhort you, Muslims, to fight unsparingly on the battlefield for the liberation of the great homeland, of all humanity, and of the Muslim world from the yoke of the fascist villains. To the men and women on the home front: do not succumb to cowardice and panic; give all of your strength to doing what is necessary for the successful conduct of the War for the Fatherland, and for the security and the lives of its people.

In this holy War for the Fatherland (*v etoi sviatoi Otechestvennaia voina*) against fascist Germany and her henchmen, show before all the world—proving your righteousness— your loyalty to your homeland. Pray in the mosques and prayer-houses for the victory of the Red Army.

We scholars of Islam and spiritual leaders living in the Soviet Union call all Muslims to the unanimous defense of the beloved homeland and the Muslim world from the German fascists and their henchmen. Pray to great and gracious God to hasten the deliverance of all humanity and the Muslim world from the tyranny of the misanthrope-fascists (*chelovekonenavistnikov-fashistov*).

There is not one true believer (*pravovernyi*) whose son, brother, or father does not fight today against the Germans, or who lags behind in taking up arms for our common homeland. Likewise, there is probably no one on the home front who has not aided in victory through their labor in the plants and factories. For we Muslims well recall the words of the Prophet Muhammad (peace be upon him!): "Love for the homeland is a part of faith."[10]

Document 6

A telegram to Stalin from Ishan Babakhanov and other leaders of the Spiritual Administration of the Muslims of Central Asia and Kazakhstan (SADUM) (October 17, 1943)

From the Representatives of the Muslim Directorates and Believers of Uzbekistan, Tajikistan, Turkmenistan, Kyrgyzstan, and Kazakhstan:

The clerical assembly of the representatives of the Muslim Directorates and Believers of Uzbekistan, Tajikistan, Turkmenistan, Kirghizstan, and Kazakhstan, which opened today in the city of Tashkent, warmly greets you, highly-respected Iusif Vissarionovich, as the head of the Soviet government and Supreme Commander-in-Chief.

From the beginning of the Great Patriotic War of the peoples of the Soviet Union against Hitlerite Germany and her allies in Europe, the Muslim clergy of Central Asia and Kazakhstan has called upon faithful Muslims to defend the dear homeland and has blessed them in their military endeavors. The Muslim clergy has offered sundry prayers for the victory of the Soviet military. In its written appeals and in its preaching before the faithful Muslims serving on the home-front, it has called and continues to summon them to honest and tenacious labor, and to provide aid to the front through the increased production of high-quality raw materials, foodstuffs, ammunition, and weapons. Today we confirm with satisfaction the fact that our fervent prayers have been heard by Almighty God—the Red Army, under your Supreme Command, is cleansing the Soviet lands of the enemy, each day liberating tens and hundreds of towns and cities.

The assembly of Representatives of the Muslim clergy and faithful assures you, highly respected Iusif Vissarionovich, that the Muslim clergy, with our prayers and preaching, will call upon faithful Muslims—both those at the front and those provisioning the front—to mercilessly eliminate the enemy, sparing neither any effort nor even, if necessary, their own lives. The Muslim clergy will also call upon men and women on the frontlines to labor with tenfold the energy in order to furnish the front with everything necessary for the prompt destruction of the insidious enemy.

Raising our fervent prayers to God, from the bottom of our hearts we wish you, our radiant sun Iusif Vissarionovich, good health and many long years of life. May Almighty God assist you in carrying out—as is now your lot—great, historic actions and the liberation of our homeland and all the peoples of Europe oppressed by Hitler's Germany. Amen.[11]

Document 7

A patriotic appeal to the Muslims of Xinjiang, on behalf of Ishan Babakhanov and other representatives of SADUM (1945)

On behalf of all Turkestan's Muslims, we appeal to the Muslim world with this letter that describes concisely our past and present [circumstances], such as they are, with the goal of dispelling various assumptions and notions about us.

Turkestan has been for millennia—and remains—the sacred fatherland of the Uzbeks, Tajiks, Turkmens, Kazakhs, Kyrgyz, Uyghurs, and Karakalpaks. Our ancestors courageously defended their fatherland from the incursions of attackers, who invaded repeatedly but failed to enslave them and annihilate our people. Our land preserves within it the remains of great men. In the Fergana Valley's Shahimardan there is the tomb of Muhammad's son-in-law, Ali. In Tashkent rest the remains of sacred ʿUkasha, one of the companions of the Prophet. In Samarkand there is Shah-i Zinda, its graves known to all, the holiest among them being that of Qusam Ibn Abbas. In Turkestan there is the grave of the holy Khwaja Ahmad Yasavi. In Bukhara there is the shrine of Baha al-Din Naqshbandi [sic], shaykh Alim al-Bakharzi, holy Kulaia, and there are tens of shrines of other saints located in other corners of our noble Turkestan. Magnificent mausoleums have been erected over many of these [sites], and the Muslims of Turkestan say prayers over the graves of these saints. May there be a place for them in paradise. Amen.

Over the course of centuries, our blessed cities of Bukhara, Samarkand, Khiva, Tashkent, and others have been epicenters of science, knowledge, and holy wisdom for Khurasan, Egypt, Arabia, Kashgar, India, Iran, and Afghanistan. Great scholars, jurists, astronomers, architects, and poets have issued from Turkestan. The wise Ibn Sina, the incomparable scholar Ulugh Beg, and others are among these outstanding pupils, and they later became teachers in Turkestan's madrasas. Our ancestors constructed magnificent buildings for the mosques and madrasas of Bibi Khanim, Khwaja Ahrar, Ulugh Beg, Shir Dor, Tillia-Kari.

The libraries of *Bukhara-i sharif*, Samarkand, Tashkent, Urgench, Alma-Ata, Frunze, and other cities hold millions of books and unique manuscripts. In the Tashkent state library alone there are around two million volumes, among which is the pearl of Muslim wisdom, the Noble Word (the Qurʾan) written by the hand of the holy Caliph ʿUthman himself, who was martyred around the time this Qurʾan [was written]. The pages of this holy book are made of gazelle skin, and one can still see spots of noble blood upon them. Muslims of Turkestan have touched their hands to this holy Qurʾan on the occasion of congresses or trade agreements. In these libraries there are authentic manuscripts of all six "Sahih" [authentic *hadith* collections]—those sacred Muslim books. There is also a manuscript of the poem *Kutadgu-bilig*, compiled in the 11th century in Kashgar by the blessed Yusuf al-Khojib [*Yusuf Khass Hajib Balasaguni*]. This manuscript is written in the Turkish "Khaqani" dialect—ancestor of the Uzbek and Uyghur literary languages. In the Tashkent library are all volumes of the dictionary of Mahmud al-Kashghari, the works of the famous scholars and theorists Abu-Nasr al-Farabi, Abu Ali Ibn Sina Bukhari, al-Biruni Khorezmi, Ahmad al-Fergani, Muhammad Ibn Musa, al-Khorezmi, at-Taftazani, and others.

Before the Great Soviet Revolution, we Muslims of Turkestan were disunited and scattered, lacking our own statehood. Under the banner of the Soviet government we united and established our free republics. The national discord which abided before the Revolution was liquidated. In Turkistan we established the independent republics of Uzbekistan, Tajikistan, Turkmenistan, Kazakhstan, and Kyrgyzstan, which have been included in the Soviet Union as equal members together with the republics of other peoples. The peoples of all these republics built their capital cities, adorned them with the magnificent buildings of state institutions, houses of culture and learning, medical institutions, universities, schools, and so on. We now have schools of higher learning for any branch of the sciences, in which thousands of Muslim youths are studying.

Shining forth for five hundred years on the threshold of the majestic madrasa of Ulugh Beg in Samarkand is a noble saying of our Prophet: "Striving for knowledge is the duty of every Muslim." Only under the Soviet government is this [saying] embodied in life itself. Now we have our own doctors, teachers, professors, agronomists, engineers, officers, pilots. Turkestan's Muslims have gained the opportunity to apply their skills in all areas of life, and to ensure their prosperity, while remaining firm in the clear faith of Islam.

Thanks to the constitution of the USSR, the basic law of our state, written by the blessed hand of the great and wise Stalin, we are the masters of our own policies, economy, culture, language, creed, customs, and private lives. Article 124 of the constitution of our state grants every citizen the right to profess whatever religion they please. The clergy and faithful of various cults have their own Directorates and in matters of the exercise of religious rites the state does not attempt any sort of obstruction (*ne chinit nikakikh prepiatstvii*).

It is known to Muslims all over the world that the stewardship of Muslim religious activities in Turkistan is entrusted to the Spiritual Directorate of the Muslims of Central Asia and Kazakhstan, elected in the great congress of Muslim clergy and believers.

At the very moment when the great friendly family of the peoples of the Soviet Union had built a peaceful life for themselves; when our people's economic power grew and strengthened and we had built the largest factories, companies, railroads, and irrigation canals in all of Central Asia; when heavy agriculture developed as we facilitated the successful mass application of new agricultural machines; when the political and cultural level of the people had increased—it was then, in 1941, that the armies of Hitler's Germany, with no declaration of war, perfidiously violated the pact between the Soviet Union and Germany and attacked our Sacred Homeland. Since the first days of the war we have blessed our sons and brothers to defend the Homeland from the treacherous enemy that has flooded Europe with blood.

The Germans want to annihilate and exterminate most of the population of our country, and to press those who remain into slavery, leaving thousands of our children crippled and orphaned. [They want] to destroy our home, trample our rights, humiliate and debase our religion, convert Muslims to Protestantism [*sic*], and leave barren our fragrant gardens, as the great irrigation canals built by the hands of the people flow—along with water, giving life and happiness to our people—with the innocent blood and tears of the elderly, women, and children.

The Germans and Romanians momentarily occupying the Crimea, which is inhabited mostly by Muslims, ravaged and devastated that flourishing region, liquidating the national self-determination of the Crimean Muslims and bringing unprecedented mockeries upon their everyday customs and religion.

In the North Caucasus, which has likewise been visited by the German monsters, they have committed atrocious crimes: they have robbed the entire population, burned and blown up the dwellings of the mountain-dwellers, and taken thousands of men and women into slavery and captivity. In Krasnodar *krai*, Kharkov, and other oblasts of the Ukraine, by the orders of German commanders, thousands of people, including the infirm, elderly, women, and children, have been poisoned by suffocating gas in tightly enclosed cars. These atrocities are confirmed by evidence from German officers and functionaries which emerged in the course of their open trials, which were conducted after the liberation of these *raions* from the invaders by Soviet troops. Numerous analogous facts are recorded in reports signed by eyewitnesses. The Germans have shot, hanged, burned, tortured and tormented soldiers and the wounded whom they have taken captive, including Muslims.

"Love for the Homeland is a part of faith"—so said our Prophet. For that reason, we spiritual shepherds of Turkestan's Muslims have called upon our flock to come forward in the advance against the villainous armies of Hitler for the defense of our honor and freedom, our faith and glory. In the words of our Lord: "Fight in the way of Allah those who fight you but do not transgress. Indeed. Allah does not like transgressors. And kill them wherever you overtake them and expel them from wherever they have expelled you" [al-Bakara 190–191; *incorrectly cited here as 186–187*]. Our soldiers on the front have performed miracles of courage, day and night exterminating the Hitlerite invaders and liberating from them hundreds of cities and thousands of villages. Many sons of Turkistani Muslims have distinguished themselves in battle and have received high awards, including the rank of Hero of the Soviet Union.

Men and women on the home front tirelessly forge weapons, offer the warfront all necessities, and supply their dear army with food and equipment, ammunition and weaponry, machine guns and armaments, tanks and airplanes. Besides this, Muslims have donated their own savings to the needs of the front, totaling tens of millions of rubles as well as clothing and food.

The troops of our allies in England and America are dealing the enemy blows from the air. They have smashed the German-Italian forces in Africa, which has been completely cleared of enemy forces, and in Italy, which has actually withdrawn from the war. The partisans in occupied countries of Europe, those national avengers, are dealing blows to the enemy every day from the rear, destroying roads and bridges, derailing trains, blowing up and burning warehouses of ammunition and supplies. A front is widening against the German invaders and their accomplices in Europe. The hour of victory against the fascists is near. To accelerate victory against the enemy, we servants of the Muslim religion pray to Allah every day, five times a day, in the mosques. We offer our appeal to all the Muslims of the world. The Hitlerites are the enemies of all freedom-loving peoples, and especially of Muslims. For that reason, we Muslim clergy living in the Soviet Union appeal to the Muslims of all the world to rise up against the wicked fascist enslavers. Those who cannot play a direct part in this great struggle with weapons in hand can provide moral support for those fighting. Our hearts are bound to yours, such that your happiness gladdens us, and your sorrow grieves us; and so should our happiness gladden you, and you should share our sorrow. Soon the sun will rise over the enslaved countries, and the day of living a free, happy life will come.

In historic days to come, we will meet you, our noble brothers, and you will be our dear guests in the house of love and friendship, in the abode of peace and security.

Our coreligionist brothers of the world! People of clean conscience, firm in faith! Pray for the prompt victory of the Soviet army, which carries banners of freedom and independence for enslaved peoples. Do not believe the various heinous slanders circulated about our country by our enemies and yours, may a curse fall upon their heads.

Raising our prayers for the prompt victory of the Allied troops over the Hitlerite invaders and their accomplices; raising our prayers and blessings for the well-being and happiness of all Muslims.

Signed:

Chairman (predsedatel) of SADUM, Mufti
Shaykh [Ishan] Babakhan Abumadzhitkhanov

Member of the presidium of SADUM, *qadi*
Murad Khodzha Salikhov

Member of the presidium of SADUM, *qadi*
Imam-Khatib Ziyatdin Kari Babakhanov[12]

Notes

Introduction

1. The war era is invariably regarded as a pivotal moment in the history of Soviet religion. Nevertheless, the immense English-language historiography of the Second World War has largely passed over questions of religion when it comes to Soviet Muslims, and Allied Muslims in general, the majority of whom fought for the Soviet Red Army. For example, Yaacov Ro'i, in his deeply researched study of Soviet bureaucratic responses to Islam, observes that the war era marked a crucial shift—indeed, the book contains the phrase "Second World War" in its subtitle—but devotes just four pages of commentary to those pivotal years (see Ro'i, *Islam in the Soviet Union: From the Second World War to Gorbachev* [New York: Columbia University Press, 2000], 102–105). Most recently, the finest book yet written on Soviet Islam, Eren Tasar's *Soviet and Muslim*, begins with a chapter titled, "Word War II and Islamically Informed Soviet Patriotism"; this insightful sixty-three-page chapter contains just eleven pages, however, discussing events that occurred specifically in the war years of 1941–45 (see Tasar, *Soviet and Muslim: The Institutionalization of Islam in Central Asia* [New York: Oxford University Press, 2017], 15–16, 46–50, 53, 57, 75–76). By contrast, at least nine books on the religious aspects of Muslim-Axis alliances have appeared in English since 2007. The best of these is David Motadel's outstanding *Islam and Nazi Germany's War* (Cambridge: Harvard University Press, 2014). Other works include David G. Dalin and John F. Rothmann, *Icon of Evil: Hitler's Mufti and the Rise of Radical Islam* (New York: Random House, 2008); Barry Rubin and Wolfgang G. Schwanitz, *Nazis, Islamists, and the Making of the Modern Middle East* (New Haven, CT: Yale University Press, 2014); Chuck Morse, *The Nazi Connection to Islamic Terrorism: Adolf Hitler and Haj Amin al-Husseini* (Washington, DC: WND, 2010); Jeffrey Harf, *Nazi Propaganda for the Arab World* (New Haven, CT: Yale University Press, 2009); Edwin Black, *The Farhud: Roots of the Arab-Nazi Alliance in the Holocaust* (Dialog Press, 2010); Klaus-Michael Mallmann and Martin Cüppers, *Nazi Palestine: The Plans for the Extermination of the Jews in Palestine* (Philadelphia: Enigma Books, 2013); Francis R. Nicosia, *Nazi Germany and the Arab World* (Cambridge: Cambridge University Press, 2014); and Matthias Küntzel, *Jihad and Jew-Hatred: Islamism, Nazism, and the Roots of 9/11* (New York: Telos Press, 2007). The largest and best-known Muslim cohort to fight alongside the Nazis was the Turkistan Legion, consisting of some thirty battalions of Muslims from the Caucasus and Central Asia. In all, perhaps 180,000 ex-Soviet Muslims fought for the Nazis. This is a considerable number, but to put this number in perspective, it amounts to fewer than half the number of Kazakh Red Army soldiers alone, the vast majority of whom were Muslims. Farther afield, Sayaka Chatani offers a fascinating study of Japanese colonial

subjects who volunteered to fight for the Japan: *Nation-Empire: Ideology and Rural Youth Mobilization in Japan and Its Colonies* (Ithaca: Cornell University Press, 2018).

2. While it is difficult to arrive at a conclusive estimation of the total number of Muslims who fought in the Red Army over the course of the war, a few estimates of the total number of soldiers drawn from Muslim-majority regions can demonstrate that they numbered in the millions overall: among Kazakhs, some 450,000 fought on the front lines; another 681,000 were drafted from Azerbaijan; and 126,000 were drafted from Dagestan (Roberto J. Carmack, Kazakhstan in World War II: Mobilization and Ethnicity in the Soviet Empire (Lawrence, KS: University Press of Kansas, 2019), 12; Martha Brill Olcott, *The Kazakhs* [Washington, DC: Hoover Press, 1987], 188; A.B. Iunusova, ed., *225 let Tsentral'nomu dukhovnomu upravleniiu musul'man rossii: Istoricheskie ocherki* [Ufa, 2013], 264). Beyond the Soviet Union, an additional 700,000 Muslims fought for the Indian Army; perhaps 900,000 colonial subjects from Muslim-majority North Africa fought for France (Xavier Bougarel, Raphaëlle Branche, and Cloé Drieu, "Introduction," in Xavier Bougarel, Raphaëlle Branche, and Cloé Drieu, eds., *Combatants of Muslim Origin in European Armies in the Twentieth Century: Far From Jihad* [London: Bloomsbury, 2017], 2–3); and a smaller—but still significant—number of Muslim soldiers from Southeast Asia, the United States, and the Balkans joined the Allied struggle.

3. AkadNkKaz MS 123 VII, 7–8.

4. Khalid, *Islam after Communism* (Berkeley: University of California Press, 2014), 78.

5. Until recent years, both evidence of and research on Soviet Muslim devotional life in the pivotal years of the 1930s to the 1940s was flimsy. This scarcity of research was not limited to religion but extended to entire Muslim-majority regions: as Eren Tasar writes, the history of Central Asia (for example) "during the 1930s and 1940s largely remains unstudied in both Western and Central Asian scholarship" (Tasar, *Soviet and Muslim*, 45). As recently as the early 2010s, meanwhile, the reasonable consensus among leading historians was that Soviet Islam was visible almost exclusively through the lens of "official" sources—that is, through the eyes of militantly atheist government agents (see Adeeb Khalid, "Searching for Muslim Voices in Post-Soviet Archives," *Ab Imperio* 4 [2008], 304; for a contrasting—and somewhat more optimistic—approach, see Paolo Sartori, "Toward a History of the Muslim's Soviet Union: A View from Central Asia," *Die Welt des Islams* 50 [2010], 325; and Michael Kemper, *Studying Islam in the Soviet Union* [Amsterdam: Amsterdam University Press, 2008]). Tasar summarizes the longstanding predicament: "many of the documents generated by Islamic scholars during the Soviet period—such as religious poetry and biographies of 'ulama—exist only in handwritten, manuscript form, and were often hidden in the private family libraries of their authors, where they largely remain today. The discovery and processing of such materials is only beginning now" (Tasar, *Soviet and Muslim*, 13).

6. In Kumyk, the last lines read: "*Taziyatda yoldashlar ëre turar. / Yasha—yasha, kommunist partiyasï, / bu zulmunu azatlyq yolgha burar!*" A.M. Adzhiev, ed., *Fol'klor narodov Dagestana o Velikoi Otechestvennoi voine* (Makhachkala: Dagestanskii nauchnyi tsentr Rossiiskoi akademii nauk Institut iazyka, literatury i isskustva im. Gamzata Tsadasy, 2006), 37.

7. At the time of writing, Allen J. Frank is completing a monograph on Kazakh Muslim wartime poetry based on hundreds of Red Army poems, each suffused with religious imagery and themes: Frank, *Faith and Trauma on the Eastern Front: Kazakh Soldiers in the Red Army, 1939–1945* (in preparation). I am very grateful to Dr. Frank for the opportunity to read a draft of this groundbreaking work-in-progress, which has been an inspiration to me in the course of writing this book.

8. This perception—unanimously rejected by historians in the past two decades—was eagerly adopted by Western Cold War–era analysts of Soviet Islam. Thus Alexandre Bennigsen and S. Enders Wimbush: "Sufi Islam is pronouncedly hostile to Soviet power; the official Islamic establishment is loyal and submissive to it"; and "Sufis view Soviet power as the devil incarnate, while Soviet authorities view the brotherhoods as a dangerous aberration that must be destroyed" (*Mystics and Commissars: Sufism in the Soviet Union* [London: C. Hurst, 1985], 40; 111). See also Bennigsen and Marie Broxup, *The Islamic Threat to the Soviet State* (London: Croom Helm, 1983).

9. For example, V.N. Basilov and K.K. Kubakov, two Soviet-era, anti-religious activists who were also prominent ethnographers, make the alarming claim that, in the nineteenth century, human sacrifice was practiced during Central Asian canal-cleaning ceremonies: "Sacrifices completed the construction and cleaning of irrigation canals in Central Asia. As a rule, the animals were killed by cutting their throats with their blood dripping into the water. Even in the last century Uzbeks and Tajiks sacrificed human life as a last resort" (Basilov and Kubakov, "Survival of Pre-Muslim Beliefs in Islam," in S.C. Dube and V.N. Basilov, eds., *Secularization in Multi-Religious Societies: Indo-Soviet Perspectives* [New Delhi: Indian Council of Social Science Research, 1983], 228). Two years later, Bennigsen and Wimbush would praise Basilov's work as "authentically scientific" (*Mystics and Commissars*, 133). See also Jeff Eden, "A Soviet Jihad against Hitler: Ishan Babakhan Calls Central Asian Muslims to War," *Journal of the Economic and Social History of the Orient* 59 (2016), 241–246.

10. Devin DeWeese, "Islam and the Legacy of Sovietology: A Review Essay on Yaacov Ro'i's *Islam in the Soviet Union,*" *Journal of Islamic Studies* 13/3 (2002), 298–330. Kemper writes: "I am inclined to argue that Soviet writings on Islam, just as their counterparts from the Cold War period in the West, should be dismissed completely unless their findings can be supported by testimonies of the Muslims themselves" (*Studying Islam in the Soviet Union,* 21).

11. See, for example, Devin DeWeese, "Survival Strategies: Reflections on the Notion of Religious 'Survivals' in Soviet Ethnographic Studies of Muslim Religious Life in Central Asia," in F. Mühlfried and S. Sokolovskiy, eds., *Exploring the Edge of Empire: Soviet Era Anthropology in the Caucasus and Central Asia* (Münster: Lit Verlag, 2011), 35–58; Devin DeWeese, "Shamanization in Central Asia," *Journal of the Economic and Social History of the Orient* 57 (2014), 326–363; Paolo Sartori, "Of Saints, Shrines, and Tractors: Untangling the Meaning of Islam in Soviet Central Asia," *Journal of Islamic Studies* 30/3 (2019), 1–40. See also Sonja Luehrmann's highly original *Religion in Secular Archives: Soviet Atheism and Historical Knowledge* (New York: Oxford University Press, 2015).

12. Longue durée conclusions are better suited to longue durée studies. Several such studies are available: see, for example, Tasar, *Soviet and Muslim*; Khalid, *Islam after Communism*; and Sartori, "Toward a History of the Muslim's Soviet Union: A View from Central Asia."

13. Thus, Karel C. Berkhoff writes, "overall the rapprochement with the leaders of religious denominations was meager. It was primarily meant to influence the Allies, who were told much more about it, and those citizens who were and had been living under German rule. Otherwise considered virtually useless, what could have been an important contribution to mobilization was not employed extensively in the media" (*Motherland in Danger: Soviet Propaganda during World War II* [Cambridge, MA: Harvard University Press, 2012], 209.

14. G. Saksin to V.M. Molotov and A.S. Shcherbakov (September 13, 1941), *PDDUM*, 137; L.A. Koroleva and A.A. Korolev, *Islam v Srednem Povolzh'e. 1940-e gg.* (Penza: Penzenskii gosudarstvennyi universitet arkhitektury i stroitel'stva, 2015), 12.

15. *PDDUM*, 17–18; Koroleva and Korolev, *Islam v Srednem Povolzh'e. 1940-e gg*, 12.

16. *PDDUM*, 44–45.

17. The document was later published and circulated in Uyghur (3,500 copies) and in Kazakh (1,500 copies) (*PDDUM*, 64–65).

18. Babakhanov, appeal to the Muslims of Xinjiang (n.d.), *PDDUM*, 309–310.

19. Babakhanov, appeal to the Muslims of Xinjiang (n.d.), *PDDUM*, 312.

20. Babakhanov, appeal to the Muslims of Xinjiang (n.d.), *PDDUM*, 312–313.

21. Babakhanov, appeal to the Muslims of Xinjiang (n.d.), *PDDUM*, 313.

22. Babakhanov, appeal to the Muslims of Xinjiang (n.d.), *PDDUM*, 314. The transcript incorrectly cites the verse as Q 2:186–187; it should properly be Q 2:190–191.

23. Babakhanov, appeal to the Muslims of Xinjiang (n.d.), *PDDUM*, 315.

24. Babakhanov, appeal to the Muslims of Xinjiang (n.d.), *PDDUM*, 315.

25. *PDDUM*, 49–50. Along with Alizada Akhund, the other main envoys were his DUMZAK colleagues Akhund Abdurrakhim-Kazy of Baku and Shaykh Mustafa-Kazy of Lankaran, Azerbaijan. The word typically translated as "Cults" here is the Russian *kul'ty*, but the common Russian usage is much more similar to—and probably drawn from—the French, in which *culte* is more properly translated as "denomination" (e.g. *le culte protestant*). In this book I have generally translated "*kul'ty*" as "denominations," but because the title "Council for the Affairs of Religious Cults" has become a standard translation in English I will maintain it here. I am grateful to Allen J. Frank for his insights into this thorny issue of translation.

26. Alizada, text of Iranian radio broadcast (June 13, 1945), *PDDUM*, 301–302.

27. Alizada, text of Iranian radio broadcast (June 13, 1945), *PDDUM*, 303.

28. Alizada, text of Iranian radio broadcast (June 13, 1945), *PDDUM*, 304.

29. Alizada, text of Iranian radio broadcast (June 13, 1945), *PDDUM*, 305.

30. Alizada, text of Iranian radio broadcast (June 13, 1945), *PDDUM*, 305.

31. Alizada, text of Iranian radio broadcast (June 13, 1945), *PDDUM*, 306.

32. Alizada, text of Iranian radio broadcast (June 13, 1945), *PDDUM*, 306.

33. Alizada, text of Iranian radio broadcast (June 13, 1945), *PDDUM*, 306, emphasis added.

34. Alizada, text of Iranian radio broadcast (June 13, 1945), *PDDUM*, 306.

35. Alizada, text of Iranian radio broadcast (June 13, 1945), *PDDUM*, 307.

36. On the religious heritage of some Soviet Muslim scientists, see Allen J. Frank, *Gulag Miracles: Sufis and Stalinist Repression in Kazakhstan* (Vienna: Austrian Academy of Sciences Press, 2019), 109–115.

37. Shkarovskii, *Russkaia Pravoslavnaia Tserkov' pri Staline i Khrushcheve*, 215–216; Aleksei Beglov, *V poiskakh "bezgreshnykh katakomb." Tserkovnoe podpol'e v SSSR* (Moscow: Izd. Sovet Russkoi Pravoslavnoi Tserkvi, 'Arefa,' 2008), 106–107.

38. M.I. Odintsov, *Russkaia pravoslavnaia tserkov' nakanune i v epokhu stalinskogo sotsializma, 1917–1953 gg.* (Moscow: Politicheskaia entsiklopediia, 2014), 267.

39. Dennis J. Dunn, *The Catholic Church and Russia: Popes, Patriarchs, Tsars, and Commissars* (Aldershot: Ashgate, 2004), 113.

40. See V.A. Alekseev, *Illiuzii i dogmy* (Moscow: Politizdat, 1991), 336; Odintsov, *Russkaia pravoslavnaia tserkov'*, 275; Nathaniel Davis, *A Long Walk to Church: A Contemporary History of Russian Orthodoxy* (Boulder, CO: Westview, 2003), 18; Roger R. Reese, "The Russian Orthodox Church and 'Patriotic' Support for the Stalinist Regime during the Great Patriotic War," *War and Society* 33/2 (2014), 143. D.V. Pospelovskii criticizes historians who dwell too resolutely on the Tehran moment as a "catchall" explanation of Stalin's religious policy in the war era (*Russkaia pravoslavnaia tserkov' v XX veke* [Moscow: Respublika, 1995], 191). See also Mikhail Shkarovskii, "Stalinskaia religioznaia politika i Russkaia Pravoslavnaia Tserkov' v 1943–1953 godakh," *Acta Slavica Iaponica* 27 (2009), 1–27.

41. Stephen Merritt Miner, *Stalin's Holy War: Religion, Nationalism, and Alliance Politics, 1941–1945* (Chapel Hill, NC: University of North Carolina Press, 2003), 110–111. Meanwhile, Stalin had also reduced propaganda efforts targeting powerful foreign religious influences—ending, for example, propaganda against the Vatican soon after the war began (Dunn, *The Catholic Church and Russia*, 111).

42. Miner, *Stalin's Holy War*, 83. The British Foreign Ministry felt much the same way, albeit with an interesting twist: many of its analysts concluded that Stalin's primary interest was to prevent the spread of British or American influence over the Caucasus (*PDDUM*, 60).

43. Miner, *Stalin's Holy War*, 221.

44. Miner, *Stalin's Holy War*, 266.

45. Shkarovskii, *Russkaia Pravoslavnaia Tserkov' pri Staline i Khrushcheve*, 197.

46. Daniela Kalkandjieva, *The Russian Orthodox Church, 1917–1948: From Decline to Resurrection* (Abingdon: Routledge, 2014), 159; see also Odintsov, *Russkaia pravoslavnaia tserkov' nakanune i v epokhu stalinskogo sotsializma, 1917–1953 gg.*, 297. Interestingly, as Daniela Kalkandjieva observes, *The Truth about Religion in Russia* also served as a strong claim for the Orthodox Church's primacy over all other forms of Christianity in the Soviet Union. Here, the Orthodox Church is indeed *the* church, the sole representative of Christian tradition in the county (Kalkandjieva, *The Russian Orthodox Church*, 156). No mention is made of Old Believers, the "Living Church," Roman Catholicism, or any other tradition. While Sergii would have been a clear beneficiary if a perception of the Orthodox monopoly over Christianity caught

on, the state also hoped to promote loyal "normative" religious institutions at home as an alternative to "sectarian" activity, which was generally regarded as suspect, subversive, and fertile ground for the emergence of anti-Soviet splinter groups. The Patriarchate later published another wartime booklet for foreign distribution, titled *The Russian Orthodox Church and the Great Patriotic War*, this one hailing the patriotic efforts of church leaders and churchgoers in the fight against Germany.

47. Miner, *Stalin's Holy War*, 99.

48. *PDDUM*, 64–65.

49. *PDDUM*, 65.

50. E.D. Abataev, "Islam v gody Velikoi Otechestvennoi voiny," *Istoriia Velikoi Pobedy: sbornik materialov mezhvuzovskoi I 89 nauchno-prakticheskoi konferentsii* (Novokuznetsk: FKOU VO Kuzbaskii institut, FSIN Rossii, 2018), 13.

51. *PDDUM*, 81; Tasar, *Soviet and Muslim*, 56.

52. *PDDUM*, 47–48. The original plans for the magazine, described in a correspondence with Polianskii, proposed article topics such as "German Imperialism: The Age-Old Enemy of Muslims," "Fascism—The Enemy of Muslim Believers," and "The Soviet Constitution and Religion" (*ISG3*, 30–31). The calendars were printed with more hesitation: the layout proposed for the 1947 calendar originally featured biographies of Muslim leaders, quotes from scripture, and religious invocations ("In the name of gracious and merciful Allah . . ."), much of which was removed. After some further delays due to the heavy workload of the printing press, the SADUM calendar was finally released in a print run of 3,000 copies (V.A. Akhmadullin, "Reglamentatsiia sovetskim gosudarstvom vypuska i raspredeleniia islamskikh kalendarei, izdannykh muftiiatami (1944–1965)," *Vestnik Moskovskogo gosudarstvennogo lingvisticheskogo universiteta* 1/794 (2018), 106–108).

53. Tatiana A. Chumachenko, *Church and State in Soviet Russia: Russian Orthodoxy from World War II to the Khrushchev Years*, trans. Edward E. Roslof (New York: M.E. Sharpe, 2002), 77–78. According to Chumachenko, the promised press run of 15,000 copies of the inaugural issue of *Journal of the Moscow Patriarchate* never came to fruition because the printing house was not provided with sufficient paper. The Church had to settle for a run of just 3,000 copies.

54. M.V. Shkarovskii, *Russkaia Pravoslavnaia Tserkov' pri Staline i Khrushcheve—Gosudarstvenno-tserkovnye otnosheniia v SSSR v 1939–1964 godakh* (Moscow: Krutitskoe Patriarshee Podvor'e; Obshchestvo liubitelei tserkovnoi istorii, 1999), 103. Defining religious policy in the occupied territories was not as simple as mere permissiveness or its absence, however. In Polish occupied territory, a recent Catholic-inspired campaign of repression against Orthodox churches served to incline Orthodox citizens in Poland closer to the Soviet occupiers—this was an opportunity the Soviets were wise enough to seize, not just by permitting the Orthodox to carry on unbothered, but by embracing the role they were expected—however naively—to play in championing the church against its Catholic oppressors. Witness, for example, the scenes of Orthodox priests, in 1939, leading celebrations of their "liberation" by the Soviets against a background of church bell towers hung with welcoming red flags. Soon enough, Moscow delegated the Orthodox Church to

help disperse Soviet influence in these and other occupied regions. Meanwhile, Soviet soldiers in the occupied territories partook actively in religious life: a rector in a western Ukrainian Orthodox cathedral observed a massive rise in baptisms once Soviet servicemen and their families arrived, and Communist Party members and NKVD (People's Commissariat for Internal Affairs) agents were among those bringing their children to receive these rites (Shkarovskii, *Russkaia Pravoslavnaia Tserkov' pri Staline i Khrushcheve*, 103–104; 109).

55. Miner, *Stalin's Holy War*, 47; Reese, "The Russian Orthodox Church and 'Patriotic' Support for the Stalinist Regime during the Great Patriotic War," 137, 143. See also Konstantin Oboznyi, "'Novyi kurs' religioznoi politiki Stalina i tserkovnaia situatsiia na okkupirovannykh territoriiakh Leningradskoi oblasti (1943–1944 gg.)," *Gosudarstvo, religiia, tserkov v Rossii i za rubezhom* 3 (2017), 360–387.

56. Miner, *Stalin's Holy War*, 53. As German forces oversaw the reopening of churches, Hitler plotted to support multiple sects in an effort to fragment Christian allegiance and prevent the dominance of any single, unified church (see Shkarovskii, *Russkaia Pravoslavnaia Tserkov' pri Staline i Khrushcheve*, 141; 144–145; 160–161). Nathaniel Davis writes, "Why did Stalin receive the hierarchs, and why did he do so when he did, more than two years after Hitler's invasion? The probable explanation starts with his limited amelioration of church policy in 1941, which was in reaction to the renaissance of church life behind German lines and his evident fear that the yearnings of Soviet believers would make them anti-Soviet activists. In the desperate months of the initial Soviet retreat and in the renewed retreats of 1942, Stalin's energies were concentrated on survival and military strategy; he probably concluded—to the extent that he thought about Sergii and his church—that additional concessions would have little effect on Sergii's already supportive public stand. By 1943, however, Stalin was thinking more about politics, and Red forces were liberating areas where newly opened Orthodox churches abounded" (*A Long Walk to Church*, 18).

57. Richard Steigmann-Gall, *The Holy Reich: Nazi Conceptions of Christianity, 1919–1945* (Cambridge, UK: Cambridge University Press, 2003), 254.

58. See Pospelovskii, *Russkaia pravoslavnaia tserkov' v XX veke*, 191.

59. On the pervasive discrimination faced by Kazakh soldiers, see Carmack, *Kazakhstan in World War II*, 30–38.

60. See, for example, Brandon Schechter, "'The People's Instructions': Indigenizing the Great Patriotic War Among 'Non-Russians,'" *Ab Imperio* 3 (2012), 109–133; Roger R. Reese, *Why Stalin's Soldiers Fought: The Red Army's Military Effectiveness in World War II* (Lawrence, KS: University of Kansas Press, 2011), 141–148; Miner, *Stalin's Holy War*, 64–65.

61. K.S. Drozdov, "Stalingrad: voennaia mashina Reikha protiv internatsionala sovetskikh narodov," in V.A. Tishkova and E.A. Pivnevoi, eds., *Istoricheskaia pamiat' i rossiiskaia identichnost'* (Moscow: RAN, 2018), 188.

62. See Carmack, *Kazakhstan in World War II*, 42–62; 92–107; Carmack, "Hero and Hero-Making: Patriotic Narratives and the Sovietization of Kazakh Front-Line Propaganda, 1941–1945," *Central Asian Survey* 33/1 (2014), 95–112; Charles Shaw, "Soldiers' Letters to Inobatxon and O'g'ulxon: Gender and Nationality in the Birth of

a Soviet Romantic Culture," *Kritika* 17/3 (2016), 517–552; Boram Shin, "Red Army Propaganda for Uzbek Soldiers and Localised Soviet Internationalism during World War II." *The Soviet and Post-Soviet Review* 42-1 (2015), 39–63; Schechter, " 'The People's Instructions.' " Since evidence for the development of self-perceptions concerning ethnic identity in this period is necessarily sketchy, the connection between wartime "identity formation" and wartime propaganda is necessarily sketchy as well. Shin, by contrast, considers whether Uzbek response to the war—and to the heavily propagandized calls for participation—show any clear evidence of agency. While Schechter emphasizes the "cookie-cutter nature of this propaganda" (Schechter, " 'The People's Instructions,' " 118) without denying its potential resonance, Shin proposes that "The localization process was much more complex than simply 'plugging-in' indigenous details to a meta-narrative dictated from the centre. The war years allowed the local cultural elites engaged in propaganda production a degree of leverage over Moscow. As a result, the local cultural elites could define their nations' own place *within* and even *beyond* the Soviet Union" (Shin, "Red Army Propaganda for Uzbek Soldiers," 41). This is a promising proposal, and one that I will explore in this book. However, the examples Shin offers to support it—mostly drawn from the canon of popular literary and artistic propaganda—do not clearly separate the "Party line" from the propaganda efforts of "local cultural elites." The fact that Uzbek playwrights and novelists produced precisely the kinds of Red Army hagiographies encouraged— even commanded—from Moscow tells us only that these literati and the Soviet government envisioned Uzbekistan's place in the Soviet Union in a remarkably similar way. To find evidence of agency, one would especially like to know if there were there wartime cases in which local elites negotiated for concessions that might not otherwise have been granted, either for themselves or for communities they represented; or in which their "local" propaganda clearly diverged from erstwhile Party policies or convictions. In the case of Islam and local Muslim elites, as this book will show, we can answer this question emphatically in the affirmative.

63. I use scare-quotes here on the word "secular" in order to recognize the fact that many "national" heroes whose stories were likely regarded as devoid of religious content by Moscow authorities may well have had religious resonance for the communities targeted by the propaganda in question. Manas, for example, the subject of the world's longest epic, was trumpeted by generations of Soviet academics and cultural coordinators as a secular national hero for the Kyrgyz people, but very rarely indeed (if ever) did Soviet-era literature on Manas point out what would be obvious to many Kyrgyz, then and now: the plot revolves not only around a hero battling enemies, but a *Muslim* hero battling *non-Muslims*.

64. Aleksandr I. Solzhenitsyn, *Letter to the Soviet Leaders* (New York: Harper & Row, 1975), 17–18.

65. Miner, *Stalin's Holy War*, 7.

66. Miner, *Stalin's Holy War*, 320; see also Shkarovskii, *Russkaia Pravoslavnaia Tserkov' pri Staline i Khrushcheve*, 199–200; Dunn, *The Catholic Church and Russia*, 108. Roger Reese writes, "The popular impression is that the Church sat impassively on the sidelines until re-established by Stalin in September 1943. What the Church did

up to that point has only recently been brought to light in Russian historiography in a handful of monographs, articles, conference proceedings, and published document collections. These works promote the Church's claim that it was motivated by patriotism, a point it uses to claim legitimacy in contemporary Russia." Reese offers a nuanced, contrasting perspective that likewise falls broadly within the "revolution from below" umbrella: "I argue, contrary to the current Russian interpretation, that the Patriarchal Church under Metropolitan Sergii was *not* essentially motivated by patriotism or the desire to show loyalty to the Soviet regime in 1941, but instead carefully designed its actions to use the war to achieve three goals: first and most important, to become relevant in the everyday life of the Soviet people by promoting Christian beliefs and values; second, to earn legitimacy in the eyes of anti-clerics and non-believers by lending moral and practical support to the war effort; and finally, to obtain legal standing by showing its trustworthiness and loyalty through displays of Russian (not Soviet) patriotism consonant with its historic role, all the while without endorsing communist ideology. Furthermore, I argue that the spontaneous grassroots response by believers and clerics in support of the Church and its wartime activities represents primarily an endorsement of the Church, Christianity, Russian patriotism, and only secondarily, if at all, loyalty to the Stalinist regime" (Reese, "The Russian Orthodox Church and 'Patriotic' Support for the Stalinist Regime during the Great Patriotic War," 132–133; 136–137).

67. Shoshana Keller, *To Moscow, Not Mecca: The Soviet Campaign Against Islam in Central Asia* (Westport, CT: Praeger, 2001), 244.

68. Victoria Smolkin, *A Sacred Space is Never Empty: A History of Soviet Atheism* (Princeton, NJ: Princeton University Press, 2018), 18; 49. Elsewhere, Smolkin writes: "The fact that the decision to bring religion back into Soviet life came from Stalin personally suggests that he perceived the political threat of religion to be effectively neutralized" (*A Sacred Space is Never Empty*, 52).

69. HPSSS sched. A, vol. 36, case 103/(NY) 1593, f. 23.

70. Interview, Ion Lazarovich Degen, https://iremember.ru/en/memoirs/tankers/degen-ion-lazarevich-/ (accessed April 10, 2020).

71. HPSSS sched. A, vol. 21, case 420, f. 7.

72. HPSSS sched. A, vol. 14, case 191, ff. 23–24.

73. HPSSS sched. A, vol. 18, case 342, f. 32.

74. HPSSS sched. A, vol. 11, case 136, f. 53.

75. See Irina Korovushkina Paert, "Memory and Survival in Stalin's Russia: Old Believers in the Urals during the 1930s–50s," in Daniel Bertaux, Paul Thompson, and Anna Rotkirch, eds., *On Living Through Soviet Russia* (New York: Routledge, 2004), 195–213.

76. See, for example, Shkarovskii, *Russkaia Pravoslavnaia Tserkov' pri Staline i Khrushcheve*, 215–216; Miner, *Stalin's Holy War*, 50; Beglov, *V poiskakh "bezgreshnykh katakomb,"* 115.

77. HPSSS sched. B, vol. 9, case 448, f. 19.

78. HPSSS sched. B, vol. 31, case 479/(NY)1108, f. 19.

79. HPSSS sched. A, vol. 13, case 159, f. 35.

80. HPSSS sched. A, vol. 22, case 434, f. 31.

81. HPSSS sched. A, vol. 14, case 275, f. 17.

82. HPSSS sched. A, vol. 32, case 176/(NY)1173, f. 17–18.

83. While the Nazis destroyed hundreds of holy places, they also backed up some of their propaganda claims with action: some estimates claim that they permitted the reopening of *thousands* of churches in the occupied borderlands (*PDDUM*, 63). See also Shkarovskii, *Russkaia Pravoslavnaia Tserkov' pri Staline i Khrushcheve*, 200.

84. See, for example, Miner, *Stalin's Holy War*, 78–79.

85. Iu.N. Guseva, *Rossiiskii musul'manin v XX veke (na materialakh Srednego Povolzh'ia)* (Samara: Ofort, 2013), 156.

86. Moreover, as Reese (discussing Soviet Christian populations in wartime) observes, "some might question whether Stalin needed to cater to the public in late 1943 when it was clear that the USSR was no longer in danger of losing the war. After all, the leaders of the Patriarchal, the Renovation, and Josephite churches already supported the war. Furthermore, Stalin had already made conciliatory gestures that could be seen as a quid pro quo for the Church's loyalty. We might therefore consider that Stalin had no functional need to formally re-establish the Church" ("The Russian Orthodox Church and 'Patriotic' Support for the Stalinist Regime during the Great Patriotic War," 142).

87. It is important to note, however, that this feeling was not unanimous. Some Soviet Muslims and Christian interviewed in the late Stalin era lamented what they regarded as an ongoing and general decline in religious life, oftentimes focusing on the decline of a few rituals that they clearly regarded as bellwethers. "People have lost religion," the grandson of Rizaetdin Fakhretdinov lamented to interviewers. "The circumcision of boys is no longer practiced and marriage is no longer a religious ceremony because it is only the civil ceremony that counts now. A man no longer needs a mullah for a wedding or a funeral" (HPSSS sched. B, vol. 8, case 228 f. 11). A Kabardian Muslim, born in 1903, noted the restriction of important funeral customs, among others: "You could not honor the dead under the Soviets as we did traditionally with the mullah; also the period of mourning is reduced because people have to work in order to increase production, and now, of course, you do not have mullahs . . . Traditionally, the mullahs registered births, deaths, and marriages. Then, too, we had circumcision of boys at the age of 2 or 3 but even as late as 8 and 10; this is not done anymore" (HPSSS sched. B, vol. 8, case 354 f. 10). A Russian bookkeeper, thirty-nine years old, told her interviewer: "It's important to bear in mind that Stalin never officially came out against any religion, but the vessels, through which spiritual life flows to the people, were destroyed. For that reason there is no church organization, as such, no priests, and no local churches" (HPSSS sched. A, vol. 35, case 355/(NY)1498 ff. 27–28).

88. "Until 1929," one Kalmyk Christian convert recalls, "I used to go to church and even when I was in the Komsomol when I went to visit my aunt she would light a light in front of the holy picture so it could not be seen from the outside, and we would pray. She made me pray . . . They say that heaven and earth are just natural phenomena. But I believe in my thoughts that God exists. Now, after I have seen the west my faith has become even firmer. I think the majority of the Soviet Union still believes in God" (HPSSS sched. A, vol. 3, case 23 f. 21).

89. This is true not only of Muslim communities, as will be described over the course of this book, but also of Soviet Orthodox Christians. M.V. Shkarovskii describes how the efflorescence of Orthodox religious activity in wartime is evidenced relentlessly in archival documents, wartime and postwar memoirs, and the testimony of eyewitnesses (*Russkaia Pravoslavnaia Tserkov' pri Staline i Khrushcheve*, 124–126). On the other hand, some historians have contested the pervasiveness of the social shift; Dennis J. Dunn, for example, writes that "Stalin's concessions had nothing to do with a change of attitude toward religion and led to no improvement in the sad state of religious conditions in most parts of the Soviet Union." Nevertheless, Dunn adds that "The minor concessions to the Russian Orthodox Church were especially telling among the Russians, who assumed that the Communists were on the verge of altering their general anti-religious policy" (*The Catholic Church and Russia*, 109; 112). Similarly, writing about SADUM, the Central Asian "muftiate" created by Stalin as an "official" Islamic institution, Eren Tasar notes that "SADUM's establishment contributed to a popular perception that the Stalinist state had turned a new page in its approach toward God-fearing folk" (*Soviet and Muslim*, 15).

90. As Catriona Kelly writes in her superb study of urban Soviet churches, during the war "the emotional status of religion had changed. During the terrible years of the [Leningrad] Blockade, even formerly skeptical members of the intelligentsia had felt wistfully drawn to religious ritual" (Kelly, *Socialist Churches: Radical Secularization and the Preservation of the Past in Petrograd and Leningrad, 1918–1988* [DeKalb, IL: Northern Illinois University Press, 2016], 147).

91. HPSSS sched. A, vol. 28, case 535, f. 37.

92. HPSSS sched. A, vol. 15, case 305, f. 36.

93. HPSSS sched. A, vol. 22, case 434, f. 32.

94. Koroleva and Korolev, *Islam v Srednem Povolzh'e*, 11–14.

95. Koroleva and Korolev are correct, nevertheless, to direct our attention toward negotiation between religious leaders and the Soviet state, even if—as with the meeting between Stalin and the Orthodox Patriarchs discussed in Chapter 1—these negotiations were often one-sided. Suffice to say that when the state gave concessions, it did not give them uniformly or all at once. This begs the question: when religious Soviet citizens were able to take advantage of the new climate, what signals inspired them to act—to petition the government, say, or to move their activities from dark basements to plain view?

Chapter 1

1. Alexander N. Yakovlev, *A Century of Violence in Soviet Russia* (New Haven: Yale University Press, 2002), 156.

2. Davis, *A Long Walk to Church*, 3. In earlier years, Lenin had courted a less violent approach to religion, as Victoria Smolkin writes: "even as Lenin demanded strict ideological discipline of party members, he was, above all, concerned with politics and maintaining the party's hold on power. Though he allowed that 'science can be

enlisted in the battle against religion, he explicitly spoke out against repression and discrimination on religious grounds. Instead, he demanded that Bolsheviks help believers see through the 'religious fog' with 'purely ideological and solely ideological weapons.' By 1922, however, Lenin was declaring open war on the clergy, twinning them with the bourgeoisie, and declared that "the greater number of representatives of the reactionary clergy and reactionary bourgeoisie we manage to shoot on this basis the better" (*A Sacred Space Is Never Empty*, 13; 29).

3. See Edward E. Rosloff, *Red Priests: Renovationism, Russian Orthodoxy, and Revolution, 1905–1946* (Bloomington: Indiana University Press, 2002). The Renovationists opposed the existence of an Orthodox Patriarchate, and they favored allowing priests to marry. They also supported a shift to the Russian language from Old Church Slavonic for church services, and the adoption of the Gregorian calendar.

4. Niccolo Pianciola, "Orthodoxy in the Kazakh Territories (1850–1943)," in *Kazakhstan: Religions and Society in the History of Central Eurasia*, ed. Gian Luca Bonora, Niccolo Pianciola, and Paolo Sartori (Turin: Umberto Allemandi, 2009), 245.

5. Previously, ten out of the eleven prelates who rose to head the Church were swiftly jailed (see Davis, *A Long Walk to Church*, 4).

6. On the one hand, anti-religious propaganda efforts and the first glimpses of Soviet administrative intervention were already underway in Muslim regions by the mid-1920s; on the other hand, even as *madrasa* education had been coming under ever-stricter control, the authority of the officially sanctioned Central Spiritual Directorate of the Muslims of Russia (TsDUM) was expanding into new territories, such that in Kazakhstan—for example—the number of mosques, *muhtasibs*, and *imams* increased steadily in the mid-1920s. See Allen J. Frank, *Gulag Miracles: Sufis and Stalinist Repression in Kazakhstan* (Vienna: Austrian Academy of Sciences Press, 2019), 74; Saduaqas Ghïlmani, *Biographies of the Islamic Scholars of Our Times*, ed. Allen J. Frank, Ashirbek Muminov, and Aitzhan Nurmanova (Istanbul: IRCICA, 2018), 35–40; 247; 477–481. On the general shift in perception toward Islam among Bolsheviks circa 1926–27, Khalid writes, "The situation changed by 1926. In the joyful world that the Bolsheviks were building, there could be (by definition) no wretchedness, no soul-less conditions, and hence no need for mournful sighing. Instead, religion was now the last redoubt for ideological opposition, a cover for 'counterrevolutionary elements' to wage their struggle against the Will of History" (*Islam after Communism*, 69).

7. Keller, *To Moscow, Not Mecca*, 113.

8. Keller, *To Moscow, Not Mecca*, 129.

9. Keller, *To Moscow, Not Mecca*, 156.

10. See, for example, AkadNkKaz Inv. 1375: N.D. Makarov, *Analargha maslahatlar*, trans. M. Rasuli (Tashkent: Özbekistan Dawlat Nashriyati; Saghliqni saqlash kutubkhanasi, 1925); *Qazaq aieldernyng otkendegysy men kazyrgy jaiy* (Kzyl-Orda: Izdanie Kazanskogo Gusudar, 1927).

11. AkadNkKaz Inv. 1571: Naʿmat Hakim, *Islamda va shura hukumatida khatun-qizlar huquqi* (Tashkent: Özbek Dawlat Nashriyati, 1925). Khalid notes that Hakim, a Tatar anti-religious propagandist, had been delivering atheist-themed lectures to Central Asian audiences as early as December 1921, in which, as Khalid writes, "he put

various aspects of Islamic belief to the test of science and disproved them to his own satisfaction" (Khalid, *Islam after Communism*, 69).

12. See Gregory J. Massell, *The Surrogate Proletariat: Moslem Women and Revolutionary Strategies in Soviet Central Asia, 1919–1929* (Princeton: Princeton University Press, 1974); Douglas Northrop, *Veiled Empire: Gender and Power in Stalinist Central Asia* (Ithaca: Cornell University Press, 2004); Marianne Kamp, *The New Woman in Uzbekistan: Islam, Modernity and Unveiling under Communism* (Seattle: University of Washington Press, 2006); Shoshanna Keller, "Trapped between State and Society: Woman's Liberation and Islam in Soviet Uzbekistan, 1926–1941," *Journal of Women's History* 10/1 (1998), 20–44; Chiara De Santi, "Cultural Revolution and Resistance in Uzbekistan during the 1920s: New Perspectives on the Woman Question," in Paolo Sartori and Tomaso Trevisani, eds., *Patterns of Transformation in and around Uzbekistan* (Reggio Emilia: Diabasis, 2007), 51–89; Adrienne Edgar, "Bolshevism, Patriarchy, and the Nation: The Soviet 'Emancipation' of Muslim Women in Pan-Islamic Perspective," *Slavic Review* 65/2 (2006), 252–272; Edgar, "Emancipation of the Unveiled: Turkmen Women under Soviet Rule, 1924–29," *Russian Review* 62/1 (2003), 132–149; Khalid, *Islam after Communism*, 73–75.

13. See Khalid, *Islam after Communism*, 72.

14. On the punitive taxation and repression of Sufi elites in Kazakhstan, see Frank, *Gulag Miracles*, 75.

15. Alfrid K. Bustanov, "Islamskii apokalipsis pri Staline" (forthcoming), 13.

16. Khalid, *Islam after Communism*, 71.

17. Keller, *To Moscow, Not Mecca*, 240.

18. Khalid, *Islam after Communism*, 73.

19. Smolkin, *A Sacred Space Is Never Empty*, 46. Among Soviet Muslims, descendants of the most esteemed "sacred lineages" were at particular risk for the double burden of condemnation for religion and class. Allen J. Frank describes, for example, how the descendants of the Sufi saint Shah-i Ahmad were charged with being *bays* (steppe tribal elites), leading to the persecution or exile of the entire family. Drawing on Kazakh Muslim hagiographies of the Stalin era, Frank observes that they "depict above all a period of more or less consistent violence, persecution, and disruption" for Kazakh families with esteemed Muslim lineages (Frank, *Gulag Miracles*, 79; 81).

20. HPSSS sched. A, vol. 13, case 159 f. 102.

21. Frank, *Gulag Miracles*, 73. The Kazakh term for "smoke hole" here (*shangïraq*) also has the sense of "families"; among native Kazakh speakers, this sentence can carry an even more direct, simultaneous meaning: "many families were extinguished." I am grateful to Allen J. Frank for describing this usage to me.

22. Shoshanna Keller, *To Moscow, Not Mecca: The Soviet Campaign against Islam in Central Asia* (Westport, CT: Praeger, 2001), 205; Khalid, *Islam after Communism*, 73. The Orthodox Church was also hard hit by these articles, which effectively ended the Church's charitable and community-support activities, including permission to operate orphanages, hospitals, psychiatric treatment facilities, and homes for the care of the disabled and elderly. The scope of activity permitted on church grounds was also severely circumscribed: according to Article 17, churches could no longer be used for

activities other than worship, which excluded functions such as religious education and study groups, casual prayer meetings, libraries, and sewing circles (see Davis, *A Long Walk to Church*, 8). Summarizing their impact, Smolkin writes, "The 1929 law was intended to bring all aspects of religious life under state control by repealing numerous provisions established in 1918: it outlawed the religious education of children and charity work, closed monasteries, and dictated that religious communities had to register with local government organs. To make sure the league faced no competition, the Bolsheviks revoked the right to 'religious propaganda' from the fourth article of the Constitution of the Russian Soviet Federal Socialist Republic (RSFSR), which had, until then, guaranteed Soviet citizens "freedom of religious and anti-religious propaganda" (*A Sacred Space Is Never Empty*, 46). See also Beglov, *V poiskakh "bezgreshnykh katakomb*," 103–104.

23. GARF f.R-393, op. 43a, d.283, l.1-2 ("Proekt instruktsii NKVD i Narkomprosa "O prepodavanii musul'manskogo veroucheniia sredi vostochnykh narodnostei, ispoveduiushchikh musul'manskoe verouchenie," *Russian Perspectives on Islam*, https://islamperspectives.org/rpi/items/show/11960 [accessed April 14, 2020]); GARF,f.R1235,op.69,d.29,l.51-51ob ("Tsirkuliar Tsentral'nogo administrativnogo upravleniia Krymskoi ASSR o poriadke prepodavaniia islama," *Russian Perspectives on Islam*, https://islamperspectives.org/rpi/items/show/21395 [accessed April 14, 2020]).

24. On this theme, see Eren Tasar, "Unregistered: Gray Spaces in the Soviet Regulation of Islam," in Pauline Jones, ed., *Islam, Society and Politics in Central Asia* (Pittsburgh: University of Pittsburgh Press, 2017), 127–148. Elsewhere, Tasar keenly appraises the naiveté of the registration system as applied to Muslim life: "Registration also constituted an ineffective means of controlling Islam because much religious practice did not center around mosques. Muslims frequented thousands of shrines, great and small, and relied on a host of figures whose activities bore no connection to mosques, such as itinerant *mullas* called in to recite prayers associated with name-giving ceremonies and circumcisions; male and female teachers in religious and linguistic subject matter; as well as shamans, sorcerers, and family specialists. Reducing the number of registered Muslim prayer houses therefore had little effect on the daily practice of most Central Asian Muslims" (*Soviet and Muslim*, 52).

25. Dilyara Usmanova, Ilnur Minnullin, and Rafik Mukhmetshin, "Islamic Education in Soviet and Post-Soviet Tatarstan," in Michael Kemper, Raoul Motika, and Stephan Reichmuth, eds., *Islamic Education in the Soviet Union and its Successor States* (New York: Routledge, 2010), 65n54. See also Michael Kemper, "From 1917 to 1937: The Mufti, the Turkologist, and Stalin's Terror," *Die Welt des Islams* 57/2 (2017), 162–191.

26. The arbitrary and illegal taxation—sometimes involving fraud—of religious elites had been a subject of complaint and concern since the early to mid-1920s, prompting both internal reviews at the Party level and petitions of protest from Soviet religious leaders. GARF fR-1235, op.120, d.22, l.1-4 ("Tsirkuliar No. 463 Nalogovogo upravleniia NK finansov RSFSR 'Ob oblozhenii nalogami i sborami tserkovnykh zdanii i sluzhitelei kul'ta' . . .," *Russian Perspectives on Islam*, https://islamperspectives.

org/rpi/items/show/11944 [accessed April 14, 2020]); GARF fR-1235, op. 120, d.22, l.8 ("Dokladnaia zapiska otdela natsional'nostei pri Prezidiume VTsIK za podpis'iu zav. otdelom Klingera i sekretaria T.Vasil'eva . . ." *Russian Perspectives on Islam*, https://islamperspectives.org/rpi/items/show/11945 [accessed April 14, 2020]). Since 1925, Fakhretdinov had been submitting petitions complaining of "outrageous insults to the religious feelings of Muslims" being perpetrated routinely by "Party youth." GARF f.R5263, op.2, d.4, l.119-120ob ("Pis'mo predsedatelia Tsentral'nogo dukhovnogo upravleniia musul'man R. Fakhreddinova M.I. Kalininu kak dukhovnogo glavy musul'man RSFSR, v tom chisle Kazakskoi ASSR," *Russian Perspectives on Islam*, https://islamperspectives.org/rpi/items/show/13015 [accessed April 14, 2020]).

27. Yakovlev, *A Century of Violence in Soviet Russia*, 164. In some regions, the proportion of closed mosques was still higher: in October, 1944, a CARC report from Georgia reported 28 "inactive" (*nedeistvuiushchii*) mosques in Akhaltsikhe *raion*, and just one registered and active mosque. The region's *madrasa* was shuttered in 1933 (NatArchGE R 1880.1.1 ff. 31; 52.).

28. Keller, *To Moscow, Not Mecca*, 211.

29. A.B. Iunusova, ed., *225 let Tsentral'nomu dukhovnomu upravleniiu musul'man Rossii: Istoricheskie ocherki*, 26.

30. A.S. Gaiazov, *Malaia i bol'shaia rodina grazhdanina. "Rakh Kazanchi."* (Ufa: "Bashkirskaia entsiklopediia," 2016), 228–229. The historical novel *Krasnaia poliana* by Anatolii Genatulin features a strikingly similar scene of mosque "decapitation," in which the narrator, then a schoolboy, joins in as a group of rural Communists lassos the crescent of a minaret with a rope and pulls it down, to shouts of opprobrium from village elders. The narrator likewise implies a kind of curse related to these events, relating that none of the children or grandchildren of those "Godless people" went on to live "full and happy" lives, but instead were struck by alcoholism, disease, and all manner of troubles (*Krasnaia poliana* [Ufa: Kitap, 2008], 367). In a more disturbing scene, some of the villagers surround an elderly neighbor who was rumored to be practicing old-fashioned "witchcraft" and poke out her eyeball with a stick! (Genatulin, *Krasnaia poliana*, 363).

31. V.A. Akhmadullin, "Deiatelnost' sovetskogo gosudarstva po organizatsii khadzha sovetskikh musul'man v 1944 g.," *Vlast'* 6 (June 2013), 161.

32. Davis, *A Long Walk to Church*, 9.

33. Smolkin, *A Sacred Space Is Never Empty*, 47.

34. Terry Martin, *The Affirmative Action Empire* (Ithaca: Cornell University Press, 2004), 439.

35. Keller, *To Moscow, Not Mecca*, 223.

36. Paert, "Memory and Survival in Stalin's Russia," 198.

37. Keller, *To Moscow, Not Mecca*, 241.

38. Yakovlev, *A Century of Violence in Soviet Russia*, 165; Shkarovskii, "Stalinskaia religioznaia politika i Russkaia Pravoslavnaia Tserkov' v 1943–1953 godakh,"; Davis, *A Long Walk to Church*, 11. Statistics on church closures are likewise approximate, but offer a general picture: of the estimated 37,000 Orthodox churches operating in 1930, 8,302 remained unclosed—but just a fraction of these were functioning as

churches, since a widespread shortage of clergy rendered many "open" churches inactive (Shkarovskii, *Russkaia Pravoslavnaia Tserkov' pri Staline i Khrushcheve*, 98). The precise arrest and death-toll figures naturally show some moderate variation in different sources; Roger Reese writes, for example: "Between 1937 and 1939, 150,000 clergy and lay officials of all faiths were arrested. About 80,000 of them ended up in the Gulag, and 70,000, including scores of archbishops and bishops, died or were executed. Approximately 8000 Orthodox churches and houses of worship were closed and most of the property confiscated and put to use by the state" ("The Russian Orthodox Church and 'Patriotic' Support for the Stalinist Regime during the Great Patriotic War," 134).

39. I.A. Zaripov and M.A. Safarov, *Akhmetzian Mustafin: iz istorii islama v SSSR* (Moscow: Medina, 2017), 59.

40. Bustanov, "Islamskii apokalipsis pri Staline," 15.

41. B.G. Fairuzov, *Istoriia islama v Rossii* (St. Petersburg: Timoshka, 2019), 230.

42. NatArchGE R 1880.1.1 f. 84.

43. NatArchGE R 1880.1.1 f. 111.

44. Tasar, *Soviet and Muslim*, 7. Even today, Central Asian Muslims routinely engage religious specialists to carry out rites in private homes, not by way of evasion, but simply by way of tradition: "Central Asian Muslims regularly call on Muslim male practitioners to recite prayers in their homes on special occasions, such as the fortieth anniversary of someone's death, or a circumcision ceremony. These *mullas* generally know the relevant Arabic prayers by heart but lack the formal training or standing of an *imam*, let alone a member of the '*ulama*" (*Soviet and Muslim*, 21–22).

45. HPSSS sched. B, vol. 7, case 106 f. 25 (emphasis added).

46. HPSSS sched. B, vol. 11, case 106 f. 354.

47. Sh.Sh. Shikhaliev, "Transformatsiia sufisma v svete religioznoi politiki i pereselenii gortsev v Dagestane 1930–1990-x gg.," *Pax Islamica* 2/11 (2013), 96.

48. Smolkin, *A Sacred Space Is Never Empty*, 48.

49. This holiday is the Festival of the Sacrifice, called Eid al-Adha in Arabic.

50. A.N. Starostin, *Islam v Sverdlovskoi oblasti* (Moscow: Logos, 2007), 75. The league's decline had been a longstanding trend since its peak in the early 1930s. By 1938, the proportion of members paying dues reportedly dipped as low as 13 percent; circulation of its trademark magazine, *Bezbozhnik*, dropped from 230,000 in 1938 to 155,000 the next year. While it is tempting to read into these figures evidence that "religious feeling" was increasing even at the tail end of the Great Terror, M.V. Shkarovskii proposes—plausibly—that Soviet citizens had simply grown tired of the organization, with its repetitive propaganda and hackneyed rhetoric (Shkarovskii, *Russkaia Pravoslavnaia Tserkov' pri Staline i Khrushcheve*, 97–98).

51. Rustam Bikbov has published this material online, along with several related digitized manuscript folios: https://rbvekpros.livejournal.com/23511.html#_ftnref2, accessed February 8, 2020.

52. G.D. Selianinova, "Musul'manskaia obshchina Prikam'ia v gody Velikoi Otehestvennoi voiny," in L.P. Markova, et al, eds., *Religioznye organizatsii verushchie Prikam'ia v gody Velikoi Otechestvennoi voiny: materialy nauchno-praktichestoi konferentsii 12 maia*

2005 g. (Perm': Bogatyrev P.G.; Gosudarstvennyi obshchestvenno-politicheskii arkhiv Permskoi oblasti, 2005), 18; D.Z. Khairetdinov, ed., *Islam na Urale: entsiklopedicheskii slovar'* (Moscow: Medina, 2009), 172.

53. This town is called "Baranga" in the Tatar language. An unusual wealth of information on the "Islamic history" of this town (and its broader religious milieu) has been preserved thanks to a remarkable source called the *Tarikh-i Barangawi*. On this source and its author, see Allen J. Frank, *Bukhara and the Muslims of Russia: Sufism, Education, and the Paradox of Islamic Prestige* (Leiden: Brill, 2012), 15–26.

54. Zaripov and Safarov, *Akhmetzian Mustafin*, 70.

55. Zaripov and Safarov, *Akhmetzian Mustafin*, 59–60.

56. Bustanov, "Islamskii apokalipsis pri Staline," 15–16.

57. Bustanov, "Islamskii apokalipsis pri Staline," 15–19.

58. Bustanov, "Islamskii apokalipsis pri Staline," 20.

59. As Nathaniel Davis explains, this should not necessarily be understood as an expansion of the rights outlined by previous constitutions: "The constitution of 1918 had given both atheists and believers the right to propagate their beliefs, but the 1929 amendment gave the right of propaganda to the atheists and allowed the believers only the opportunity to profess their beliefs and engage in worship. The 1936 Stalin constitution gave them only the right to worship." By Davis' timeline, 1936 also marked the beginning of a new wave of church closings (Davis, *A Long Walk to Church*, 8–9; 10). As early as 1925, Rizaetdin Fakhretdinov had sent a letter of complaint to Moscow observing that the two freedoms (religious and anti-religious expression) were, in practice, manifested in a "completely unilateral" preponderance of anti-religious propaganda while Muslim faithful were "deprived of any opportunity to refute" their assailants in the Soviet press or other public venues. GARF f.R-1235, op.120, d.22, l.11–12 ("Obrashchenie Tsentral'nogo dukhovnogo upravleniia musul'man vnutrennei Rossii za podpis'iu muftiia R.Fakhreddinova k predsedateliu VTsIK M.I. Kalininu . . . ," *Russian Perspectives on Islam*, https://islamperspectives.org/rpi/items/show/11946 [accessed April 14, 2020]). On the 1936 Constitution, see Samantha Lamb, *Stalin's Constitution: Soviet Participatory Politics and the Discussion of the 1936 Draft Constitution* (Milton: Routledge, 2017).

60. *VRGV*, 8.

61. *VRGV*, 7.

62. *VRGV*, 8.

63. *VRGV*, 9 (emphasis added).

64. *VRGV*, 9.

65. *VRGV*, 11.

66. *VRGV*, 12. Tasar offers insightful commentary on these dynamics in the postwar period: see, for example, *Soviet and Muslim*, 78–102.

67. *VRGV*, 11.

68. *VRGV*, 12.

69. *VRGV*, 13. It is important to remember that the "soft line" on policy does not correlate to a more "accommodating" vision of Marxist-Leninist ideology. On this point,

Iaroslavskii was clear: "One cannot be a Leninist and believe in God," he declared (Smolkin, *A Sacred Space Is Never Empty*, 43).

70. On the census and its production, see: V.B. Zhiromskaia, "Religioznost' naroda v 1937 godu," *Istoricheskii vestnik* 5/1 (2000); Tatiana Chumakova, "'Karta religii' dlia neudavsheisia Vsesoiuznoi perepisi 1937 g.: zabytaia stranitsa sovetskogo religiovedeniia," *Gosudarstvo, religiia, tserkov* 3–4/30 (2012), 106–133; Chumakova, "Podgotovka k Vsesoiuznoi perepisi 1937 g. Sozdanie karty religii SSSR," *Dialog so vremenem* 41 (2012), 296–316.

71. E.F. Krinko, "Vera i sueveriia na fronte i v tylu v usloviiakh voennogo vremeni (1941–1945)," *Bylye Gody* 29/3 (2013), 53–54. The remaining reported religious affiliations, in descending order of incidence, were: "traditional beliefs," 3.62 percent; Catholic, 0.49 percent; Protestant, 0.47 percent; Old Believer, 0.40 percent; Gregorian, 0.14 percent; Jewish, 0.29 percent; Buddhist, 0.08 percent. We may presume that the first category includes the religions of Siberia and the Arctic Circle, for example, though it also seems possible that some citizens reported in this way to avow personal belief without confessing a specific affiliation.

72. Krinko, "Vera i sueveriia na fronte i v tylu v usloviiakh voennogo vremeni (1941–1945)," 54. Among younger respondents, the proportion of atheists rose significantly, albeit not quite precipitously. Respondents 20–29 years old were, as a whole, atheists by a small majority: 55.3 percent. The trend toward atheism was more pronounced among teenagers 16–19 years old, 62.3 percent of whom reported an atheist orientation. Older respondents, meanwhile, were overwhelmingly affiliated with a specific religion: among citizens in their fifties, some 78 percent reported a religious orientation (cf. Krinko, "Vera i sueveriia na fronte i v tylu v usloviiakh voennogo vremeni (1941–1945)," 54; Miner, *Stalin's Holy War*, 33). These numbers support the frequent claim of Soviet anti-religious authorities, voiced throughout the 1940s and 50s, that religion was generally a phenomenon restricted to older citizens, but they undermine the insistence of some that religion was almost *exclusively* sustained among "elders."

73. Chumakova, "'Karta religii' dlia neudavsheisia Vsesoiuznoi perepisi 1937 g.," 108. The researchers involved in developing the census were well aware of precisely these issues, and documented both their concerns about respondents' reluctance to confess religious affiliation and detailed instructions for those giving the census to explain to each that if he or she was an "unbeliever" (*neveruiushchii*), they should write down this word, and otherwise to write down the name of their particular religious affiliation (Chumakova, "'Karta religii' dlia neudavsheisia Vsesoiuznoi perepisi 1937 g.," 110).

74. Chumakova, "'Karta religii' dlia neudavsheisia Vsesoiuznoi perepisi 1937 g.," 106–110.

75. Krinko, "Vera i sueveriia na fronte i v tylu v usloviiakh voennogo vremeni (1941–1945)," 55.

76. Miner, *Stalin's Holy War*, 53.

77. Odintsov, *Russkaia pravoslavnaia tserkov' nakanune i v epokhu stalinskogo sotsializma, 1917–1953 gg.*, 258.

78. HPSSS sched. A, vol. 34, case 148/(NY)1398 f. 23.

79. Miner, *Stalin's Holy War*, 47.
80. Miner, *Stalin's Holy War*, 50. Meanwhile, however, anti-religious propaganda con-tinued to be published and widely circulated in the Soviet Union until just a few days before the German invasion. In a June 1941 article titled "Patriotism and Religion," published in *Bezbozhnik*, the flagging flagship journal of the League of Militant Atheists, readers learned that "Religion is the worst enemy of Soviet patri-otism . . . History does not confirm the merits of the church in developing authentic patriotism." A couple months earlier, in the spring, Metropolitan Sergii had expressed his agitation over the ongoing religious repression, notwithstanding the church's pa-triotic labors in the occupied borderlands. Churches continued to be shuttered in Russia and, according to Shkarovskii, priests continued to be arrested until August 1941—at which point the arrests abruptly and decisively ended. (Shkarovskii, *Russkaia Pravoslavnaia Tserkov' pri Staline i Khrushcheve*, 112–113; 115–116; 196.)
81. Reese, "The Russian Orthodox Church and 'Patriotic' Support for the Stalinist Regime during the Great Patriotic War," 135.
82. Odintsov, Odintsov, *Russkaia pravoslavnaia tserkov'*, 252; Alekseev, *Illiuzii i dogmy*, 333–334.
83. Shkarovskii, *Russkaia Pravoslavnaia Tserkov' pri Staline i Khrushcheve*, 121.
84. Odintsov, Odintsov, *Russkaia pravoslavnaia tserkov'*, 253.
85. *PDDUM*, 15.
86. Odintsov, *Russkaia pravoslavnaia tserkov'*, 260; VRGV, 64.
87. Odintsov, *Russkaia pravoslavnaia tserkov'*, 260–261; VRGV, 64.
88. Shkarovskii, *Russkaia Pravoslavnaia Tserkov' pri Staline i Khrushcheve*, 123.
89. Odintsov, *Russkaia pravoslavnaia tserkov'*, 264–265.
90. Odintsov, *Russkaia pravoslavnaia tserkov'*, 260. Roger Reese gives a sense for the disproportionate church demographics when comparing the borderlands to Russia: "In the RSFSR, twenty-five of its oblasts had no churches whatsoever, and twenty other oblasts were down to only two or three churches. Seven oblasts of the Ukraine were devoid of Orthodox churches, and three others had only one each. The Renovation Church also had hundreds of its churches closed. Only in the areas of western Ukraine and Belorussia and the Baltic States newly acquired by conquest in 1939–40 did substantial numbers of churches remain. Stalin had refrained from closing most of these out of fears that it would drive the people into the arms of the Germans in the event of war" ("The Russian Orthodox Church and 'Patriotic' Support for the Stalinist Regime during the Great Patriotic War," 134).
91. *PDDUM*, 17–18. Meanwhile, Sergii was keenly aware that the religious complexity of the borderlands could emerge as a source of strength and leverage for the Orthodox Church in relation to Stalin's government. In a memorandum written by Sergii in Riga, dated November 12, 1941, the Metropolitan explained for a German (!) audi-ence that a vibrant and robust "secret" religious life persisted in Russia; that atheist agitation and propaganda had been an utter failure; and that the destruction of the Orthodox Church Patriarchate and its elites would only empower the uncontrol-lable underground. Therefore, Sergii shrewdly concluded, the Soviet government had not—and, he implied, would not—be inclined to utterly destroy his preeminent

Church. Sergii's optimism was also nurtured by recent experience: based in the Baltic, he had watched as thousands of Orthodox churches remained open under Soviet occupation in 1939–41. Sergii had been detained by the Germans for four days in Riga, and his motive in addressing them directly was evidently to convince them that it would be in their best interests to support the Orthodox Church—whatever its Russian ties—over the rival Ecumenical Church, whose Patriarch enjoyed close connections to the British government and was at that time living in London. (Shkarovskii, *Russkaia Pravoslavnaia Tserkov' pri Staline i Khrushcheve*, 100; 148.) Previously, in 1940, Sergii had cooperated with the Soviet government in the expropriation of lands and churches from the rival Uniate Church in Ukraine (see Dunn, *The Catholic Church and Russia*, 105).

92. *VRGV*, 69.

93. Odintsov, *Russkaia pravoslavnaia tserkov'*, 274. Stalin had "raised the issue of normalizing relations with the Church in the Sovnarkom early in 1943" (Reese, "The Russian Orthodox Church and 'Patriotic' Support for the Stalinist Regime during the Great Patriotic War," 141).

94. On this meeting, see also: Chumachenko, *Church and State in Soviet Russia*, 15–16; Shkarovskii, *Russkaia Pravoslavnaia Tserkov' pri Staline i Khrushcheve*, 203–205. Some historians list the date of the meeting as September 5, and this is not incorrect: as we shall see, while the meeting began in the evening of September 4, it ran very late, not wrapping up until early the next morning.

95. Odintsov, *Russkaia pravoslavnaia tserkov'*, 272.

96. *VRGV*, 306.

97. *VRGV*, 306.

98. *VRGV*, 306.

99. *VRGV*, 307.

100. *VRGV*, 307.

101. *VRGV*, 307.

102. *VRGV*, 307.

103. *VRGV*, 309. Nevertheless, churches were reopening with or without Stalin's permission. "In the months preceding the meeting with the hierarchs," Reese writes, "reports by the People's Commissariat of State Security (NKGB) noted that in the aftermath of the Battle of Stalingrad, in spring and summer 1943, priests had begun to agitate among the faithful, encouraging them to demand the opening up of local churches. Between 1942 and mid-1943, in Iaroslavl' oblast parishioners had illegally reopened fifty-one village churches. At the same time, soviet authorities in Krasnoiarsk succumbed to local pressure and permitted two churches to open" ("The Russian Orthodox Church and 'Patriotic' Support for the Stalinist Regime during the Great Patriotic War," 142–143).

104. *VRGV*, 310.

105. Here, Stalin was onto something. Aleksii, in particular, had suffered terrible privations in recent years. A witness describes his circumstances during the brutal Siege of Leningrad, during which the Metropolitan was noted for holding processions with icons outside the church even during German air-raids: "In

the meantime the members of the Cathedral choir were dying one by one, until the choirmaster himself collapsed and died in the middle of a church service . . . The three surviving women in the choir grew so weak that they could no longer climb to the choir loft, but they continued to sing as best they could from a low platform in the sanctuary . . . Aleksi himself was wasting away, looking increasingly waxy . . . The last remaining deacon in Leningrad continued to serve until he, too, died. Thereafter Aleksi celebrated the liturgy alone." The scene in Leningrad before the war had been much more cheerful: a memoir of this period describes churches overflowing with visitors on weekends and holidays, and a crush of thousands one Easter—a crowd blithely heedless of the police calling on them to disperse (Shkarovskii, *Russkaia Pravoslavnaia Tserkov' pri Staline i Khrushcheve*, 109).

As for Sergii, a hint of his previous circumstances can be gleaned from the story of his evacuation from the Baltic back to Russia. As the Nazis invaded, Sergii was packed into a train-car with the one-eyed Old Believer archbishop of Moscow and All Russia, some Baptist leaders, and hierarchs from the Renovationist church. During the journey, Sergii ran a fever of 104 and became delirious. Two of the Renovationists fought violently, and Sergii had to hide himself away from them in a corner of the train compartment. When they reached their destination of Ulyanovsk, no place had been arranged for Sergii to stay, and only the local parish-society chairman came to greet him. He slept for a few more days in the train car. (Davis, *A Long Walk to Church*, 13–14; 16.)

106. *VRGV*, 311.
107. *VRGV*, 311.
108. The next such occasion occurred in April 1988, when Mikhail Gorbachev met with Patriarch Pimen (see Smolkin, *A Sacred Space Is Never Empty*, 1).
109. *VRGV*, 311.
110. *VRGV*, 311.
111. *VRGV*, 312.
112. *VRGV*, 312; see also Odintsov, *Russkaia pravoslavnaia tserkov'*, 275–277.
113. Odintsov, *Russkaia pravoslavnaia tserkov'*, 277; Chumachenko, *Church and State in Soviet Russia*, 17–18. Chumachenko writes that "During the first months of its existence," CAROC was "plagued by the lack of simple things such as glue, paper, envelopes, and file folders. The problem of providing the Council with folders continued until the end of 1945 when, at a conference with the Council's chairman, Senior Inspector V. Spiridonov noted that approximately *three hundred* files on request to open churches had not been properly set up due to the lack of file folders." Finding good people to staff the organization was also a problem: only a mere handful of employees had more than a secondary education (Chumachenko, *Church and State in Soviet Russia*, 18–19.)
114. Odintsov, *Russkaia pravoslavnaia tserkov'*, 305.
115. Krinko, "Vera i sueveriia na fronte i v tylu v usloviiakh voennogo vremeni (1941–1945)," 58.
116. HPSSS sched. A, vol. 35, case 355/(NY)1498 ff. 27–28.
117. HPSSS sched. A, vol. 11, case 139 f. 35.

118. *VRGV*, 84.
119. *VRGV*, 89 (emphasis added).
120. *VRGV*, 90; Chumachenko, *Church and State in Soviet Russia*, 57. Meanwhile, Orthodox Church leaders cooperated with CAROC and Stalin in destroying the remnants of their former rival, the Renovationist Church. On October 7, 1943, soon after concluding his "new deal" with the three Metropolitans, Stalin signed off on an ominous note from Karpov. The CAROC chief wrote: "The renovationist movement earlier played a constructive role but in recent years has lost its significance and base of support. On this basis, and taking into account the patriotic stance of the Sergiite church, the Council . . . has decided not to prevent either the dissolution of the renovationist church or the transfer of renovationist clergy and parishes to the patriarchal, Sergiite church." Stalin replied in a note written alongside this paragraph: "Comrade Karpov, I agree with you." Granted, the Renovationists had already been on shaky ground: of the six Renovationist churches formerly in Moscow, only one remained, and its cleric, according to Karpov, was constantly the subject of complaints for "conducting church services while obviously drunk, using foul language, and causing a scandal" (Chumachenko, *Church and State in Soviet Russia*, 37–38; see also Dunn, *The Catholic Church and Russia*, 109).
121. *VRGV*, 93; see also Chumachenko, *Church and State in Soviet Russia*, 58–60; Shkarovskii, *Russkaia Pravoslavnaia Tserkov' pri Staline i Khrushcheve*, 215 (Shkarovskii gives the tally of 6,702 rather than 6,402).
122. In Tbilisi, historically one of Eurasia's most religiously-diverse capitals, the landscape of officially sanctioned holy places was threadbare as of January 1944. In that month, a CARC report tallied the "active" religious buildings of its religious minority communities as follows: Muslim, 0; Jewish, 2; "Armenian-Gregorian," 1; "Greek-Catholic," 4; Evangelical, 3.The list of "inactive" (*nedeistvuiushchii*) sites includes, for example, seventeen "Armenian-Gregorian" churches (NatArchGE R 1880.1.1 ff. 3–4). By November, two mosques were operating in Tbilisi—one Sunni and one Shiʿa—though both, according to CARC documents, lacked what officials considered to be a *mulla* ("*mulla mechet' ne imeet*") (NatArchGE R 1880.1.1 f. 112).
123. *VRGV*, 92.

Chapter 2

1. S.A. Kildin, S.Sh. Yarmullin, and F.F. Ghaysina, eds., *Bashkortostan—aulialar ile* (Ufa: Kitap, 2012), 225. The "order not to retreat" is most likely intended as a reference to Stalin's famous Order No. 27 of July 1942, in which he forbade troops to retreat under any circumstances, commanding the Red Army to take "not a single step back." In this folktale, it is the Sufi master, and not Stalin, who gets credit for the notorious formula—and, by extension, for the famous (and tragic) steadfastness of the Soviet military. This may also be a reference, however, to a famous Qur'anic passage on steadfastness in battle, quoted later in this chapter by Ishan Babakhanov. Orthodox Christian folktales of a similar character have also been preserved from

the war years. In one such tale, set during the siege of Moscow, an embarrassed Stalin recalls the half-finished seminary training of his youth and summons clergy to the Kremlin to lead a prayer service for victory. At that same moment, a plane carrying a miraculous icon circled Moscow, and the city was saved from the Nazis. (Shkarovskii, *Russkaia Pravoslavnaia Tserkov' pri Staline i Khrushcheve*, 125–126.)

2. Muslim and Christian communities were not the only Soviet religious groups targeted by the religious propaganda effort. The Appendix offers samples of wartime appeals to two other communities: one directed to Buryat-speaking Buddhists and the other to Soviet Jews.

3. See Hamid Algar, "Shaykh Zaynullah Rasulev: The Last Great Naqshbandi Shaykh of the Volga-Urals Region," in Jo-Ann Gross, ed., *Muslims in Central Asia: Expressions of Identity and Change* (Durham, NC: Duke University Press, 1992), 112–133.

4. Building on his Sufi pedigree, Gabdrahman Rasulev made his name as an intermediary between Volga-Ural Muslim communities and the Tsarist Russian state: as a member of the Third All-Russian Muslim Congress, convened in 1906, he had helped to reorder the Tsarist Administration of Muslim Affairs.

5. Ro'i, *Islam in the Soviet Union*, 103n15; Tasar, "Soviet and Muslim," 101–105; Kolarz, *Religion in the Soviet Union*, 426.

6. S.G. Rakhmankulova, *Muftii Gabdrakhman Rasulev—starshii syn Ishan Khazrata Rasuleva* (Cheliabinsk, 2000), 121.

7. R.Sh. Khakimov, "Musul'manskie obshchiny na Urale v gody liberalizatsii gosudarstvenno-religioznoi politiki v SSSR," *Vestnik Cheliabinskogo Gosudarstvennogo Universiteta* 22/237 (2011), 94. There is limited evidence of ongoing antireligious propaganda in the Soviet press during the war years. For example, a May, 1944 propaganda article in the Uzbek-language journal *Qizil askar haqiqati*, penned by an Uzbek officer, alleges in passing that Islam was forcibly introduced to Central Asians by the Arabs as a means of oppression: "O'zbek xalqining qahramonona o'tmishi," *Ikkinchi jahon urushi va front gazetalari. Birinchi kitob*, ed. Rustam Shamsutdinov (Tashkent: Akademnashr, 2017), 438.

8. Khakimov, "Musul'manskie obshchiny na Urale v gody liberalizatsii gosudarstvenno-religioznoi politiki v SSSR," 94.

9. R.A. Raev and R.I. Iaqubov, eds., *Islam iuldarynda: Sufyisylyk habaqtary häm shäiekh Zäinulla Räsülev shäzhäräne. Islam dine tarikhy, äthärthär häm khalyq izhady* (Ufa: MÜDN RF, 2011), 65–68. On this appeal, cf. also: Rakhmankulova, *Muftii Gabdrakhman Rasulev—starshii syn Ishan Khazrata Rasuleva*, 122; S. Evans, *The Churches of the USSR* (London: Cobbett, 1943), 158–159; Motadel, *Islam and Nazi Germany's War*, 174; Koroleva and Korolev, *Islam v Srednem Povolzh'e. 1940-e gg.*, 33.

10. The idea that the Germans are taking "revenge" appears to be a reference to a common trope in Soviet wartime propaganda depicting the Soviet peoples as having spoiled previous German attempts at colonial domination.

11. Rakhmankulova, *Muftii Gabdrakhman Rasulev—starshii syn Ishan Khazrata Rasuleva*, 122.

12. Shin, "Red Army Propaganda for Uzbek Soldiers and Localised Soviet Internationalism during World War II," 46.

13. Schechter, "'The People's Instructions,'" 112.
14. Shin, "Red Army Propaganda for Uzbek Soldiers and Localised Soviet Internationalism during World War II," 46.
15. Shin, "Red Army Propaganda for Uzbek Soldiers and Localised Soviet Internationalism during World War II," 46.
16. Schechter, "'The People's Instructions,'" 116.
17. Shechter, "'The People's Instructions,'" 112.
18. Khakimov, "Musul'manskie obshchiny na Urale v gody liberalizatsii gosudarstvenno-religioznoi politiki v SSSR," 93.
19. Schechter, "'The People's Instructions,'" 114.
20. Motadel, *Islam and Nazi Germany's War*, 25–28.
21. Schechter, "'The People's Instructions,'" 115n27.
22. Raev and Iaqubov, eds., *Islam iuldarynda*, 65–68. See also Khakimov, "Musul'manskie obshchiny na Urale v gody liberalizatsii gosudarstvenno-religioznoi politiki v SSSR," 94; Guseva, *Rossiiskii musul'manin v XX veke (na materialakh Srednego Povolzh'ia)*, 153; Iunusova, ed., *225 let Tsentral'nomu dukhovnomu upravleniiu musul'man rossii: Istoricheskie ocherki*, 262; Koroleva and Korolev, *Islam v Srednem Povolzh'e. 1940-e gg.*, 34.
23. AkadNkTat MS 4046: fol. 1. This conference is mentioned in Ro'i, *Islam in the Soviet Union*, 103 and T.S. Saidbaev, *Islam i obshchestvo* (Moscow: Nauka, 1984), 188. Cf. also Walter Kolarz, *Religion in the Soviet Union* (New York: St. Martin's, 1961), 427; V.A. Akhmadullin, "Deiatel'nost' organov gosudarstvennogo upravleniia SSSR i rukovoditelei dukhovnykh upravlenii musul'man po sozdaniiu vsesoiuznogo musul'manskogo tsentra," *Vlast'* 8 (2015), 2–3.
24. AkadNkTat MS 4046: fol. 2.
25. AkadNkTat MS 4046: fol. 3.
26. AkadNkTat MS 4046: fol. 4. I am grateful to Alfrid K. Bustanov for deciphering this line of the text for me.
27. AkadNkTat MS 4046, fol. 4.
28. AkadNkTat MS 4046, fols. 5–6. The verses Rasulev quotes are: "Fight in the cause of Allah those who fight you but do not transgress limits; for Allah loveth not transgressors" (Q 2:189); "And slay them wherever ye catch them, and turn them out from where they have turned you out; for tumult and oppression are worse than slaughter" (Q 2:191); "For the present, Allah hath lightened your (task), for He knoweth that there is a weak spot in you: But (even so), if there are a hundred of you, patient and persevering, they will vanquish two hundred, and if a thousand, they will vanquish two thousand, with the leave of Allah: for Allah is with those who patiently persevere" (Q 8:66); "Those who reject Allah, and hinder (men) from the Path of Allah, then die rejecting Allah—Allah will not forgive them" (Q 47:34); "Against them make ready your strength to the utmost of your power, including steeds of war, to strike terror into (the hearts of) the enemies of Allah and your enemies and others besides whom ye may not know but whom Allah doth know. Whatever ye shall spend in the cause of Allah, shall be repaid unto you, and ye shall not be treated unjustly" (Q 8:60); "Go ye forth, (whether equipped) lightly or heavily, and strive and struggle,

with your goods and your persons in the Cause of Allah. That is best for you if ye (but knew)" (Q 9:41).)

29. AkadNkTat MS 4046, fols. 7–8.

30. Motadel, *Islam and Nazi Germany's War*, 52.

31. Motadel, *Islam and Nazi Germany's War*, 139–140; 149–150. Rasulev did not hesitate to voice his disgust for those Muslim leaders who supported the Nazis; of Amīn al-Ḥusayn, the so-called "Grand Mufti of Jerusalem" who had called on Arabs to side with Hitler, he said, "The facts are that the German and Italian fascists have been doing their utmost to secure the Near East, an important strategical base. The 'Grand Mufti' . . . is a despicable traitor and Gestapo agent. He is merely serving his masters" (M. Dolgopolov, "Soviet Mufti Exposes Hitler Mufti," *Soviet War News*, October 24, 1942).

32. The vision of colonialism as a crusade against Islam has a long heritage in the region's anti-colonial discourses, and Rasulev's comments on the Italians in Libya call to mind reflections on the same subject in the diary of the famous Bukharan jurist Sadr-i Ziya. Here is how the latter renders the comments of a (fictional) Italian soldier heading off to Tripoli: "Oh mummy! . . . This war is against Islam. It suits virgin girls, as well, to go to that war. I shall fight as well as I can for eliminating the Qurʾan and shall kill for my fatherland." Ṣadr-i Ẓiya, *The Personal History of a Bukharan Intellectual: The Diary of Muḥammad Sharīf-i Ṣadr-i Ẓiyā*, ed. Edward A. Allworth et al. (Leiden: Brill, 2003), 289. I am grateful to Paolo Sartori for calling my attention to this passage.

33. See Motadel, *Islam and Nazi Germany's War*, 83, 157–158.

34. Nabiev, *Islam i gosudarstvo*, 99.

35. Nabiev, *Islam i gosudarstvo*, 99. The state's goal in shepherding these "muftiates" into existence, as Tasar writes, likely had much to do with creating infrastructure for a more "institutionalized" Islam that would be easier to patrol, and to incorporate into a dominant bureaucratic hierarchy: "Above all the colonial authorities sought to situate Islam within stationary bodies, figures, and institutions susceptible to centralization and/or monitoring: mosques, *madrasas*, libraries, and major shrine complexes featuring all three on their grounds" (*Soviet and Muslim*, 32).

36. Nabiev, *Islam i gosudarstvo*, 99.

37. I.Kh. Sulaev, "Musul'manskoe dukhovenstvo v Velikoi Otechestvennoi Voine 1941–1945 gg.," *Voenno-istoricheskii zhurnal* 5 (2007), 25.

38. Tasar, "Soviet and Muslim," 26.

39. GARF, f.6991s, op.3s, d.6, l.34-36 ("Prvetstvie dukhovnogo s'ezda predstavitelei musul'manskogo dukhovenstva I veruiushchikh Uzbekistana, Tadzhikistana, Turkmenistana, Kirgizstana i Kazakhstana I.V. Stalinu s vyrazheniem gotovnosti musul'manskogo dukhovenstva prizyvat' v propovediakh veruiushchikh k bor'be s Germaniei," *Russian Perspectives on Islam*, https://islamperspectives.org/rpi/items/show/19566 [accessed April 14, 2020]).

40. Nabiev, *Islam i gosudarstvo*, 99.

41. Tasar, *Soviet and Muslim*, 49. M.A. Alibaev, *Islam v sovietskom Kazakhstane: strategii vyzhivaniia* (Astana: ENU im. L.N. Gumileva, 2015), 28–29.

42. Tasar, *Soviet and Muslim*, 49.

43. Not all historians can believe it either: Zaripov and Safarov write that it is "unlikely" that Stalin and Babakhanov really had a personal meeting. They do not specify the reason for their skepticism, however (*Akhmetzian Mustafin*, 64).

44. Jeremy Black, ed., *The Second World War, Volume II: The German War*, 1943–1945 (Burlington, VT: Ashgate: 2007), 65.

45. G.F. Krivosheev, *Soviet Casualties and Combat Losses in the Twentieth Century* (London: Greenhill, 1997).

46. Frank, *Gulag Miracles*, 106.

47. A cousin of the Prophet Muhammad, whose shrine is at Shah-i Zinda and in honor of whom the shrine complex is named.

48. Khwaja ʿUbaydallah Ahrar (d. 1490), a Naqshbandi master (*pīr*) of fifteenth-century Central Asia, was among the most powerful figures of his era in the region and is often credited with the rapid expansion of Naqshbandi influence in his lifetime. He is still widely revered in Central and South Asia.

49. Al-Bukhari (d. 870) wrote the *Ṣaḥīḥ al-Bukhārī*, one of the six major collections of hadith in the Sunni tradition.

50. Bahaʾ al-Din Naqshband (d. 1389), from whom the Naqshbandiyya take their name, is regarded as having begun a new Sufi lineage when he broke from his teachers and predecessors (including Amir Kulal) in preferring silent *dhikr* to the vocal *dhikr* practiced by them. Naqshbandi influence remains prominent throughout the Islamic world, from Central and South Asia to the Middle East and beyond.

51. Amir Kulal (d. ca. 1370) is widely remembered as the *pīr* of Bahaʾ al-Din Naqshband.

52. Sayf al-Din Bakharzi (d. 1260), a disciple of Najm al-Din Kubra, has been credited, among other things, with influencing the religious development of Berke Khan, ruler of the Golden Horde, who famously converted to Islam.

53. Agha-yi Buzurg was a sixteenth-century female Transoxianian saint; see Aziza Shanazarova, "A Female Saint in Muslim Polemics: Aghā-yi Buzurg and Her Legacy in Early Modern Central Asia," PhD diss. (Indiana University, 2019); Gulnora Aminova, "Removing the Veil of *Taqiyya*: Dimensions of the Biography of Agha-yi Buzurg," PhD diss. (Harvard University, 2009).

54. Ali b. Abi Ṭalib is meant here, but this shrine—located in what is presently an exclave of Uzbekistan—is not to be confused with the better-known shrine complex of Mazar-i Sharif, in northern Afghanistan.

55. Yasavi, for whom the Yasaviyya order is named, is a famed Sufi mystic of the twelfth century.

56. I have been unable to find useful biographical information on this saint.

57. I have been unable to find any biographical information on this saint.

58. Imam Qaffal (or Kaffal) Shashi (d. 976) was a renowned scholar and poet whose works were particularly influential among Shafiʿi jurists. Khwaja Ahrar claimed descent from a companion of this scholar; see J.A. Gross and A. Urunbaev, eds., *The Letters of Khwāja ʿUbayd Allāh Aḥrār and His Associates* (Leiden: Brill, 2002), 11. The Babakhanov family also claimed descent from him, and SADUM's Tashkent headquarters were located near his shrine, which is called "Hast-imam."

59. Khavand-i Ṭahur (d. 1354) is a well-known saint of Tashkent and a maternal ancestor of Khwaja Ahrar; cf. Devin DeWeese, "Spiritual Practice and Corporate Identity in Medieval Sufi Communities of Iran, Central Asia, and India: The Khalvatī/ʿIshqī/Shattārī Continuum," in Stephen E. Lindquist, ed., *Religion and Identity in South Asia and Beyond: Essays in Honor of Patrick Olivelle* (London: Anthem Press, 2011), 264.

60. A genealogical tradition claims that Shaykh Zayn al-Din is the son of Shihab al-Din ʿUmar Suhrawardi (d. 1234), who reportedly sent Zayn al-Dīn to Tashkent to popularize his teachings there.

61. ʿUkasha b. Muhsin (known in Central Asia as Ükasha Ata) was a companion of the Prophet Muhammad who is mentioned in hadith. I know of no grave site for this saint in the vicinity of Tashkent, though he has a site near Turkistan (the city in Kazakhstan) and another in Balkh (in Afghanistan).

62. AkadNkKaz MS 123 VII, 4–5.

63. AkadNkKaz MS 123 VII, 6.

64. Q 9:12: "But if they violate their oaths after their covenant, and attack for your Faith—fight ye the chiefs of Unfaith: for their oaths are nothing to them: that thus they may be restrained." Offering this and subsequent Qurʾanic verses in Arabic, Babakhanov then provides an exegesis in Turkic: "That is, God has addressed Muslims thus: 'If, after making an oath with you, they violate this oath, and taunt your religion, then of course (*albatta*) make war upon them and annihilate the leaders of those who came against your religion and your freedom, because among them there are no oaths or promises, and thus may you act, that your treacherous enemy will cease its vile works.'"

65. AkadNkKaz MS 123 VII, 6–7.

66. AkadNkKaz MS 123 VII, 7–8.

67. Q 2:190–191: "Fight in the cause of Allah those who fight you but do not transgress limits; for Allah loveth not transgressors. And slay them wherever ye catch them, and turn them out from where they have turned you out; for tumult and oppression are worse than slaughter." Babakhanov explains this verse as follows: "That is, 'Fight against those who fight you in the cause of God, but do not be one who transgresses or starts a war. God does not love the transgressor and the intemperate one. Slay them where you find them and destroy them, and drive them from your homeland (*vaṭan*) in whatever manner they drove you from your homeland. Disorder and oppression are as awful and disastrous as slaughter.'"

68. AkadNkKaz MS 123 VII, 9.

69. "The person who flees from battle at the time of the struggle is deserving of God's strict punishment, and his place on the Day of Judgment is in hell" (*dushman bilän kürāsh zamānida urushdan qachqan kishi khudāning qattiq jazāsiga mustahiq bolip uning jāyi ākhiratda dūzakhdur*).

70. In fact, state pressure on collective farms had already exceeded their potential in many parts of the region. In Kazakhstan, unreasonable wartime quotas went unmet, inspiring the state to punish "slacking" *kolkhoz* workers with lower pay and procurement prices, which in turn led some *kolkhozniki* simply to refuse to store any seed for future crops. By the time of Babakhanov's speech, it would already have been clear that the 1943 crop was disastrously meager; see Olcott, *The Kazakhs*, 189–190.

71. Q 8:60: "Against them make ready your strength to the utmost of your power, including steeds of war, to strike terror into (the hearts of) the enemies of Allah and your enemies and others besides whom ye may not know but whom Allah doth know. Whatever ye shall spend in the cause of Allah, shall be repaid unto you, and ye shall not be treated unjustly." Babakhanov explains the verse as follows: "That is, 'In order to gain victory over the enemy, reinforce your battle lines with all your strength, and ready your infantry and your cavalry to enter the battle. In this manner will you defeat and put to flight your enemies and the enemies of God and others whom you do not know but whom God Himself knows. A reward for your expenditures in the path of God will be returned to you, and you will justly be given your due.'"

72. AkadNkKaz MS 123 VII, 11.

73. *Ay khudā azzawajall, ādamkhwar razīl waḥshī dushmanning qabīḥ jināyatlaridan ādam balalarini āzād wa khalāṣ qil.*

74. AkadNkKaz MS 123 VII, 11.

75. "Mohammedans Greet Marshall Stalin," *Soviet War News*, May 31, 1944. In this same letter, they hail Stalin as the "God-sent, wise head of the Soviet Government, Supreme Commander-in-Chief, great defender of the peoples from the Fascist miscreants!" See also Kolarz, *Religion in the Soviet Union*, 428; Ro'i, *Islam in the Soviet Union*, 105; Motadel, *Islam and Nazi Germany's War*, 175. The first "patriotic appeal" to Muslims produced by the North Caucasus muftiate was published in a range of languages that showcases the region's diversity: Avar, Kumyk, Dargin, Lezgin, Lak, Tabasaran, Kabardian, Ossetian, Adyghe, Circassian, and Noghai (*PDDUM*, 44).

76. Sulaev, "Musul'manskoe dukhovenstvo v Velikoi Otechestvennoi Voine 1941–1945 gg.," 25.

77. Plans were drafted—and, in 1945, tentatively approved by the leaders of the muftiates—to combine them into a single "All-Union Muslim Center"—a kind of Vatican of Soviet Islam. The plans never came to pass, however. See R.I. Bekkin, "Muftiiaty i gosudarstvo v sovetskuiu epokhu: evolutsiia otnoshenii / The Muftiates and the State in the Soviet Times: The Evolution of the Relationship," in *Rossiiskii islam v transformatsionnykh protsessakh sovremennosti: novye vyzovy i tendentsii razvitiia v XXI veke*, ed. Z.R. Khabibullina (Ufa: Dialog, 2017), 64.

78. Tasar, *Soviet and Muslim*, 44. A refugee from Tajikistan interviewed in the late Stalin era alleges that the Badakhshan Ismaʿilis were known to make their way secretly back and forth across the Soviet border in order to complete the *hajj* pilgrimage to Mecca (HPSSS sched. B, vol. 9, case 448 ff. 20–21).

79. RGASPI,f.62, op.2, d.1145, l.83 ("Postanovlenie Plenuma Sredazbiuro o musdukhovenstve," *Russian Perspectives on Islam*, https://islamperspectives.org/rpi/items/show/11079 [accessed April 14, 2020]).

80. RGASPI, f.62, op.2, d.1145, l.35–68 ("Musul'manskoe dukhovenstvo Srednei Azii v 1927 g. [po dokladu polnomochnogo predstavitelia OGPU v Srednei Azii] [4 iunia 1927 g.]," *Russian Perspectives on Islam*, https://islamperspectives.org/rpi/items/show/16797 [accessed April 14, 2020]).

81. Guseva, *Rossiiskii musul'manin v XX veke (na materialakh Srednego Povolzh'ia*, 156.

82. Yayoi Kawahara and Umed Mamadsherzodoshev, *Documents from Private Archives in Right-Bank Badakhshan* (Tokyo: University of Tokyo, TIAS Central Eurasian Research Series, 2015).
83. The document is signed by a number of Ismaili leaders: Sayyid Kazim Sayyid Shahidzada, Shahnam Sayyid Mursilzada, Mazhab Shah, Sayyid Murad ʿAli Sayyid Mirza, Sayyid Sharif Sayyid ʿAshur, Shahnazar ʿAtaligh Shahzada, and Mahrambeg Rizazada.
84. Kawahara and Mamadsherzodoshev, *Documents from Private Archives in Right-Bank Badakhshan*.
85. Kawahara and Mamadsherzodoshev, *Documents from Private Archives in Right-Bank Badakhshan*.
86. Kawahara and Mamadsherzodoshev, *Documents from Private Archives in Right-Bank Badakhshan*.
87. Kawahara and Mamadsherzodoshev, *Documents from Private Archives in Right-Bank Badakhshan*.
88. Kawahara and Mamadsherzodoshev, *Documents from Private Archives in Right-Bank Badakhshan*.
89. Kawahara and Mamadsherzodoshev, *Documents from Private Archives in Right-Bank Badakhshan*.
90. Kawahara and Mamadsherzodoshev, *Documents from Private Archives in Right-Bank Badakhshan*.
91. RGASPI, f.17, op.127, d.163, l.63 ("Zapiska zam. nachal'nika Upravleniia kadrov TsK VKP(b) N.V. Kiseleva sekretariam TsK VKP(b) A.A. Andreevu, G.M. Malenkovu, A.S. Shcherbakovu o rabote partiinoi organizatsii Tadzhikistana (o vliianiia islama v prigranichnykh raionakh," *Russian Perspectives on Islam*, https://islamperspectives.org/rpi/items/show/17798 [accessed April 14, 2020]).
92. RGASPI, f.17, op.88, d.632, l. 73 ("Dokladnaia zapiska zamestitelia zaveduiushchego Organizatsionno-instruktorskim otdelom TsK VKP(b) L.A. Slepova sekretariu TsK VKP(b) G.M. Malenkovu o vystuplenii sekretaria TsK KP(b) Tadzhikistana D.Z. Protopopova na plenume TsK KP(b) Tadzhikistana o roli musul'manskogo dukhovenstva v gody Velikoi Otechestvennoi voiny," *Russian Perspectives on Islam*, https://islamperspectives.org/rpi/items/show/16169 [accessed April 12, 2020]).
93. Kildin, Yarmullin, and Ghaysina, eds, *Bashkortostan—aulialar ile*, 226.

Chapter 3

1. Raev and Iaqubov eds., *Islam yuldarynda: Sufiysïlïk habaqtari häm shäyekh Zäynulla Räsülev shäjärähe*, 68–69.
2. Franklyn D. Holzman, "Soviet Inflationary Pressures, 1928–1957: Causes and Cures," *The Quarterly Journal of Economics* 74/2 (May, 1960), 168; *PDDUM*, 66. Cash contributions received by the muftiate-affiliated mosques were typically turned over to banks, which provided receipts (Khakimov, "Musul'mane Urala v gody Velikoi Otechestvennoi voiny (1941–1945)," 147. It is worth noting that

wartime fundraising was also a function of the Tsarist-era Orenburg Muslim Spiritual Assembly (OMSA)—a function exercised robustly during the First World War. I am grateful to Allen J. Frank for this observation.

3. Khakimov, "Musul'manskie obshchiny na Urale v gody liberalizatsii gosudarstvenno-religioznoi politiki v SSSR," 94; cf. also D.N. Denisov and K.A. Morgunov, *130 let tsentral'noi sobornoi mecheti Orenburga* (Orenburg: OGAU, 2009; "Etnoregional'nye issledovaniia" v. 6), 26–27.

4. A.A. Nurullaev, "Musul'mane Sovetskogo Soiuza v Velikoi Otechestvennoi voine," in N.A. Trofimchuk ed., *Religioznye organizatsii Sovetskogo Soiuza v gody Velikoi Otechestvennoi voiny 1941–1945 gg.* (Moscow: RAGS, 1995), 61.

5. Nurullaev, "Musul'mane Sovetskogo Soiuza v Velikoi Otechestvennoi voine," 61

6. *PDDUM*, 28–29.

7. *PDDUM*, 48; see also Akhmadullin, "Deiatel'nost' organov gosudarstvennogo upravleniia SSSR i rukovoditelei dukhovnykh upravlenii musul'man po sozdaniiu vsesoiuznogo musul'manskogo tsentra," 3–4. On donations made through the Orthodox Church, see Shkarovskii, *Russkaia Pravoslavnaia Tserkov' pri Staline i Khrushcheve*, 129–131; Alekseev, *Illiuzii i dogmy*, 335; Reese, "The Russian Orthodox Church and 'Patriotic' Support for the Stalinist Regime during the Great Patriotic War," 138.

8. Daniel Peris writes: "In a typical [petition] example from mid-1943, peasants from a rural area of Ivanovo oblast' complained of their difficulty in getting their priest registered. They wrote that they wished to help the Motherland in difficult times, had already donated 12,500 rubles to the Defense Fund and 6,115 rubles in bonds to the Dmitrii Donskoi Tank Column, but argued, '[w]e could give much more if we had a pastor'" ("'God is Now on Our Side,'" 106).

9. Rakhmankulova, *Muftii Gabdrakhman Rasulev—starshii syn Ishan Khazrata Rasuleva*, 122. Eren Tasar offers an insightful appraisal of the significance of charitable donations in the context of Central Asian Muslim tradition: "The practice of giving charity, especially during the two major annual Muslim holidays ('*eid*), carried enormous symbolic significance. In Central Asia, almsgiving was traditionally centered around the mosque and took place in a heavily ritualized atmosphere. Often accompanied by his sons, the male head of household made a payment on behalf of his family to an *imam*, who recited a formulaic Arabic prayer, followed by an indigenous-language plea to God (in Kyrgyz, Tajik, Uzbek, etc.). This concluded with the *basmala*, or bringing both hands to the face. Ordinary people understood alms not only as a mean of supporting the mosque (and, through its offices, needy Muslims in the community, such as individuals widowed or orphaned by the war), but they also perceived such beneficence as a vehicle for beseeching the Almighty to have mercy on one's deceased ancestors (Uzbek, *ajdodlar* or *eski bobolar*) and most especially one's parents (*ota-onalar*). Charitable contributions were loaded with multiple layers of meaning" (*Soviet and Muslim*, 64).

10. Khakimov, "Musul'manskie obshchiny na Urale v gody liberalizatsii gosudarstvenno-religioznoi politiki v SSSR," 94.

11. Denisov and Morgunov, *130 let tsentral'noi sobornoi mecheti Orenburga*, 26.

12. Just a few examples—all from among the personnel of a single mosque—will suffice here to demonstrate the diversity of jobs taken up by former religious elites when religious work was scarce (many others are offered in Ghïlmani, *Biographies of the Islamic Scholars of Our Times*, which profiles in detail the lives of major steppe Islamic figures such as Momaqan Äliyev):

Abdulgaziz Sibagatullovich Murtazin—originally billed to take over as imam at the Orenburg (then called Chkalov) mosque on December 25, 1952—was one figure who endured a winding path back to religious officialdom. Born in 1885 in the village of Shishma, Murtazin was the son of a muezzin. He became the chief imam of a local mosque at the young age of twenty-six, but the mosque was shuttered in 1930. For the next fifteen years, Murtazin labored as an itinerant mason. In 1945 he settled with his son in Kazan. He tried his hand as a beekeeper and construction worker on a collective farm between 1948 and 1952 before being summoned back to work as an imam—only to be blocked, for unknown reasons, from taking over that post (Denisov and Morgunov, *130 let tsentral'noi sobornoi mecheti Orenburga*, 36).

The man who got the job of imam at the Orenburg (Chkalov) mosque instead of Murtazin, Faruk Sharafutdinovich Sharafutdinov, had suffered a more difficult journey. Sharafutdinov was born into an esteemed family of imams in the Tyulyachinsky district of Tatarstan in 1891. After finishing his madrasa training in 1920, he served as imam in the nearby village of Kovali. He was arrested in October 1929, reportedly for speaking in defense of a fellow imam, and in February of the next year he was formally charged with "religious agitation" and sentenced to five years' hard labor in Kotlas, notorious for its brutal logging camps. He returned to work in mosques only after the end of the war, serving as an imam in Chistopol, Kazan, and Troitsk before his appointment in Chkalov (Denisov and Morgunov, *130 let tsentral'noi sobornoi mecheti Orenburga*, 38).

The mosque's other personnel had followed similarly winding roads over the previous decades. Ibragim Zarifovich Iskhakov, who became the muezzin (*azancha*) at Orenburg's Chkalov Mosque after its reopening, grew up in a small village in Orenburg *oblast*, where as a child he studied at a maktab from 1891 to 1894. Afterward he worked as a hired hand in wealthy households for a decade before being called up for military service in 1904. For three years he served in the Second Orenburg Cossack Regiment, stationed in Warsaw. Demobilized in 1907, he spent seven years laboring on his father's land as a peasant farmer. In 1914 he was drafted once again, and he deployed to the Western front with the Fourteenth Orenburg Cossack Regiment, in which he served as a blacksmith. Demobilized in 1917, he returned to his father's farm, but was soon enlisted by the White Army and wounded at Aktobe. After five months' recovery in Omsk, he went back to peasant farming. In 1920, a new opportunity came along: Iskhakov found work as a guard at the Eighth Mosque of Orenburg, a position he would occupy for the next fifteen years, until the mosque's forced closure in 1935, after which he found work as a shepherd in a local cooperative. In 1939, at the invitation of his wife's relatives, he moved to the village of Angren in Uzbekistan, where he worked as an infirmary guard at a coal mine and found some additional income doing freelance work at a prison camp. After just three years he returned home to Orenburg *oblast* and labored in a cooperative in the nearby village of Chkalov. When the Chkalov Mosque was reopened in April 1945, he finally returned to the job he had previously held for fifteen years: he served as a guard there, where his voice must have attracted appreciative attention, as he soon found himself promoted to the post of muezzin (Denisov and Morgunov, *130 let tsentral'noi sobornoi mecheti Orenburga*, 39–40).

Another muezzin at the mosque, Masnavi Ahunzyanovich Aminov, had formerly performed the job "unofficially"—and perhaps illegally—in another of the city's mosques, from 1928 to 1931. After that mosque was shuttered by the government, he had worked as a mechanical technician in locksmiths' workshops. He also found work in a home for disabled Orenburg residents. With the reopening of the mosque led by Rakhmankulov, Aminov was immediately confirmed as muezzin by the Central Spiritual Directorate, returning to visible public service in the religious community for the first time in fifteen years. He soon found himself loaded with additional responsibilities: although he seems to have had no prior accounting or bookkeeping experience, Aminov was put in charge of managing the mosque community's finances; he took over for Rakhmankulov on days when the imam was absent; and he took up the solemn business of washing the dead (Denisov and Morgunov, *130 let tsentral'noi sobornoi mecheti Orenburga*, 29).

13. Rakhmankulova, *Muftii Gabdrakhman Rasulev—starshii syn Ishan Khazrata Rasuleva*, 122

14. Rakhmankulova, *Muftii Gabdrakhman Rasulev—starshii syn Ishan Khazrata Rasuleva*, 124

15. Ro'i, *Islam in the Soviet Union*, 11.

16. Ro'i, *Islam in the Soviet Union*, 12.

17. Sergey Abashin has observed that such partnerships between "official" and "unofficial" religious authorities were the norm rather than the exception—a relationship he calls the "double game" of opportunistic religious politics. One result of this "game" was the persistence of some traditional rituals (albeit sometimes in slightly altered forms) with the full cooperation of the same "official" institutions that sometimes condemned them. This was possible because, as Abashin writes, "Sovietness was not uniform or built like a hierarchical pyramid where directives would only flow from the top to the bottom; it implied a perpetual negotiation process where agreements between different groups were made and unmade. Local practices and symbols were not infrequently at stake in these negotiations; and administrators could either Sovietize (or nationalize) them and use them to their own ends, or conceal and silence them, or else censure and abuse them. The choice of this or that strategy depended on a multiplicity of factors which were constantly changing" (Sergei Abashin, "Prayer for Rain: Practicing being Soviet and Muslim," *Journal of Islamic Studies* 25/2 (2014), 199).

18. As Tasar observes, "A mosque's status as registered or unregistered had no bearing on the validity of prayers performed within its walls . . . Moreover, although Muslims traditionally performed congregational prayers in mosques, they were not required to do so. Registration also constituted an ineffective means of controlling Islam because much religious practice did not center around mosques" (*Soviet and Muslim*, 52).

19. Khakimov, "Musul'manskie obshchiny na Urale v gody liberalizatsii gosudarstvenno-religioznoi politiki v SSSR," 96.

20. Khakimov, "Musul'manskie obshchiny na Urale v gody liberalizatsii gosudarstvenno-religioznoi politiki v SSSR," 96.

21. Denisov and Morgunov, *130 let tsentral'noi sobornoi mecheti Orenburga*, 28. A prior decree by the SNK had paved the way: on July 30, 1944, the SNK had authorized—in approved cases—the transfer of buildings, property, and objects that had been "nationalized" to registered religious communities, to be used by those communities in perpetuity (Khakimov, "Musul'manskie obshchiny na Urale v gody liberalizatsii gosudarstvenno-religioznoi politiki v SSSR," 95).

22. Denisov and Morgunov, *130 let tsentral'noi sobornoi mecheti Orenburga*, 28–29.

23. It was no easy job, however. In the Tsarist era, Chkalov (then—and now again—called Orenburg) hosted several mosques, and each imam would typically lead prayers two or perhaps three times per day. In the newly reopened Chkalov Mosque, by contrast, Rakhmankulov's presence was required five times per day. Forty or fifty people would visit the mosque for noon prayers on a typical day, but on Fridays the crowd would swell to some two hundred and fifty. During the major holidays of Uraza Bayram ('Eid al-Fitr) and Kurban Bayram ('Eid al-Adha), three or four thousand Muslims overflowed the mosque and had to be accommodated in the outdoor courtyard (Denisov and Morgunov, *130 let tsentral'noi sobornoi mecheti Orenburga*, 33).

24. Khakimov, "Musul'mane Urala v gody Velikoi Otechestvennoi voiny (1941–1945)," 150

25. On Ishan Babakhanov's prestigious background and its significance, see Tasar, *Soviet and Muslim*, 49.

26. Rakhmankulova, *Muftii Gabdrakhman Rasulev—starshii syn Ishan Khazrata Rasuleva*, 124.

27. Khakimov, "Musul'mane Urala v gody Velikoi Otechestvennoi voiny (1941–1945)," 150.

28. Rakhmankulova, *Muftii Gabdrakhman Rasulev—starshii syn Ishan Khazrata Rasuleva*, 124.

29. Rakhmankulova, *Muftii Gabdrakhman Rasulev—starshii syn Ishan Khazrata Rasuleva*, 124.

30. Rakhmankulova, *Muftii Gabdrakhman Rasulev—starshii syn Ishan Khazrata Rasuleva*, 125

31. *Islam yuldarynda*, 69; Guseva, *Rossiiskii musul'manin v XX veke (na materialakh Srednego Povolzh'ia)*, 153.

32. Sulaev, "Musul'manskoe dukhovenstvo v Velikoi Otechestvennoi voine 1941–1945 gg.," 26.

33. Sulaev, "Musul'manskoe dukhovenstvo v Velikoi Otechestvennoi voine 1941–1945 gg.," 26.

34. Sulaev, "Musul'manskoe dukhovenstvo v Velikoi Otechestvennoi voine 1941–1945 gg.," 26.

35. Rakhmankulova, *Muftii Gabdrakhman Rasulev—starshii syn Ishan Khazrata Rasuleva*, 125.

36. Sulaev, "Musul'manskoe dukhovenstvo v Velikoi Otechestvennoi voine 1941–1945 gg.," 26.

37. Sulaev, "Musul'manskoe dukhovenstvo v Velikoi Otechestvennoi voine 1941–1945 gg.," 26. Eren Tasar offers two similar wartime vignettes from Central Asia: "In one telling instance immediately after Germany's defeat, an unregistered *mulla* named Bokoleev attended collective meetings in two separate *kolkhozes* dedicated to discussing Victory Day. At his initiative, those present assented to including a resolution in the meetings' protocols highlighting the beneficial character of religion for humanity. Both protocols passed reviews by the district Communist Party committee; only at the provincial level did Party officials 'note the inappropriateness of referencing religious propaganda in a resolution dedicated to Victory Day.'" The second vignette shows an unregistered *mulla* wearing multiple hats, so to speak: "Around the same time, an unregistered *mulla* in rural Osh district, Zaynuddin Sulaymanov, delivered a lecture entitled 'The Restoration and Development of the USSR's National Economy' at gatherings of several village soviets upon the Party district committee's request. Such an invitation would have been unthinkable during the Great Terror less than a decade earlier" (*Soviet and Muslim*, 53–54).

38. Khakimov, "Musul'manskie obshchiny na Urale v gody liberalizatsii gosudarstvenno-religioznoi politiki v SSSR," 95.

39. Sulaev, "Musul'manskoe dukhovenstvo v Velikoi Otechestvennoi voine 1941–1945 gg.," 25. Italics mine.

40. R.A. Nabiev, *Islam i gosudarstvo: Kul'turno-istoricheskaia evoliutsiia musul'manskoi religii na Evropeiskom Vostoke* (Kazan: Kazanskii Gos. Universitet, 2002), 98.

41. Sulaev, "Musul'manskoe dukhovenstvo v Velikoi Otechestvennoi voine 1941–1945 gg.," 25.

42. See, for example, Sulaev, "Musul'manskoe dukhovenstvo v Velikoi Otechestvennoi voine 1941–1945 gg.," 26.

43. Sulaev, "Musul'manskoe dukhovenstvo v Velikoi Otechestvennoi voine 1941–1945 gg.," 25. In May 1947, I.V. Polianskii consented to have them decorated with honors "for valiant labor in the Great Patriotic War" (see also Tasar, *Soviet and Muslim*, 55). Russian Orthodox leaders got their share, of course: Patriarch (formerly Metropolitan) Aleksei, for example, received a medal "for the Defense of Leningrad" (*PDDUM*, 87; Akhmadullin, "Deiatel'nost' organov gosudarstvennogo upravleniia SSSR i rukovoditelei dukhovnykh upravlenii musul'man po sozdaniiu vsesoiuznogo musul'manskogo tsentra," 5–6; Alekseev, *Illiuzii i dogmy*, 334).

44. Sulaev, "Musul'manskoe dukhovenstvo v Velikoi Otechestvennoi voine 1941–1945 gg.," 24.

45. Khakimov, "Musul'manskie obshchiny na Urale v gody liberalizatsii gosudarstvenno-religioznoi politiki v SSSR," 95.

46. *PDDUM*, 30; A.A. Nurullaev, "Musul'mane Sovetskogo Soiuza v Velikoi Otechestvennoi voine," 64.

47. A.A. Nurullaev, "Musul'mane Sovetskogo Soiuza v Velikoi Otechestvennoi voine," 64–65.

48. A.A. Nurullaev, "Musul'mane Sovetskogo Soiuza v Velikoi Otechestvennoi voine," 65.

49. Nabiev, *Islam i gosudarstvo*, 99–100.

50. The journal in question would become the official propaganda journal *Muslims of the Soviet East*. This journal enjoyed a short run in 1946 and was revived in 1968, eventually having a global circulation of up to 30,000 copies per issue (see Tasar, *Soviet and Muslim*, 259).

51. Raev, and Iaqubov, eds., *Islam yuldarynda*, 70. Rasulev penned the work only as a backup plan, however; originally, he had hoped to develop a full training program for imams. With Ufa's madrasas shuttered, Rasulev had approached the local government with a request to hold courses in a nearby Catholic church. He designed the program of study himself, including units on the basics of Islam, its rites and customs, the study of the Qur'an and hadith, and—somewhat desperately—the constitution of the Soviet Union. The local government in Ufa was unpersuaded. Rasulev tried again in 1946, this time submitting his proposal and his curriculum to Moscow. Once again, he got the thumbs down. It was in lieu of the training program he had designed that he ventured to write his elementary textbook on Islam. Published soon after the end of the war, it was—strangely—printed only in Arabic script, which, as Rasulev's daughter explains, was known only to certain elderly people in the region. Nevertheless, a woman named Rabita-Khanum, who was charged with publishing the Islamic calendar called for by the decree, printed a Cyrillic copy of Rasulev's book—and then, over the course of several months, she printed twenty-eight more of them. Rasulev, evidently delighted, personally sent these copies to select recipients. Just to be safe, he also sent copies to the local government, to the council for religious affairs in Ufa, and to I.V. Polianskii (the top bureaucrat of CARC). But why had he printed the book in Arabic script in the first place? Perhaps Rasulev was hoping to inspire a rededication to the older script among younger generations of Muslims, or at least Muslim imams in training. Or perhaps he simply felt that such material was better suited to the Arabic script, in which the correspondences and other internal documents of the directorates were still frequently composed. Or did Rasulev delegate the Cyrillic version to his colleague in hopes of reducing his personal culpability should officials deem this an unacceptably broad dissemination of religious literature? In any event, Rasulev's tract on the basics of the faith remains in print to this day.

52. Nabiev, *Islam i gosudarstvo*, 100.

53. HPSSS sched. B, vol. 9, case 448 ff. 20–21.

54. Consul R.W. Bullard to Mr. MacDonald, "Jeddah Report. July 31–August 30, 1924," *Political Diaries of the Arab World: Saudi Arabia: The Jeddah Diaries, 1919–1940 (Vol. 2: 1922–1927)*, ed. Robert L. Jarman (Oxford: Archive Editions, 1990), 231 (henceforth "*Jeddah Diaries*").

55. Bullard to MacDonald, "Jeddah Report. July 31–August 30, 1924," *Jeddah Diaries*, 231.

56. R.W. Bullard to Austen Chamberlain, "Report for the Period March 20-April 11, 1925," *Jeddah Diaries*, 297.

57. R.W. Bullard to Austen Chamberlain, "Report for the Period April 12–30, 1925," *Jeddah Diaries*, 300.

58. V.A. Akhmadullin, *Patrioticheskaia deiatel'nost' dukhovnykh upravlenii musul'man v gody velikoi otechestvennoi voiny* (Moscow: Islamskaia kniga, 2015), 161.

59. One of Polianskii's letters to Molotov reads: "Taking into account the fact that the Muslim pilgrimage from the USSR has not taken place over the last 20 years, the Council for the Affairs of Religious Cults under the SNK SSSR considers that satisfying the petition of the Spiritual Directorate of the Muslims of Central Asia and Kazakhstan could have positive value, especially within the USSR, raising the authority of the Spiritual Directorate among Muslims. On the other hand, in the Muslim countries of the Near East the fact of pilgrimage from the USSR will also be perceived in a positive light. This fact would indicate the freedom of religion existing in the USSR. Considering this, and also having no data of any kind [supporting the] denial of the petition of the Spiritual Directorate of the Muslims of Central Asia and Kazakhstan, the Council for the Affairs of Religious Cults considers it expedient to support the petition specified" (ISG3, 34–35). According to Akhmadullin, some CARC officials were themselves surprised that permission for the hajj was granted, as they believed such indulgences and concessions would no longer be necessary now that the war had been won! (V.A. Akhmadullin, "Kharakternye oshibki issledovatelei pri analize khadzha sovetskikh musul'man v 1945 g.," *Vlast'* 7 [2013], 156).

60. Akhmadullin, *Patrioticheskaia deiatel'nost' dukhovnykh upravlenii musul'man v gody velikoi otechestvennoi voiny*, 162.

61. Akhmadullin, *Patrioticheskaia deiatel'nost' dukhovnykh upravlenii musul'man v gody velikoi otechestvennoi voiny*, 162; Koroleva and Korolev, *Islam v Srednem Povolzh'e. 1940-e gg.*, 47

62. Rakhmankulova, *Muftii Gabdrakhman Rasulev—starshii syn Ishan Khazrata Rasuleva*, 127–128.

63. Akhmadullin, "Kharakternye oshibki issledovatelei pri analize khadzha sovetskikh musul'man v 1945 g.," 157–158.

64. Denisov and Morgunov, *130 let tsentral'noi sobornoi mecheti Orenburga*, 32.

65. Denisov and Morgunov, *130 let tsentral'noi sobornoi mecheti Orenburga*, 31; see also Koroleva and Korolev, *Islam v Srednem Povolzh'e. 1940-e gg.*, 48. Koroleva and Korolev note that, on at least one pilgrimage, the pilgrims were charged a small fortune: 3,500 rubles payable to the Spiritual Directorate's coffers.

66. Khakimov, "Musul'manskie obshchiny na Urale v gody liberalizatsii gosudarstvenno-religioznoi politiki v SSSR," 97; Denisov and Morgunov, *130 let tsentral'noi sobornoi mecheti Orenburga*, 30.

67. Nabiev, *Islam i gosudarstvo*, 100. In December 1947, permission was tentatively given to open a madrasa in Baku, with an enrollment of 40. The plans evaporated, however; the official reasons were "lack of space" and "due to the small number of people who expressed a desire to study" (Damir, Mukhetdinov, *Istoriia islama v Rossii* [Moscow: Medina, 2019], 239).

68. Denisov and Morgunov, *130 let tsentral'noi sobornoi mecheti Orenburga*, 30–31.

69. Denisov and Morgunov, *130 let tsentral'noi sobornoi mecheti Orenburga*, 30.

70. Denisov and Morgunov, *130 let tsentral'noi sobornoi mecheti Orenburga*, 30.

71. Khakimov, "Musul'manskie obshchiny na Urale v gody liberalizatsii gosudarstvenno-religioznoi politiki v SSSR," 97.

72. Based on the table in Orenburg mosque, 100. Even in the more generous years of 1944–45, local Muslim elites did not have carte blanche to open mosques: in every instance, negotiations were necessary, and requests could be denied under suspicious pretexts. Petitioners could be told, for example, that the buildings available for religious gatherings were unsuitable because they lacked sufficient space to accommodate worshippers. In 1946–47, all ten of the applications submitted from the villages and towns of Sverdlovsk *oblast'* were rejected on these dubious grounds (Denisov and Morgunov, *130 let tsentral'noi sobornoi mecheti Orenburga*, 97; cf. also V.P. Kliueva, "Zhizn' v ateisticheskom gosudarstve: musul'manskie obshchiny Tiumenskoi oblasti [1940–1960-e gg.]," *Vestnik arkheologii, antropologii i etnografii* 10 [2009], 117).

73. Denisov and Morgunov, *130 let tsentral'noi sobornoi mecheti Orenburga*, 33; Khakimov, "Musul'manskie obshchiny na Urale v gody liberalizatsii gosudarstvenno-religioznoi politiki v SSSR," 97.

74. Kliueva, "Zhizn' v ateisticheskom gosudarstve: musul'manskie obshchiny Tiumenskoi oblasti [1940-1960-e gg.]," 117.

Chapter 4

1. Nuriia Älmieva, ed., *Möselmannar böek vatan sugyshynda* (Kazan: Khozur-Spokoistvie, 1436/2015), 100.

2. Älmieva, ed., *Möselmannar böek vatan sugyshynda*, 100.

3. Älmieva, ed., *Möselmannar böek vatan sugyshynda*, 101.

4. This refers to the opening *surah* of the Qur'an (*al-Fātiḥa*), which is often recited in its entirety as a stand-alone prayer.

5. Älmieva, ed., *Möselmannar böek vatan sugyshynda*, 102.

6. Älmieva, ed., *Möselmannar böek vatan sugyshynda*, 102. An infantryman stationed in Kiev was less indulgent of his Muslim comrades' penchant for group prayers, complaining: "All those men from Central Asia, when it was their mealtime, or after a bit anyway, they'd throw themselves on the ground and start up with their "O Allah!" (Catherine Merridale, *Ivan's War: Life and Death in the Red Army, 1939-1945* [New York: Picador, 2006], 154).

7. Älmieva, ed., *Möselmannar böek vatan sugyshynda*, 103.

8. Christian and atheist veterans likewise recall witnessing the religious devotions of Muslim soldiers at the front. The artillerist Ivan Grubov recalls Uzbek, Kazakh, and Turkmen soldiers stopping mid-battle to recite prayers over fallen comrades, holding fast even under German fire until their prayers were finished (interview, Ivan Vladimirovich Grubov, https://iremember.ru/memoirs/artilleristi/grubov-ivan-vladimirovich/ [accessed April 10, 2020]). Combat engineer Georgii Strelkov had an Uzbek soldier in his platoon who would do his daily prayers so diligently that they were reluctant to appoint him as a sentry, since he would request a prayer-break (interview, Georgii Aleksandrovich Strelkov, https://iremember.ru/memoirs/saperi/strelkov-georgiy-aleksandrovich/ [accessed April 10, 2020]). Infantryman Yuri Komov recalled Central Asian soldiers as generally more religious than their Slavic

counterparts, with many—but not all—of them praying together in a group (interview, Yuri Il'ich Komov, https://iremember.ru/memoirs/pekhotintsi/komov-uriy-ilich/ [accessed April 11, 2020]).

9. The opening words of the Qur'an (as well as traditional Muslim compositions in general), usually translated as, "In the name of God, the Compassionate, the Merciful."

10. R.Sh. Khakimov, "Musul'mane Urala v gody Velikoi Otechestvennoi voiny (1941–1945)," in *Religioznoe mnogoobrazie Ural'skogo regiona. Materialy Vserossiiskoi nauchnoi Prakticheskoi konferentsii* (Orenburg: OOO IPK "Universitet," 2014), 151. Prayer offering salvation from bombardment is also a common theme in interviews with Christian veterans and survivors of the war. A fifty-six-year-old Russian woman interviewed in the late Stalin era recalls: "I know that we are alive only because of our prayers to God. Once in Germany we sat in a bunker while the Americans were dropping bombs. Three bombs fell near the bunker but didn't hit us. We remained alive because I was praying all the time. Then another time an English plane dropped a bomb on the house in which we were living and it began to burn but because we had an ikon of Saint Nikolai, our most precious things were saved" (HPSSS sched. A, vol. 14, case 273 f. 26). A Ukrainian tractor mechanic told an interviewer, a few years after the war: "One cannot live without God. I remember that during some bombing attacks, I used to pray, but a friend of mine, who did not believe in God, ran for cover and was killed" (HPSSS sched. A, vol. 36, case 103/[NY]1593), f. 46).

11. "There is no God but God, and Muhammad is His messenger; I seek protection in Allah, the Merciful One . . . Allah is greatest!" Khakimov, "Musul'mane Urala v gody Velikoi Otechestvennoi voiny (1941–1945)," 150.

12. Älmieva, ed., *Möselmannar böek vatan sugyshynda*, 105–106.

13. "Praise be to God."

14. Khakimov, "Musul'mane Urala v gody Velikoi Otechestvennoi voiny (1941–1945)," 151.

15. Khakimov, "Musul'mane Urala v gody Velikoi Otechestvennoi voiny (1941–1945)," 151.

16. Khakimov, "Musul'mane Urala v gody Velikoi Otechestvennoi voiny (1941–1945)," 152.

17. Älmieva, ed., *Möselmannar böek vatan sugyshynda*, 129.

18. Älmieva, ed., *Möselmannar böek vatan sugyshynda*, 129–130.

19. "There is no God but God."

20. Älmieva, ed., *Möselmannar böek vatan sugyshynda*, 103–104.

21. Merridale, *Ivan's War*, 194. Brandon M. Schechter observes that "Religious items, such as Bibles, crosses, and prayers wrapped in leather, were often found among soldiers' belongings. . . Pëtr Liubarov, who worked for a frontline newspaper, noted in his diary in August 1943, that crosses and semipublic expressions of faith had become common during the war. . . Many soldiers mention talismans, some of which took the form of *oberegi* (amulets, often prayers wrapped in leather) or crosses, but which also could simply be 'lucky' objects with no religious connection, such as a broken cigarette holder" (*The Stuff of Soldiers: A History of the Red Army in World War II through Objects* [Ithaca: Cornell University Press, 2019], 187).

22. Interview, Vladimir Tikhonovich Annenkov, https://iremember.ru/memoirs/kavaleristi/annenkov-vladimir-tikhonovich/ (accessed April 11, 2020).

23. Interview, Stepan Aleksandrovich Stiazhkin, https://iremember.ru/memoirs/pekhotintsi/styazhkin-stepan-aleksandrovich/ (accessed April 11, 2020).

24. Krinko, "Vera i sueveriia na fronte i v tylu v usloviiakh voennogo vremeni (1941–1945)," 56; 59. Artillerist Mikhail Shurakov had a cross and the ninetieth psalm blessed by his mother, which he carried with him the entire war, fastened to his undergarments (interview, Mikhail Nikolaevich Shurakov, https://iremember.ru/memoirs/artilleristi/shurakov-mikhail-nikolaevich/ [accessed April 10, 2020]). Signalist Anatoly Krylov likewise recalls being given a piece of paper with the "Living Aid" psalm by his sister, and receiving a fresh copy from a Ukrainian woman later in the war. He credits the recitation of this psalm with saving his life while he was hiding in a roadside ditch under bombardment (interview, Anatoly Pavlovich Krylov, https://iremember.ru/memoirs/svyazisti/krylov-anatoliy-pavlovich/ [accessed April 11, 2020]). Infantryman Ivan Garshtia carried with him a small book called *Mother of God's Dream*, given to him by his grandmother, to which he attributed amulet-like qualities (interview, Ivan Garshtia, https://iremember.ru/en/memoirs/infantrymen/ivan-garshtia/ [accessed April 10, 2020]). Antonina Komaritsyna credits her cross (given to her by her mother) and a prayer titled "God has risen" with saving her in battle (interview, Antonina Maksimovna Komaritsyna (Baranova), https://iremember.ru/memoirs/drugie-voyska/komaritsina-baranova-antonina-maksimovna/ [accessed April 10, 2020]).

   There was also a fashion for "non-traditional" amulets without explicit Christian content. The famous sentimental poem "Wait for Me" (*Zhdi menia*) by Konstantin Simonov was often used in this manner, as some soldiers attributed to it magical protective qualities. Photographs, letters, and relatives' gifts could also have "protective powers" attributed to them (Krinko, "Vera i sueveriia na fronte i v tylu v usloviiakh voennogo vremeni (1941–1945)," 58–59).

25. HPSSS, sched. B, vol. 15, case 147 f. 14.

26. Khakimov, "Musul'mane Urala v gody Velikoi Otechestvennoi voiny (1941–1945)," 151.

27. Krinko, "Vera i sueveriia na fronte i v tylu v usloviiakh voennogo vremeni (1941–1945)," 56. Krinko's essay recounts other, similar memories of "sudden" Christian feeling, including the memories of a woman raised in a staunch atheist household who, in wartime, began attending church with her children, where they improvised prayers, as they "did not know how" to pray.

28. Interview, Degen Ion Lazarevich, https://iremember.ru/en/memoirs/tankers/degen-ion-lazarevich-/ (accessed April 8, 2020).

29. See, for example: interview, Arsenij Zonov, https://iremember.ru/en/memoirs/tankers/arsenij-zonov/ (accessed April 8, 2020); interview, Naum Aronovich Orlov, https://iremember.ru/memoirs/minometchiki/orlov-naum-aronovich/ (accessed April 8, 2020).

30. Interview, Fedor Ivanovich Beliaev, https://iremember.ru/memoirs/razvedchiki/belyaev-fedor-ivanovich/ (accessed April 5, 2020).

31. Shkarovskii, *Russkaia Pravoslavnaia Tserkov' pri Staline i Khrushcheve*, 123–124.

32. Interview, Grigorii Sergeevich Krasnonos, https://iremember.ru/memoirs/razvedchiki/krasnonos-grigoriy-sergeevich/ (accessed April 10, 2020).

33. Krinko, "Vera i sueveriia na fronte i v tylu v usloviiakh voennogo vremeni (1941–1945)," 56. Christian veterans' interviews oftentimes touch on the theme of battlefield salvation thanks to the prayers of others. A twenty-three year-old Russian student interviewed shortly after the war recalled: "I had a cousin who was on the front during the war. He asked my grandfather to pray for him, and he did. Later my cousin told us that his comrades fighting around him were all killed. They did not believe in God. But he remained unhurt, untouched. It does help to pray" (HPSSS sched. A, vol. 20, case 393 f. 25).

34. E.F. Krinko observes that, of 311,942 "negative" (that is, impermissible or suspect) statements flagged by NKVD censors of the "Stalingrad Front" during a two week period (!) in July 1942, only nineteen were flagged due to religious content. C.f. Krinko, "Vera i sueveriia na fronte i v tylu v usloviiakh voennogo vremeni (1941–1945)," 56. In the correspondences of Christian soldiers, meanwhile, according to M.V. Shkarovskii, one encounters requests from soldiers that the transcripts of sermons by their hometown priests be sent to them at the front (Shkarovskii, *Russkaia Pravoslavnaia Tserkov' pri Staline i Khrushcheve*, 124–125). One officer expressed exasperation that his soldiers had a habit of beginning "their letters home with the words *Long live Jesus Christ*. One soldier," the officer went on, "received an icon in the mail from his mother in front of which, before going to sleep, he prays" (Merridale, *Ivan's War*, 75).

35. Älmieva, ed., *Möselmannar böek vatan sugyshynda*, 159.

36. Älmieva, ed., *Möselmannar böek vatan sugyshynda*, 160–161.

37. Khakimov, "Musul'mane Urala v gody Velikoi Otechestvennoi voiny (1941–1945)," 151.

38. See, for example, K.M. Mingullin, M.Kh. Väliev, I.I. Iamaltdinov, and L. Kh. Mökhämmätcanova, eds., *Milli-mädäni mirasybyz: Samara ölkäse tatarlary* (Kazan: G.I. Ibrahimov isem. Tel, ädäbiyat häm sängat' instituty, 2015); K.M. Mingullin, I.G. Nuriev, and M.I. Äkhmätjanov, eds., *Milli-mädäni mirasybyz: Archa* (Kazan: G.I. Ibrahimov isem. Tel, ädäbiyat häm sängat' instituty, 2017); K.M. Mingullin, O.R. Khisamov, and L.Sh. Däulätshina, eds., *Milli-mädäni mirasybyz: Tomsk ölkäse tatarlary* (Kazan: G.I. Ibrahimov isem. Tel, ädäbiyat häm sängat' instituty, 2016); and K.M. Mingullin, I.I. Iamaltdinov, and L.Sh. Däulätshina, eds., *Milli-mädäni mirasybyz: Orenburg ölkäse tatarlary* (Kazan: G.I. Ibrahimov isem. Tel, ädäbiyat häm sängat' instituty, 2016).

39. Allen J. Frank, *Faith and Trauma on the Eastern Front: Kazakh Soldiers in the Red Army, 1935–1945* (in preparation). I am very grateful to Dr. Frank for sharing his work-in-preparation with me and for the permission to quote his translation of this poem. The theme of a child departing for the front is a common one in Soviet Muslim war poetry. Oftentimes the sentiment of sad parting is rendered in touchingly plain-spoken terms, as in these quatrains from Dagestan recorded, respectively, in 1948 and 1974: "At the hour when you / Take leave of the village, / Your mother will pray: / 'May Allah guard you!'"; "Dear son, you're going to war, / And I want peace to come! / Day and night I will pray / That Allah will protect you" (Adzhiev, ed., *Fol'klor narodov Dagestana o Velikoi Otechestvennoi voine*, 16; 56).

40. Mingullin, Väliev, Iamaltdinov, and Mökhämmätcanova, eds., *Milli-mädäni mirasybyz: Samara ölkäse tatarlary*, 248.

41. A village in Bugulma district, Samara *guberniia*.

42. That is, soldiers like this mulla were given lodging (billeted) in locals' homes or other non-military buildings.

43. Adzhiev, ed., *Fol'klor narodov Dagestana o Velikoi Otechestvennoi voine*, 36–37.

44. In this context, a traditional Muslim prayer of mourning for the dead.

45. Adzhiev, ed., *Fol'klor narodov Dagestana o Velikoi Otechestvennoi voine*, 57–58.

46. Adzhiev, ed., *Fol'klor narodov Dagestana o Velikoi Otechestvennoi voine*, 57.

47. Adzhiev, ed., *Fol'klor narodov Dagestana o Velikoi Otechestvennoi voine*, 19; 80. The first verse was composed by Batul Gadzhieva in the village of Tissi-Akhitli and copied down by Asiiat Suraeva; the second was copied down by F.M. Ibragimova in the village of Rutul, among the many quatrains remembered and recited by local women Kh. Navruzbekova, Z.R. Magomedragimova, and Z. Babaeva.

48. Adzhiev, ed., *Fol'klor narodov Dagestana o Velikoi Otechestvennoi voine*, 84.

49. Adzhiev, ed., *Fol'klor narodov Dagestana o Velikoi Otechestvennoi voine*, 143. This poem, titled "A Brother's Cry" (translated here from Russian), was copied down by F.M. Ibragimova in village of Rutul in 1970, from the words of Z.K. Babaeva.

50. Frank, *Faith and Trauma on the Eastern Front*.

51. Mingullin, Väliev, Iamaltdinov, and Mökhämmätcanova, eds., *Milli-mädäni mirasybyz: Samara ölkäse tatarlary*, 251. I am grateful to Allen J. Frank for his kind, diligent help in correcting and improving my translation of this Tatar text.

52. "In the name of God."

53. *Bashkort khalyk ijady, 11 tom: bäyettär / Bashkirskoe narodnoe tvorchestvo, tom 11: bayty*, ed. B.S. Baimov (Ufa: Kitap, 2004), 234.

54. M.C.-G. Albogachieva, *Islam v Ingushetii: etnografiia i istoriko-kul'turnye aspekty* (St. Petersburg: MAZ RAN, 2017), 34–35. According to Albogachieva, Muslim leaders played a crucial role in supporting and sustaining deported communities; some of the Muslim elites in the Caucasus, however, played a darker part in the deportations: documents reveal that certain "clergy" cooperated actively with the NKVD in the expulsion of Chechens and Ingushetians. Albogachieva prefers a sympathetic reading of these events, suggesting that Muslim leaders were in some cases able to negotiate the peaceful disarmament of resisters who would otherwise would have been killed (52–54). Nevertheless, this charitable view rings with an off-note of desperation.

55. Albogachieva., *Islam v Ingushetii: etnografiia i istoriko-kul'turnye aspekty*, 36. On the theme of folkloric memory, Albogachieva documents a tale in which the deportations were foreseen in a mystical vision by an Ingush shaykh (76). Kakagasanov notes that among non-deported populations, many "patriotic" speeches and calls to battle were delivered by Muslim leaders throughout the war era; local atheist officials recognized the role of the region's muftiate in encouraging these developments, listing them among the "many positive changes" they had noted in the region's religious milieu (G.I. Kakagasanov, "Vzaimootnosheniia vlasti i religii v Dagestane v gody Velikoi Otechestvennoi voiny (1941–1945 gg.)," *Vestnik instituta IAE* 2 [2011], 42–43).

56. Galim'ianova, "Cheremkhovskii Mulla," http://islamrb.ru/cheremkhovskij-mulla/ (accessed January 1, 2020).

57. Eren Tasar describes the appraisal of a CARC representative in Kyrgyzstan and offers some wartime examples from other layers of Central Asian society as well: "For Akhtiamov, the rise in Muslim religiosity as a result of the war was indisputable. 'Clearly some of the participants in the war made a pledge during the heat of battle, that they would "respect God" if He let them live. I find no other explanation for the fact that one encounters former *frontoviki* among the belivers attending prayers.' Mirzakulov, a mechanic at an MTS decorated for bravery during the war, applied for admission to one of SADUM's *madrasas* immediately upon his return home. G'ulomov, a Komsomol member and Stakhanovite, wrote to Stalin vowing to gather eighty-eight *tsentners* (8,800 kg) of cotton per hectare. Afterward, he started attending the mosque and 'praying to God for His "help" in fulfilling the promise'" (*Soviet and Muslim*, 52–53).

58. R.Kh. Kinziabaeva, "Vklad religioznykh organizatsii BASSR v pobedu v Velikoi Otechestvennoi voine," *Iadkiar* 1 (2008), 85.

59. Zaripov and Safarov, *Akhmetzian Mustafin: iz istorii islama v SSSR*, 61. Zaripov and Safarov's work makes a fine companion for Catriona Kelly's *Socialist Churches*, an important study of urban Soviet churches in Petrograd/Leningrad.

60. Zaripov and Safarov, *Akhmetzian Mustafin*, 62.

61. Vladimir Bobrovnikov, "Withering Heights: The Re-Islamization of a Kolkhoz Village in Dagestan: a MicroHistory," in Stéphane A. Dudoignon and Christian Noack, eds., *Allah's Kolkhozes. Migration, DeStalinisation, Privatisation, and the New Muslim Congregations in the Soviet Realm (1950s–2000s)* (Berlin: Klaus Schwarz, 2014; Islamkundliche Untersuchungen. Bd. 314), 375. Uraza Bairam is the Festival of the Breaking of the Fast, called ʿEid al-Fitr in Arabic. *Tarawih* refers to special prayers performed by Muslims only during the month of Ramadan. *Dhikr* is a distinctly Sufi practice involving the repetition of devotional phrases, either silently as meditative, repetitious thoughts or out loud in "chanted" form. Non-Muslims too could find themselves enjoying the hospitality of the Ramadan rituals: a young woman named Zoia Likholobova, evacuated to Uzbekistan from the West, recalls working twelve-hour days at a plant that entirely stopped production for the Muslim celebration she calls "the big bairam" (*bol'shoi bairam*); she was welcomed to join a foreman's large family as they enjoyed "a wonderful Uzbek plov, fragrant melons, and other delicacies" ("Likholobova Zoia Grigor'evna," in V.I. Podmarkov, et al, eds., *Pamiat': Vospominaniia rabotnikov Donetskogo natsional'nogo universiteta o Velikoi Otechestvennoi voine 1941–1945 gody* (Donetsk: Iugo-Vostok, 2011), 135–136.

62. Miner, *Stalin's Holy War*, 141.

63. *RPTs*, 493.

64. See, for example, DeWeese, "Islam and the Legacy of Sovietology."

65. Bobrovnikov, "Withering Heights: The Re-Islamization of a Kolkhoz Village in Dagestan," 375.

66. Bobrovnikov, "Withering Heights: The Re-Islamization of a Kolkhoz Village in Dagestan," 374.

67. DeWeese, "Shamanization in Central Asia"; see also Devin DeWeese, "'Dis-ordering' Sufism in Early Modern Central Asia: Suggestions for Rethinking the Sources and Social Structures of Sufi History in the 18th and 19th Centuries," in B. Babadjanov and Y. Kawahara, eds., *History and Culture of Central Asia/Istoriia i kul'tura Tsentral'noi Azii* (Tokyo: The University of Tokyo, 2012), 259–279.

68. Shikhaliev, "Transformatsiia sufisma v svete religioznoi politiki i pereselenii gortsev v Dagestane 1930–1990-x gg.," 102.

69. Zaripov and Safarov, *Akhmetzian Mustafin*, 80. On women's traditional role in the life of the mosque, Eren Tasar writes: "The mosque was a male-dominated setting and largely remains so (in Central Asia, at least) to the present day. What about Muslim women? With very few exceptions, they did not venture into mosques, nor was their attendance at congregational prayers required. Instead, women participated in a vibrant sphere of religious life off limits to men under the leadership of an *otin* . . . [a phrase which] refers to prominent female authority figures who combine the roles of prayer leader, scholar, teacher, healer, and therapist" (*Soviet and Muslim*, 20).

70. Zaripov and Safarov, *Akhmetzian Mustafin*, 62.

71. Kinziabaeva, "Vklad religioznykh organizatsii BASSR v pobedu v Velikoi Otechestvennoi voine," 85.

72. Koroleva and Korolev, *Islam v Srednem Povolzh'e*, 23.

73. Koroleva and Korolev, *Islam v Srednem Povolzh'e*, 97.

74. During this session, the faithful typically request God's help for issues that have no clear solution.

75. Khairetdinov, *Islam na Urale: entsiklopedicheskii slovar'* (Moscow: Medina, 2009), 80.

76. Kinziabaeva, "Vklad religioznykh organizatsii BASSR v pobedu v Velikoi Otechestvennoi voine," 85.

77. Khakimov, "Musul'mane Urala v gody Velikoi Otechestvennoi voiny (1941–1945)."

78. M.D. Butaev, G.I. Kakagasanov, and A.I. Osmanov, eds., *Vlast' i musul'manskaia religiia v Dagestane (Noiabr' 1917 g.–dekabr' 1991 g.). Dokumenty i materialy* (Makhachkala: IIAE DNTs RAN, 2007), 154.

79. *RPTs*, 501–502.

80. *RPTs*, 497. The report goes on to note a similar wave of circumcisions taking place in the Severo-Kazakhstan oblast', among both babies and adolescents.

81. See for example, Koroleva and Korolev, *Islam v Srednem Povolzh'e*, 18. A report by local atheist authorities in the Penza region claimed that other strata of the population—specifically, craftsmen, laborers, and intelligentsia—"stand apart from religion as if on the sidelines" (18).

82. O.R. Khasianov, "Religioznye praktiki predstavitelei kommunisticheskoi partii na sele v poslevoennoe desiatiletnie (na materialakh Kuybyshevskoy i Ul'ianovskoi oblastei)," in T.V. Petukhovoi, ed., *Patriotizm: istoriia, sovremennost', obraz budushchego. Mezhdunarodnaia nauchno-prakticheskaia konferentsiia, posviashchennaia 70-letiiu Pobedy v Velikoi Otechestvennoi voine: sbornik nauchnykh trudov* (Ul'ianovsk: UlGTU, 2015), 287.

83. Khakimov, "Musul'mane Urala v gody Velikoi Otechestvennoi voiny (1941–1945)," 153; Khairetdinov, *Islam na Urale: entsiklopedicheskii slovar'*, 173.

84. Zaripov and Safarov, *Akhmetzian Mustafin*, 82.
85. Zaripov and Safarov, *Akhmetzian Mustafin*, 73.
86. Zaripov and Safarov, *Akhmetzian Mustafin*, 72. The authors observe that officials involved in anti-religious activities were much less concerned about cemetery visitation and funeral rites than about traditional Muslim wedding ceremonies (*nikāh*), for example, as the incidence of Muslim weddings was regarded as a bellwether of religiosity among younger populations and therefore a predicter of long-term trends (Zaripov and Safarov, *Akhmetzian Mustafin*, 75).
87. Starostin, *Islam v Sverdlovskoi oblasti*, 77.
88. Khairetdinov, *Islam na Urale: entsiklopedicheskii slovar'*, 365.
89. Michael Kemper and Shamil Shikhaliev, "Qadimism and Jadidism in Twentieth-Century Daghestan," *Asiatische Studien / Etudes Asiatiques* 69/3 (2015), 609.
90. Älmieva, ed., *Möselmannar böek vatan sugyshynda*, 131.
91. Zaripov and Safarov, *Akhmetzian Mustafin*, 80–81n.

Chapter 5

1. Koroleva and Korolev, *Islam v Srednem Povolzh'e. 1940-e gg,* 63–64.
2. Koroleva and Korolev, *Islam v Srednem Povolzh'e*, 93.
3. Koroleva and Korolev, *Islam v Srednem Povolzh'e*, 16.
4. Koroleva and Korolev, *Islam v Srednem Povolzh'e*, 18.
5. For example, one official in Ul'ianovsk estimated that over 70 percent of the "practicing" religious population in the district was over the age of 60 (Koroleva and Korolev, *Islam v Srednem Povolzh'e*, 19). Some Soviet Christians and atheists interviewed in the late Stalin era as part of the Harvard Project on the Soviet Social System offered a similar assessment of the demographics of devoutly religious citizens. "There are still many people who do feel religious," noted one Russian electrical engineer. "Especially those over 40 or 45 years ... Religious has not died out" (HPSSS sched. A, vol. 26, case 517 f. 33). "In general," a twenty-five-year-old Russian student recalled, "only the middle-aged and the old went to church. And the priests were very suspicious of young people" (HPSSS sched. A, vol. 32, case 642/(NY)1109 f. 10).
6. Koroleva and Korolev, *Islam v Srednem Povolzh'e*, 18.
7. Koroleva and Korolev, *Islam v Srednem Povolzh'e*, 24–25.
8. "*v protsesse etoi p'ianki byla ustroena draka*" (Koroleva and Korolev, *Islam v Srednem Povolzh'e*, 24).
9. Kulmagambetov to the Pavlodar *oblispolkom*, September 17, 1944, V.D. Boltina and L.V. Sheveleva, eds., *Iz istorii islama v Pavlodarskom Priirtysh'e 1919–1999: sbornik dokumentov* (Pavlodar: EKO, 2001) (henceforth *IIIPP*), 72–73, doc. 52.
10. N. Guliaeva to Sh. Kenzhebaev, December 15, 1944, *IIIPP*, 74, doc 54.
11. Kulmagambetov, Tarchakov, and Mamyrov to K. Makin, December 19, 1944, *IIIPP*, 74–75, doc. 55.
12. T. Morshchinin, "Decision of the Pavlodar *oblispolkom*," December 22, 1944, *IIIPP*, 75–76, doc. 56.

13. A. Zagovel'ev to N. Guliaev, February 10, 1945, *IIIPP*, 78, doc. 58.

14. Iadryshnikova, "Memo from Pavlodar Gorispolkom," February 26, 1945, *IIIPP*, 79, doc 59.

15. Kulmagambetov and Tarchakov to I. Kalinin, February 27, 1945, *IIIPP*, 79, doc. 60.

16. N. Guliaeva to N. Sabitov, April 13, 1945, *IIIPP*, 83, doc. 66.

17. N. Guliaeva to N. Sabitov, April 13, 1945, *IIIPP*, 83, doc. 66.

18. N. Sabitov to N. Guliaeva, May 30, 1945, *IIIPP*, 85, doc. 69; N. Guliaeva, "Memo on the opening of registered mosques in Pavlodar," June 8, 1945, *IIIPP*, 86, doc. 70.

19. N. Guliaeva to S. Artamonov, June 9, 1945, *IIIPP*, 87, doc. 71.

20. Simonenko, Mamyrov, and Kulmagambetov, "Certificate of transfer for the mosque in Pavlodar," June 12, 1945, *IIIPP*, 87, doc 72. These developments were facilitated by a decree (No. 801 from June 30th, 1944) permitting the return or donation of devotional objects to religious communities. This was followed in August 1944 by a decision to allow registered religious organizations to open accounts with the state bank and, one year later, a decision granting these organizations representation as "legal entities" in the purchase, leasing, or constructing of buildings for religious use (*PDDUM*, 56). It was on the strength of these decrees that SADUM, for example, petitioned Polianskii for the transfer of seven shrine complexes—including such major pilgrimage sites as Shah-i zinda and Shahimardan—into their care that had previously been overseen by the Directorate of the Affairs of Architecture (*ISG3*, 36–37). On the impacts of these reforms on the Russian Orthodox Church, see Chumachenko, *Church and State in Soviet Russia*, 79–80. Chumachenko notes that these laws also relieved the clergy of tax burdens that were sometimes not only harsh, but vaguely absurd: previously, rural clergy were asked to deliver taxes in the form of meat and eggs—even if they did not own any livestock or chickens (Chumachenko, *Church and State in Soviet Russia*, 79–80).

21. "Contract with the Muslim community of Pavlodar," June 14, 1945, *IIIPP*, 88, doc. 73.

22. N. Guliaeva to N. Sabitov, June 28, 1945, *IIIPP*, 91, doc. 75.

23. Kolarz, *Religion in the Soviet Union*.

24. N. Guliaeva to N. Sabitov, June 28, 1945, *IIIPP*, 91, doc. 76 (emphasis added).

25. N. Guliaeva to *raispolkom* representatives, June 28, 1945, *IIIPP*, 92–93, doc. 77.

26. N. Sabitov to N. Guliaeva, July 10, 1945, *IIIPP*, 94–95, doc. 80.

27. It is not clear from Guliaeva's letter whether this holiday—which she calls "Ramazan-Eid," was ʿEid al-Fitr or ʿEid al-Adha.

28. N. Guliaeva to N. Sabitov, "not before October, 1945," *IIIPP*, 95, doc. 81.

29. N. Guliaeva to N. Sabitov, "not before October, 1945," *IIIPP*, 95, doc. 81.

30. N. Guliaeva to N. Sabitov, "not before October, 1945," *IIIPP*, 95, doc. 81.

31. N. Guliaeva to N. Sabitov, "not before October, 1945," *IIIPP*, 95, doc. 81.

32. N. Sabitov, "On Work from the Time of Appointment," November 16, 1945, *IIIPP*, 96–97, doc. 82.

33. N. Guliaeva to N. Sabitov, December 15, 1945, *IIIPP*, 100, doc. 85.

34. N. Guliaeva to N. Sabitov, December 15, 1945, *IIIPP*, 100–101, doc. 85.

35. N. Guliaeva to N. Sabitov, December 15, 1945, *IIIPP*, 101, doc. 85 (emphasis added).

36. N. Guliaeva to N. Sabitov, December 15, 1945, *IIIPP*, 100, doc. 85.

37. N. Guliaeva to N. Sabitov, January 10, 1946, *IIIPP*, 102, doc. 86.

38. N. Guliaeva to N. Sabitov, January 10, 1946, *IIIPP*, 102–103, doc. 86.

39. N. Guliaeva to N. Sabitov, January 10, 1946, *IIIPP*, 103, doc. 86.

40. Iu. Sadovskii to N. Sabitov, February 14, 1946, *IIIPP*, 106–107, doc. 88.

41. N. Guliaeva to N. Sabitov, April 2, 1946, *IIIPP*, 108, doc. 89.

42. N. Guliaeva to N. Sabitov, April 2, 1946, *IIIPP*, 108, doc. 89.

43. N. Guliaeva to N. Sabitov, April 2, 1946, *IIIPP*, 108, doc. 89.

44. N. Sabitov, "On the Conduct of [Religious] Rites in Auls without Mosques," November 16, 1945, *IIIPP*, 97–98, doc. 83.

45. Koroleva and Korolev, *Islam v Srednem Povolzh'e*, 60.

46. N. Sabitov, "On the Conduct of [Religious] Rites in Auls without Mosques," November 16, 1945, *IIIPP*, 97–98, doc. 83.

47. N. Guliaeva to N. Sabitov, January 10, 1946, *IIIPP*, 101, doc. 86.

48. Koroleva and Korolev, *Islam v Srednem Povolzh'e*, 50; cf. also Denisov and Morgunov, *130 let Tsentral'noi sobornoi mecheti Orenburga*, 36.

49. Koroleva and Korolev, *Islam v Srednem Povolzh'e*, 23; 50. In the Hanafi Muslim legal tradition that predominates in Central Asia, it is licit for women to lead other women in prayer. However, as Tasar observes, "with very few exceptions, they did not venture into the mosques" (*Soviet and Muslim*, 20).

50. Koroleva and Korolev, *Islam v Srednem Povolzh'e*, 22.

51. "Report on the Activities of Religious Denominations in the City of Kuibyshev and Kuibyshev Oblast in 1945," Koroleva and Korolev, *Islam v Srednem Povolzh'e*, 97.

52. "Report on the Activities of Religious Denominations in the City of Kuibyshev and Kuibyshev Oblast in 1945," Koroleva and Korolev, *Islam v Srednem Povolzh'e*, 97; cf. also Koroleva and Korolev, *Islam v Srednem Povolzh'e*, 56.

53. Here, the agent offers an "honor roll" of loyal Muslim leaders: "For example, the mullah of the Blagodarov mosque, Sabirov Valiakht, born in 1869, who has worked as a mullah in this mosque since 1928, is a member of the collective farm, and during the Great Patriotic War he continuously worked in the collective farm fields as an ordinary farmer, combining this work with service in the mosque. Among the believers as well as the rest of the population of the village of Blagodarov, he commands great respect and influence. The mullah of the Kamyshlinskii mosque, Sharipov Mugamedgali, has also been a member of the *kolkhoz*, and he himself works on the *kolkhoz*. His sermons also relate to the issues facing the collective farm. The mullah of the mosque in Denichenko Shentalinsky *raion*, Shamardanov, in his free time from worship, works in the village as a stovemaker, carpenter, tinsmith (*zhestianshchik*), and in other labors. And a number of other mullahs conduct themselves like honest citizens of the Soviet state" ("Report on the Activities of Religious Denominations in the City of Kuibyshev and Kuibyshev Oblast in 1945," Koroleva and Korolev, *Islam v Srednem Povolzh'e*, 97).

54. Koroleva and Korolev, *Islam v Srednem Povolzh'e*, 50.

55. Koroleva and Korolev, *Islam v Srednem Povolzh'e*, 62.

56. N. Guliaeva, "[Report] on Works during the Second Quarter of 1946," June 28, 1946, *IIIPP*, 114–115, doc. 95.

57. Kliueva, "Zhizn' v ateisticheskom gosudarstve: musul'manskie obshchiny Tiumenskoi oblasti (1940–1960-e)." gg.)," 117.

58. Specifically, Kulmagambetov had sought to attain the functions of imam for the entire *oblast'*, in keeping with an arrangement from the 1920s under TsDUM, by which Pavlodar imams would serve in that capacity. In this ambition, Kulmagambetov had the support of SADUM's qadi (*kazi*) for the Kazakh SSR. I am grateful to Allen J. Frank for sharing this information.

59. N. Sabitov to N. Guliaeva, November 22, 1945, *IIIPP*, 99, doc. 84.

60. N. Guliaeva, "[Report] on Works during the Second Quarter of 1946," June 28, 1946, *IIIPP*, 113, doc. 95.

61. Koroleva and Korolev, *Islam v Srednem Povolzh'e*, 62.

62. Koroleva and Korolev, *Islam v Srednem Povolzh'e*, 62.

63. Sulaev, "Musul'manskoe dukhovenstvo v Velikoi Otechestvennoi Voine 1941–1945 gg.," 24.

64. Khakimov, "Musul'manskie obshchiny na Urale v gody liberalizatsii gosudarstvenno-religioznoi politiki v SSSR," 97.

65. Nabiev, *Islam i gosudarstvo*, 100. Molotov personally approved the opening of these two madrasas in October, 1945. His note of permission has been published: see *ISG3*, 40.

66. Ro'i proposes a "legitimation of religion" between 1943 and 1947, a slight doubling back from 1947 to 1954, a "further liberalization" from 1955 to 1958, and a new anti-religious campaign from 1959 to 1964 (Ro'i, *Islam in the Soviet Union*, 10). The idea that anti-religious policies resumed around 1946–47 is also supported by Babazhanov, who mentions a renewed push against "survivals" (*perezhitki*), such as shrine pilgrimage, around this time; see his "O fetvakh SADUM protiv 'neislamskikh obychaev,'" in A. Malashenko and M.B. Olcott, eds., *Islam na postsovetskom prostranstve: vzgliad iznutri* (Moscow: Carnegie Center, 2001), 171.

67. I. Stalin and Ia. Chadaev, "On the Prayer-Houses of Religious Communities," January 28, 1946, *IIIPP*, 103, doc. 87.

68. Denisov and Morgunov, *130 let Tsentral'noi sobornoi mecheti Orenburga*, 33.

69. Eren Tasar aptly sums up the predicament: "The new climate was also furthered by nonexistent controls of Islam. Official regulation of religion across the country was in a state of chaos during and after the war. Stalin did not articulate any clear direction for religious policy after the Great Terror's conclusion. To make matters worse, the Party-state offered little or no guidance to regional bureaucrats concerning implementation of the religious reforms of 1943–44. As a result, officials saw little incentive in clamping down on religion, turning their energies elsewhere" (*Soviet and Muslim*, 50–51).

70. I. Stalin and Ia. Chadaev, "On the Prayer-Houses of Religious Communities," January 28, 1946, *IIIPP*, 103, doc. 87.

Conclusion

1. *"Za chto vy voevali?" "Za Rodinu, za Stalina. Stalin—eto tot chelovek, blagodaria komu strana krepko stoiala. Krepkii chelovek byl." "Na fronte verili v Allakha?" "Allakha my ne zabyvaem. I na fronte tozhe Allakh."* Interview, Asral Kalychev, https://iremember.ru/memoirs/pulemetchiki/kalichev-asral/ (accessed April 11, 2020).
2. See also Reese's valuable discussion in *Why Stalin's Soldiers Fought*, 14–27.
3. George Gibian, "World War 2 in Russian National Consciousness: Pristavkin (1981–7) and Kondratyev (1990)," in John Garrard and Alison Healicon, eds., *World War 2 and the Soviet People: Selected Papers from the Fourth World Congress for Soviet and East European Studies* (London: Palgrage, 1990), 155.
4. Berkhoff, *Motherland in Danger*, 209; 216.
5. See Adeeb Khalid, Review of *Soviet and Muslim: The Institutionalization of Islam in Central Asia*, by Eren Tasar, *Slavic Review* 77/4 (2018), 1035–1037.
6. Berkhoff, *Motherland in Danger*, 4.
7. See Paolo Sartori and Bakhtiyar Babajanov, "Being Soviet, Muslim, Modernist, and Fundamentalist in 1950s Central Asia," *Journal of the Economic and Social History of the Orient* 62 (2019), 110.
8. See DeWeese, "Islam and the Legacy of Sovietology."
9. Zaripov and Safarov, *Akhmetzian Mustafin*, 67–68. The authors add: "Moreover, as historian A. B. Yunusov notes, by 1950 Mufti G. Rasulev personally issued 917 certificates to unregistered imams for the right to perform rituals, drawing the disapproval of the Council for Religious Cults."
10. Bobrovnikov, "Withering Heights," 376. On the blurred lines between "official" and "unofficial" spheres, see Tasar, *Soviet and Muslim*, and "Islamically Informed Soviet Patriotism in Postwar Kyrgyzstan," *Cahiers du monde russe* 52/2–3 (2011), 387–404; Kemper and Shikhaliev, "Administrative Islam: Two Soviet Fatwas from the North Caucasus"; and Abashin, "A Prayer for Rain: Practicing Being Soviet and Muslim."
11. See Ghīlmani, *Biographies of the Islamic Scholars of Our Times*; Frank, *Gulag Miracles*, 105–116; Ashirbek Muminov, "From Revived Tradition to Innovation: Kolkhoz Islam in the Southern Kazakhstan Region and Religious Leadership (through the Cases of Zhartï-Töbe and Oranghay since the 1950s)" in Stéphane A. Dudoignon and Christian Noack, eds., *Allah's Kolkhozes. Migration, DeStalinisation, Privatisation, and the New Muslim Congregations in the Soviet Realm (1950s–2000s)* (Berlin: Klaus Schwarz, 2014; Islamkundliche Untersuchungen. Bd. 314), 307–366.
12. Tasar, *Soviet and Muslim*, 29; 35; see also Sartori and Babajanov, "Being Soviet, Muslim, Modernist, and Fundamentalist in 1950s Central Asia," 113.
13. Khalid, *Islam after Communism*, 111.
14. Sartori and Babajanov, "Being Soviet, Muslim, Modernist, and Fundamentalist in 1950s Central Asia."
15. Sartori and Babajanov, "Being Soviet, Muslim, Modernist, and Fundamentalist in 1950s Central Asia," 135.
16. See Tasar, *Soviet and Muslim*, 36–37; Frank, *Gulag Miracles*, 105. On the Orenburg Muslim Spiritual Assembly and Tsarist religious policy, see Robert Crews, *For Prophet*

and Tsar: Islam and Empire in Russia and Central Asia (Cambridge, MA: Harvard University Pres, 2009); Mustafa Tuna, Imperial Russia's Muslims: Islam, Empire and European Modernity, 1788–1914 (New York: Cambridge University Press, 2015); Firouzeh Mostashari, On the Religious Frontier: Tsarist Russia and Islam in the Caucasus (New York: I.B. Tauris, 2006); Paul W. Werth, The Tsar's Foreign Faiths: Toleration and the Fate of Religious Freedom in Imperial Russia (New York: Oxford University Press, 2014).

17. Tasar, Soviet and Muslim, 36.

18. This appointment came on the heels of large public demonstrations in Tashkent against the incoming mufti's predecessor—indicative, perhaps, of broad popular interest in the institution of the muftiate itself. See Tasar, Soviet and Muslim, 365.

19. Sartori and Babajanov, "Being Soviet, Muslim, Modernist, and Fundamentalist in 1950s Central Asia," 109. I have added numbers to their list here for clarity in the discussion that follows.

20. On the legacy and persistence of Sufi tradition in Central Asia, see DeWeese's recent, landmark essay, "Sufism in Central Asia: New Perspectives on Sufi Traditions, 15th-21st Centuries," in Devin DeWeese and Jo-Ann Gross, eds., Re-Envisioning the History of Sufi Communities in Central Asia: Continuity and Adaptation in Sources and Social Frameworks, 16th–20th Centuries (Leiden: Brill, 2018), 21–74.

21. DeWeese, "Shamanization in Central Asia," 358.

22. Khalid, Islam after Communism, 70–71; Devin DeWeese, Review: Islam after Communism: Religion and Politics in Central Asia by Adeeb Khalid, Journal of Islamic Studies 19/1 (2008), 135; Sartori, "Toward a History of the Muslim's Soviet Union," 322.

23. HPSSS sched. B, vol. 8, case 224, f. 15.

24. Interview, Grigorii Konstantinovich Kudriavtsev, https://iremember.ru/memoirs/razvedchiki/kudryavtsev-grigoriy-konstantinovich/ (accessed May 20, 2020).

25. Interview, Farit Minrahmanovich Kagarmanov, https://iremember.ru/memoirs/svyazisti/kagarmanov-farit-minrakhmanovich/ (accessed May 20, 2020).

26. HPSSS sched. A, vol. 31, case 445/(NY)1007, f. 57–58.

Appendix

1. The verse is cited in the document as Q 2:186–187, but this is incorrect; the lines are actually a slight garbling of Q 2:190–191.

2. The verse is cited in the document as Q 8:62 but is actually from Q 8:60.

3. PDDUM, 275–280.

4. These lines do not appear anywhere in the Qur'an.

5. GARF f. R-6991, op. 3, d. 20, ll. 61–69 (PDDUM, 301–307).

6. See glossary at end of speech.

7. See glossary at end of speech.

8. PDDUM, 216. The glossary following the speech is reproduced from the original document.

9. *PDDUM*, 251–253.
10. *Islam yuldarynda: Sufïysïlïk habaqtari häm shäyekh Zäynulla Räsülev shäjärähe*, 65–68.
11. GARF f. R-6991, op. 3, d. 6, l. 34–36 (*PDDUM*, 199–201).
12. *PDDUM*, 310–316.

Bibliography

Archival Abbreviations

AkadNkKaz: The National Academy of Sciences of the Republic of Kazakhstan, Almaty.
AkadNkTat: The Academy of Sciences of the Republic of Tatarstan, Kazan.
GARF: State Archive of the Russian Federation, Moscow.
HPSSS: The Harvard Project on the Soviet Social System, Cambridge, MA.
NatArchGE: National Archives of Georgia, Tbilisi.
RGASPI: Russian State Archive of Socio-Political History, Moscow.

Interviews, www.iremember.ru

Annenkov, Vladimir Tikhonovich
Belyaev, Fedor Ivanovich
Degen, Ion Lazarevich
Garshtia, Ivan
Grubov, Ivan Vladimirovich
Kalychev, Asral
Komaritsyna (Baranova), Antonina Maksimovna
Komov, Yuri Ilyich
Krasnonos, Grigory Sergeevich
Krylov, Anatoly Pavlovich
Shurakov Mikhail Nikolaevich
Strelkov, Georgii Aleksandrovich
Styazhkin, Stepan Alexandrovich
Zonov, Arsenij

Websites

https://rbvekpros.livejournal.com/23511.html#_ftnref2
https://islamperspectives.org/rpi/
http://islamrb.ru/cheremkhovskij-mulla/

Published Primary and Secondary Sources

Abashin, Sergei. "A Prayer for Rain: Practicing Being Soviet and Muslim." *Journal of Islamic Studies* 25/2 (2014), 178–200.

Abataev, E.D. "Islam v gody Velikoi Otechestvennoi voiny." In *Istoriia Velikoi Pobedy: sbornik materialov mezhvuzovskoi I 89 nauchno-prakticheskoi konferentsii*, 11–15. Novokuznetsk: FKOU VO Kuzbaskii institut, FSIN Rossii, 2018.

Adzhiev, A.M. ed. *Fol'klor narodov Dagestana o Velikoi Otechestvennoi voine*. Makhachkala: Dagestanskii nauchnyi tsentr Rossiiskoi akademii nauk Institut iazyka, literatury i isskustva im. Gamzata Tsadasy, 2006.

Akhmadullin, V.A. *Patrioticheskaia deiatel'nost' dukhovnykh upravlenii musul'man v gody velikoi otechestvennoi voiny*. Moscow: Islamskaia kniga, 2015.

Akhmadullin, V.A. "Deiatel'nost' organov gosudarstvennogo upravleniia SSSR i rukovoditelei dukhovnykh upravlenii musul'man po sozdaniiu vsesoiuznogo musul'manskogo tsentra." *Vlast'* 8 (2015), 154–158.

Akhmadullin, V.A. "Deiatel'nost' sovetskogo gosudarstva po nagrazhdeniiu musul'man za razgrom gitlerovskoi Germanii: uroki dlia natsional'noi bezopasnosti Rossii." *Gumanitarnyi vestnik* 4 (2016), 1–13.

Akhmadullin, V.A. "Deiatel'nost' sovetskogo gosudarstva po organizatsii khadzha sovetskikh musul'man v 1944 g." *Vlast'* 6 (June 2013), 162–164.

Akhmadullin, V.A. "Kharakternye oshibki issledovatelei pri analize khadzha sovetskikh musul'man v 1945 g." *Vlast'* 7 (2013), 156–158.

Akhmadullin, V.A., "Reglamentatsiia sovetskim gosudarstvom vypuska i raspredeleniia islamskikh kalendarei, izdannykh muftiiatami (1944–1965)." *Vestnik Moskovskogo gosudarstvennogo lingvisticheskogo universiteta* 1/794 (2018), 103–119.

Albogachieva, M.C.-G. *Islam v Ingushetii: etnografiia i istoriko-kul'turnye aspekty*. St. Petersburg: MAZ RAN, 2017.

Alekseev, V.A. *Illiuzii i dogmy*. Moscow: Politizdat, 1991.

Algar, Hamid. "Shaykh Zaynullah Rasulev: The Last Great Naqshbandi Shaykh of the Volga-Urals Region." In *Muslims in Central Asia: Expressions of Identity and Change*, edited by Jo-Ann Gross, 112–133. Durham, NC: Duke University Press, 1992.

Alibaev, M.A. *Islam v sovetskom Kazakhstane: strategii vyzhivaniia*. Astana: ENU im. L.N. Gumileva, 2015.

Älmieva, Nuriia, ed. *Möselmannar böek vatan sugyshynda*. Kazan: Khozur-Spokoistvie, 1436/2015.

Aminova, Gulnora. "Removing the Veil of *Taqiyya*: Dimensions of the Biography of Āghā-yi Buzurg." PhD dissertation, Harvard University, 2009.

Anonymous. "Mohammedans Greet Marshall Stalin." *Soviet War News*, May 31, 1944.

Arapov, D.Iu., and G.G. Kosach, eds. *Islam i sovetskoe gosudarstvo (1944–1990). Sbornik Dokumentov. Vypusk 3*. Moscow: Mardzhani, 2011.

Arapov, D.Iu. "Mozhno otmetit' riad vysokikh podvigov voinskoi doblesti, proiavlennykh musul'manami." *Voenno-istoricheskii zhurnal* 11 (2004), 42–44.

Arapov, D.Iu. "Musul'manskii triptikh: islam i sovetskaia vlast'. 1917–1949–1982." *Pax Islamica* 1/2 (2009), 248–266.

Arapov, D.Iu. "'Prizyvaite pravovernykh otvagoi i geroistvom na fronte, chestnym i samootverzhennym trudom v tylu uskorit' chas pobedy.' S'ezd musul'man Srednei Azii i Kazakhstana o zadachakh borby s fashistskoi agressiei. Oktiabr 1943 g." *Pax Islamica* 1/10 (2013), 152–160.

As-Salam 9/478, May 1, 2015 / Rajab 1436.

Babazhanov, Bakhtiyar. "O fetvakh SADUM protiv 'neislamskikh obychaev.'" In *Islam na postsovetskom prostranstve: vzgliad iznutri*, edited by Alexei Malashenko and Martha Brill Olcott, 65–78. Moscow: Carnegie Center, 2001.

Baimov, B.S. *Bashkort khalyk ijady, 11 tom: bäyettär / Bashkirskoe narodnoe tvorchestvo, tom 11: bayty*. Ufa: Kitap, 2004.

Basilov, V.N., and K.K. Kubakov. "Survival of Pre-Muslim Beliefs in Islam." In *Secularization in Multi-Religious Societies: Indo-Soviet Perspectives*, edited by S.C. Dube and V.N. Basilov, 227–240. New Delhi: Indian Council of Social Science Research, 1983.

Beglov, Aleksei. *V poiskakh "bezgreshnykh katakomb." Tserkovnoe podpol'e v SSSR.* Moscow: Izd. Sovet Russkoi Pravoslavnoi Tserkvi, 'Arefa,' 2008.

Bekkin, R.I. "Muftiiaty i gosudarstvo v sovetskuiu epokhu: evolutsiia otnoshenii." In *Rossiiskii islam v transformatsionnykh protsessakh sovremennosti: novye vyzovy i tendentsii razvitiia v XXI veka*, edited by Z.R. Khabibullina et al, 54–74. Ufa: Dialog, 2017.

Bennigsen, Alexandre, and Marie Broxup. *The Islamic Threat to the Soviet State.* London: Croom Helm, 1983.

Bennigsen, Alexandre, and S. Enders Wimbush. *Mystics and Commissars: Sufism in the Soviet Union.* London: C. Hurst, 1985.

Berkhoff, Karel C. *Motherland in Danger: Soviet Propaganda during World War II.* Cambridge, MA: Harvard University Press, 2012.

Black, Edwin. *The Farhud: Roots of the Arab-Nazi Alliance in the Holocaust.* Dialog Press, 2010.

Black, Jeremy ed., *The Second World War, Volume II: The German War, 1943–1945.* Burlington, VT: Ashgate: 2007.

Bobrovnikov, Vladimir. "'Traditionalist' versus 'Islamist' Identities in a Dagestani Collective Farm." *Central Asian Survey* 25/3 (2006), 287–302.

Bobrovnikov, Vladimir. "Withering Heights. The Re-Islamization of a Kolkhoz Village in Dagestan: a Microhistory." In *Allah's Kolkhozes. Migration, DeStalinisation, Privatisation, and the New Muslim Congregations in the Soviet Realm (1950s–2000s)*, edited by Stéphane A. Dudoignon and Christian Noack, 367–397. Berlin: Klaus Schwarz, 2014; Islamkundliche Untersuchungen. Bd. 314.

Bobrovnikov, V.O., A.R. Navruzov, and Sh.Sh. Shikhaliev. "Islamskoe obrazovanie v sovetskom Dagestane (konets 1920-x–1980-e gg.)." *Pax Islamica* 1/4 (2010), 72–75.

Boltina, V.D., and L.V. Sheveleva. *Iz istorii islama v Pavlodarskom Priirtysh'e 1919–1999: sbornik dokumentov.* Pavlodar: EKO, 2001.

Bustanov, Alfrid K. "Against Leviathan: On the Ethics of Islamic Poetry in Soviet Russia." In *The Piety of Learning: Islamic Studies in Honor of Stefan Reichmuth*, edited by Michael Kemper and Ralf Elger, 199–224. Leiden: Brill, 2017.

Bustanov, Alfrid K. *Biblioteka Zainap Maksudovoi.* Moscow: Mardjani Foundation, 2019.

Bustanov, Alfrid K. *Islamskaia poeziia v epokhu Stalina: sbornik stikhov Kyiametdina al-Kadyirii.* Kazan: Institut istorii im. Sh. Mardzhani AN RT, 2018.

Bustanov, Alfrid K. "Islamskii apokalipsis pri Staline" (forthcoming).

Bustanov, Alfrid K., and Michael Kemper. "Administrative Islam: Two Soviet Fatwas from the North Caucasus." In *Islamic Authority and the Russian Language: Studies on Texts from European Russia, the North Caucasus and West Siberia*, edited by Alfrid K. Bustanov and Michael Kemper, 55–103. Amsterdam: Pegasus, 2012; Pegasus Oost-Europese Studies 19.

Butaev, M.D., G.I. Kakagasanov, and A.I. Osmanov, eds. *Vlast' i musul'manskaia religiia v Dagestane (Noiabr' 1917 g.–dekabr' 1991 g.). Dokumenty i materialy.* Makhachkala: IIAE DNTs RAN, 2007.

Carmack, Roberto J. "Hero and Hero-Making: Patriotic Narratives and the Sovietization of Kazakh Front-Line Propaganda, 1941–1945." *Central Asian Survey* 33/1 (2014), 95–112.

Carmack, Roberto J. *Kazakhstan in World War II: Mobilization and Ethnicity in the Soviet Empire.* Lawrence, KS: University of Kansas Press, 2019.

Chatani, Sayaka, *Nation-Empire: Ideology and Rural Youth Mobilization in Japan and Its Colonies.* Ithaca: Cornell University Press, 2018.

Chumachenko, Tatiana A. *Church and State in Soviet Russia: Russian Orthodoxy from World War II to the Khrushchev Years.* Translated by Edward E. Roslof. New York: M.E. Sharpe, 2002.

Chumakova, Tatiana. "'Karta religii' dlia neudavsheisia Vsesoiuznoi perepisi 1937 g.: zabytaia stranitsa sovetskogo religiovedeniia." *Gosudarstvo, religiia, tserkov* 3–4/30 (2012), 106–133.

Chumakova, Tatiana. "Podgotovka k Vsesoiuznoi perepisi 1937 g. Sozdanie karty religii SSSR." *Dialog so vremenem* 41 (2012), 296–316.

Dalin, David G., and John F. Rothmann. *Icon of Evil: Hitler's Mufti and the Rise of Radical Islam.* New York: Random House, 2008.

Davis, Nathaniel. *A Long Walk to Church: A Contemporary History of Russian Orthodoxy.* Boulder, CO: Westview, 2003.

Denisov, D.N., and K.A. Morgunov. *130 let tsentral'noi sobornoi mecheti Orenburga.* Orenburg: OGAU, 2009; "Etnoregional'nye issledovaniia" v. 6.

De Santi, Chiara. "Cultural Revolution and Resistance in Uzbekistan during the 1920s: New Perspectives on the Woman Question." In *Patterns of Transformation in and around Uzbekistan*, edited by Paolo Sartori and Tomaso Trevisani, 51–89. Reggio Emilia: Diabasis, 2007.

DeWeese, Devin. "'Dis-ordering' Sufism in Early Modern Central Asia: Suggestions for Rethinking the Sources and Social Structures of Sufi History in the 18th and 19th Centuries." In *History and Culture of Central Asia/Istoriia i kul'tura Tsentral'noi Azii*, edited by B. Babadjanov and Y. Kawahara, 259–279. Tokyo: The University of Tokyo, 2012.

DeWeese, Devin. "Islam and the Legacy of Sovietology: A Review Essay on Yaacov Ro'i's *Islam in the Soviet Union.*" *Journal of Islamic Studies* 13/3 (2002), 298–330.

DeWeese, Devin. "Shamanization in Central Asia." *Journal of the Economic and Social History of the Orient* 57 (2014), 326–363.

DeWeese, Devin. "Spiritual Practice and Corporate Identity in Medieval Sufi Communities of Iran, Central Asia, and India: The Khalvatī/ʿIshqī/Shattārī Continuum." In *Religion and Identity in South Asia and Beyond: Essays in Honor of Patrick Olivelle*, edited by Stephen E. Lindquist, 251–300. London: Anthem Press, 2011.

DeWeese, Devin. "Survival Strategies: Reflections on the Notion of Religious 'Survivals' in Soviet Ethnographic Studies of Muslim Religious Life in Central Asia." In *Exploring the Edge of Empire: Soviet Era Anthropology in the Caucasus and Central Asia*, edited by F. Mühlfriedand and S. Sokolovskiy, 35–58. Münster: Lit Verlag.

Dolgopolov, M. "Soviet Mufti Exposes Hitler Mufti." *Soviet War News.* October 24, 1942.

Drozdov, K.S. "Stalingrad: voennaia mashina Reikha protiv internatsionala sovetskikh narodov." In *Istoricheskaia pamiat' i rossiiskaia identichnost'*, edited by V.A. Tishkova and E.A. Pivnevoi, 185–202. Moscow: RAN, 2018.

Dunn, Dennis J. *The Catholic Church and Russia: Popes, Patriarchs, Tsars, and Commissars*. Aldershot: Ashgate, 2004.

ad-Durgeli, Nazir. *Uslada umov v biografiiakh Dagestanskikh uchenykh (Nuzkhat al-azkhan fi taradzhim 'ulama' Dagistan)*. Edited and translated by A.R. Shikhsaidov, M. Kemper, and A.K. Bustanov. Moscow: Mardzhani, 2012.

Eden, Jeff. "A Soviet Jihad against Hitler: Ishan Babakhan Calls Central Asian Muslims to War." *Journal of the Economic and Social History of the Orient* 59 (2016), 241–246.

Edgar, Adrienne. "Bolshevism, Patriarchy, and the Nation: The Soviet 'Emancipation' of Muslim Women in Pan-Islamic Perspective." *Slavic Review* 65/2 (2006), 252–272.

Edgar, Adrienne. "Emancipation of the Unveiled: Turkmen Women under Soviet Rule, 1924–29." *Russian Review* 62/1 (2003), 132–149.

Evans, S. *The Churches of the USSR*. London: Cobbett, 1943.

Fairuzov, B.G. *Istoriia islama v Rossii*. St. Petersburg: Timoshka, 2019.

Frank, Allen J. *Bukhara and the Muslims of Russia: Sufism, Education, and the Paradox of Islamic Prestige*. Leiden: Brill, 2012.

Fefermen, Kirill. "Between 'Non-Russian Nationalities' and Muslim Identity: Perceptions and Self-Perceptions of Soviet Central Asian Soldiers in the Red Army, 1941–1945." In *Combatants of Muslim Origin*, 121–136.

Florin, Moritz. "Becoming Soviet through War: The Kyrgyz and the Great Fatherland War." *Kritika*, 17/3 (Summer 2016), 495–516.

Frank, Allen J. *Gulag Miracles: Sufis and Stalinist Repression in Kazakhstan*. Vienna: Austrian Academy of Sciences Press, 2019.

Frank, Allen J. *Faith and Trauma on the Eastern Front: Kazakh Soldiers in the Red Army, 1935–1945* (in preparation).

Froese, Paul. *The Plot to Kill God: Findings from the Soviet Experiment in Secularization*. Berkeley: University of California Press, 2008.

Gaiazov, A.S. *Malaia i bol'shaia rodina grazhdanina. "Rakh Kazanchi."* Ufa: "Bashkirskaia entsiklopediia," 2016.

Genatulin, Anatolii. *Krasnaia poliana*. Ufa: Kitap, 2008.

Ghïlmani, Saduaqas. *Biographies of the Islamic Scholars of Our Times*. Edited by Allen J. Frank, Ashirbek Muminov, and Aitzhan Nurmanova. Istanbul: IRCICA, 2018.

Gibian, George. "World War 2 in Russian National Consciousness: Pristavkin (1981–7) and Kondratyev (1990)." In *World War 2 and the Soviet People: Selected Papers from the Fourth World Congress for Soviet and East European Studies*, edited by John Garrard and Alison Healicon, 147–160. London: Palgrage, 1990.

Gross, J.A., and A. Urunbaev, eds. *The Letters of Khwāja ʿUbayd Allāh Aḥrār and His Associates*. Leiden: Brill, 2002.

Guseva, Iu.N. "Mrachnoe ekho 'Dela TsDUM': 'Tsep' korana' i repressii protiv musul'manskoi elity v SSSR (1940 god)." *Novyi istoricheskii vestnik* 2/52 (2017), 85–102.

Guseva, Iu.N. *Rossiiskii musul'manin v XX veke (na materialakh Srednego Povolzh'ia)*. Samara: Ofort, 2013.

Hakim, Naʿmat. *Islamda va shura hukumatida khatun-qizlar huquqi*. Tashkent: Uzbek Dawlat Nashriyati, 1925.

Hammond, Kelly. "Managing Muslims: Imperial Japan, Islamic Policy, and Axis Connections during the Second World War." *Journal of Global History* 12 (2017), 251–273.

Harf, Jeffrey. *Nazi Propaganda for the Arab World*. Yale University Press, 2009.

Hoare, Marko Attila. *The Bosnian Muslims in the Second World War: A History*. New York: Oxford University Press, 2013.

Holzman, Franklyn D. "Soviet Inflationary Pressures, 1928–1957: Causes and Cures." *The Quarterly Journal of Economics* 74/2 (May, 1960), 167–188.

Ibragimov, Ruslan R. "Activities of the Commissioners of the Council on Russian Orthodox Church and the Council on Religious Faiths under the Council of People's Commissars of the USSR on the Tatar Autonomous Soviet Socialist Republic during the Great Patriotic War and Early Post-War Years." *Journal of Sustainable Development* 8/5 (2015), 184–190.

Ibragimova, Zaira Bagautdinovna. "Prodolzhenie bogoslovskoi polemiki nachala XX v. v Dagestanskikh arabograficheskikh sochineniiakh sovetskogo perioda." *Istoriia, arkheologiia i etnografiia Kavkaza* 14/3 (2018), 34–39.

Imy, Kate. *Faithful Fighters: Identity and Power in the British Indian Army*. Palo Alto: Stanford University Press, 2019.

Iunusova, A.B, ed. *225 let Tsentral'nomu dukhovnomu upravleniiu musul'man Rossii: Istoricheskie ocherki*. Ufa, 2013.

Iunusova, A.B. *Islam v Bashkortostane*. Ufa: Ufimskii poligrafkombinat, 1999.

Jarman, Robert L., ed. *Political Diaries of the Arab World: Saudi Arabia: The Jeddah Diaries, 1919–1940 (Vol. 2: 1922–1927)*. Oxford: Archive Editions, 1990.

Kabirova, A.Sh., E.G. Krivonozhkina, and A.S. Bushuev. *Nam zhit' i pomnit': Tatarskaia ASSR v gody Velikoi Otechestvennoi voiny (1941–1945 gg.)*. Kazan: Foliant, 2016.

Kalkandjieva, Daniela. *The Russian Orthodox Church, 1917–1948: From Decline to Resurrection*. Abingdon: Routledge, 2014.

Kakagasanov, G.I. "Vzaimootnosheniia vlasti i religii v Dagestane v gody Velikoi Otechestvennoi voiny (1941–1945 gg.)." *Vestnik instituta IAE* 2 (2011), 40–45.

Kamp, Marianne. *The New Woman in Uzbekistan: Islam, Modernity and Unveiling under Communism*. Seattle: University of Washington Press, 2006.

Kawahara, Yayoi, and Umed Mamadsherzodoshev. *Documents from Private Archives in Right-Bank Badakhshan*. Tokyo: University of Tokyo, TIAS Central Eurasian Research Series, 2015.

Keller, Shoshana. *To Moscow, Not Mecca: The Soviet Campaign against Islam in Central Asia*. Westport, CT: Praeger, 2001.

Keller, Shoshanna. "Trapped between State and Society: Woman's Liberation and Islam in Soviet Uzbekistan, 1926–1941." *Journal of Women's History* 10/1 (1998), 20–44.

Kelly, Catriona. *Socialist Churches: Radical Secularization and the Preservation of the Past in Petrograd and Leningrad, 1918–1988*. DeKalb, IL: Northern Illinois University Press, 2016.

Kemper, Michael. *Studying Islam in the Soviet Union*. Amsterdam: Vossiuspers UvA, 2009.

Kemper, Michael, and Shamil Shikhaliev. "Administrative Islam: Two Soviet Fatwas from the North Caucasus." In *Islamic Authority and the Russian Language: Studies on Texts from European Russia, the North Caucasus and West Siberia*, edited by Alfrid K. Bustanov and Michael Kemper, 55–102. Amsterdam: Pegasus, 2012.

Kemper, Michael, and Shamil Shikhaliev. "Qadimism and Jadidism in Twentieth-Century Daghestan," *Asiatische Studien / Etudes Asiatiques* 69/3 (2015), 593–624.

Kemper, Michael. "From 1917 to 1937: The Mufti, the Turkologist, and Stalin's Terror." *Die Welt des Islams* 57/2 (2017), 162–191.

Khairetdinov, D.Z. *Islam na Urale: entsiklopedicheskii slovar'*. Moscow: Medina, 2009.

Khakimov, R.Sh. "Musul'manskie obshchiny na Urale v gody liberalizatsii gosudarstvenno-religioznoi politiki v SSSR." *Vestnik Cheliabinskogo Gosudarstvennogo Universiteta* 22/237 (2011), 93–99.

Khakimov, R.Sh. "Musul'mane Urala v gody Velikoi Otechestvennoi voiny (1941–1945)." In *Religioznoe mnogoobrazie Ural'skogo regiona. Materialy Vserossiiskoi nauchnoi Prakticheskoi konferentsii*, 145–153. Orenburg: OOO IPK "Universitet," 2014.

Khalid, Adeeb. "Being Muslim in Soviet Central Asia, or an Alternative History of Muslim Modernity." *Journal of the Canadian Historical Association / Revue de la Société historique du Canada* 18/2 (2007), 123–143.

Khalid, Adeeb. *Islam after Communism: Religion and Politics in Central Asia*. Berkeley: University of California Press, 2007.

Khalid, Adeeb. Review of *Soviet and Muslim: The Institutionalization of Islam in Central Asia*, by Eren Tasar. *Slavic Review* 77/4 (2018), 1035–1037.

Khalid, Adeeb. "Searching for Muslim Voices in Post-Soviet Archives." *Ab Imperio* 4 (2008), 302–312.

Khalidova, O.B. "Religiia, dukhovenstvo i gosudarstvo v gody Velikoi Otechestvennoi voiny v severo-kavkazskom regione." *Vestnik instituta IAE* 3 (2016), 58–65.

Khasianov, O.R. "Religioznye praktiki predstavitelei kommunisticheskoi partii na sele v poslevoennoe desiatiletnie (na materialakh Kuybyshevskoy i Ul'ianovskoi oblastei)." In *Patriotizm: istoriia, sovremennost', obraz budushchego. Mezhdunarodnaia nauchno-prakticheskaia konferentsiia, posviashchennaia 70-letiiu Pobedy v Velikoi Otechestvennoi voine: sbornik nauchnykh trudov*, edited by T.V. Petukhovoi, 284–289. Ul'ianovsk: UlGTU, 2015.

Kildin, S.A., S.Sh. Yarmullin, and F.F. Ghaysina, eds. *Bashkortostan—aulialar ile*. Ufa: Kitap, 2012.

Kinziabaeva, R.Kh. "Vklad religioznykh organizatsii BASSR v pobedu v Velikoi Otechestvennoi voine." *Iadkiar* 1 (2008), 83–86.

Kisriev, E.F. *Islam v Dagestane*. Moscow: Logos, 2007.

Kliueva, V.P. "Zhizn' v ateisticheskom gosudarstve: musul'manskie obshchiny Tiumenskoi oblasti (1940–1960-e gg.)." *Vestnik arkheologii antropologii, i etnografii* 10 (2009), 117–121.

Kokebayeval, Gulzhaukhar, Yerke Kartabayeval, and Aigul Sadykoval. "The Evolution of Soviet Power's Religious Policy during the Great Patriotic War." *Asian Social Science* 11/13 (2015), 235–239.

Kolarz, M. *Religion in the Soviet Union*. New York: St. Martin's Press, 1961.

Koroleva, L.A., and A.A. Korolev. *Islam v Srednem Povolzh'e. 1940-e gg*. Penza: Penzenskii gosudarstvennyi universitet arkhitektury i stroitel'stva, 2015.

Koroleva, L.A., and A.A. Korolev. "Vlast' i musul'mane v SSSR v velikoi otechestvennoi voine (po materialam penzenskoi oblasti)." *Vestnik Permskogo Universiteta* 1/13 (2010), 30–34.

Krinko, E.F. "Vera i sueveriia na fronte i v tylu v usloviiakh voennogo vremeni (1941–1945)." *Bylye Gody* 29/3 (2013), 53–61.

Krivosheev, G.F. *Soviet Casualties and Combat Losses in the Twentieth Century*. London: Greenhill, 1997.

Küntzel, Matthias. *Jihad and Jew-Hatred: Islamism, Nazism, and the Roots of 9/11*. New York: Telos Press, 2007.

Lamb, Samantha. *Stalin's Constitution: Soviet Participatory Politics and the Discussion of the 1936 Draft Constitution*. Milton: Routledge, 2017.

Le Gac, Julie. "Haunted by Jinns: Dealing with War Neuroses among Muslim Soldiers during the Second World War." In *Combatants of Muslim Origin in European Armies in the Twentieth Century: Far From Jihad*, edited by Xavier Bougarel, Raphaëlle Branche, and Cloé Drieu, 183–204. London: Bloomsbury, 2017.

Luehrmann, Sonja. *Religion in Secular Archives: Soviet Atheism and Historical Knowledge*. New York: Oxford University Press, 2015.

Makarov, N.D. *Analargha maslakhatlar*. Translated by M. Rasuli. Tashkent: Uzbekistan Dawlat Nashriyati; Saghliqni saqlash kutubkhanasi, 1925.

Mallmann, Klaus-Michael, and Martin Cüppers. *Nazi Palestine: The Plans for the Extermination of the Jews in Palestine*. Philadelphia: Enigma Books, 2013.

Martin, Terry. *The Affirmative Action Empire*. Ithaca: Cornell University Press, 2004.

Massell, Gregory J. *The Surrogate Proletariat: Moslem Women and Revolutionary Strategies in Soviet Central Asia, 1919–1929*. Princeton: Princeton University Press, 1974.

Merridale, Catherine. *Ivan's War: Life and Death in the Red Army, 1939–1945*. New York: Picador, 2006.

Miner, Stephen Merritt. *Stalin's Holy War: Religion, Nationalism, and Alliance Politics, 1941–1945*. Chapel Hill, NC: University of North Carolina Press, 2003.

Mingullin, K.M., I.I. Iamaltdinov, and L.Sh. Däulätshina, eds. *Milli-mädäni mirasybyz: Orenburg ölkäse tatarlary*. Kazan: G.I. Ibrahimov isem. Tel, ädäbiyat häm sängat' instituty, 2016; Fänni ekpeditsiialär khäzinäsennän.

Mingullin, K.M., O.R. Khisamov, and L.Sh. Däulätshina, eds. *Milli-mädäni mirasybyz: Tomsk ölkäse tatarlary*. Kazan: G.I. Ibrahimov isem. Tel, ädäbiyat häm sängat' instituty, 2016; Fänni ekpeditsiialär khäzinäsennän.

Mingullin, K.M., I.G. Nuriev, and M.I. Äkhmätjanov, eds. *Milli-mädäni mirasybyz: Archa*. Kazan: G.I. Ibrahimov isem. Tel, ädäbiyat häm sängat' instituty, 2017; Fänni ekpeditsiialär khäzinäsennän.

Mingullin, K.M., M.Kh. Väliev, I.I. Iamaltdinov, and L. Kh. Mökhämmätcanova, eds. *Milli-mädäni mirasybyz: Samara ölkäse tatarlary*. Kazan: G.I. Ibrahimov isem. Tel, ädäbiyat häm sängat' instituty, 2015; Fänni ekpeditsiialär khäzinäsennän.

Minnullin, Il'nur. *Musul'manskoe dukhovenstvo i vlast' v Tatarstane (1920–1930 gg.)*. Kazan: Institut Istorii, 2006.

Minnullin, Il'nur. *Musul'manskoe dukhovenstvo Tatarstana v usloviiakh politicheskikh repressii 1920–1930-x gg*. Nizhnii Novgorod, 2007.

Morse, Chuck. *The Nazi Connection to Islamic Terrorism: Adolf Hitler and Haj Amin al-Husseini*. Washington, DC: WND, 2010.

Motadel, David. *Islam and Nazi Germany's War*. Cambridge: Harvard University Press, 2014.

Murashko, G.P., and M.I. Odintsov, eds. *Vlast' i tserkov v SSSR i stranakh Vostochnoi Evropy 1939–1958. Diskussionnye aspekty*. Moscow, 2003.

Nabiev, R.A. *Gosudarstvenno-konfessional'nye otnosheniia v Rossii*. Kazan: Kazanskii Gos. Universitet, 2013.

Nabiev, R.A. *Islam i gosudarstvo: Kul'turno-istoricheskaia evoliutsiia musul'manskoi religii na Evropeiskom Vostoke.* Kazan: Kazanskii Gos. Universitet, 2002.

Nicosia, Francis R. *Nazi Germany and the Arab World.* Cambridge: Cambridge University Press, 2014.

Northrop, Douglas. *Veiled Empire: Gender and Power in Stailinist Central Asia.* Ithaca: Cornell University Press, 2003.

Nurullaev, A.A. "Musul'mane Sovetskogo Soiuza v Velikoi Otechestvennoi voine." In *Religioznye organizatsii Sovetskogo Soiuza v gody Velikoi Otechestvennoi voiny 1941–1945 gg.*, edited by N.A. Trofimchuk, 57–69. Moscow: RAGS, 1995.

Oboznyi, Konstantin. "'Novyi kurs' religioznoi politiki Stalina i tserkovnaia situatsiia na okkupirovannykh territoriiakh Leningradskoi oblasti (1943–1944 gg.)." *Gosudarstvo, religiia, tserkov v Rossii i za rubezhom* 3 (2017), 360–387.

Odintsov, M.I. *Russkaia pravoslavnaia tserkov' nakanune i v epokhu stalinskogo sotsializma, 1917–1953 gg.* Moscow: Politicheskaia entsiklopediia, 2014.

Odintsov, M.I. *Velikaia Otechestvennaia voina (1941–1945) i religioznye organizatsii v SSSR.* Moscow: Pravoslavnaia Entsiklopediia t. 7, Varshavskaia eparkhiia—Veroterpimost', 2004.

Odintsov, M.I. *Vlast' i religiia v gody voiny. Gosudarstvo i religioznye organizatsii v SSSR v gody Velikoi Otechestvennoi voiny. 1941–1945.* Moscow: OOO "Favorit," 2005.

Odintsov, M.I., and A.S. Kochetova. *Konfessional'naia politika v Sovetskom Soiuze v gody Velikoi Otechestvennoi voiny 1941–1945 gg.* Moscow: Nauchno-politicheskaia kniga; Politicheskaia entsiklopedia, 2014.

Olcott, Martha Brill. *The Kazakhs.* Washington, DC: Hoover Press, 1987.

Paert, Irina Korovushkina. "Memory and Survival in Stalin's Russia: Old Believers in the Urals during the 1930s–50s." In *On Living Through Soviet Russia*, edited by Daniel Bertaux, Paul Thompson, and Anna Rotkirch, 195–213. New York: Routledge, 2004.

Paert, Irina Korovushkina. "Popular Religion and Local Identity during the Stalin Revolution: Old Believers in the Urals, 1928–1941." In *Provincial Landscapes: Local Dimensions of Soviet Power, 1917–1953*, edited by Donald J. Raleigh, 171–193. Pittsburgh: University of Pittsburgh Press, 2001.

Pasherstnik, A.E. *Buiuk Vatan urushi va yangi ishchilar.* Tashkent: O'zSSR davlat nashriyoti, 1942.

Pianciola, Niccolo. "Orthodoxy in the Kazakh Territories (1850–1943)." In *Kazakhstan: Religions and Society in the History of Central Eurasia*, edited by Gian Luca Bonora, Niccolo Pianciola, and Paolo Sartori, 237–254. Turin: Umberto Allemandi, 2009.

Podmarkov, V.I., A.N. But, L.V. Gnedenko, T.A. Medvedkina, and V.I. Shabel'nikov, eds. *Pamiat': Vospominaniia rabotnikov Donetskogo natsional'nogo universiteta o Velikoi Otechestvennoi voine 1941–1945 gody.* Donetsk: Iugo-Vostok, 2011.

Pospelovskii, D.V. *Russkaia pravoslavnaia tserkov' v XX veke.* Moscow: Respublika, 1995.

Privratsky, Bruce. *Muslim Turkistan: Kazak Religion and Collective Memory.* Richmond, Surrey: Curzon, 2001.

Privratsky, Bruce. "Turkistan: Kazak Religion and Collective Memory." Ph.D. dissertation, University of Tennessee, 1998.

Qazaq aieldernyng otkendegysy men kazyrgy jaiy. Kzyl-Orda: Izdanie Kazanskogo Gusudar, 1927.

Raev, R.A., and R.I. Iaqubov, eds. *Islam yuldarynda: Sufïysïlïk habaqtari häm shäyekh Zäynulla Räsülev shäjärähe. Islam dine tarikhï, äthärdhär häm khalïq izhadï.* Ufa: MÜDN RF, 2011.

Rakhmankulova, S.G. *Muftii Gabdrakhman Rasulev—starshii syn Ishan Khazrata Rasuleva.* Cheliabinsk, 2000.

Reese, Roger. R. "The Russian Orthodox Church and 'Patriotic' Support for the Stalinist Regime during the Great Patriotic War." *War and Society* 33/2 (2014), 131–153.

Reese, Roger R. *Why Stalin's Soldiers Fought: The Red Army's Military Effectiveness in World War II.* Lawrence: University of Kansas Press, 2011.

Ro'i, Yaacov. *Islam in the Soviet Union: From the Second World War to Gorbachev.* New York: Columbia University Press, 2000.

Rosloff, Edward E. *Red Priests: Renovationism, Russian Orthodoxy, and Revolution, 1905–1946.* Bloomington: Indiana University Press, 2002.

Rubin, Barry, and Wolfgang G. Schwanitz. *Nazis, Islamists, and the Making of the Modern Middle East.* New Haven: Yale University Press, 2014.

Ṣadr-i Ẕiyā, Muḥammad Sharīf-i. *The Personal History of a Bukharan Intellectual: The Diary of Muḥammad Sharīf-i Ṣadr-i Ẕiyā.* Edited and translated by Rustam M. Shukurov, Muhammadjon Shakuri (Shukurov), Shahrbanou Tadjbakhsh, and Edward A. Allworth. Leiden: Brill, 2003.

Saidbaev, T.S. *Islam i obshchestvo.* Moscow: Nauka, 1984.

Sartori, Paolo. "Of Saints, Shrines, and Tractors: Untangling the Meaning of Islam in Soviet Central Asia." *Journal of Islamic Studies* 30/3 (2019), 1–40.

Sartori, Paolo. "Toward a History of the Muslim's Soviet Union: A View from Central Asia." *Die Welt des Islams* 50 (2010), 315–334.

Schechter, Brandon M. "'The People's Instructions': Indigenizing the Great Patriotic War Among 'Non-Russians.'" *Ab Imperio* 3 (2012), 109–133.

Schechter, Brandon M. *The Stuff of Soldiers: A History of the Red Army in World War II through Objects.* Ithaca: Cornell University Press, 2019.

Sartori, Paolo and Bakhtiyar Babajanov. "Being Soviet, Muslim, Modernist, and Fundamentalist in 1950s Central Asia." *Journal of the Economic and Social History of the Orient* 62 (2019), 108–165.

Selianinova, G.D. "Musul'manskaia obshchina Prikam'ia v gody Velikoi Otehestvennoi voiny." In *Religioznye organizatsii verushchie Prikam'ia v gody Velikoi Otechestvennoi voiny: materialy nauchno-praktichestoi konferentsii 12 maia 2005 g.,* edited by L.P. Markova, M.G. Nechaev, L.V. Masalkina, and S.A. Plotnikov, 18–22. Perm': Bogatyrev P.G.; Gosudarstvennyi obshchestvenno-politicheskii arkhiv Permskoi oblasti, 2005.

Shamsutidinov, Rustam. *Ikkinchi jahon urushi va front gazetalari.* Tashkent: Akademnashr, 2017.

Shanazarova, Aziza. "A Female Saint in Muslim Polemics: Aghā-yi Buzurg and Her Legacy in Early Modern Central Asia." PhD dissertation, Indiana University, 2019. Shaw, Charles. "Soldiers' Letters to Inobatxon and O'g'ulxon: Gender and Nationality in the Birth of a Soviet Romantic Culture." *Kritika* 17/3 (2016), 517–552.

Shikhaliev, Sh.Sh. "Transformatsiia sufisma v svete religioznoi politiki i pereselenii gortsev v Dagestane 1930–1990-x gg." *Pax Islamica* 2/11 (2013), 93–109.

Shin, Boram. "Red Army Propaganda for Uzbek Soldiers and Localised Soviet Internationalism during World War II." *The Soviet and Post-Soviet Review* 42/1 (2015), 39–63.

Shkarovskii, M.V. "Stalinskaia religioznaia politika i Russkaia Pravoslavnaia Tserkov' v 1943–1953 godakh." *Acta Slavica Iaponica* 27 (2009), 1–27.

Shkarovskii, M.V. *Russkaia Pravoslavnaia Tserkov' pri Staline i Khrushcheve— Gosudarstvenno-tserkovnye otnosheniia v SSSR v 1939-1964 godakh.* Moscow: Krutitskoe Patriarshee Podvor'e; Obshchestvo liubitelei tserkovnoi istorii, 1999.

Smolkin, Victoria. *A Sacred Space is Never Empty*: A History of Soviet Atheism. Princeton, NJ: Princeton University Press, 2018.

Solzhenitsyn, Aleksandr I. *Letter to the Soviet Leaders*. New York: Harper & Row, 1975.

Starostin, A.N. *Islam v Sverdlovskoi oblasti*. Moscow: Logos, 2007.

Steigmann-Gall, Richard. *The Holy Reich: Nazi Conceptions of Christianity, 1919–1945.* Cambridge, UK: Cambridge University Press, 2003.

Sulaev, I.Kh. "Musul'manskoe dukhovenstvo v Velikoi Otechestvennoi Voine 1941–1945 gg." *Voenno-istoricheskii zhurnal* 5 (2007), 24–26.

Tasar, Eren. "Soviet and Muslim: The Institutionalization of Islam in Central Asia, 1943–1991." PhD dissertation, Harvard University, 2010.

Tasar, Eren. *Soviet and Muslim: The Institutionalization of Islam in Central Asia.* New York: Oxford University Press, 2017.

Tasar, Eren. "Unregistered: Gray Spaces in the Soviet Regulation of Islam." In *Islam, Society and Politics in Central Asia*, edited by Pauline Jones, 127–148. Pittsburgh: University of Pittsburgh Press, 2017.

Tasar, Eren. "Islamically Informed Soviet Patriotism in Postwar Kyrgyzstan," *Cahiers du monde russe* 52/2–3 (2011), 387–404.

Usmanova, Dilyara, Ilnur Minnullin, and Rafik Mukhmetshin. "Islamic Education in Soviet and Post-Soviet Tatarstan." In *Islamic Education in the Soviet Union and its Successor States*, edited by Michael Kemper, Raoul Motika, and Stephan Reichmuth, 21–67. New York: Routledge, 2010.

Vasil'eva, O.Iu., I.I. Kudriavtsev, and L.A. Lykova, eds. *Russkaia pravoslavnaia tserkov v gody Velikoi Otechestvennoi voiny, 1941–1945 gg. Sbornik documentov.* Moscow: Izd. Krutitskogo podvor'ia Obshchestvo liubitelei tserkovnoi istorii, 2009.

Werth, Paul W. *The Tsar's Foreign Faiths: Toleration and the Fate of Religious Freedom in Imperial Russia. New York: Oxford University Press, 2014.*

Werth, Paul W. "Conformity and Defiance in a Religious Key." *Kritika* 17/4 (2016), 869–896.

Yakovlev, Alexander N. *A Century of Violence in Soviet Russia*. New Haven: Yale University Press, 2002.

Yakupov, R.I. *Russian Islamic University CSDM of Russia: History and Nowadays.* Ufa: RIU, 2011.

Zaripov, I.A., and M.A. Safarov. *Akhmetzian Mustafin: iz istorii islama v SSSR.* Moscow: Medina, 2017.

Zhiromskaia, V.B. "Religioznost' naroda v 1937 godu." *Istoricheskii vestnik* 5/1 (2000), 105–114.

Index

For the benefit of digital users, indexed terms that span two pages (e.g., 52–53) may, on occasion, appear on only one of those pages.